WITCHCRAFT, VIOLENCE, AND DEMOCRACY IN SOUTH AFRICA

WITCHCRAFT, VIOLENCE, AND DEMOCRACY IN SOUTH AFRICA

ADAM ASHFORTH

THE UNIVERSITY OF CHICAGO PRESS
CHICAGO AND LONDON

The University of Chicago Press, Chicago 60637
The University of Chicago Press, Ltd., London
© 2005 by The University of Chicago
All rights reserved. Published 2005
Printed in the United States of America

14 13 12 11 10 09 08 07   5 4 3 2

ISBN (cloth): 0-226-02973-5
ISBN (paper): 0-226-02974-3

Library of Congress Cataloging-in-Publication Data

Ashforth, Adam.
    Witchcraft, violence, and democracy in South Africa / Adam Ashforth.
        p.   cm.
    Includes bibliographical references and index.
    ISBN 0-226-02973-5 (hardcover : alk. paper) — ISBN 0-226-02974-3
(pbk. : alk. paper)
        1. Witchcraft—South Africa—Soweto.   2. Witchcraft—Political
aspects—South Africa—Soweto.   I. Title.
    BF1584.S6A84   2005
    133.4′3′0968221—dc22

                                                2004011326

IN MEMORY OF TSELANE ADELINA SELLO MTHEMBU

Contents

Preface

My engagement with Soweto began accidentally. I was visiting South Africa in 1990 researching the politics of the transition to democracy when I was invited to visit Soweto by friends and family of a Sowetan friend in the United States. Those were the days when freedom seemed close at hand. Mandela and his comrades in the African National Congress had been released from prison. The liberation movements, banned since 1961, had been "unbanned." The streets of Soweto were a tumult of triumph and euphoria over a struggle that at the time seemed as good as won. I only intended to stay overnight. But I failed to reckon with the fascination of the place and the warmth of the life I would be welcomed into. Over the course of the decade I spent about thirty-six months in Soweto. Most years I was there during the June to September summer vacation from my teaching job in New York. My longest stay was from October 1992 until August 1994, for the lead-up to the elections of April 1994 and the inauguration of the Government of National Unity in May of that year.

Before visiting Soweto in 1990, like most outsiders I had an image of Soweto as a place marked by unrelieved poverty, oppression, misery, violence, and struggle. When I arrived in Soweto in 1990, though, I found myself in a world that was dynamic and joyful, where life was lived on its own terms—terms that virtually everyone insisted, in all their joy as well as pain, were in defiance of the oppressive "apartheid regime." From the start of my first visit on June 16, my hosts in Soweto embarked upon a project of "exposing" me (their term) to all aspects of Soweto life. Before long I became utterly absorbed in, and by, the place and the people. I was "adopted" (their term) into a family and made to feel at home as a brother and son. Such expansive kinship—"fictive" hardly does the connection justice—is unremarkable in African families. The Mfete family who adopted me already contained another "sister" unrelated by ties of blood. It took a long time for me to be able to acknowledge this relationship outside Soweto without feeling pretentious. That the Mfetes should have a tall white son and brother was a source of some amusement to their friends, relatives, and neighbors—though it was never a matter for doubt or disputation. Over time I was integrated into the life of a whole community. After more than a decade, I know none of my "family" will disagree if I say that family life is not always easy.

Despite the appalling legacy of white racism in South Africa I was never unduly troubled in Soweto for being a white man. By the time I arrived in 1990 it was no longer necessary for white people to apply for a permit to visit Soweto and there were no laws preventing them from sleeping overnight. Few did in those days, however. Having had little experience of living with racial differences before encountering Soweto, it took me some time to become accustomed to the fact that I was living in the body of a *white* man and that this had consequences independent of my own sense of self, such as it is. The status of white people in Soweto has changed over the years, along with everything else. At first I was welcomed to Soweto as a symbol of the "new" South Africa, a sign that Black and White could in fact live together despite the racist strictures of apartheid. Over the years since 1990, racial attitudes in Soweto have hardened somewhat, and a white stranger is more likely to encounter resentment now than when I was first a stranger there. Yet I consider it a testament to the depth of black South Africa's commitment to "nonracialism" that although the fact of physical difference has always been with me in Soweto, it has never been presented to me as the only relevant fact of my being in Soweto.

My original research plan focused upon the politics of representation in a transition to democracy. I was intending to develop ideas elaborated in my first book (Ashforth 1990) by examining how social categories defined by the state as "ethnic" and "racial" were reconfigured in the course of crafting a democratic, all-inclusive constitution. This worthy plan fell by the wayside as I became ever more engrossed in the task of learning about life in Soweto and learning how to live in a place like Soweto. At the time I embarked on this course I had no idea how time-consuming, challenging, and rewarding it would prove. Fortunately, from my first day in Soweto I was blessed with remarkable friends who guided me through the pleasures and perils of life in the township. They steered me toward what little understanding of their world I can now claim, though they do not always agree with the way I have come to understand this place. I have read widely in the years since I began getting to know Soweto, but the essence of whatever I know about this place I have learned through my friends; how I know it is by being there as a friend. This is both the strength and the weakness of what follows. For what I came to understand—dimly, slowly, over many years of fumbling in the dark—is that their world is my world, and mine theirs, and yet we also live in worlds apart. While a good deal of what is presented in this book is less than lovely, the reason I keep returning to Soweto, as I have every year but one since 1990, is for the company of friends in a place that I came to think of as home. That I feel a little sadder each time I return is perhaps because we are all getting older, and are burying too many loved ones, as the euphoria of 1990 fades into the distance.

The life in Soweto that I first encountered in 1990 was strangely familiar to me. Both strange and familiar. Soweto was a place of working people struggling to make ends meet, with parents raising their children in difficult circumstances while striving to build a secure future. People were poor and many slept hungry but no one was starving. Houses were crowded, but most people slept with some kind of roof over their heads. I had little difficulty adapting to the family life I found in Mapetla Extension (a section of Soweto) with the Mfetes. Anchored in basic norms of sharing, reciprocity, mutual aid, and understanding—in a word, love—it was not much different from what I had known at home in Australia or with my relatives in Ireland and England, although people in Soweto were a bit more emphatic in their talk of kinship. When those who were not kin insisted on calling me "brother," however, I knew basically what they meant. But I had had little preparation in my previous life for the times when this talk of "brotherhood" would be tested in a willingness to face death on each other's behalf. This book, despite its faults, is testament to the strength of those bonds.

When I consider how outsiders are so often despised in polite "white" society for ignorance of middle-class mores and social norms, it shames me to think of how generous people in Soweto were when faced with my cultural imbecility over the years I lived there. It took a long time for me to acquire my small proficiency in the complex mixtures of languages that swirl through Sowetan conversations. These include isiZulu, isiXhosa, seSotho, seTswana, sePedi, English, Afrikaans, and the slang argots of Isicamtho and Tsotsitaal, as well as the less common languages of xiChangana and tshiVenda. In what follows I shall use as far as possible the standard forms of Zulu and Sotho, occasionally Xhosa, although I shall not use prefixes and suffixes since they tend to confuse people unfamiliar with these languages. Hence, the language is "Zulu" and not "isiZulu"; the people are "Zulus," not "amaZulu." Most people in Soweto can speak English if they need to and were unfailingly generous with my linguistic incompetence. Virtually everyone over the age of about fifteen (when they attend secondary schools and become accustomed to English as the medium of instruction) is at least trilingual and can switch readily between Zulu, Sotho (or their related languages), and English. The variety of language spoken under each of these names, however, differs from the "standard" versions (Caltreaux 1996). Linguistic purists, whether of African or European descent, are regularly appalled by what young Sowetans do to their languages.

Since most of my friends' grasp of English was more sophisticated than my own command of their languages, most of our more complex discussions took place in that language. This would be a more serious problem were it not the case that all of the terms through which life is understood here are already translated, and retranslated, in everyday usage. From time to time in what follows I shall try to describe ordinary linguistic usages, in various vernaculars, English and African alike, but I shall not privilege one over the others as a pristine repository of authentic meaning.

While much was familiar for me in my encounter with Soweto, and readily assimilable to my experiences of life in other places—not to mention scholarly understandings of how the world works—two features of life there struck me as radically different from anything I had known previously. In the first place, I had never encountered a world where violence and the threat of violence were always present, where the vicissitudes of everyday injustice had to be suffered without reference to a meaningful idea of Law standing above all, without the comforting sense of a righteous power—a system of institutions embodying real rights belonging to real persons—awaiting the call to set wrongs to right. Certainly, the people I met had a powerful sense of the injustice of the "apartheid system" and the historic destiny of the "liberation struggle" as a quest for justice. But the everyday sense of justice of the sort that comes from living in security under a legitimate regime was virtually unknown, even after several years of democratic government. "There is no justice here," MaMfete, the mother of the family with whom I stay, once told me. I was slow in understanding what she meant. For her, and many like her, "God" was the name of the only righteous power, and justice was a hope only for the afterlife.

In the second place, I had never before lived in a world with witches. Before living in Soweto I had never encountered a world where people were presumed to have capacities for causing harm to others by supernatural means. I had never known people who feared sickness and death by witchcraft. I had never had friends accused of killing others by witchcraft. I had never had someone I loved hounded to an untimely death as a witch. I

had never been a subject of witchcraft myself. The issue of witchcraft became particularly pressing for me in 1997 when I returned to Soweto and
found my old friend Madumo in a crisis of witchcraft. His mother had died
the year before and shortly after the funeral, his younger brother accused
Madumo of killing her by means of witchcraft. The brother had been informed of this crime by a "prophet" in the Zion Christian Church. Prophets, of whom there are hundreds of thousands in South Africa, are individuals in the "indigenous" African Christian churches who, inspired by the
power of the Holy Spirit and other spirits, claim the ability to divine the future and to see the hidden causes of misfortune. This one told Madumo's
brother that the mother's death was an "inside job." Madumo was chased
away from his family home. When I found him, he was in the depths of de-
spair. He knew that the misfortunes he was suffering must be a product of
supernatural forces, but he did not know how to overcome them. Nor had
he the money to employ the services of professionals, of whom there are
thousands in Soweto. After long discussions about his predicament and
prospects, I agreed to finance Madumo's quest for a cure. He engaged the
services of a Zulu healer, an *inyanga* by the name of Mr. Zondi, and began
a long struggle to overcome the forces of witchcraft that were afflicting his
life. He also decided that we should make a "case study" of his plight, which
we did and which was published by the University of Chicago Press and
by David Philip in Cape Town in 2000 under the title *Madumo, a Man Bewitched.* The present book emerges in large part from the experiences documented in *Madumo.*

Witchcraft, as I have said, is a commonplace feature of life in Soweto, as
it is in Africa more generally. No one can understand life in Africa without
understanding witchcraft and the related aspects of spiritual insecurity. For
those of us who derive our understanding of the world from the heritage
of the European Enlightenment, however, witchcraft in the everyday life
of Africa is enormously difficult to fathom. Many Africans insist that we
should not even try, arguing that the outsider's interest in African witchcraft is merely a voyeuristic trifling with the exotic, a distraction from the
more important issues of poverty, violence, and disease pressing upon the
continent. They remind us that throughout the history of colonialism, not
only were European attitudes to African spirituality derogatory, but the colonial fascination with African witchcraft served to perpetuate stereotypes
of African irrationality and grounded colonial claims that Africans were incapable of governing themselves without white overlords. I might be inclined to agree with them were it not for the fact that I have seen too much

of the damage that the fear of witchcraft can cause. This book is an attempt by an outsider to think about the connection between living in a world without justice and living in a world with witches and how these two features of life might affect the cause of democracy. I write with an intense consciousness of the danger of being misunderstood but have no doubt that the issues are too important to ignore.

Perhaps the most difficult challenge I have faced in dealing with issues of spiritual insecurity has arisen from the necessity of taking seriously (and by this I mean treating as literal statements) propositions about witchcraft that seem evidently absurd and nonsensical without thereby denigrating the people who utter them as idiotic or stupid. This I believe is one of the greatest challenges facing anyone who would write about spiritual insecurity. It is far too easy to dismiss such propositions as mere ignorance and almost as easy to assert that they should not be taken literally but should be interpreted as figurative or metaphorical statements about something else. Tolerant secular humanists, such as myself, find it extremely difficult to accept that otherwise reasonable people really believe as literally true impossibilities such as propositions about virgin birth, spaceships behind the Hale-Bopp comet, or healers living seven years under the water of a lake. And we find it difficult to understand how matters such as blasphemy or apostasy (differences that should be treated as disagreements about belief, faith, or identity about which reasonable people can agree to disagree) can be treated as matters of public safety for which offenders must be put to death. But unless we make the imaginative leap to treat propositions about invisible forces seriously, the social and political dynamics of vast portions of humanity will remain incomprehensible.

Experience of life in Soweto, then, exposed me to the fact that the threat of violence—occult, spiritual, and supernatural as well as physical—permeates all aspects of life in that place. This sad fact is by no means all there is to life in Soweto. But the reality of this insecurity shapes all else. The insecurity of life in Soweto is not simply a case of Hobbes's war "of every man, against every man"—the predicament of life when there exists no "common Power to keep them all in awe." For a powerful state in South Africa, a "common Power" in Hobbes's terms, standing above all, had long claimed sovereignty over all in these parts. And the men who governed that state were never shy about invoking the power of the Almighty as the ultimate ground of their authority. From the point of view of the people I first met in Soweto in 1990, however, this power standing above all was in no sense a righteous power bestowing justice and serving the interests of its subjects, and certainly not the embodiment of the common will or the expression of the consent of the governed, but rather the very font and origin of injustice and oppression. It is by no means certain that the new regime will ultimately succeed in creating a sense of the state as a public power embodying justice, righteousness, and security for all. Underpinning the argument of this book is a conviction that the ways in which the insecurity aroused by fears of witchcraft and the general condition of spiritual insecurity are handled by political authorities over the long run will have profound significance for the long-term legitimacy of the democratic state. The AIDS pandemic only makes these issues more urgent.

It was not by research alone, in the sense of a systematic program of methodical inquiry, that I arrived at what little understanding I can claim in the matters discussed in this book. It was rather from years spent gossiping at the kitchen table, drinking in shebeens, downing countless cups of tea and bottles of beer, and drifting in the currents of stories that sweep friends, family, and neighbors—along with a multitude of strangers more distant— through life, becoming part of the trials and tragedies, glories and joys of everyday life while sitting out the endless days of simple boring rounds until the sudden explosion of anger that shatters all routine like the violence of a summer thunderstorm. I lived in Soweto long enough for the exotic to become commonplace, becoming a brother while remaining an outsider, watching friends die from what they recognized as witchcraft, mourning others killed in the violence we make sense of by calling it "senseless" or bewitched by others' jealousy, learning of comrades murdered for their body parts to be used in magic medicines, witnessing the suffering of infants said to be bewitched, struggling with loved ones over the proper cure for ailments unknown at the clinic, becoming an object of gossip myself and a target of violence and witchcraft, like everyone else.

Stories of those times are threaded through the loose patchwork of argument in this book. They are told from the perspective of a white man who wandered into an apartheid township at a time when a page of world history was turning, the last page in the annals of white supremacy in Africa. The book speaks little, however, of that "small miracle"—as Mandela called it—of the struggle for freedom and the birth of the new South Africa. Nor does it dwell upon the many horrors of apartheid. Others have done that, and will continue to do so. Nor do I seek to essay policy recommendations for the new regime. This book seeks rather to suggest approaches to thinking about the perplexing problems of spiritual insecurity and speculate upon implications for the future of democracy. As well as presenting the problems and puzzles of Sowetan life, however, I will try to make it clear throughout—and will state it here in black and white—that this book would not exist, nor, indeed, would its author, without the love and support of the people of whom I write, people who have shared their lives with me and were prepared to risk their lives for mine—who opened their homes and lives to me and afforded me security in Soweto at a time when a white man had no right to expect it.

Acknowledgments

I owe far too many debts to far too many people for shelter, companionship, knowledge, insight, love, money, and all the other forms of aid I have been the fortunate beneficiary of over the past decade since I began this book to be able to adequately acknowledge them here, and the fulsomeness of my gratitude would probably embarrass us all, so I shall merely say *thank you* to Abdoumaliq Simone, Abraham Dladla, Abraham Zondi, Achille Mbembe, Adelina Sello, Alan Mabin, Alastair Davidson, Albert Hirschman, Alcinda Honwana, Amy Calvo, Andrew Apter, Angus Deaton, Anna Rubbo, Anne Case, Anthony Minaar, Ari Zolberg, Ayanda Koetle, Beatrice Hibou, Belina Mavuso, Belinda Bozzoli, Bheki Masilo, Boetie Nkosimang, Boetumelo Ramakgale, Bontle Makua, Charles Tilly, Charles van Onselen, Christina Scott, Clifford Geertz, Courtney Jung, Daphne Mfete, David Brent, David Coplan, David Webster, Debra Keates, Debbie Koehler, Debbie Posel, Dianne Ciekawy, Donne Petito, Dumisani Ntshangase, Edwin Ritchken, Elaine Wolfensohn, Eric Maskin, Ethel Gorham, Fila More, Gavin Williams, Halton Cheadle, Harriet Perlman, Harry West, Helen Epstein, Helen Nissenbaum, Hendry Mfete, Ikobeng Molapo, Isak Niehaus, James Der Derian, Janet Gornick, Janet Roitman, Jean Comaroff, Jean-François Bayart, Jeff Peires, Joan Scott, John Comaroff, John Philip Santos, Karen Colvard, Kate Monahan, Katherine Lee, Keitumetse Moeketsi, Kenosi Gaboutwelwe, Kgomotso More, Kirsty Venanzi, Macheli Motingoe, Madumo Tsoku, Mamama Masetla, Mamphela Ramphele, Manuel Delanda, Marcia Reid-Grant, Marcia Tucker, Marcus Wood, Marks Chabedi, Matiro Gaboutwelwe, Mercy Lebakeng, Michael Bennish, Michael Gilsenan, Michael Taussig, Michael Walzer, Michel Vaillaud, Modiehe Moumakwe, Moeketsi Mosheshe, Mogomotse Lubisi, Moleboheng Sello, Mpho Mathebula, Nancy Cotterman, Njabulo Ndebele, Noise Khan-

yile, Nomampondomise Koetle, Pamela J. Bruton, Paul LaHausse de La-
louvière, Peter Delius, Peter Geschiere, Philip Bonner, Philip Corrigan,
Santu Mofokeng, Steve Caton, Susan Parnell, Terence Ashforth, Teresa
Ashforth, Thabo Mfete, Tico Taussig, Tom Halper, Tom Karis, Tom Levin,
Tom Lodge, Tshikala K. Biaya, Seipati Mfete, Veena Das, Vera Zolberg,
Vivian Gornick, Vivien Koech, Wendy Brown, Willis Ngobe, and Ximena
Vargas while apologizing for neglecting the hundreds of friends who made
possible my long sojourns in Soweto and remembering with love those who
have passed away.

I am also most grateful for funding provided by the American Council
of Learned Societies, Baruch College in the City University of New York,
the Harry Frank Guggenheim Foundation, the Institute for Advanced
Study, the John D. and Catherine T. MacArthur Foundation, the Professional Staff Congress of the City University of New York, and the Social
Science Research Council.

Plates 1–3 are from the author's collection. All photographs are by the
author.

A Note on Nomenclature

A note on nomenclature is still necessary when writing of the country known as South Africa and the people who live there. At the end of the apartheid era four official categories of population—Black, Coloured, Indian, and White—were enshrined in law. These categories had mutated in various ways throughout the course of the century in response to efforts to impose social order, meet the objections of those so ordered, and represent something resembling reality (Ashforth 1990, 1). In the dying days of apartheid, when the authorities decided that the people otherwise designated by an ethnic-national tag such as "Zulu," "Xhosa," or "Sotho" were collectively to be called "Black," the Black Consciousness movement insisted that *all* oppressed people were black (which they usually spelled with a small *b*) a category including Coloureds, in those days also known as "so-called Coloured," and "Indians."

Throughout the twentieth century, many of the people who were officially designated at various times as "Natives," "Bantu," and "Blacks" preferred the term "African" as a way of reclaiming indigenous roots without privileging ethnic identities—a claim Afrikaner nationalists were displeased with, as their own self-designation was Dutch for "African," while their program of apartheid was nothing if not a privileging of ethnic identity (Jung 2000). For the Nationalists, a person who spoke isiZulu as a first language was a Zulu first, a Bantu or Black second, and only tangentially a South African.

In the postapartheid era public discourse sometimes becomes rather confusing when referring to matters of race since the official ideology of "nonracialism" is premised on the denial of significance to "racial" differences. One term in vogue in official circles that attempts to sidestep the question of race is "historically disadvantaged person," or HDP. I have yet

to meet anyone who answers to that name. In Soweto the favored labels
of self-identification when race or color is invoked are "black" (as in "we
blacks") and "African." The term "African" is also proving somewhat contentious in postapartheid public discourse, as many white South Africans
insist they are Africans, too, particularly after Thabo Mbeki made his declaration "I am an African" on the occasion of the adoption of the new constitution in 1996 in an affirmation of identity that left many of his paler
compatriots feeling somewhat excluded (Mbeki 1996).

    When referring to categories of discourse, I shall use one of the con-
ventional terms in capitalized form: Blacks, Whites, Africans, etc.; when referring to actual people, I shall use color terms as adjectives: black people,
white people, etc. Since virtually everyone in Soweto is black, because the
place was built for Blacks, and few people other than Africans (or HDPs)
remain, when I speak of Sowetans I shall usually just refer to "people."

Introduction

The chapters of this book have been organized into three parts. The first
part deals with the social dimensions of spiritual insecurity in Soweto at the
turn of the twenty-first century. These chapters examine how issues of spiritual insecurity—the dangers, doubts, and fears arising from the sense of
being exposed to invisible evil forces—relate to other dimensions of insecurity in everyday life such as those arising from poverty, violence, political oppression, and disease. They chart the contours of seismic changes
in Sowetan social life corresponding with the end of apartheid, such as increasing socioeconomic inequality, declining community solidarity, rampant violent crime, and the AIDS epidemic, all of which have contributed
to a widespread sense that witchcraft is increasing. And they examine the
social dynamics of life in a world with witches. These dynamics are premised upon a presumption of malice underpinning community life. This
presumption constitutes what I describe as a negative corollary of the doctrine of *ubuntu,* the foundational principle of what is sometimes described
as African humanism. That is, where the philosophy of *ubuntu* proclaims
that "a person is a person through other persons," everyday life teaches that
life in a world of witches must be lived in terms of a presumption of malice
that adds: *because they can kill you.*

Part 1 ends with an examination of the implications of believing in witchcraft at the start of the twenty-first century in places like Soweto. I discuss
the limitations of conventional social scientific approaches to understanding issues of spiritual insecurity in terms of concepts of "rationality" and
"modernity" and argue that contemporary Sowetans generally approach issues of witchcraft with a sense that it is better not to believe in witches, while
suffering problems of spiritual insecurity nonetheless for that.

Part 2 begins a discussion of the ways in which people in contemporary Soweto interpret and attempt to manage the invisible forces they experience as acting upon their lives. It investigates the nature of the various agencies that people interact with in the course of their everyday lives, agencies inherent in substances, objects, images, persons, and spirits or other invisible beings. The central aim here is to illuminate how everyday statements about witchcraft and other forms of harm involving invisible forces can be taken by reasonable people living in the modern world as plausible accounts of reality. This involves consideration of the ways people interpret the agency of substances and the dialectics of health and harm implicit in the category *muthi* — the generic label for both "poison" and "medicine" and the central term in discourses of power linking human action with invisible agencies.

Part 2 also examines ways of interpreting the dangers of pollution inherent in various forms of dirt, particularly those associated with death. I argue that issues of pollution are central to understanding the stigma and denial associated with AIDS. As well as describing the sources of spiritual insecurity in everyday life, part 2 also examines conceptions of spiritual power said to afford protection to individuals, families, and communities. I describe how the quest for spiritual security has been transformed by colonial conquest, urbanization, transformations of kinship, and Christian evangelization. Part 2 concludes by raising questions about how the pervasive spiritual insecurity of everyday life contributes to what I call vulnerabilities of the soul that complicate issues of personal responsibility and individual autonomy.

Part 3 examines how issues of spiritual insecurity intrude upon political agendas at the level of the state and present difficult challenges for democratic government. Foremost among these is the problem of justice that arises from the fact that among a large portion of the South African citizenry, witchcraft is the name for a form of harm, a criminal violence inflicted upon innocent victims. Since colonial times, however, indigenous judicial procedures aimed at managing the problem of witchcraft in African communities have been outlawed, leaving victims to improvise informal, ad hoc, or purely private modes of seeking justice in response. Part 3 examines some examples of efforts to seek justice in relation to witchcraft and raises the question of how the sense of invisible powers operative in witchcraft discourses might transpose onto interpretations of state power in the political domain. I offer a reading of the Truth and Reconciliation Commission, widely portrayed as an exercise in "national healing," viewed through the lens of the witchcraft paradigm and principles of traditional healing.

In the absence of formal institutions serving the ends of justice in cases of witchcraft, people finding themselves the victims of witches have been left mostly to seek justice through practices of healing that also offer the promise of revenge by turning the evil forces afflicting a person back onto the malefactor who dispatched them. Traditional healing, however, though widespread and diverse in form, is technically illegal under the terms of colonial-era legislation. Part 3 examines efforts by the African National Congress government to recognize and regulate healers and analyzes the underlying contradictions between forms of authority invoked in healing and those institutionalized within modern states. These contradictions make it unlikely that regulatory efforts will be successful in the manner in which they are currently being proposed. Ironically, however, the related official investment currently under way in efforts to scientifically substantiate the claims of "traditional medicine" may succeed in lending greater credence to suppositions about witchcraft as a form of parallel, secret, and illicit "African science."

Part 3 concludes with an examination of the history of efforts to eradicate the belief in witchcraft by means of African education in South Africa and the implications of current efforts to revise the curriculum.

Spiritual insecurity may be a universal feature of human life. It is related to, but not reducible to, other forms of insecurity such as poverty, violence, political oppression, and disease.[1] It is not merely a form of benightedness that disappears with enlightenment and modernization. Nor is it simply a matter of belief that can be relegated to a distinct sphere of human concerns: religion. I have found that few people can hear tell of witchcraft in Soweto without seeking historical and ethnographic comparisons or drawing parallels with their own experience. I shall not, in this present work, explore in any detail the philosophical, historical, or comparative dimensions of these issues other than to insist that previous approaches to these issues as matters simply of "belief" are inadequate for understanding the complex sets of relations that constitute the lived world of humanity. I will also insist that the predicament of spiritual insecurity experienced by people such as those I have known in Soweto cannot be adequately comprehended in the

---

1. For a good elaboration of the concept of "human security" that the concept of spiritual insecurity I am using here builds on, see UNDP 1994.

shopworn language of "tradition" and "modernity"—however those terms may be refined and redefined.

In this book I focus primarily upon the spiritual insecurity experienced by particular people in a particular place at a particular time: in Soweto, South Africa, at the turn of the millennium. I do this from a conviction that many of the frames of reference within which the historical, comparative, and philosophical questions have commonly been posed are no longer relevant to the experience of people living in places like Soweto or to the challenges facing those who would seek to govern them. Rather, the questions that matter are those emerging in the course of everyday life in places like Soweto. This book is an attempt to bring some of these questions into focus.

Part One

SOWETO

1

SPIRITUAL INSECURITY AND
POLITICAL POWER

"Evil Forces" and the Problem of Justice

In September 2000, the Portfolio Committee on Arts, Culture, Science, and Technology of the South African Parliament issued a report on its public hearings on "a Bill on the protection and promotion of Indigenous Knowledge Systems." During its investigations into "traditional medicine," which is one of the principal domains of indigenous knowledge systems identified in the bill, the committee met with numerous representatives of traditional healers' organizations and found themselves drawn into consideration of matters referred to as "witchcraft." Puzzled by the distinction between "traditional medicine" and "witchcraft," a distinction which they were told colonial and apartheid authorities had failed to heed, the Committee asked the healers to explain: "Often," the healers told the Committee, "their patients consult them for health reasons, and during the consultation and diagnosis, it transpires that there is involvement of evil forces. It is then their duty to protect their patient in this regard. The manner applied for protection purposes [*sic*] then distinguishes witches from healers. Witches intentionally harm and kill people or cause harm or death to people. Healers heal by protecting people from harm and death through the spirit and ancestors" (Portfolio Committee on Arts 2000, para. 24.2). The healers testifying before the committee did not say that *all* the suffering experienced by their clients as health problems is caused by witchcraft. This is only "often" the case. So how often is "often"? How many witches are out there causing "harm and death" in their communities, and how much harm are they causing? What sort of a problem is this?

The committee did not address these questions directly, but they are worth considering in order to gauge the significance of issues I shall be describing as pertaining to spiritual insecurity. One way of assessing the extent of perceived witchcraft in postapartheid South Africa is to estimate the scale of endeavors by healers engaged in efforts to counteract it. Traditional healing is a big business.[1] According to another parliamentary committee, "there are about 350,000 traditional practitioners in South Africa, providing their services to 60–80% of their communities" (Select Committee on Social Services 1998, 2). In addition to these "traditional practitioners," healers known as "prophets" (*maprofeti*), who belong to African Initiated Churches (AICs),[2] are active in work against "evil forces" in the same communities in numbers that would most likely approximate those of traditional healers (Allan Anderson 2000b; Kiernan 1990b; Oosthuizen 1992). A rough estimate would be that at least half a million African healers are at work outside the formal biomedical system in South Africa and are dealing with problems of witchcraft.[3] If the hundreds of thousands of nonmedical healers at work in South Africa are, in the Portfolio Committee's words, *often* consulting with patients who are victims of witches intent upon causing harm and death, then "witchcraft" must be taken as the name of a problem affecting millions of people.

Another way of approaching the question of the significance of witchcraft is to ponder the extent of the health problems that people are taking to traditional healers and that could be diagnosed as involving evil forces. At the turn of the twenty-first century, the most significant health problem facing South Africans was HIV/AIDS. In 1990, the South African Department of Health began an annual survey of the HIV status of pregnant women attending prenatal clinics. The results of these surveys show a dramatic increase in infections in the middle of the decade, coinciding with the election of the ANC government. Death rates began increasing about five years later (Department of Health 2001, fig. 1). In 1999, according to city officials in Durban and Johannesburg, twice as many people were buried as

---

1. I have been unable to find plausible estimates of the value of nonmedical healing endeavors to the national economy. A recent study, however, estimates the value of the national trade in plant and animal substances for medicinal purposes at 270 million rand per year (Mander 1998). The total expended upon healers' fees, medicines, ancestral feasts, and donations to faith-healing churches would be many times that.

2. Indigenous African Christian churches are now variously denominated "Independent," "Indigenous," "Instituted," or "Initiated" and known collectively by the initialism AIC. See chapter 8.

3. The total population of the country at the time was about 40 million people, of whom the 1996 census classified 31,127,631 as "African/Black"—the principal consumers of services offered by traditional healers and prophets (Statistics South Africa 1999, fig. 2.5).

five years previously (B. Jordan 2000). The Medical Research Council estimated in 2001 that AIDS will have killed between five and seven million South Africans by 2010 (Dorrington et al. 2001, 6, also table 5).[4] The
same researchers projected that life expectancy in South Africa would
drop from fifty-five in 2000 to forty by 2010 (Bradshaw et al. 2001, 25). Most
of the people infected with HIV and dying of AIDS are young adults in
what should be their most fertile and productive years. The death of such
persons has long been associated with witchcraft in these parts (Molema
1920, 175).

Symptoms of illness associated with the onset of AIDS, such as persistent coughing, diarrhea, abdominal pains, and wasting, have long been associated in this part of the world with the malicious assaults of witches. One
of the most common forms of such witchcraft is known in Zulu as *idliso*
and in Sotho as *sejeso,* both deriving from the root verb "to eat" (*ukudlisa,*
Zulu; *ho ja,* Sotho). These terms and the conditions associated with them
are usually translated into English as "poison" and "poisoning," but the understandings of the power of substances to cause harm that are typically
engaged in notions of *idliso/sejeso* and the substances that serve as the
medium of engagement between the witch and his or her victim (called
muthi) are much broader than the concepts of "poison" that inform biomedical notions of infection or basic principles of toxicology. The witch deploying *muthi* in the manner of *idliso* manufactures a creature that mani-
fests itself in the body of the victim in a form resembling a snake, lizard, or
crab and devours the victim from within, causing all manner of misfortune
to befall the person in the process.[5]

Other ways of using *muthi* are also said to kill in a manner similar to
AIDS. AIDS-awareness accounts of HIV as an invisible agency inhering in

4. The publication of the Medical Research Council report, following President Mbeki's
insistence that HIV/AIDS was not a major cause of death, stirred a controversy over the
accuracy of mortality statistics in South Africa. The report was based upon demographic
projections. Statistics South Africa, the official statistics office, sampled death notification
forms to explain the increasing mortality noticed between 1997 and 2001 and found that
HIV/AIDS was already the leading cause of death for African females and that there was
a "pronounced" pattern of mortality from HIV and related diseases "amongst children and
the reproductive and economically active population group (i.e., the population between
15–49)" (Statistics South Africa 2002, 22).

5. For a description of *idliso* in relation to biomedical interpretations of symptoms, see
Conco 1972; for a psychological study of suffering from what was considered to be *idliso,*
see Farrand 1988; and for accounts of traditional healers and AIC prophets comparing
idliso with tuberculosis, see Wilkinson, Gcabashe, and Lurie 1999 and Oosthuizen 1992,
100, respectively.

the already potentially dangerous mess of bodily fluids that is the medium of exchange of sex resonate powerfully with local understandings of invisible agents involved in witchcraft that contaminate a victim and then begin to "attack" the victim by destroying the person's defenses, precipitating illness, misfortune, and death. The language of "attack" and "defense" common in virology and AIDS-awareness discourses is precisely the same language used in describing the actions of poison and poisoners spoken of as "witchcraft."

I am not suggesting that all Africans infected with HIV will come to believe that they have been bewitched. Nor will everyone who worries about witchcraft be worrying about the same thing. I am, however, going to argue that the repertoire of available interpretations for misfortunes such as AIDS includes concepts of witchcraft and understandings of invisible agency that are substantially different from those of Western biomedicine. This has major cultural and political implications. Understanding these dimensions of agency is crucial if the battle against this epidemic is going to succeed. The central mysteries of the epidemic in this part of the world—the extent of stigma, denial, and risky behavior by people aware of the dangers of infection—cannot be understood unless the dimensions of spiritual insecurity in everyday life are comprehended. Similarly, the social and political consequences of AIDS mortality will remain mysterious unless these dimensions are considered.

As the healers pointed out to the committee, for every person suffering a problem caused by the evil forces of witchcraft another person is responsible. Traditional healers pride themselves on being able to distinguish between the ordinary "health reasons" that might drive a client to consult them and the harm and death intentionally caused by others. Sometimes, as we shall see in more detail later, illnesses are considered by healers as simply natural occurrences; deaths can also be an ordinary consequence of life. But when witches and their evil forces are at work, suffering is not simply natural and unavoidable. In those instances, suffering is harm. That is, illness, death, and other misfortunes become forms of unjust injury, damage deliberately inflicted on an innocent victim. Viewed from the perspective of traditional healers and their clients, then, witchcraft undoubtedly constitutes a serious social problem. Multitudes of people are experiencing harm and death caused by witchcraft, and similar numbers are falling under suspicion of being responsible for the suffering. Legions of healers are battling these evil forces. HIV/AIDS is part of this struggle.

Witchcraft tends to surface in public discourse in South Africa only when reports of witch killings arise, as they do periodically. "Witchcraft" is

then taken to be a "problem" insofar as it pertains to the killing of inno-
cents—a "human rights abuse" in the current parlance. The fact that the
vast majority of people killed as witches have been older women also engages discourses of gender equity in the need to contain antiwitchcraft violence (Commission on Gender Equality 2000). Yet, although action against
witches is almost universally conducted in terms of demands for justice,
public discourse in national political forums or print and electronic media
rarely, if ever, engages with questions of justice for those who, like the
clients of the healers interviewed by the Portfolio Committee, see themselves as suffering at the hands of others causing "harm and death" by
means of evil forces. For people who live in a world with witches, these issues of justice are of the utmost importance in everyday life. The central
question this book seeks to address, then, is: What implications might this
have for democratic governance within a modern liberal state?

Addressing this question demands that we try to understand what it is
like to live in a world with witches while not presuming that such people live
in a world entirely alien from that enjoyed by those of us who do not fear
witchcraft.[6] For those readers who have not known themselves or those
they love as exposed to witchcraft, or not had to cope with others' struggles
in this domain, this requires an effort of imagination and a willingness to
suspend judgment that can, I should warn, be taxing since it requires treating as open a mess of ontological questions that are ordinarily lived as if
they are resolved. The varieties of spiritual insecurity expressed in the term
"witchcraft" represent a sort of ontological fault line at the heart of the
South African state. In the discourses of statecraft enshrined in the new
constitutional order and taken for granted by a good proportion of the citizenry—not all of whom, it should be noted, are of European descent—
witchcraft is a matter of belief, a property of the mind. For most South
Africans, however, witchcraft is a matter of action leading to real, material
consequences for living human beings—action, moreover, that creates injustice. Life in a world with witches, then, raises problems that are not easily
sequestered in the institutional categories—particularly those of politics,
law, medicine, and religion—that are taken for granted in liberal demo-

6. For an excellent recent treatment of the literature on witchcraft in Africa, see Moore
and Sanders 2001a. For earlier surveys, see Geschiere 1997 and Douglas 1970a. South
Africans almost never refer to "sorcery" or insist on the analytical distinction made famous
by Evans-Pritchard (1937) between "witchcraft" (as an innate capacity of persons) and
"sorcery" (as a skill in manipulating the powers of material substances). I shall follow their
practice.

cratic thought. The problem of justice posed by witchcraft cannot easily be resolved in the terms of liberal democracy in its secular guise.

In the chapters that follow I focus mostly on the social relations that make fears of witchcraft and other forms of spiritual insecurity seem plausible to people in Soweto at the turn of the twenty-first century and the problems of everyday epistemology faced by people living with these fears. I am acutely aware, however, that this approach barely scratches the surface of the situations I am trying to represent and leaves untouched a host of existential questions faced by those who live them. I shall not, however, attempt to describe the complexity of Sowetans' lives in the fullness they deserve or to resolve the philosophical questions arising from what I am calling the problems of everyday epistemology. Nor shall I attempt to reprise the centuries of argument underpinning the practice of democratic governance and the nature of liberalism, presuming instead that my readers are familiar with the basic outlines of liberal democratic thought. This is not a work of political theory, though I hope it will cause political theorists and others interested in arguments about government and political legitimacy to rethink some of their assumptions. Rather, I hope to be able to show how these matters constitute part of the very stuff of politics in this African context. And I shall insist that unless the dimensions of spiritual insecurity are understood, politics in Africa is incomprehensible.

Witchcraft in Everyday Life: An Epistemological Double Bind

In the course of everyday life in Soweto, witchcraft accusations are the exception rather than the rule. When gossiping about other people's misfortunes, for example, particularly when the suffering is serious, Sowetans rarely find it necessary to utter the words "witch" or "witchcraft"—neither in English nor in any other local language. Witchcraft discourse, with all the possibilities of nefarious interactions with invisible agencies it expresses, serves primarily as subtext—that which is not said but without which one cannot comprehend what is spoken. To say "the wife is to blame" when a husband dies, for example, is automatically to invoke witchcraft. If the connection is not patently obvious, it might be said openly that she "used *muthi.*" To say more than this about how she killed him, however, would be to seem to know too much about witchcraft. For someone other than a healer, this might be dangerous.

Everyday life in Soweto—as in most of Africa, most of the time—is lived more in a mode of suspicion and fear of occult assault rather than open accusation and persecution of witches. Witches are seldom denounced and punished. Yet the sense that life is continually exposed to people deploying evil forces to harm and kill is palpable, the fear of occult assault is real, and the enterprise of healing devoted to protection from evil forces is enormous. The abiding presence of occult assault in a world of witches arouses a pervasive sense of insecurity and injustice resulting from the experience of suffering as harm.

The essential predicament of living in a world with witches was once summarized for me in a conversation with MaMfete, the woman I call "Mother" in Soweto: "You know, Adam, this thing [witchcraft] comes from a bitterness in somebody's heart, like a poison, causing jealousy and hatred. And you can never know what's inside someone's heart. Truly, you never know. You can think you know somebody, but you don't. And people who have this spirit of hatred, this bitterness, they can do anything" (Ashforth 2000a, 74). Most of the time, this possibility that people harboring malice can do anything exists merely as a background fact of life in a place like Soweto—no cause for undue worry. Sometimes, however, when suffering and misfortune become acute and demand action, the possibility that they have been deliberately inflicted by malicious others is cause for serious alarm. The presumption, such as the one MaMfete operates on, that the people among whom one lives have capacities for extraordinary action in the form of witchcraft creates an epistemological double bind. On the one hand, one can never really know who has a motive for malicious action. The "bitterness" in the heart, to adopt MaMfete's terms, is secret. On the other hand, because their modes and means are also secret, one can never really know what they are capable of other than that they might be capable of anything. The possibility of extraordinary action by people who are otherwise experienced as utterly ordinary makes the smiles of the villainous neighbor masks of extraordinary complexity.

In his classic essay on secrecy, Georg Simmel suggested that the awareness of secrecy in social life expands the field of imagination and action enormously: "From secrecy, which shades all that is profound and significant, grows the typical error according to which everything mysterious is something important and essential. Before the unknown, man's natural impulse to idealize and his natural fearfulness cooperate toward the same goal: to intensify the unknown through imagination, and to pay attention to it with an emphasis that is not usually accorded to patent reality" (1950, 333). Simmel also pointed out that "the secret puts a barrier between men but, at the same time, it creates the tempting challenge to break through it, by gossip or confession—and this challenge accompanies its psychology like a constant overtone" (1950, 334). As well as encouraging gossip and confession, secrecy—the hiding, presumed deliberate, of the realities that shape life's most important contours—creates the need for revealing the unseen through access to more perspicacious powers: divination. Divination is at the heart of all African healing, traditional and spiritual, and, as we have seen, healing is an enormous enterprise in contemporary South Africa. The investment in secrecy that lies at the heart of both witchcraft and healing is the foundation of the social power of the occult in this part of the world.[7]

While this secrecy can rarely be breached comprehensively, in everyday life two modes of discourse serve to elaborate forms of knowledge relevant to the task. The mode of discourse through which the secrets of other people's "hearts" are plumbed is conventionally known, in Soweto as elsewhere, as "gossip." The mode of discourse through which the "anything" of which witches are capable is analyzed, and within which their doings are separated out from those of other invisible powers, is the discourse of idle speculation. Divination and confession are the two other modes of penetrating secrets, the one offering access to hidden truths by means of access to higher powers of perspicacity, the other promising direct expression of inner secrets. Both are essential for evidence of culpability in the perpetration of witchcraft. Amid the poverty, violence, and general hardship of life in Soweto, plausible evidence abounds of "evil forces" at work. And despite the fact that the secrecy of witchcraft precludes certainty, when witches are experienced as posing a real and present danger, their potential for causing harm makes discovering what they are up to imperative.

Talk of witches and their craft in Soweto is mostly conducted with the warm convivial malice of good gossip accompanied by plentiful laughter and jokes. People rarely feel free to talk of such things when they do not feel free to laugh. Stories of witches, as with most stories, are recounted with deliberate efforts to stimulate laughter. Good stories are rewarded with guffaws. The fact of laughter, however, does not detract from the importance of the information. When matters of witchcraft become serious, however, when lives are at stake or deaths need to be explained, words about witches are seldom spoken. And when people tell their intimate friends and family about their troubles, they rarely need to explain the reasons for them. Silence about witches at such times is more than eloquent —for the silence is not just an absence but an acknowledgment of understanding implicitly that which need not be said. The latticework of local

7. For discussion of the dynamics of secrecy and healing in a Latin American context, see Taussig 1986, 1993.

knowledge supporting such silence, the tracery of suppositions through which conjectures of responsibility for evil can be surmised, is made from the skeins of gossip and idle speculation — oft-repeated, half-remembered — that are the living history of a community. These skeins are also the materials which I shall use in an endeavor to interpret the sources of spiritual insecurity in contemporary Soweto.

The Challenge for Democracy

Though the world has changed since Chief Pakati wrote to the governor of Natal more than a century ago complaining that the colonial authorities were providing sanctuary to accused witches, the challenge for government remains the same: "Let government beware lest it protect murderers at the expense of the lives of innocent people" (Casalis 1861, 281). Or, to put it another way: if there are people in the community who, in the words of the Portfolio Committee on Arts, Culture, Science, and Technology, "intentionally harm and kill people" by means of witchcraft, should not government do something about them in the same way it seeks to protect people from violent criminals? And if, as the Portfolio Committee also reports, mysterious evil forces are often involved in causing harm and death, should not a government that cares for its citizens find out what these forces are and do something about them or, at the very least, do something to assist the healers who are working to protect people from them?

African democrats who know these evil forces of witchcraft as real and present dangers cannot deny that government has a role to play in these matters, a role akin to that of providing safety, security, and justice in relation to ordinary crimes and violence. Yet they also face difficulties in devising ways of responding to the problem of witchcraft without compromising the elemental democratic ideals of human rights and the rule of law. Democrats who deny the reality of such threats face difficulties as well. They risk alienating themselves from the everyday concerns of their citizens, citizens who find themselves living in a world with witches. Leaders who are alienated in this way may find themselves struggling to create an image of the democratic state as a regime embodying the true interests of the people they are governing. If they neglect to deal with the witches, those who seek to rule may end up being perceived as agents of evil forces themselves. Thus, the challenge for those who would govern a democratic state in a world of witches, is to promote doctrines of human rights while not being perceived as protectors of witches, who perpetrate occult violence within communities.

In South Africa during the 1980s and 1990s, suspicions that governing authorities were protecting witches became a staple of politics in regions governed by the former Homeland authorities. In 1996, for example, the Commission of Inquiry into Witchcraft Violence and Ritual Murders in the Northern Province of the Republic of South Africa (the Ralushai Commission) reported of the Venda Homeland: "To politicise rural communities, the revolutionary forces chose witchcraft and ritual killing to destabilise these communities. One finding is that the reason why this route was chosen was due to the fact that the revolutionary forces were fully aware that the local communities were dissatisfied with the manner in which such cases were being handled by the authorities, for example, as witches could not be tried, the government was seen as a protector of witches" (Ralushai Commission 1996, 270; see also 273 for a similar report regarding the Lebowa Homeland). There is no guarantee that the postapartheid regime will remain immune to this taint of being "a protector of witches."

The concepts of "security" and "protection" are the elemental notions involved in thinking about relationships with invisible powers in this part of the world (Doke et al. 1990). In Soweto, "security" is often spoken of in Sotho as *tshiriletso,* from *ho tshira,* "to conceal from view" (Mabille and Dieterlen 1961); in Zulu they commonly speak of *ukuvikela,* from *ukuvika,* "to ward off blows." Ancestors provide protection for their descendants from invisible evil forces. Healers of every variety also offer protection. A great deal of activity in Christian churches, too, is directly concerned with questions of security from invisible evil forces, among other things (Kiernan 1994). Security in all its senses is a primary concern of everyone in places like Soweto, and a great deal of discursive effort goes into distinguishing between legitimate and illegitimate uses of force. The central promise at the heart of the social contract founding the democratic state is also the dream of security for all. The key to linking concerns such as those surrounding spiritual insecurity in everyday life with the politics of the state, then, lies in taking seriously the questions of security and justice that arise from efforts to manage relations with invisible forces acting upon life.

The core of this book is an examination of ways of understanding the forces impinging upon people's lives that make them feel unsafe and the ways in which they seek protection, safety, and meaning in response. I focus upon these problems of insecurity from the conviction, grown out of my years living in Soweto, that it is only when the forces threatening harm are either mastered or kept at bay that there is any possibility of freedom and autonomy. Much has been written about the debilitating effects of violence, oppression, racism, and poverty upon Soweto life, less about other sources of perceived harm. My intention here is to take seriously the notions of "force" that people use when they worry about invisible forces or evil forces—implicated in matters such as witchcraft, the action of evil spirits, or the wrath of the ancestors—and investigate the dynamics of relations wherein worries about these forces arise. My principal aim will be to examine the sorts of questions that arise in the course of everyday life concerning the dangers posed by these forces and to anatomize the features of what William James called "live hypotheses" that can plausibly address them (James 1897, 2). To this end I shall delineate the principal patterns of questions regarding invisible forces that arise in the course of everyday life, suggest why they are important, examine the frameworks within which plausible answers to these questions can be produced, and investigate the forms of authority that both produce these answers and are produced in the course of seeking answers.

My examination of the quest for spiritual security in Soweto reveals a pervasive sense of social injustice that is difficult to express in the ordinary terms of conventional political discourse but that nonetheless has real political effects. This is most apparent in relation to those forms of spiritual insecurity usually summarized under the rubric "witchcraft," that is, forms of occult assault perpetrated by other persons, usually persons disguising their malicious motives while using secret means. The ubiquity of the fear of witchcraft in Africa is also an exposure to injustice, for when suffering is caused by witchcraft, it is a form of *harm,* harm perpetrated by some*one.* For this reason I labor long in the following pages over the terms of everyday analogy conjoining witchcraft and violence as parallel uses of occult and physical force, showing how similar principles govern the understandings of legitimate and illegitimate uses of both. These parallels are informed by a common conception of justice. (In the most simple terms, witchcraft is the illegitimate use of occult force; healing is its legitimate purpose. Often the two forms are combined in the same person, just as the corrupt police officer can be both a force for justice and a perpetrator of injustice.) The desire for justice arising from the experience of spiritual insecurity, however, unlike that arising from exposure to violent crime, is difficult for political leaders to satisfy or even express as part of any political agenda in the liberal democratic state in its modernist configurations. This is the heart of the conundrum of spiritual insecurity and political power in contemporary Africa.

My central contention is that the sense of injustice that arises from forms of spiritual insecurity in everyday life is as important to the political process in African contexts as the sense of injustice that arises from the experience of illegitimate violence and exploitation. This is especially important in the context of the HIV/AIDS pandemic. For if, as I shall argue, AIDS is interpreted in a discourse of witchcraft (which need not exclude talk of HIV; witches and viruses are not mutually exclusive concepts, at least from the perspective of the witchcraft paradigm), the implications for community relations and political power are profound. In that case the epidemic is a product of malicious human action and not just the impersonal agency of a virus. As AIDS decimates the population, families and communities are being and will continue to be riven by a desire for justice which the state cannot provide.

In South Africa during the later decades of the twentieth century, the struggle for justice in the face of apartheid became expressed in a quest for democracy. Political democracy, however, is not a deeply rooted cultural form in this region. The long-term prospects for democracy, most observers agree, will depend in large part upon the ability of the new regime to instill in the population a widespread conviction that government really exists to serve the people: to meet demands for physical security and economic well-being and to serve the ends of justice. Spiritual insecurity, which, as I shall show, is closely related to but not reducible to poverty and violence, creates further problems of injustice for the democratic regime. How these are addressed, or ignored, will also affect the future of democracy.

Readers who come to these pages with a sense of their own political agency will perhaps find themselves asking as they read: What is to be done? Those with an awareness of the sorry history of colonialism and apartheid in Africa may also be troubled by these discussions of spiritual insecurity. The colonialists long emphasized talk of witchcraft in Africa as evidence of Africans' inherent irrationality, serving thereby as grounds for excluding them from rights of citizenship. In a context such as South Africa, where rights of citizenship have only recently been granted to the majority of the African population after a long and painful struggle, even to raise questions about the political implications of witchcraft and other forms of spiritual insecurity can seem to cast doubt upon the project of liberation. Moreover, the new political elites in that country are extremely sensitive to suggestions that Africans are any less able to solve their social problems through political action than anyone else, particularly the white people who proclaim their form of rule—democracy!—as the best. These are valid concerns. My experience of spiritual insecurity in Soweto, however, persuades me that these questions cannot be ignored.

Other readers may be inclined to view the matters that I am describing as spiritual insecurity as simply forms of superstition that have persisted because of the inadequate educational opportunities afforded Africans in this part of the world—yet another legacy of colonialism, racism, and apartheid. This may be true. But even if these superstitions could be eradicated in classrooms dedicated to instilling "enlightenment" and modernity and all the other intellectual tools necessary for learners to thrive in the twenty-first century, there is little chance of such education becoming the norm anytime soon. If there are political consequences to spiritual insecurity, as I am convinced there are, they will remain. Moreover, the experience of other societies striving to educate people out of their superstitions—think of religion in the Soviet Union or the teaching of evolution in the United States—makes the prospect of universal enlightenment seem dim. Rather than eradicating superstition, I shall argue, education creates new possibilities for shaping structures of plausibility within which the dangers contributing to spiritual insecurity are interpreted.

Spiritual insecurity arising from fears of witchcraft will surely persist in these parts for the foreseeable future. I shall not, however, presume to dispense policy advice on how to deal with it, other than to point out that it informs virtually every aspect of social life and thus impinges upon virtually every aspect of politics. I shall, however, devote much attention to examining ways in which spiritual insecurity affects political life through the changing distributions of social jealousy, the pervasive presence of injustice, the presumption of malice in community life, and habits of interpretation conducive to distrust of power. The fact that these complications make many aspects of government unpredictable and difficult to explain, however, is no reason to diminish a commitment to democracy—even if only, in a Churchillian phrase, as the least worst political system or, in Robert Dahl's less pessimistic view, the "best feasible" one (Dahl 1989, 84).

2

DIMENSIONS OF INSECURITY
IN CONTEMPORARY SOWETO

Why Soweto?

Most of the literature on witchcraft in Africa has focused on the experience of life in rural communities and villages. Indeed, a rural bias inflects most of the scholarship on Africa in general. Even the more recent contributions to the study of African witchcraft have tended to avoid the complex dynamics of urban life, particularly in large cosmopolitan cities such as Johannesburg. When black South Africans talk of witchcraft in their country, they almost always point to rural areas as the heart of the problem. Some suggest that these places, being economically underdeveloped, are thus backward and the people there more subject to ignorance and superstition. Others, including most of the people I have talked with about this in Soweto, point to witchcraft as more of a problem in the countryside because there are more witches there.

Yet, as with the rest of humanity, African lives are increasingly lived in cities. In South Africa, moreover, not only do most people live in cities—of which Johannesburg is the largest—but much of the African population in the countryside is housed in urban-style "townships" while being financially dependent upon urban economies and culturally focused upon urban lifestyles. To understand the significance of spiritual insecurity for the development of South African democracy, therefore, it is necessary to focus primarily upon urban experiences. There is no better place to begin than Soweto. As Walter Sisulu, veteran leader of the African National Congress (ANC) and lifelong Sowetan, once put it, with only slight exaggeration:

"the history of Soweto is the history of South Africa" (1998, 7).[1] The future of South Africa, I would add, lies in places like Soweto, too.

Soweto is a conglomeration of dormitory townships to the southwest of Johannesburg—hence the name, coined by committee in 1963: *South Western Townships* (Pirie 1984). Home to around a million and a half people, Soweto stretches from a point about twelve miles from the Johannesburg city center to cover an area of about thirty square miles, although the precise delimitations depend upon how one conceives of "Soweto." The area commonly known as Soweto incorporates Black Townships that were originally built and administered by three different sets of authorities: the Johannesburg City Council, the Roodeport City Council, and the Natives Resettlement Board of the national government. Adjacent to Soweto are areas once known as Coloured Townships (Noordgesigt and Eldorado Park) and the Indian Township of Lenasia. To the untrained eye, these latter settlements are hard to distinguish from "Soweto," but they are not usually thought of by residents as part of that place.

When the first democratically elected mayor of Soweto, Danny Kekana, took office in 1995, he discovered he was presiding over the government of an area about which basic social data were both scarce and inaccurate. Nobody could offer even an accurate count of its population. Mayor Kekana commissioned the Department of Sociology at the University of the Witwatersrand to survey Soweto (hereafter referred to as the Wits Survey), and they estimated the population in 1997 to be about 1 million people (A. Morris 1999b, 5). Official figures from the previous regime put the population at less than 1 million (Statistics South Africa 1998). Popular estimates typically reckoned the number nearer 4–5 million.[2] Such numbers are absurd, inflated by a sense of Soweto's significance. If they were true, it would mean that more than 10 percent of the country's population live in Soweto. They don't. Soweto is no less significant for all that.

Most Sowetans are young. A quarter of the population is under the age of fifteen, one-third are younger than twenty, and 57 percent are younger

1. I quote Sisulu's remark from his foreword to *Soweto: A History* (1998), a book based on the six-part television documentary produced by the History Workshop at the University of the Witwatersrand and Free Filmmakers, directed by Angus Gibson. For an overview of Soweto's place in the Johannesburg metropolitan region, see Beavon 1997.

2. In 1999, for example, at a ceremony marking the handing over of title deeds to houses in Soweto, Paul Mashatile, the minister of housing in Gauteng Province, the region incorporating Soweto, claimed that Soweto "has an estimated population of no less [than] 4 million" (Mashatile 1999).

than thirty (A. Morris 1999b, table 2.2). This is a lower proportion of youth than the national demographic profile for Africans in South Africa generally, particularly in rural areas, and is considerably lower than is usual in less developed countries and than was probably the case here in the past (A. Morris 1999b, 6). Nonetheless, the youthfulness of the place is striking. Only 7 percent of the population is over sixty, most of whom are women—which accounts for the slight gender imbalance in the population, which is 51.8 percent female (A. Morris 1999b, 26).[3] Sixty is considered very old by young people in Soweto. With the AIDS epidemic gaining strength, United Nations demographers estimate that fewer than half of the fifteen-year-old children alive in South Africa at the turn of the century will live to see their sixtieth birthday (UNAIDS 2000).

The language of everyday life, particularly among younger people in Soweto, while based upon the predominant Nguni and Sotho/Tswana languages, has a distinct character of its own, blending vocabulary and grammar from English and Afrikaans into a mixture known as *isicamtho,* which is barely comprehensible by someone schooled in the "standard" forms of the indigenous languages of the region that predominate in rural areas (Ntshangase 1993). Another urban argot, known as *tsotsitaal* (gangster-speak), is based upon Afrikaans and tends to be more common among older people and residents of Meadowlands (where people were settled after the demolition of Sophiatown). Most urban people in Johannesburg speak forms of the local languages that are broadly similar in their patterns of borrowing from other languages. Slang vocabularies, however, change very rapidly and can be quite local in scope. Sowetan youths, for example, sometimes find themselves speaking in codes unrecognizable to black youths from townships on the other side of Johannesburg, although with the explosion of *kwaito* music in the 1990s, *isicamtho* has gained a much wider currency nationally than it had previously.[4]

3. By contrast, 16.2 percent of white South African females and 12.6 percent of males are over sixty (A. Morris 1999b, 7).

4. Until recently there has been very little sociolinguistic study of urban language use in South Africa, with the result that although the majority of urban dwellers speak distinctive language varieties, differing from standard forms of regional and European languages in vocabulary, semantics, phonology, and morphology (Caltreaux 1996), the thrust of language policy formation has been framed in terms of standard rural versions of the languages, with which most urban dwellers have limited formal competence. The 1996 report of the Language Plan Task Group, for example, presents a plan for fostering the development of African languages to challenge the "hegemony" of English but says nothing about the place of the nonstandard language forms, such as *isicamtho,* that people actually speak (Lan-

Built far from the exclusive White suburbs to the north of the city and separated from the less-expensive southern suburbs by mine dumps and vacant land, the major part of Soweto was erected by White authorities pursuing the twin objectives of segregating black people from white while providing cheap housing for workers and their families employed for low wages in white-owned firms in an industrial city. The first "Native Location" was built there in 1904; the first "properly planned township," known as Orlando Township, was settled in 1930; the bulk of "Greater Soweto" was constructed in the 1950s and 1960s. The sections built after 1954 were ethnically segregated. In apartheid South Africa, Soweto was the biggest, most diverse (both ethnically and socioeconomically), and the most politically significant of the Black Townships.[5]

Soweto, it must be stressed, is not some sort of blighted inner-city ghetto. Though created as a public housing project by white officials responding to the challenges of African urbanization and the demands of white industrialists, farmers, and merchants (not to underestimate the prejudices of white electors), in shape and character the South Western Townships came in time to resemble something living. The severe crenellations of the original streetscape, bare but for the symmetrical rows of 70,000 "matchbox" houses, softened as trees grew, outhouses sprang up, and, after the administrators lost control, the mass-produced dwellings were expanded to fit the comfort and means of their occupants. Some Sowetan families are quite prosperous. The roads are jammed with late-model cars, as well as pedestrians too poor to afford the bus fare. Despite its inauspicious beginnings, Soweto became a place of homes for families and communities. And the lives that people have made for themselves in these homes and streets have shaped the world far beyond the confines of the South Western Townships.

Soweto is best known as the principal seat of resistance to apartheid and the struggle for freedom. In 1976 the schoolchildren of Soweto began protests that sparked a countrywide conflagration and the beginning of the end of apartheid (Brink et al. 2001; Hirson 1979; Kane-Berman 1978; Ndlovu 1997). After the Soweto schoolchildren's uprising of June 16, 1976, the word "Soweto" became a symbol of resistance to racism around the world. For almost two decades prior to the dawning of democracy, Soweto was con-

---

guage Plan Task Group 1996). It should also be noted that the eleven "official" languages enshrined in the Constitution are products of a history of missionary translation and apartheid-era notions of ethnicity, which eradicated a great deal of linguistic diversity in pursuit of a model of protonational ethnic "cultures."

5. For a survey of the literature on Soweto, see Appendix 1.

sumed by an oftentimes violent struggle against the security forces of the apartheid regime. Few Sowetans in those years saw the institutions of the state as anything other than agents of racist oppression, even those institutions such as hospitals, clinics, and schools that were ostensibly geared to providing services to township dwellers. Township revolt was spearheaded by young people. These youths were largely contemptuous of the seeming quiescence of their elders, and in their struggle to make the townships of apartheid "ungovernable," they challenged the authority of parents, elders, and teachers as well as their enemy, "the apartheid system." The legacy of this revolt remains evident in youth culture today. But Soweto, now, is also just another suburb of Johannesburg. Its matchbox houses, icons of apartheid, are now valuable real estate.

From its beginning in 1904, the place that became known as Soweto was created with the imperatives of governance in mind. The history of Soweto is also the history of efforts to govern Africans in cities and the history of ways of resisting that governance. For most of the twentieth century, Africans in urban areas posed acute problems for those who would govern cities in a state wherein black people were denied rights of full citizenship (Ashforth 1997). In the postapartheid era, following the first democratic elections in 1994, the place known as Soweto is no longer a "Native Location" or a "Bantu Township," as the terminologies of the past described it. The townships that were once the South Western Townships are now referred to as "historically disadvantaged communities," and for purposes of local government the place is divided into administrative regions named Doornkop/Soweto and Diepkloof/Meadowlands within the "megacity" of Johannesburg (Office of the City Manager 2000). Problems of governance remain. Though it no longer refers to a distinct administrative entity, "Soweto" is a name that still lives. What it names is something more than just a place on a map.

In 1990, the first time I visited Soweto, I learned what all Sowetans know and relearn each day if they forget: be careful. Although the fact that I was a white man staying in an apartheid township colored the question of security for myself at that time, as it still does when I visit, *everyone* in Soweto lives with a pressing sense of exposure to dangers. Everyone has his or her own requirements for managing relations with others so as to minimize risk of harm. Even children playing on the street constantly remind themselves to avoid the dangers of passing cars. My friend Madumo summed up the situation well when he told me back in 1991 that "here in Soweto life is too much exposed." Life is indeed exposed: exposed to the gaze of others in crowded homes, streets, taxis, shebeens, and all the other loci of the dense sociality that is Sowetan life; exposed to the goodwill of others to meet basic needs of shelter, food, and clothing; exposed to the resentment, rage, and violence of others (violence that is feared in both physical and occult forms); and now, more than ever before, exposed to the ravages of disease in the form of HIV/AIDS. I have suggested that spiritual insecurity informs every aspect of life and is related to, but not reducible to, other forms of insecurity. Circumstances that can be summarized under the rubrics of poverty, violence, and disease produce misfortunes demanding interpretation. These interpretations typically invoke the action of mysterious invisible forces, including those manifest in persons. They also produce relationships among people that are stressed by feelings of envy, resentment, and revenge, feelings that are taken as conducive to motivating people to perpetrate occult violence. In this and the following two chapters I shall examine some aspects of the general insecurities of social relations in Soweto and the ways people try to manage the dangers of poverty, violence, and disease by drawing upon resources of family, community, the state, and healing specialists.

Poverty and the Burdens of Reciprocity

Most Sowetans are poor. About 60 percent of households surveyed by a team of sociologists from the University of the Witwatersrand had incomes less than R 1,500 per month. The R 1,500 per month which many Sowetan households subsisted upon in 1997 was about the average wage for an urban semiskilled worker in formal employment at the time.[6] In 1997, the estimated subsistence level in the region for a family of five was R 1,293 (A. Morris 1999b, 9). A loaf of bread at the time cost about R 2.50, a bottle of beer in a shebeen was R 3.50, a medium-sized television was around R 3,000, and a late-model used car cost about R 40,000–50,000. The exchange rate was about five rand to the U.S. dollar. A household earning R 1,500 in the mid- to late 1990s could survive reasonably comfortably, depending upon who was earning the money and how responsible they were in their duties of support, but there would not have been enough money in the house for the consumer items many of the family would consider necessities.

Conditions in many places in South Africa, however, are far worse than in Soweto. Black people in rural areas, for example, have much lower house-

---

6. A countrywide survey at the time found that 42 percent of Africans earned less than R 1,000 per month (May 1998).

hold incomes: less than R 1,000 per year at the end of the 1990s (Whiteford and Van Seventer 1999). Rural services are much worse. Indeed, Sowetans enjoy a position roughly in the middle of the socioeconomic spectrum of the country as a whole, with a slightly higher socioeconomic profile and a more substantial middle class than most other Black Townships (A. Morris 1999b, 11). In comparison with the formerly "Whites-only" suburbs, however, conditions in Soweto—even in the relatively desirable parts of the township—are inferior. Suburban incomes are higher. Services are better. Properties are more secure. Most Sowetan families who could afford suburban life moved out in the late 1990s. Houses in the suburbs are bigger, and services better, but life is vastly more expensive.[7] Despite all the difficulties, however, it is not impossible to live well in Soweto.

Most people in Soweto are not regularly employed in paying work. Of the people in Soweto who are over sixteen and neither studying full-time, disabled, nor retired, only 40.5 percent are employed in full-time work (A. Morris 1999b, 7). Most of those who are working are not earning high wages. Among Sowetans in paid employment, about two-thirds work in unskilled or semiskilled occupations. Of those surveyed by the Witwatersrand team, 8.9 percent defined themselves as "professionals," most of whom were teachers employed in local schools. Only 0.8 percent of Sowetans who were employed in 1997 occupied managerial positions (A. Morris 1999b, table 2.1). Everyone earning income in Soweto is under strong pressure to share with family members, friends, and neighbors. Without this sharing, many would not survive.

Earning a regular income, from any source and at any level, is enough to put a person into the category of the comparatively well-off in Soweto. Few people there, however, enjoy careers they find satisfying and rewarding. In conversational exchanges among new acquaintances in Soweto, the polite inquiry "What do you do?" is seldom heard. People are either working or they are not, and it is not always polite to inquire. The job itself is hardly relevant. It is rare to find a person in Soweto for whom work provides a sense of identity invested with more significance than access to cash in the pocket. In the place of inquiries about work and professions, new acquaintances more often ask one another, "Where do you stay?" Being able to locate a person geographically is far more useful than knowing what they do.

7. A rough measure of the inequality between suburb and township can be gauged from the fact that, according to the 1996 census, white households (predominantly suburban) earned on average nine times the income of black households (Whiteford and Van Seventer 1999). A black family would find suburban life difficult if they earned less.

A great many people try to make money from time to time by "business," mostly by selling groceries, sweets, or beer or plying trades such as shoe repair or welding for which the formal economy has little use. Many households have backyard rooms that they rent out. Three rooms in the yard, the maximum that can fit on most stands, rented at the maximum rate would bring in the equivalent of about half of an average worker's pay packet. Few participants in these informal economies make anything like the income that a proper job in the formal sector would earn, and most are just trying to make ends meet until they find full-time work (Piazza-Georgi 2000, 11).

About 10 percent of the adult population receive an old-age pension, which women qualify for at the age of sixty and men at sixty-five (Piazza-Georgi 2000, 11). In the mid-1990s pensions were equalized at R 520 across all the former "population groups," resulting in a significant increase in income for black pensioners—about twice the median income for black people—in many cases granting them more money than they had earned during their working lives (Case and Deaton 1998, 1330). Pensions are a significant source of income for many families, and it is a rare pensioner who does not have to share her monthly payout with children and grandchildren. By 2003 pensions had risen to R 700. As well as pensions, public assistance is available in the form of child support grants, which pay R 160 (2003) per month for each child under nine, disability grants, and various other social grants.[8]

Unemployed Sowetans have pitifully few opportunities for employment. Not only has the number of unskilled and semiskilled jobs that sustained their parents declined, but they face competition for such "menial" jobs as do exist from migrants coming from neighboring states. Employers in Sowetan shops and small businesses generally prefer to employ migrants from rural areas and neighboring states. Employers are not afraid to express a strong prejudice that Sowetans, particularly young men, are— to quote a prominent shopkeeper in Mapetla Extension who will remain nameless—"lazy and unreliable." Most of the small businesses in Soweto employ illegal immigrants, mostly from Mozambique, who can be paid minimal wages and subjected to closer control in the workplace than Sowetans will tolerate. Nonetheless, and despite the odds, virtually everyone hopes to find a job one day, if not soon.

8. For details on grants, see the Department of Social Development's pamphlet *You and Your Grant*, available at www.socdev.gov.za/services/servo1.htm. Figures here are taken from the 2003 edition.

In short, about half of all adults are financially dependent to some extent, and at least some of the time, on others, when, according to the prevailing norms of adulthood, they should not be. These relations of dependence are of the utmost importance in family and community life, for as well as being dependent themselves, these people are generally unable to meet the requirements of supporting those who are supposed to be dependent upon *them,* namely their children. Long-term structural unemployment and the virtually permanent state of dependency it entails have corrosive effects in families and communities. Although there are deeply rooted norms of sharing and reciprocity within families and communities, these function best when capacities for giving are relatively evenly distributed. When one person's needs today might be the other's tomorrow, it makes sense to share and share alike, to recognize the interdependency of persons expressed in the concept of *ubuntu:* "a person is a person through other people." But when some people's needs are permanent and their capacities for reciprocity limited, habits and ethics of sharing come under strain.

To be a member of a family, even a distant relative, is to enjoy rights to shelter and food. And to be a member of a family is to know an obligation to share. Considering how little there is to go around, the fact that it gets shared out relatively equitably most of the time is little short of miraculous. And considering that in almost all families, certainly every one that I know intimately, the burdens of providing for parents and siblings require the earners within the family to regularly forgo significant opportunities for personal pleasure and fulfillment, the fact that family life continues with as few ruptures as it does is tribute to a fundamental generosity and is the source of tremendous social resilience. When these relations of amity and comity in a family break down, however, the results can be devastating.

Images and objects celebrating affluence invade life in Soweto from all sides, reminders of the fact that while many black South Africans are thriving in this postapartheid era of Black Economic Empowerment (BEE), most Sowetans are poor. Many go to sleep hungry from time to time. Some are hungry much of the time. Hardly anyone, even those with good jobs, has cash to spare. All could use the "better life" they were promised in elections past. Everyone complains of trouble paying their debts, and were one not to complain so, others would insist on more help with theirs. But nearly everyone manages to get by, somehow. In the mid- and late 1990s, the tenor of life in Soweto seemed agitated by nothing so much as the desire to go shopping, as if the political energies of the previous decade had been channeled into consumerism. In 1990, for example, when the first June 16 rally commemorating the 1976 Soweto Uprising was held following the unbanning of the ANC and the release of political prisoners, 50,000 people crammed Jabulani Amphitheatre in Soweto to savor the moment of victory close at hand. By June 16, 1997, the uprising was being commemorated in Soweto by a handful of dedicated activists accompanied by a couple of hundred fans of the *kwaito* star Arthur Mafokate, the featured musical act. The fans threatened rebellion when ANC dignitaries tried to prevent their idol from performing his hit single "AmaGents," celebrating the criminal life. A week later, the opening of a new shopping center on the outskirts of Soweto drew a crowd of 50,000 clamoring for the possibility of a bargain.

This burst of consumer excitement in the late 1990s came after decades of steady transformation in the financial complexity of urban black life. Consider a brief history of the financial affairs of the family I stayed with. It is emblematic of the transformation of domestic finances for a great many Sowetans. In 1964, at the height of what is sometimes called the "golden age of apartheid" (O'Meara 1996, 116), the newly married Hendry and Daphne Mfete moved into their new house in Mapetla Extension. He was a carpet-layer and she was a domestic servant working for a white family in the suburbs. Despite the fact that their wages were low when compared with white workers with similar skills and diligence, they were accustomed to paying their rent for six months in advance without particular sacrifice. They had been married in church, and *lobola* (bride-wealth) had been paid in full. The house they called home was owned and had been built by the Johannesburg City Council (in accordance with the National Institute of Building Research design NE51/9). They were permitted to make only minor changes or improvements, such as installing burglar bars over the windows, concreting the dirt floor, or erecting a fence and a gate. None of their friends and family had a better house. None lived in anything notably worse. Only a small minority of township dwellers in the 1960s enjoyed houses better than the ubiquitous matchboxes identical to the Mfetes' home. The slums and shantytowns of the cities had mostly been cleared by then. Most of the poorest people were stuck in the Homelands and were forcibly prevented from migrating to towns.

More money, were it to have been available to the Mfetes in the 1960s, would have had only limited utility after the rent was paid and groceries bought. There were only limited opportunities for spending in those days. The money they had was sufficient to mark a degree of social distinction by expenditure on clothes (especially for the children at Christmas), furniture (though not electrical appliances, as there was no electricity available), and, most important, a car. Hendry never tires of recalling the cars he owned in the seventies and his journeys "up and down" the country. They were able to help relatives, friends, and neighbors in distress. Had they been so inclined, they might have been able to impress the neighbors by the scale and regularity of feasts in honor of their ancestors or with parties to mark birthdays and special occasions. They could have bought a lot of drinks, because in 1962 the government abolished the liquor laws prohibiting sale of "European" liquor to Africans. But they were modest people. If they had been first-generation migrants to town with close ties to family and land in rural places they thought of as "home," they might have been inclined to invest in cattle or homesteads in a Homeland. But they were urban people, with urban parents, making urban lives for their children. Their prospects looked good.

In their early married life, the sorts of investments in health care, housing, place of abode, and schooling for children that contribute significantly to the life chances of future generations of the middle classes were prohibited to people like Daphne and Hendry by the architects of apartheid. Nonetheless, they strove to be what they are happy to describe as "respectable" and to bring their children up "right," even if an occasional neighbor criticized them for trying to be like white people—"black *umlungus*" was the taunt. They considered themselves lucky to have the house they had in the quiet street of Mapetla Extension—which was fortunate, for they had no chance of moving. Nor had they any choice in the 1970s and 1980s but to send their children to the local public schools to be taught, for a modest fee, according to the National Party's doctrines of "Bantu Education." When sick, they went to the public clinic or Chris Hani Baragwanath Hospital. Fees at both places were minimal.

In the early 1980s, when the strictures of apartheid began to be relaxed following the 1976 Soweto Uprising, the Mfetes bought the ninety-nine-year lease on their home that was offered in lieu of full ownership (since the regime was still insisting that black people really belonged in the Homelands) and began to improve it "bit by bit." Most of their money then went into the house. When electricity services began, they were able to start buying appliances. They were fortunate in the late eighties to be able to participate in the boycotts of electricity and service charges that the Civic Associations mounted in protest against apartheid.[9] For the better part of a decade they, like most Sowetans, enjoyed free electricity and water. They

9. After 1983, following the lead of community organizations in the Eastern Cape town of Craddock, a network of Street Committees and Civic Associations was established in Soweto. In the mid-1980s these operated as attempts to create "organs of people's power" taking over some of the functions of local government. For an account of the politics of these organizations in the 1980s, see Mayekiso 1996.

were able to connect a phone when service became available in the late 1980s and to pay the bill.

When Mandela was released from prison in 1990 and negotiations began for a "new" South Africa, the Mfete family seemed poised to enjoy the fruits of freedom in the form of a comfortable middle-class life. The two daughters were studying to become schoolteachers, and the son was beginning a career in retail sales. Life could only get better. But the price of entry to middle-class life was beginning to rise, and the costs of remaining comfortable were becoming prohibitive. Everything that had been either provided or prohibited for the parents in the 1960s had to be bought and was expensive for the children in the 1990s. Houses were no longer provided by the state and rent paid for six months in advance but bought through private sales with mortgages paid over thirty years at exorbitant interest rates. Cars were no longer a luxury but a necessity for transport to work. Local schools were still available but were hopelessly outclassed by expensive "multiracial" schools in the suburbs to which black children were now admitted. Health insurance was necessary to avoid the lines at clinics and the dreadful conditions of public hospitals. Water and electricity had to be paid for in full. Cell phones were essential. Houses had to be stocked full of electrical appliances. The television, a medium that was introduced to the country only in 1976, kept pumping images of more desirable things and the people who have them into the home. And the demands of less fortunate family members and friends never ceased. By the end of the 1990s, though they all enjoyed comforts unknown to the parents in the 1960s, the family found themselves struggling to make ends meet and all too often unhappy about their failure to do so.

Sometimes the worry of making ends meet can be unbearable and the burden of failure to meet financial obligations can be crushing. Suicides and clinical depression seem to be increasing. When two sisters I know were hospitalized for "stress" and "depression" in the late 1990s, their mother told me that she had never known of "this thing depression." In her day, she said, people were often unhappy and sad but she had never encountered a person suffering from the depression she had come to know as a serious illness.[10] But day after day, month after month, life goes on. And life can be good. Laughter and joy are known in Soweto as well as suffering. The

10. A survey of "attitudes toward mental health in an urban black population" conducted among patients at Soweto's Baragwanath Hospital in 1967 confirms this recollection, finding that only 29 percent of respondents "stated that they had seen people in a state of depression," of whom 32 percent considered the symptoms "normal" (Fisher and Hurst 1967).

struggle for life, however, is unending, and the stresses and the strains of securing food, clothing, and shelter shape every aspect of life within households, families, and communities.

Most people survive because others feel obliged to share and support them as members of their families, as neighbors, and as friends. Reciprocity is a norm that has been handed down in the name of ancient "African tradition," reinforced by Christian teachings, and learned anew a generation at a time from the exigencies of urban life. Sharing and redistribution, however, as well as expressing love and interpersonal commitment, can engender complex relations of power and domination that breed resentments. Among these resentments is the jealousy that is said to give rise to witchcraft.

Norms of reciprocity and principles of distribution within families and fictive kin relationships provide people with a strong expectation, based on a sense of entitlement if not always an enforceable right, that within the networks to which they belong resources will be distributed equitably and according to need. This sense is particularly strong within families, although it can also be found in other social groupings such as cohorts of lifelong friends, church groups, or gangs of young men bonded together in the solidarities of violence — groups that will all typically express their relationships in terms of the language of kinship. One of the key lessons I learned when living in Soweto was that to survive there, if you do not have family, particularly "brothers" who are prepared to risk their lives for yours, you must invent one.

Within networks where relations are premised upon principles of reciprocity, the metaphor of "family" serves to establish a structure of redistribution that incorporates the core of the network into obligatory transfers in the name of "kinship" while simultaneously excluding others on the same grounds. That is, one has to share with kin but not with non-kin; one should share more with a sibling than with a cousin; and so on. If a person with money in a family or network of reciprocity makes a major purchase, or even if she begins to enjoy a manifestly better standard of living than the rest, such as by wearing expensive clothes or moving out of the family home to a place of her own, then it is in a sense true to say that she benefits at the expense of the others in something like a zero-sum fashion. Her gain is the others' loss. Moreover, since only a minority of people are earning income, for most people their standard of living depends upon having access to people willing to share. When someone moves into a new relationship with someone possessing financial means, it is true to say that he benefits at someone else's expense. A person who alienates the affections of a financially sound person from others who depend on him can cause considerable harm.

Within informal financial networks, the most egregious infraction of social norms consists of using money as an excuse for ignoring the obligations deriving from hierarchical relations, such as when "children," conscious of their father's financial dependence on them, neglect to pay him sufficient deference. Similarly, taking advantage of financial prosperity to transform relations that should be horizontal, reciprocal, and egalitarian into vertical structures of dominance and dependence is a serious breach of propriety and will be deeply resented. A young man who buys a car, for example, will be able to impose his social agenda on his friends, but he does so at his peril. In the realities of everyday life, both of these types of infraction are virtually impossible to avoid because far too many people are dependent on others when they should be providers, and most are unable to meet the requirements of reciprocity. Thus, virtually everyone is resentful to some extent of others and their uses of money or has others angry and resentful at them.

People with access to money in a context of generalized poverty such as Soweto find themselves in positions of significant power, whether they wish to be or not. To a large extent their social situation will depend upon how they manage the relations of power that grow out of the financial dependence of those around them. Generosity, magnanimity, liberality, open-handedness, and all the other virtues of benevolence are necessary for the survival of the fortunate—at the very least to secure themselves against robbery and theft. These same virtues, however, can persuade others that the benefactor is "a stupid" who deserves to be taken advantage of, a lesson I learned the hard way when I discovered that a couple of the neighborhood boys had been pilfering my cash while enjoying my hospitality. Practices of reciprocity and benevolence always run up against the problem of how to manage relations with those not included in the network—such as when my brother's brother is not also my brother. I experienced an instance of this when I encountered deep resentment between Madumo and his brother over my support for Madumo's studies. This was compounded by the fact that over the years, while Madumo had seemed to be benefiting from my largesse, his brother had had to fend for himself (Ashforth 2000a, 218–220). No matter how generous people with money might be, they are always vulnerable living among the poor, vulnerable to theft, to resentment, and to imprecation. No matter how wealthy you are when you live in Soweto, no matter how many you make happy with your helping hand, many more will be excluded from your beneficence and largesse and feel themselves harmed thereby.

This vulnerability partly explains one of the phenomena that I found puzzling in my early years in Soweto: the fact that even those friends with decent jobs never seemed to have any money. Over the years I too learned that the safest way to protect one's income was to hide it. No one will tell you truthfully how much money they earn or have. And the safest way to save money is to spend it. At first I found the famous institution of the *stokvel* particularly puzzling. The *stokvel* is a rotating credit association in which a group of a dozen or so people combine, agree to contribute a set amount monthly, and meet each month to make their contributions and celebrate at a member's house, who usually sells the *stokvel* members and their guests food and liquor; each month a designated member takes the whole pot. Apart from the obvious attraction of the camaraderie involved in the *stokvel,* the risks of participating are considerable compared to putting the equivalent sum into a savings account in a bank each month. People die, disappear, and renege on their obligations to *stokvels.* But the advantage of the *stokvel* as a means of saving, in addition to the discipline it imposes, is that it allows the member to restrict money that would otherwise be subject to obligations to family and kin. Everyone recognizes the importance of the obligation involved in membership in a *stokvel.* This allows members to legitimately deny requests for financial support that would otherwise be unavoidable, a matter of the utmost importance to people with the modest incomes available to most working Sowetans. The rotating nature of the payout allows members to plan in advance for substantial expenditures, which can be protected from others' demands.[11]

By the late 1990s, the skewed distribution of good fortune among those who expected liberation to "uplift" all was beginning to be registered in the language of "jealousy," the elemental motive of witchcraft. Here is a typical example. The conversation was between myself and Modiehe, a grandmother and retired schoolteacher, in her neighbor MaMfete's kitchen in 1998:

> "Amongst us, jealousy is increasing tremendously. They don't want to see you progressing. If you are progressing they say, 'She thinks she's better than us.' Like now, you see we are doing this small business. They're not happy

---

11. For a discussion of the history and practice of the *stokvel* in South Africa, see Lukhele 1990; Schultze 1997; Verhoef 2002. For a comparative account of rotating credit associations, see Geertz 1962.

for it, most of them. And you would just hear from the things they say. Like, someone will just stop you in the street and say, 'Are you still selling?' Because last week they saw us selling but this week they didn't. What kind of question is that? 'Are you still selling?' Oh! And then the other one would tell me funny things like 'I heard your meat wasn't very nice. Somebody bought it and they didn't like it.' So that is jealousy."

"And it didn't used to be like this?" I asked.

"Now lately it's more. It has never been as bad as it is now."

"Why?"

"It's because most of the people don't work and they don't have money and now seeing that they don't have and if you are doing something and prospering then they become jealous. They ask themselves, 'How? How is she progressing while other people are not?' And then they just make a mountain out of a molehill."

I asked Modiehe if she were afraid that the jealous people would do something to harm her. "I don't care about them, if they are jealous," she scoffed. "So long as my business will go on, that won't harm me." She had also told me once that when people build a new house, others say, "Now that the house is finished, someone must die" (Ashforth 2000a, 73). But she had built a house some years earlier and nothing untoward had happened. Two years later this lady and her family moved to a new house in the suburbs north of Johannesburg. A year after that she was dead. The women who had said those "funny things" about my friend would not have been surprised. From their point of view she was proud. And to be proud is to be a veritable magnet for witchcraft. To be successful in a place like Soweto and not be considered proud, however, is virtually impossible.

Violence, Crime, and Justice: Legitimating the Use of Force

Soweto is a dangerous place. Each year, according to police statistics, more than a thousand people are murdered in and around Soweto.[12] Another fifteen hundred attempted murders are reported to the police. Approximately 13,000 violent assaults are reported to the police each year and

12. The South African Police Service "Police Area" of Soweto includes police stations in Eldorado Park and Lenasia, which are not generally thought of as part of Soweto (and are not so considered in this book), so the actual numbers for the former Black Townships would be slightly lower. Crime statistics here are taken from numbers published by the police in 2001 (South African Police Service 1998, 2001). For reasons discussed below, they should not be treated as accurate.

2,500 or more rapes; both numbers would be far higher were all incidents of violence reported and recorded.[13] South Africa has the highest incidence of reported rape in the world, and Soweto has some of the highest rates in South Africa (Human Rights Watch 2001). In excess of 4,000 burglaries of residential properties are reported each year. Until 1994, political murders and repressive state violence were also endemic.[14] A survey of crime in the Johannesburg region, including Soweto, conducted in 1996 as part of a United Nations international study of crime victimization found that "over the past five years 67.8 percent of all the respondents were victims of crime and 37.8 percent were victims of more than one offense" (Naudé, Grobbelaar, and Snyman 1996, 13).

I can think of no way to adequately convey the sense of insecurity that the prevalence of violence in Soweto arouses other than to report that the only friends I have mourned as murdered have died in that place and no one I have known there over the past decade has seen a year go by without being called to a funeral of someone connected to them who died at another's hand. In comparison, the chances of getting murdered or knowing a murder victim in the other places I have lived, such as New York City and Perth, Western Australia, are slight. New York City, for example, with a population of 7.6 million, suffered 767 murders in 1997 (New York City Police Department CompStat Unit 2002); Western Australia, with a population of 1.8 million, almost twice the population of Soweto, had 30 (Ferrante, Fernandez, and Loh 1999, table V). But 995 Sowetans were murdered that year (South African Police Service 2001). All this violence creates a great deal of hardship and suffering, misfortunes that demand interpretation. Nobody takes physical security for granted in Soweto, and considerations of security suffuse every aspect of everyday life.

Officers of the state upholding the authority of the law have never offered much in the way of a sense of safety for people living in Soweto. In the absence of effective formal policing over many decades, the forms of discipline and socialization of young men that had developed in rural communities also proved inadequate to the task of urban industrial society, where the sanctions available to fathers and other elders, other than ad hoc

13. A survey of women in the south of Johannesburg, the region encompassing Soweto, found that 20 percent of young women had experienced sexual abuse by the age of eighteen (N. Anderson et al. 2000).

14. In the first four years of the 1990s, 6,361 deaths were attributed to political violence in the region around Soweto (Bornman, Eeden, and Wentzel 1998, 18).

violence, were negligible (Glaser 2000, chap. 1).[15] During the apartheid era, when "public order policing" was the preoccupation of the police force, it was difficult to live in a place like Soweto and believe that the police existed to prevent or solve crimes and serve the people.[16] Police were universally despised and feared as the brutal servants of the apartheid regime. In the words of an antiapartheid activist who was eventually to become justice minister, the police represented "the grossest evils the white minority regimes have been capable of" (Maduna 1993, 41). Everyone knew someone who had been their victim, if they had not been one themselves. Before the pass laws, which controlled black access to white areas, were suspended in 1986, millions of black people were arrested and imprisoned for trifling bureaucratic infringements (Frankel 1979b). Prior to the liberalization of the liquor laws in 1962, similar numbers were arbitrarily arrested for drinking or selling "European" liquor (Horrell 1960). The idea of Law carried little moral authority in everyday life; the "rule of law" was a concept known only by a small coterie of political intellectuals who had discovered the notion in books, not in the experience of life. The aura surrounding the police, dominated in the apartheid era by Afrikaners, was that of arbitrariness and brutality.

After the new government took office in May 1994, the police were represented to the community as if miraculously transformed into servants of the people. The South African Police of old were renamed the South African Police *Service*. In 2001 a new police force, the Metropolitan Police, was established by the city of Johannesburg to bring together traffic officers, policing of municipal regulations, crime prevention, and crime investigation under a central municipal command. Seven police stations serve Soweto. Three more can be found in contiguous areas. As the legacy of their reputation as enforcers of apartheid, the officers working in them battle against crime in a context shaped by a generalized disregard for lawfulness produced by apartheid (Brewer 1994). Effective policing is also hampered by inadequate resources and the widespread perception, deriving from experience and reinforced by persistent media reports, that police and criminal justice officials are corrupt and incompetent (M. Shaw 2002). One of the unintended effects of efforts to transform policing was that the po-

15. For an account of the socialization of young men in a rural context, Sekhukuneland in the 1940s and 1950s, see Pitje 1950a, 1950b, 1950c.

16. For a history of policing in South Africa, see Brewer 1994. For a discussion of efforts at police transformation in the postapartheid era, see M. Shaw 2002.

lice lost some of the capacity to arouse fear that had been the hallmark of apartheid-era policing. No longer afraid of the police themselves, the ordinary citizens of Soweto assumed that the criminals, when not actually in league with the police in organized syndicates, were equally unafraid. This contributed to a growing sense of exposure to criminals.[17]

Victims of violent crime in Soweto rarely approach officers of the police and courts with their grievances expecting to witness justice being served. Mostly police involvement in lives affected by crime is incidental, unpredictable, and unreliable. Unless an insured automobile is stolen, in which case a police report will be needed, there is little point in approaching the police. The 1996 crime victimization survey found that while most crimes against property were reported to the police (90.5 percent of car thefts; 59.3 percent of "burglary with entry"), few crimes against persons were (25.6 percent of assaults or threats of assault; 27.5 percent of rapes) (Naudé, Grobbelaar, and Snyman 1996, 17). Considering that the survey incorporated respondents from white middle-class suburbs along with subjects in the townships, figures for Soweto alone would probably be lower. When people feeling wronged do approach officers of the state, they are usually disappointed. For example, on March 19, 2002, the minister for safety and security, answering a question in Parliament, reported that of the 15,680 cases of rape and attempted rape of children in South Africa reported to the police in the first nine months of 2001, only 1,539 resulted in convictions (SAPA 2002). Thus, in nine out of ten cases in which parents and other family members believed their child had been raped and were prepared to put her through the trauma of a trial to seek justice, they were disappointed.

No one I have ever known in Soweto expects truth to emerge from the course of criminal investigations or to govern judicial proceedings. Nor have I heard of anyone referring a matter to the police and expecting investigative or detective work in pursuit of unknown perpetrators except for the time when a friend was hijacked in a rental car equipped with a radio locating device. When people do approach the police to "open a docket," police involvement tends to be seen as but one of a variety of possible tactics of revenge ranging from personal vendetta to community vigilante

17. More than two-thirds of respondents to the Wits Survey in 1997 thought that crime had increased in the previous five years. The crimes that most people were most worried about were rape (34.1 percent of respondents placed it at the top of their list of worries) and murder (26.4 percent) (A. Morris 1999b, table 7.2).

action. In many instances, the act of involving police in conflicts where parties are known to one another is construed by the person charged, as well as by his or her family and friends, as an aggressive action. In many quarters a strong ethic remains that conflicts should be handled within the community.

When a friend's mother had a beer bottle broken over her head by a drinking partner with whom she had fallen out, for example, she laid a charge at the police station against the other woman. She had no husband in the house or grown sons, so she felt she had no choice. The next day her assailant's sons and their friends paid my friend and her family a visit, brandishing guns and demanding that the assault charge be dropped. Knowing that even if they did not follow through on their threat to shoot, the boys could easily bribe the police to "lose" the docket, my friend's mother agreed to accept one hundred rand (equivalent to about fifteen dollars at the time) to cover medical expenses. The fact that her assailant had been arrested and held overnight was, she told me, about as far as a person could expect justice to go.

Alcohol abuse contributes significantly to the general scourge of violence in homes and neighborhoods (Parry and Bennetts 1999). Researchers at the Medical Research Council report that South Africans are among the heaviest drinkers in the world and that some 30 percent of urban Africans are at risk from alcohol abuse (Parry 1997). My experience in Sowetan shebeens (those unlicensed drinking houses, one of which can be found within about one hundred yards of any given point in the township) confirms this finding. Surveys of criminal suspects and crime victims show a strong correlation between alcohol consumption and violent crime, with one survey reporting more than 70 percent of victims and suspects in assault cases under the influence of alcohol (M. Shaw and Gastrow 2001, 246). Serious drug abuse most often involves Mandrax tablets (methaqualone, a.k.a. "quaaludes"), a heavy tranquilizer that, when crushed and smoked with *dagga* (marijuana), produces hallucinations and is addictive. The combination is known as Bubu Mala, after the dope-smoking reggae genius Bob Marley, and is favored by young men and boys in Soweto because it is a cheaper high than alcohol. A 1999 survey of drug use among criminal offenders in metropolitan areas of South Africa conducted by the Medical Research Council and the Institute of Security Studies found that 56 percent of young male offenders under the age of twenty were using this combination (A. Louw and Parry 1999). Violence is by no means an exclusively male preserve, though victims and perpetrators are overwhelmingly male and young. The

National Non-natural Mortality Surveillance System estimated that in the first quarter of 1999 in South Africa, slightly more than 91 percent of all homicide victims between the ages of fifteen and thirty-four (the age-group comprising the vast bulk of the total) were male (Peden and Butchart 2000, table 1).

The high prevalence of violence, often exacerbated by the volatility of intoxication, coupled with the limited availability of state resources serving the ends of justice, means that individuals, families, and communities are commonly driven to seek private redress for harms caused by other people's violence. Where justice is not possible, such as in situations where the victim of an injury is unable to recruit forces sufficient to right a wrong, the victim either suffers in silence or seeks occult revenge. Similar principles govern the interpretation of the legitimacy of such acts.

Two primary motives for inflicting harm upon a person by means of physical violence or the use of invisible forces are universally admitted as legitimate in Soweto, as elsewhere: defense and punishment, or "discipline" as it is mostly called here. Judgment about the legitimacy of a particular act of physical or occult violence is almost always made according to how well the act can be interpreted in either or both of these terms. Most narratives relating accounts of violent conflict or witchcraft struggles in everyday life are framed in the language of defense against an unwarranted aggression or punishment for an inexcusable infraction.

A third motive for violence, the desire to compel a person to speak the truth, is ambiguous because it blurs the distinction between voluntary confession and punishment. If the violence induces a confession to a crime worthy of punishment, it is justifiable as punishment. If not, it is unjust. At a kangaroo court I witnessed in 1992, one of the community leaders insisted that he could make the man accused of theft confess by beating him with a whip fashioned from a car's fan belt and coat hanger wire. Other members of the Street Committee restrained him, however, arguing that, once the suspect had been beaten, even if he confessed to the crime the beating itself would be taken by the culprit and the community as constituting "payment in full" for the crime and thus preclude any chance of retrieving the stolen goods.

Aggressive violence may be understandable but is rarely unambiguously legitimate. Boys and young men are considered by most in these parts, with considerable reason, to be inherently aggressive and prone to fighting—a propensity that all agree should be disciplined by their elders but rarely is. Contemporary forms of violent sociability for young men draw their inspiration from three primary sources: accounts of African warrior traditions (Pitje 1950a, 1950b, 1950c); the contingencies of urban working-class life in a context marked by an inadequate institutional capacity for disciplining youthful energies and by a vibrant culture of youth gangs (Glaser 2000); and the legacy of political struggle against an oppressive regime (Everatt 2000). Even in these postapartheid times, when young men are no longer at war with the forces of the state, no boy can grow to manhood in Soweto without witnessing or participating in serious violent conflict and attending the funerals of peers killed in such conflict. Young men, however, have their reasons for fighting. Aggression aimed merely at causing harm and destruction is almost always interpreted as arising from "jealousy" in the same way that witchcraft is understood to be motivated. Aggression aimed at ends other than mere destruction is mostly aimed at theft and is judged according to whether it is motivated by need or greed. From the point of view of his peers, a thug's thieving can be perfectly acceptable when it is merely the redistribution of ill-gotten wealth from Whites. If he begins preying on his neighbors, however, his thefts become crimes. For many young men rape is also a form of theft: a taking by force of what would otherwise have to be paid for (Ashforth 1999).

Using the occult force that is believed to be mobilized through *muthi* to gain wealth or power at other people's expense is a similar form of aggression and theft since the wealth or power is obtained at the expense of others who should rightfully share in it. Three forms of occult action predominate in talk about illegitimate wealth: the use of *muthi* made with human body parts, intercourse (in all senses of the word) with mystical creatures, and the use of zombies. Body parts harvested through killings that are colloquially referred to as "*muthi* murders" are reputed to contain the most powerful substances for use in wealth-creating *muthi*. I have never heard of body parts being used in *muthi* designed to bring other types of harm to others. The illegitimacy of these uses derives from the fact of killing an innocent person in order to advance oneself—the height of selfishness. Another commonly spoken of form of witchcraft that involves human sacrifice in pursuit of illicit wealth and power involves connection with the mystical snake MaMlambo. MaMlambo is said to be able to bring great riches to the person who possesses her, but she demands the sacrifice of a family member to satiate her appetite. Few wealthy people can live long in a black township or rural area without someone suspecting them of using *muthi* from body parts or keeping a MaMlambo. Zombies, persons who have been robbed of their free will by occult means known in Zulu as *ukuthwebula,* a process that is said to involve the killing of a real person and the fashioning of his or her double, assist in the creation of illicit wealth by being set to work in the manner of slavery (Niehaus 1997).

The primary and unambiguously legitimate motivation to violence, both physical and occult, is defense. For a man to be considered a man he must be able and willing to defend his property, his women, his family, his comrades, and his manhood—to kill those who would try to kill him and those he cares for. The same applies to the use of *muthi.* In a 1999 survey of attitudes to the Suppression of Witchcraft Act among "Black/African" people in Northern Province, Karl Peltzer found that while the overwhelming majority of people surveyed agreed that a "traditional healer practicing witchcraft or supplying *muti*" should be banned by law, only 29 percent agreed that it should be illegal to use "witchcraft or charms to identify thieves" (Peltzer 2000a, 316). Similar attitudes would be found in Soweto. For a healer to be a healer, he or she must be able to formulate *muthi* capable of defending a person from occult attack in such a way that it reverses the direction of the forces responsible for the attack and kills whoever dispatched them. Healers also regularly dispense *muthi* to protect property from theft and attack by ordinary burglars as well as by occult forces such as the *tokoloshe* (witch's familiar).[18]

Legitimate punishment is typically spoken of as "discipline." The verb "to discipline" is one of those English words that gained currency in Soweto during the times of political struggle ("to organize"—as in "let's organize some few beers"—is another). It bears overtones from the struggle propaganda extolling the virtues of the "disciplined comrade" and carries memories of the scores of people punished by activists in those days for political infractions. Practices of punishment, however, and the forms of obedience and discipline they are meant to sustain have a much longer history, particularly in the organization of young men into regiments for collective labor duties and military purposes (Pitje 1950b, 105ff.). Discipline is something that one imposes upon one's own. The police were never said to "discipline" comrades no matter how many they beat or killed in punishment.

"Discipline" is something meted out to children by their parents and to "comrades" by their leaders when they misbehave—and to women by their men. Despite new laws granting equal status to women married in customary unions and protection from domestic violence, along with numerous spirited campaigns by government and civil society groups to end violence against women, the attitude among men that women are properly subject

18. For a description of such a treatment in Soweto, see Ashforth 2000a, 46–49.

to their command remains entrenched at the start of the twenty-first century. The authors of the Wits Survey, noting that their figures probably represented an underestimation of the extent of marital violence, reported that 21.7 percent of women interviewed were prepared to admit to having been beaten by their spouse or partner. Half of these women said they were beaten regularly or severely (A. Morris 1999b, table 5.6). The survey authors also noted that although one in five "married" women reported being beaten, 96.1 percent of all respondents claimed that no one in their household had been "attacked by someone known to them," suggesting that domestic violence or spouse abuse was not thought of in the same way as violent crime (A. Morris 1999b, 33). Among young men, even those without strong ties to patriarchal forms of custom and tradition, the perception of wives and girlfriends as "property" under their control is strong (Ashforth 1999).

Although outlawed in schools by the Schools Act of 1996, corporal punishment is the rule rather than exception in everyday life here. Children are regularly beaten for disobedience and unruliness, and it is a rare parent who accepts the proposition that beating children is harmful and wrong. Indeed, children playing among themselves constantly inflict physical punishments—mostly mock, though sometimes severe—in the course of their games. One of the first phrases small children in my neighborhood learn, picked up from the play of their elders in the streets and backyards, is "Ke tla ua shapa!" ("I am going to beat you!" in Zulu-speaking neighborhoods, "Ngizok'shaya wena").

Just as no monopoly of physical violence exists in Soweto, so no monopoly, hierarchy, or even centralization of discursive authority can be found there within which the truth of interpretations of violent acts can be pronounced and confirmed. Certainly the institutions of criminal justice produce and adjudicate stories of violence on a regular basis, stories that are frequently reported in the news media, but these are a small fraction of the violent events that impinge upon people's lives. The general lack of confidence in the police and courts, moreover, tends to undermine the veracity of particular official judgments of criminal motive and purpose. Acts of violence that are unimpeachably proper within the bounds of one discursive community, among a criminal's friends, say, can quite easily be transformed through the words of a different narrator for another audience, such as the schoolchildren who have been his victim, into a story of injury and offense, becoming in the process the occasion for violent acts of justified revenge. Where the use of *muthi* is suspected as the instrument of harm, the problems of interpretation are even more complex, for the actors in the event are not only humans—acting secretly, of course—but also invisible beings such as spirits and ancestors. Before engaging in any healing work, therefore, a healer or other concerned person must be able to distinguish whether the evident misfortunes that signify the action of invisible forces are a product of malicious attack with *muthi,* a form of legitimate punishment by spiritual agencies such as the ancestors, a product of pollution from invisible substances or evil spirits, a natural disease, or just bad luck.

Health, Disease, and the Onslaught of AIDS

Before the arrival of the HIV/AIDS epidemic, Sowetans were free of the calamitous public health problems afflicting many African cities, such as malaria (the elevation is too high) or cholera and other illnesses arising from impure water and poor sanitation. Though planned under the shadow of racism and political exclusion, Soweto was built according to the best principles of public housing and sanitation current in the middle decades of the twentieth century, with piped potable water on each plot and waterborne sewage systems.[19] Most of the housing constructed since the 1930s is still standing and still occupied. Despite the official apartheid ideology premised upon the principle that Africans were only "temporary sojourners" in urban areas, township residents were also provided with health care services, albeit of a quality inferior to those available to white people. These remain the foundation of the biomedical health care infrastructure of the township in the postapartheid era. Soweto is also home to tens of thousands of traditional healers and Christian faith-healing prophets.

The foundational distinction in everyday understandings of health in Soweto, as in the rest of black South Africa, is between "natural" illnesses (*mkhuhlane,* Zulu; *mokotlane,* Sotho) and "man-made" or "African" diseases (*ukufa wa Bantu* or *imisebenzi yabantu; mesebetsi ya batho*), or, in the common manner of Sowetan English, between "a natural sick" and "things of we blacks." Sometimes a further distinction among natural ailments is made between diseases of "whites" and other natural ones known to Af-

19. The National Building Research Institute, part of the Council for Scientific and Industrial Research, conducted many studies trying to determine the proper dimensions for "Bantu housing" and the requirements of space and light for families as well as the economics of large-scale housing construction. Although blighted by the legacy of political racism, the achievements of public housing for Africans in the mid–twentieth century were quite remarkable. For examples of this research, see National Building Research Institute 1954.

ricans of old. As an everyday rule of thumb, natural illnesses are thought susceptible to treatment by Western medicine, and man-made afflictions are immune to such treatment and require the intervention of healers deploying spiritual powers. Natural afflictions are also typically spoken of as "God's will," particularly when they prove to be terminal. African diseases, on the other hand, are spoken of as involving "evil forces"—typically either the man-made forces of *muthi* or the ill effects of encounters with pollution. These disease categories are not necessarily dependent upon symptoms, for the same physical symptoms can be indicative of entirely different categories of affliction.[20] This poses serious problems of interpretation, especially for ailments that cannot be decisively remedied by Western medicine. Where medical treatment is definitive, suspicions regarding the involvement of evil forces can sometimes be allayed.

By far the most common forms of illness in Soweto are respiratory complaints. Of respondents in the Wits Survey reporting health problems over the previous twelve months, 39.6 percent had suffered respiratory problems (A. Morris 1999b, table 6.1). Soweto, particularly in winter, is hard on the lungs. Regular congregation of random strangers in closed confines such as commuter vans aids the spread of respiratory infections, and wide temperature fluctuations of as much as 15 degrees Celsius between night and day, the dry high-altitude climate, high levels of wind-borne dust, heavy pollution from coal stoves used in cooking, and high levels of indoor tobacco smoking conspire to produce breathing misery. Children, of whom 50 percent were reported to have suffered in the previous year, and the elderly are the most seriously afflicted (A. Morris 1999b, 35). Ordinary coughs and colds are usually referred to as *isifuba* (Zulu for "chest") or "flu," and most people will seek medical attention if they can. Local doctors seem inclined to prescribe antibiotics to patients presenting with colds or flu: I have never seen anyone return from such a visit to the clinic without some antibiotic "tablets to drink." More persistent coughs, such as those associated with tuberculosis, which has long been epidemic in South Africa and has become more prevalent as an AIDS-related infection, raise questions about the possible involvement of witchcraft, notably in the form of *idliso* (*sejeso*), or pollution from contact with death.

In the Wits Survey, "other infections" is the next most common source of disease (10.2 percent of illnesses), followed by injuries and violence (7.9 percent of overall health problems and 13.6 percent of men's problems;

20. For an account of some common ways of interpreting symptoms, see Conco 1972.

A. Morris 1999b, table 6.1 and p. 35). Overall, 13.7 percent of respondents reported requiring eight or more days off from their usual activities because of ill health (A. Morris 1999b, table 6.1).[21] People suffering chronic conditions such as high blood pressure (known as "high blood"), diabetes (referred to as "sugar"), or arthritis tend to treat them as natural indispositions and oscillate between medical treatments and traditional or faith healers' remedies as finances and inclinations permit.

The most pernicious source of untoward injury in Soweto is the street. On top of all the dangers of crime, the streets of Soweto are part of a network of roads throughout South Africa that have one of the world's highest rates of death per vehicle mile traveled. About 10,000 people die on South African roads annually. Between 35,000 and 40,000 suffer serious injuries, and approximately twice that number suffer minor injuries (Ministry of Transport 1997, table 5.1). I have no specific figures for Soweto but have seen enough carnage on the roads there to suspect that the Sowetan rates of road death and injury are commensurate with those of the rest of the country. South African traffic fatalities include an unusually high number of pedestrian victims compared to other countries, and a high proportion of these victims were drunk at the time of their deaths.[22] No one injured in

21. When the researchers conducting the Wits Survey asked respondents to describe their health over the last month, 76.7 percent described it as "fairly good" or "very good"; 13.4 percent described their health as "bad" or "very bad." Not surprisingly, these numbers were higher in housing domains where more elderly and poorer people lived. In the older "Council"-type houses of Soweto, 21.1 percent of respondents reported their health status as "bad." Given that the average number of people in these houses is 5.5, the chances are that virtually every household had some member who considered his or her health to be bad, most likely an older person. Almost one in every three women and one in every five men over the age of fifty said that their health had been bad in the past month. See A. Morris 1999b, tables 2.1 and 6.12 and p. 41. These figures accord with my observations over the years.

22. A national study testing pedestrians for alcohol as they walked by the side of the road between the hours of 1730 and 1900 found that 12.5 percent had blood alcohol readings above the legal driving limit at the time (0.08 percent). Drivers tested in the same study, who were stopped at random roadblocks, tested over the legal limit at the rate of 5.5 percent (Peden and Butchart 2000). Sunday evening is the most dangerous time to be on the road in Soweto, especially at the end of the month (more so during the Festive Season in December), because the roads are overrun with drunken drivers. Unfortunately, protecting oneself against the risks posed by drunk drivers is exceedingly difficult. Throughout the 1990s, the police in Soweto displayed no discernible interest in enforcing drunk-driving laws. (In fact, in my experience and that of all my motorist friends, traffic police were more inclined to ask for bribes in order to buy themselves a beer.) Without public efforts to control drunk driving, the individual motorist must rely on vigilance. For passengers, riding

an accident would insist on seeking primary treatment from a nonmedical healer. Victims of accidents and their families, however, will be strongly inclined to seek answers to the question "Why me?" from healers with spiritual connections, especially if their injuries are slow to heal.

Coinciding with the achievement of democracy in South Africa in the mid-1990s, the explosion of the HIV/AIDS epidemic was a cruel irony of history. The new government was engaged in its historic and long-awaited mission of "reconstruction and development," devising policies and reorganizing institutions of government in an effort to redress the injustices and inequities of the past. At the same time an invisible enemy was wreaking havoc with the future. Concerted action against this threat could have been mounted only by trusted authorities within a legitimate state. Had the new ANC government recognized the scale of this danger and deployed adequate resources and attention to halt the explosion of the epidemic, however, they would most likely have found themselves berated for neglecting the real tasks of reconstruction and "transformation" that they had been elected to pursue. For in 1994, although the danger posed by the HIV/AIDS epidemic was recognized by the many South Africans who heeded the warning signs evident in countries to the north, where many of the exiled ANC leaders had witnessed the emergence of the epidemic, most of the constituents of the ANC in places like Soweto were still unpersuaded of its significance. Indeed, many doubted the reality of this strange new disease that was often spoken of but seldom seen.

When I first started talking with people in Soweto about AIDS in the early 1990s, the disease was laughingly referred to as the "American invention to discourage sex." In 1991, on the wall of a shop in Mapetla, someone painted in dripping white paint with a heavy brush "AIDS MY FAVRIT KIND OF SICK."[23] People were generally skeptical about the existence of such a disease, since they had never buried anyone who died of it, and most treated the whole subject as a joke. By the late 1990s, however, most Sowetans had a basic level of what had come to be known as "AIDS awareness." They knew the disease was spread through sex, and they knew they should use condoms to protect themselves against infection. But AIDS was just

---

with a drunk driver is often the lesser of two evils since public transport is unsafe because of crime and unreliable after dark. Moreover, suggesting to a male driver that he is too drunk to drive can be perilous, given that he is likely to consider his manhood impugned. For most drinkers, to be too drunk to drive is to be too drunk to stand.

23. Though English is seldom used in everyday talk, the sign was written in English because although students learn to read and write a "vernacular" (i.e., African) language in the course of their schooling, most are more comfortable writing English or variants thereof.

one of many dangers in a dangerous world, and protection was a far more complex business than slipping on a sheath of rubber. People who were at little risk of infection with HIV, such as the grandmother MaMfete, seemed more interested in the issue than those who faced the real risks. They tended to view my stories of AIDS calamities in East and Central Africa as yet more grim harbingers of things to come, further evidence of the general moral decline of the world around them, and confirmation of their gloomy aphorism that Africans were born to suffer.

Medical facilities in Soweto are overburdened and underfunded, particularly as the impact of AIDS deaths begins to be felt. The main public hospital for the region, Chris Hani Baragwanath Hospital, is reputedly the biggest hospital in the world, with more than 3,000 beds and a staff of about 5,000, and serves almost 150,000 inpatients and 650,000 outpatients each year (Chris Hani Baragwanath Hospital 2002). The hospital, named after a Cornish trader who ran a hostel in the area in the late nineteenth century (John Baragwanath) and with the name of an assassinated ANC leader (Chris Hani) appended in 1997, was built for the British army during the Second World War and sold to the South African government in 1947 (Huddle and Dubb 1994). During the apartheid era it was a Black hospital serving Africans throughout the region around Soweto, and although there are no longer any racial restrictions upon hospital admissions, "Bara" patients in the postapartheid era are almost exclusively black. One of the many ironies of the apartheid era was the fact that while the police were shooting people protesting in the streets, doctors and nurses were healing wounds in a public hospital funded by the same regime. And one of the sad ironies of the postapartheid regime is that despite a government in office committed to improving life for the poor, conditions in Chris Hani Baragwanath Hospital have deteriorated as a result of poor management and endemic corruption (Landman, Mouton, and Nevhutalu 2001). Funding shortages also mean that while people can gain access to basic services, expensive diagnostic tests, drugs, and surgery are often unavailable. Despite the inadequacy of facilities and provisions, however, a modern biomedical system exists in Soweto with a network of private surgeries of general practitioners and public clinics. It is possible for people living in this region to receive medical care, even if not always of the highest standard, which is more than can be said for most of Africa.

Mental health services in Soweto are minimal. Like everything else in South Africa, mental health services have historically been skewed toward the rich and pale, with little more than custodial "care" for the severely ill and disabled available for black people (Flisher, Fisher, and Subedar 2000).[24] Three public clinics in Soweto currently provide psychiatric services on an outpatient basis, and Chris Hani Baragwanath Hospital has 150 beds for such patients, which are usually fully occupied. Considering the size of the population that the hospital serves, this is hardly adequate. In the words of the director of the Psychiatry Department, writing on the hospital's official Web site, "the Psychiatry Department in this hospital has expanded to the extent that the wards are overcrowded, in need of repair and, in many ways, unsuitable for psychiatric patients."[25] Lesedi Clinic, a private hospital across the Old Potch Road from Baragwanath, also has small psychiatric wards.

Apart from the shortage of services, the practice of mental health professionals in places like Soweto is rendered virtually impossible by two sets of factors. First, the material situation of many, if not all, Sowetans is such that the more common ailments of anxiety, depression, and all the disorders consequent to trauma and stress are frequently an all-too-reasonable response to desperate circumstances that are unlikely to change. Second, many of the symptoms that Western medicine treats as "mental illnesses" (e.g., visual and auditory hallucinations, a sense of being taken over by alien beings) at least in their milder forms are often considered in these parts to possess a different kind of reality from "psychological" processes.[26] Dreams, visions, and unseen voices can, at times, be interpreted as deceased ancestors or other invisible beings seeking to communicate with the living (Jedrej and Shaw 1992). Fits or loss of bodily control, rather than constituting an illness of an individual brain or mind requiring treatment, can be interpreted, if the signs so portend, as spirit possession and, possibly, a call to become a healer. Witches, too, can interfere with the proper functioning of a person's mind to cause hysteria and madness.

24. This may be an instance where the inequalities imposed upon Africans were a blessing in disguise. For examples of the sort of thinking informing the psychiatric care that was routinely inflicted upon African patients, see Laubscher 1937.

25. See http://www.chrishanibaragwanathhospital.co.za/departments.shtml#medicine (accessed April 12, 2002).

26. A small, but important, body of literature over the past seventy years seeks to describe the categories of African spirituality and psychic disorders in terms consonant with Western psychology. For examples, see Bührmann 1986; Cheetham and Griffiths 1980; Holdstock 2000; Laubscher 1937. One of the most perceptive books on African life in this part of the world in the past century is the biography of a traditional healer written by the Viennese psychiatrist Wulf Sachs (1947).

In ordinary talk in Soweto, a distinction is made between being "mad" (*uhlanya* in Zulu) and "not normal." People with obvious "mental" problems of a more or less permanent kind are said to be "not normal" (sometimes "abnormal")—the English expression being the predominant usage —while temporary indispositions are forms of madness. "Mad" is also an everyday term of affectionate abuse. Interruptions of ordinary psychological health accompanied by dramatic symptoms are typically interpreted as resulting from witchcraft. Recurrent ailments and neuroses are usually described by the capacious category of "nerves." In these days, when clinics are visited regularly, "nerves" are usually taken to be caused by "stress" or "thinking too much." "Depression" has also become a more widely used term of self-diagnosis. When symptoms that psychologists would interpret as mental illness or psychological disturbances are deemed serious by sufferers and their families, they are usually treated by traditional healers. These symptoms can be deeply disturbing to the people experiencing them and usually drive them to seek help. Even if a person in such distress were able to find treatment with Western-trained mental health professionals, however, his or her chances of satisfaction would be slight. As Len Holdstock has argued, "Western techniques are, with a few exceptions, culturally too different to offer a psychological approach toward healing that would be meaningful for the majority of South Africans" (1979, 119).[27]

Sages, Charlatans, and the Business of Traditional Healing

Although the term "traditional healer" is widely used in South Africa these days in place of the colonial-era "witch doctor," it is something of a misnomer because it conjures up a sense of timeless unchanging traditions practiced by adherents of fixed and systematic customs and procedures. In reality, most "traditional" healers are constantly innovating in their healing practices and enjoy a great deal of flexibility in their approaches to alleviating suffering.[28] Thousands of these innovative healers are at work in

27. Holdstock has been a strong advocate of the ability of traditional healers to treat mental health problems (Holdstock 1981, 2000). In recent years a number of psychologists and medical practitioners have argued that the principal value of traditional healing lies in its psychotherapeutic dimensions (Bührmann 1977; Mkhwanazi 1989).

28. In a report for the Food and Agriculture Organization on the marketing of medicinal plants in KwaZulu Province, Myles Mander has argued: "The healing practices used, while originating in African culture, are not purely traditional. The practice is dynamic, addressing new illnesses like AIDS, and adopts new technologies and new medicines. The healers also deal with all manner of urban social problems, which are not traditional" (1998,

South Africa in an extraordinarily dynamic and vibrant market fed by unceasing suffering. Nonetheless, insofar as this domain of healing is marked by practitioners who invoke African "ancestors" as their central source of therapeutic knowledge and power, and as the ground of their claims to authority, then "traditional healing" is as useful a term as any.

Most black South Africans consult traditional healers, or are taken as children to healers, at some time in their lives. Reliable data on the extent of their use of these services, however, are scant. I have tried to track the source of the commonplace assertion that 60–80 percent of black South Africans consult traditional healers. However, whenever the ubiquitous locution "it has been estimated that . . ." comes with a citation, the reference inevitably turns out to be to another author claiming, without proper attribution, that "research has also shown. . . ." [29] Sometimes the number is cited as the percentage of Africans who consult traditional healers *before* attending medical practitioners; sometimes it seems to refer to the proportion of Africans who have ever consulted a traditional healer. These numbers are regularly recycled by government officials—"it has been found that over 60% of (black) Africans . . . consult traditional methods of healing" claimed Mondli Gungubele, the chair of the Gauteng legislature's committee on health, on June 4, 1997—as well as the pages of august medical journals such as the *Lancet* (Baleta 1998). All this repetition gives the numbers a patina of scientific authority when in fact they are really just reasonable guesses. Nor is it clear, when these numbers are cited, what "providing services" means. Given the difficulties of classifying traditional healers and the fact that many people who qualify to heal by way of undergoing treatment for their own afflictions in a process known as *ukuthwasa* do not practice as professional healers, *all* quantifications must be merely approximate.

A great variety of practitioners, drawing upon diverse traditions, fashions, and bodies of knowledge, fall under the general rubric "traditional." In later chapters we shall consider some of the analogous practices of African Christian faith healing in more detail; here I shall outline some of the main features of traditional healing as it is currently practiced in places like

chap. 4, sec. 3, n. 3). For these reasons, Mander argues that they should be termed "indigenous" rather than "traditional" healers, although he provides no solution to the problem of exorcizing the presumption of "traditional" implicit in the use of "indigenous." Chris Simon and Masilo Lamla have described similarly "incorporative pharmacopoeial processes" among Xhosa healers in the Transkei (Simon 1991; Simon and Lamla 1991).

29. See, e.g., E. Pretorius 1999, 250, which cites Chipfakacha 1994, 861; Centre for Health Policy 1991, 1; and an article in a local newspaper, the *Sowetan*—all of which invoke mysterious "research" without specifying who did it or where and when it was done.

Soweto. Most discussions of traditional healers generalize the Zulu usage of *sangoma* and *inyanga* to cover all traditional healers serving Africans in the region, regardless of ethnicity. Other commonly encountered local terms include the Sotho *ngaka* (*dingaka*) and Xhosa *igqirha* (*amagqirha*). Common usage in Soweto also favors the Zulu terms, and in everyday parlance *inyanga* and *sangoma* are often used interchangeably. Sowetans, particularly younger people, typically make no distinction between *inyangas* and *sangomas* when thinking about healers, though if pressed, they will recognize as a distinct category healers who engage in the activity of drumming. I shall follow a similar procedure here and refer generically to "traditional healers" unless the context requires specification, in which case I shall distinguish healers according to whether or not they participate in rituals of drumming.

Since colonial times, thinking and writing on the subject of healing in this part of the world have been powerfully shaped by the drive to assert a fundamental similarity between local institutions and customs dealing with matters of spiritual insecurity and the human endeavors known as "medicine" and "religion" brought by the colonists in the form of powerful institutions with global reach. For many generations, "traditional medicine" and "traditional religion" have served as frameworks facilitating the translation of local African practices into readily understandable constructs for outsiders while affording the colonized Africans grounds for asserting the validity of and demanding respect for local customs as particular instances of universal human capacities and distinct ways of meeting universal human needs. These are powerful imperatives, but they sometimes distort appreciation of how people are actually meeting their needs in particular instances.

Academic literature on traditional healing in South Africa conventionally distinguishes between two types of traditional healers: "diviners" and "herbalists." Harriet Ngubane, for example, writes: "An African in South Africa who requires medical attention has available [as well as Western-trained doctors] indigenous healers of two main kinds—the *inyanga*, who is male and uses African medicines but has no clairvoyance, and the *isangoma*, who is usually female and has clairvoyant powers as well as a comprehensive knowledge of African medicines" (1981, 361). Since *sangoma* rituals center on communication with ancestors and other spiritual beings, many writers believe it is more appropriate to consider *sangomas* as religious practitioners rather than simply functionaries in a putative "traditional health system." The *inyanga*, thus, can be treated as a medical practitioner, whereas the *sangoma* belongs primarily in the field of religious activity.[30]

The functional distinction between herbalist and diviner has been widely endorsed in the discourse of new African elites in postapartheid South Africa. In 1998, for example, the Select Committee on Social Services of the National Council of Provinces proposed granting official recognition to the following basic categories of healers:

(a) Inyanga (herbalist or traditional doctor). This is usually a person who uses herbal and other medicinal preparations for treating disease.
(b) Sangoma (diviners). They are trained to communicate with and utilise the powers of ancestors in diagnosing a disease or mishap. (Select Committee on Social Services 1998, 6)

This distinction serves the purposes of state regulation nicely because it posits a distinct mode of authority underlying each form of healing practice. On the one hand, *inyangas* are presumed to have access to a putatively ancient set of ideas, information, and practices, now referred to as "indigenous knowledge systems," that can be systematized, tested, and regulated through institutional procedures analogous to those applied to medical practitioners using "modern" knowledge. On the other hand, as members of cults, *sangomas* can be thought of as participating in networks founded upon the authority of those who have trained them to communicate with ancestors and thus as being subject to the same sorts of regulatory authority the state exercises in relation to churches. To accord *sangomas* a religious status helps avoid the problem that the art of divination, which involves revealing secrets of the past as well as foretelling events yet to come, is to the modern rationalist irredeemably bogus. As Griffiths and Cheetham argue, the *sangoma* is a "'healer' *because* she is 'priest' *and* social psychiatrist, sociologist, ecologist, parapsychologist and an intelligent and highly perceptive member of the community" (1982). And this is all she is only because her roles in law, justice, and government have been limited by more

30. Freeman and Motsei, for example, in their efforts to identify issues pertinent to the integration of traditional healers into the medical system in South Africa, described the *sangoma* in religious terms as acting "as a medium with the ancestral shades" in a "traditional religious supernatural context" (1992, 1183). An extensive literature treats traditional healers as firmly within the purview of the "ancestor cult," the central feature of the somewhat dubious construct "traditional African religion." For an account of the many problems surrounding the concept of African traditional religion and the history of its academic study, see R. Shaw 1990.

than a century of colonial and apartheid rule. The *inyangas*, however, are also dependent upon connection with ancestors for their healing powers. All healers rely on connections with invisible beings in order to divine the true cause of suffering and to foretell the perils that lie ahead for their clients and divine the proper course of treatment.

Many *inyangas* legitimate their healing work by reference to having been "called" to heal by ancestral spirits or empowered in their healing gifts by them, and virtually all claim ancestral inspiration for their *muthi*. And while *sangomas* do not always use medicinal substances in their activities while "doing *ngoma*," they almost always do use *muthi* in their work as healers treating members of the public. Indeed, when treating members of the public, the *sangoma* is virtually indistinguishable from the *inyanga*, and in everyday usage in places like Soweto, either term can be applied, particularly to healers who are—as they say in Soweto—"in business." In the era of AIDS, business for healers is booming.

As the missionary ethnographer A. T. Bryant pointed out almost a century ago, while the "medicine man [*inyanga*] is a personage totally distinct from the Zulu diviner or so-called witchdoctor . . . the two professions do still considerably overlap," with the medicine man dealing extensively in "magic and charms" and the witch doctor dispensing "curative herbs" (1970, 13). Monica Hunter agreed, arguing on the basis of her fieldwork in Pondoland in the 1930s that the distinction between "herbalist" and "diviner" is "based on a difference in initiation rather than in function, for their functions overlap." Virtually all healers "communicate with and utilize the power of" ancestors or other invisible beings in some way (Hunter 1961, 320). Indeed, healing in Africa generally is inconceivable without the healer invoking spiritual beings of some variety as part of the healing practice, either as the source of diagnosis and prescription or as the origin of medicinal remedies (Feierman and Janzen 1992). Diagnosis of ailments by traditional healers is typically predicated upon an ability to discern the hidden realities of illness and misfortune, realities that are not accessible to ordinary human beings without the intercession of higher powers. Even healers who merely dispense their concoctions, decoctions, powders, and potions in bulk will typically claim (like the minister for public works in the national government, Stella Sigcau, who brewed up an AIDS remedy on her farm in the Eastern Cape) that the recipes for their medicines come from ancestors via visions or dreams.[31]

31. On July 22, 2001, the *Sunday Times* reported that the public works minister, Stella Sigcau, had perfected an anti-AIDS remedy based on ground, sun-dried, peach leaves and

Rather than categorizing healers as functionaries within putative religious and medicine systems, another way of understanding the enterprise of healing emphasizes the extent to which healers have been initiated into and participate in the rituals of what John Janzen has identified as the *"ngoma* cult." For Janzen, the *ngoma* cult, represented in southern Africa in the person of the *sangoma,* is a centuries-old "unique" institution that is informed by definite rules, norms, and ritual practices and stretches from Central Africa to the Cape, albeit with significant regional and ethnic variations (Janzen 1992). Members are recruited to *ngoma* (thereby becoming *sangomas*) by virtue of suffering a serious illness that is diagnosed by a *sangoma* as a call from the ancestors for the afflicted person to become a healer via a process known in Zulu as *ukuthwasa.* The *ngoma* cult involves, among other things, drumming, singing, and dancing as modes of interaction with ancestors and other spirits (Friedson 1996). The word *ngoma* is the Bantu root meaning "drum." Whereas *sangomas* and *inyangas* typically engage in divination and work with herbs, only *sangomas* participate in the rituals that Janzen calls "doing *ngoma,"* which involve the public (or semipublic) activities of drumming and dancing within a community of healers, initiates, and their families.[32]

For outsiders, *ngoma* rituals seem to embody something elemental and essential in African culture and tradition. Many Africans in search of cultural authenticity also find such rituals appealing, even while others find them embarrassing and troubling. *Sangoma* ceremonies involve prolonged sessions of drumming, singing, and dancing. People fall into trances and become possessed by spirits. Beasts are slaughtered. Initiates into the *ngoma* cult drink the blood of these slaughtered beasts. For the uninitiated, these scenes can be quite dramatic. Christians of the born-again variety denounce the whole enterprise as demonic. Only a few people, mostly older women, suffer an illness that is interpreted as a call from the ancestors to join *ngoma* as their means of healing. Of those who go through *ukuthwasa,* only a mi-

---

other, "secret" ingredients. According to the minister's housekeeper: "Stella is excited. She says it is her late father who is helping her" (Govender 2001). The minister told the *Sunday Times* reporter that her AIDS medicine was in its "early stages" but that she would be applying for a patent: "I don't want the whole world to know the ingredients. That's why I am keeping it a secret. I believe traditional medicine may have a role to play in combating viral diseases and should be assessed." In response to this report, the health spokesperson of the Pan Africanist Congress denounced the minister for "meddling at the fringes of science" and insisted she take her concoction to the Medicines Control Council for testing (SAPA 2001).

32. The classic ethnographic description of *ngoma* rituals is to be found in Turner 1968.

nority proceed to practice healing arts as a profession. Most just drift away from the whole business. In my neighborhood of Mapetla Extension a few years ago I counted six *sangomas* in about fifty houses—five women and one man—of whom only one, the man, was active in the work of healing. The heavy lifting of professional healing, the work that is referred to as *traditional* healing, is performed mostly by *inyangas* operating outside the *ngoma* cults.

Inyangas typically do not participate in *ngoma* cults as regular members of a healing community, nor do they all necessarily undergo the rituals of *ukuthwasa*—the period of illness and instruction through which a healer is born. Unlike *sangomas, inyangas* tend to work alone. *Inyangas* tend to claim the authority to heal either by virtue of inheriting special capacities and knowledge from ancestors or by serving long apprenticeships with notable healers, from whom they learn the arts of making *muthi* (which can be translated, according to context, as "medicine," "herbs," also "poison"), or both. While there are certain conventional techniques of healing (purgation, enemas, steaming, incising, and bloodletting being the most common) and conventions of applying particular commonplace herbs to treat certain ailments (about four hundred herbs are commonly available in the commercial *muthi* market; Mander 1998), most of the *inyanga*'s knowledge, particularly when it comes to treating major illness and "evil forces," is secret and jealously guarded. When asked the source of his recipes, almost without exception an *inyanga* will state: "My ancestors."

In the literature on traditional healing, the healing practices of contemporary *inyangas* are sorely underresearched. The weight of the imperative of discovering the indigenous wisdom underpinning their practice as *traditional* healers (which we shall consider later in the light of the recent awakening of interest in what are now called "indigenous knowledge systems"), coupled with the presumption that *inyangas* are engaged in traditional *healing* in a manner similar to "modern medicine," has resulted in gaps in the understanding of their activities. In the context of the HIV/AIDS pandemic, particularly as antiretroviral treatments become commonplace as a medical "cure" for the disease, this deficiency is becoming ever more serious. Most of the literature, proceeding from the presumption of homology between "modern" and "traditional" medicine, assumes that the use of *muthi* by *inyangas* is but an herbal analogy to the medicinal use of drugs in the treatment of disease manifest in particular symptoms. Herbal medicine in these terms, however, is only a small part of the enterprise. The logic of this kind of healing at times engages—not consistently or uniformly—entirely different ontological and epistemological principles from those of Western medicine. The medical doctor, for example, may know how to repair a gun-shot wound but will be useless in protecting someone from bullets in the first place.

Traditional healing almost always involves divination of some sort in which the healer purports to be able to divine secrets of his or her client's past, the nature of the client's present problems, and the future course of events—both with and without treatments to make them fortunate for the client.[33] The occasion of divination is usually experienced by people suf-fering some perceived misfortune, often but not exclusively health related. The standard divinatory procedure is for the healer, drawing on access to the superior knowledge and capacities of spirits, to demonstrate his or her power by recounting facts about the client's past that could not have been known to the healer, by accurately identifying the particular problem that has brought the sufferer to the healer's door, and then by identifying its cause and likely future course. Divination in this context, however, rarely takes the form of singular, authoritative, oracular pronouncements. Rather, it is almost always performed as a sort of multiparty conversation between the healer, the client, and the unseen spirits both of the healer and of the client, through which the past, present, and future emerge as a consensus assessment. Techniques of divination serve to both stimulate this conversa-tion and manifest the presence of the invisible parties. Although the rep-ertoire of conventional divination procedures used in traditional healing is fairly standard—"throwing bones" being the most common—the particu-lar technique used to communicate with beings in other realms is less im-portant than the structure of the communication between client (and the client's therapeutic community) and healer, and between healer and spirits (and among the various spirits interested in the particular case).

Since Henry Callaway sat in on Zulu divinations in the late nineteenth century, most observers of divination in this part of the world have noted that successful divinations almost always take the form of dialogue or con-versation between healer and client rather than a single, awe-inspiring, au-thoritative pronouncement (Callaway 1970). The client corrects the diviner and suggests, somewhat in the manner of the old guessing game "Hot and Cold," directions of inquiry. As James Kiernan has argued, "diviners are particularly attentive to the nuances of their clients' (believers') situations and to the complexities of the social symptoms, in order to produce a mea-

---

33. For detailed accounts of divination in this region over the past century or so, see Callaway 1970; Eiselen 1932a, 1932b; Fernandez 1967; Hammond-Tooke 2002; Kiernan 1995b; Kohler 1941; Lambprecht 2002; Watt and Van Warmelo 1930.

sure of fit between what the belief system allows and what the clients perceive to be their needs. Consequently, specialist and client enter into a protracted process of negotiation in order to establish within the parameters of shared beliefs a truth that is both palatable and actionable" (1995b, 11). Diviners work on the not unreasonable presumption that a person appearing before them both has a particular problem or problems for which he or she needs help and is amenable to the suggestion that such problems relate to "African" matters, such as witchcraft and ancestral inclinations.

Given the limited opportunities and experiences open to ordinary Sowetans, to "divine" reasonably accurately the sorts of problems troubling any particular client is not terribly difficult. For example, a young woman seeking assistance is almost certain to have a child or children with a man from whom she is not receiving adequate support; a young man similarly will have children with a woman or women who are most likely angry with him. Both might be impressed to hear tell of such things from a stranger such as the diviner. My own experiences with diviners, who are usually only too happy to demonstrate their skills on a white man, have been uniformly disappointing. I have been inaccurately diagnosed with a host of nonexistent ailments. I am willing to accept, however, that the experience of divination can establish a bond of confidence between healer and client that might allow the healer to perform important work in restoring a sense of health and wholeness in a sufferer's life, particularly in the commodious realms of those malaises known as "psychological." No doubt, too, effective diviners are skilled in working with states of consciousness that defy easy categorization in Western psychological terms (Hund 2000).

Sowetans who consult traditional healers generally combine a healthy skepticism about particular diviners with a deep faith in the necessity and possibility of divination, of perceiving the nature of invisible forces operating in and on the manifest visible world. Evans-Pritchard famously noted similar attitudes in Zandeland in the 1920s (Evans-Pritchard 1937).[34] The necessity of divination derives from the unassailable conviction that the forces ultimately shaping life and fortune are not accessible by ordinary human perception.[35] The possibility of perceiving them, and managing their impact on ordinary human affairs, derives from perceived access to spiri-

34. For a discussion of similar skepticism among the Gisu people in Kenya and Uganda, see Heald 1991.

35. The famous, and famously maverick, South African diviner Credo Mutwa has a theory that diviners are able to perceive the future because they access, via the ancestors, different scales of temporality so that what is the future for mere mortals is the present for them. See Mutwa 2002.

tual powers such as ancestors. Everyone experiences a feeling of connection with ancestors from time to time through troubling dreams (though, as we shall see in later chapters, many African Christians interpret these as visitations by evil spirits). Some people, however, namely those called to be healers by the spirits or those fulfilling family traditions of healing, possess—perhaps—a greater facility in connecting and communicating with spiritual powers and, by virtue of such communication, in perceiving things that ordinary people cannot. However, although the action of invisible forces and the existence of spiritual beings engaged in meaningful relations with the living are taken as axiomatic by virtually everyone here, the claims of particular individuals to be able to access these powers at will, regardless of whatever "training" they may have undergone, are treated with caution. Everyone knows stories of hopeless diviners; everyone enjoys a laugh at an *inyanga*'s expense. And it is only when a particular divination session produces a narrative about a person's suffering that rings true that the attitude of skepticism diminishes.

Perceptions of the powers of healers are underpinned not only by the private experience of suffering alleviated and the public reputations of prowess in healing but also by the uncomfortable relationship the whole enterprise of healing has with the primary source of suffering: witchcraft. The presumption that people can gain access to substances and evil powers capable of wreaking havoc in the world—a presumption underpinning most of the work of traditional healing—is buttressed by the presumption that certain individuals make their capacities for evil available on a commercial basis. And the popular supposition is that those who know how to use substances (*muthi*) and rituals to heal probably also know how to use the same to cause harm.

In the early 1990s, a healer by the name of Dr. Kalongha was reputed to be one of the most powerful *inyangas* in Soweto. His unorthodox methods illustrate the general innovation featured by successful healers. I first went to his surgery when a friend in the Snake Park shack settlement on the outskirts of Soweto suffered the theft of a spray-painting machine from her shack. In an attempt to apprehend the culprit and secure the return of the machine, a meeting of the Street Committee was convened and a delegation of residents dispatched to consult an *inyanga*.

Dr. Kalongha was the unanimous choice because residents had heard not only that he hailed from a far-off place (Malawi, they thought, or Kenya perhaps, some place to the north in that country they call here "Africa") but that he practiced a strange religion, Islam. He was also reputed to possess a large and terrifying snake (evidence for the existence of which I was never able to find). The services he advertised, listed on a photocopied flier (see figs. 1–2), were typical of those offered by *inyangas* and included (in addition to professing to cure virtually everything that has ever ailed a body) herbs to repel burglars from the home, defend against knife and bullet wounds, protect cars from accidents and thieves, and guard against nasty creatures like the *tokoloshe.* Dr. Kalongha also advertised medicines to advance what might be thought of as more positive, perhaps even aggressive, goals, such as securing the "love of whites" (*moriana wa ho rata ke makgowa;* i.e., "to find favor with employers"), attracting prospective lovers, or keeping the father of a child attentive to his duties. On top of all this, Dr. Kalongha boasted he could solve each and every problem brought to him—including "this thing of AIDS." Dr. Kalongha divined by means of magic writing.

On entering the "doctor's surgery," patients were issued a metal disk with a number welded onto it and told to wait until their number was called on the intercom, a public address system that doubled as a piped music system. After a long wait in the waiting room (a large covered-over area that conveniently doubled as a shebeen, so patients or their companions could enjoy a health-giving beer or brandy while they waited), patients were given "papers" in the manner of a public clinic and told to follow a tiny wizened old woman to a little room at the bottom of the yard made from an old canopy from a *bakkie* (pickup truck). Clients were told to climb into the dark room and speak to their ancestors, telling them all their problems.

After communing with their ancestors in the dark for a few minutes, clients were then taken to the doctor's "office" inside the house, a room lined with shelves laden with dusty jars. The doctor, wearing the long robes and skullcap of a Muslim, would then instruct clients to remove their shoes and socks (if they had them) and place their bare feet upon a plain sheet of white photocopying paper, whereupon he would pronounce a litany of words sounding to my ears like Arabic—a language not widely spoken in Soweto.

After the incantation, the foot-imprinted paper would be wafted briefly through smoke arising from incense on a small coal brazier beside the doctor's desk. Miraculously, writing would appear on the paper. A few words in one of the local languages would be surrounded by Arabic writing. These words were the words of the ancestors, reporting the very same problems told to them a few minutes earlier in the secrecy of the dark room at the bottom of the garden. Skeptic that I am, I could not help but wonder if the same intercom system that the busy doctor was using to call patients according to number was not also wired up to listen to the murmurings at the bottom of the garden. My friends from Snake Park, however, were de-lighted with the perspicacity of the divination and confident that the pack-age of herbs they were instructed to burn in the evening would bring the stolen machine to their door and the thief to book promptly. Unfortunately, they were disappointed and a further visit to Dr. Kalongha found them wondering whether his story about the power of the herbs being diluted by their talking too much was not just a lie to hide his incompetence.

The stolen spray-painting machine was never found. Majola, the main suspect, talked his way out of the kangaroo court. A few years later he talked his way out of custody after he was found raping a five-year-old girl. Dr. Kalongha disappeared from his place in Rockville. I never found out what had happened to him because my friend Madumo had impregnated a girl in Kalongha's neighbor's house whom he had come to know when we were hanging around the "surgery," and we did not dare return to that place.

Dr. Kalongha was a diviner, an herbalist, a religious figure, and, most probably, an opportunist. I have no doubt, however, that he was sincere in his work and perhaps even effective in helping people. Everyone I knew spoke of him as an *inyanga*. They would happily call him a "traditional healer" or "witch doctor," too. Nor would most people I know in Soweto quibble about describing this outlandish healer as a *sangoma*. He is by no means representative of traditional healing as portrayed in the literature or in the imagery of contemporary political discourse. He is, however, typical of the sorts of healers plying their trade in Soweto and a thousand other places in South Africa at the turn of the twenty-first century.

In sum, Soweto is a place where life is tough but not impossible, though it is getting harder under the impact of HIV/AIDS. Generally, people are poor but most live in a solid house and have access to drinkable water and elec-tricity. Children have access to schools, though these are not the finest one could wish for. The sick can get to clinics and a hospital, though they could be much better cared for than they are. And the elderly, the disabled, and parents of young children are entitled to pensions or other financial as-sistance, though the administration of such payments could be much im-proved. Most households also have a phone or a family member with a cell phone; all have access to public phones in the near vicinity (which is one of the more common "informal" businesses in the township). Many Sowetans are thriving, but with the earnings of some 60 percent of households barely at subsistence levels, most people live a financially precarious existence. Those who are not financially desperate have relatives whom they are expected to assist with financial support, far too many to help them all. The relationships of reciprocity and generosity within households, families, and communities that support those who are unable to support themselves also produce relations of dependence and spawn feelings of resentment that can be fatal to amity and peace. When people begin to wonder whether witchcraft is affecting their fortunes, they have access to innumerable healers willing to endorse and inflame their suspicions.

3

ON LIVING IN A WORLD WITH WITCHES

The Witches of Mapetla: Local Knowledge, Public Secrets

At a party in a neighbor's house in Mapetla Extension some years ago, a group of young women, fueled by a few good drinks, began entertaining themselves with songs. They sang hymns and wedding songs for a while — at the top of their voices, of course — before one of them started up an old melody with a new, improvised, ironic refrain: "the women of Mapetla are witches . . ." Hearing the lyrics, an old lady from a nearby street became agitated. "You speak the truth," she cried. "It's true! The women of Mapetla *are* witches. *Witches!*" The singers laughed so much they could no longer sing. Someone shouted, "No!" The singers laughed louder. The old lady disappeared from the house.

To an outside eye, that afternoon's revelry would have seemed like the ordinary raucousness of cheerful community life. And it was. To appreciate the joke, however, you would have needed to know what everybody already knew, to wit: the old lady was a witch herself. Among her many crimes, the witch's neighbors can list the murders of her daughter-in-law, her granddaughter, and a neighbor's child and the insanity of another neighbor — not to mention dozens of odd and suspicious sightings and events in the neighborhood. None of this, however, is reason not to laugh on a sunny Sunday afternoon when the drinks are flowing, at least for those who have escaped her evil works unscathed. Nor is laughter a sign that the witch is not to be feared.

None of the young women singing about the witches of Mapetla would dream of making an outright accusation against their neighbor, nor would they repeat what everyone else knows to her face. To the best of my knowledge, no one has ever openly accused that old lady of being a witch, certainly not in the decade or so that I have known her. We know what we know about her witchcraft, just as we know we all know it—and we know she knows that we know—through gossip. And though her neighbors may laugh at her as a witch, they are careful nonetheless. For hers is the name that comes to mind when suspicions of malefaction arise or when a healer specifies an unnamed "neighbor" as the source of illness or misfortune. She is the embodiment of her neighbors' generalized fears of evil forces at work in the world.

In a place like Soweto, evidence of witches' handiwork is everywhere to be seen for those who know what to look for. Knowing what to look for means knowing the history of gossip around the place. In the older neighborhoods, where families have been settled for three generations or more, the melding of individual fates into the life of a community creates dense networks of suspicion animated by memories of past suffering. Knowledge of who was responsible for particular calamities filters slowly down through the generations, making it difficult for anyone to say how they came to know what everybody knows: that so-and-so over there is a witch. I learned what everyone knew about that neighbor they call the witch only after I discovered, accidentally, that I had been spared by my friends, perhaps, from what seemed at the time to have been a possible attack: this same neighbor had sent over a pot of sorghum beer for the enjoyment of the men of our house who could not attend the neighbor's feast, but the suspicious women in our house poured it down the drain before any of the family could be harmed (Ashforth 2000a, chap. 11). That old lady, though she is the most well known witch in our neighborhood, is not the only one. Anyone can perpetrate acts of witchcraft. When living in a world with witches, it is not wise to fear only the well-known witch.

When I have talked with friends in the neighborhood about what makes that old lady a witch, no one can say for sure what her powers are. Being old, my friends assume she has learned secrets of witchcraft, recipes for dangerous *muthi,* over time. Perhaps she inherited evil powers at birth, probably from her mother; suppositions about genes can be applied to witchcraft abilities as well as other family traits. Perhaps she was taught her deadly skills by a relative. When people talk of these possibilities, they do not often mention male forebears. Mothers and grandmothers are usually blamed. The possibility of a male line of malefaction, however, cannot be ruled out, especially since many male healers claim powers descending from their fathers and grandfathers. On several occasions I have enjoyed a good laugh with friends of this witch's granddaughters while speculating about which of our mutual friends might be slated as the future witch. Despite the laughter, they did not doubt that one of the girls was a potential killer.

One night long ago, as the local gossip has it, a neighbor witnessed the old woman performing some strange ritual with one of the children in the dark in the yard—a clear sign that she was up to something. Everyone who heard the story as the gossip spread through the neighborhood agreed that the incident was deeply suspicious. No one could say for sure, however, what the witch was up to, other than "witchcraft." And no one seemed inclined to consider the incident innocent—an ordinary healing procedure, for example, perhaps the cleansing of a child who had encountered dangerous pollution. Perhaps the old woman had made a secret pact with Satan, the generally acknowledged ultimate source of evil. When I have pointed out that the old lady is a regular churchgoer, a Lutheran, my friends have pointed out that such devotion is the best cover for a witch. In short, when it comes to imagining the powers of a witch, anything is possible. In the end, except for professionals involved in the business of healing and their clients who are victims of witchcraft, the details do not matter. A witch is a witch. And only the witch knows how witchcraft works.

Witchcraft and Gossip

Witchcraft is both a subject of gossip and a product of gossip. Gossip is the medium within which it lives. Through the pleasurable exchanges of gossip and idle speculation in the chance encounters of everyday life, much valuable information can be transmitted from which motives can be surmised and the dangers lurking beneath the surface of amicable community life revealed. In the idle talk that is gossip, the motives of seemingly virtuous neighbors, friends, relatives, and others can be minutely scrutinized for signs of malice. Reputations and the public images that others thought they had cunningly constructed can be taken apart piece by piece and the outward appearance of everyday life turned, in the words of Marcel Proust, "inside out with the magic dexterity of an idealist philosopher" (Proust 1983, 1082). Through gossip, "backstage" behavior, to use Erving Goffman's phrase, can be brought to light and subjected to scrutiny (Goffman 1959).

Writing of her experiences with witchcraft in central and eastern Gonja, Ghana, in the 1960s, Esther Goody distinguishes between gossip, allegations, and accusations concerning witchcraft attacks. Gossip she treats as instances "where an attack or misfortune is attributed to witchcraft, but the identity of the witch is not specified"; allegations arise when "both victim and witch are named, but no publicly sanctioned counteraction occurs";

and accusations occur when "a witch is named as responsible for a given attack, and some form of publicly sanctioned counteraction follows" (1970, 229). For Goody, the allegation is an intermediate phase in the process of counteracting witchcraft aggression. In contemporary Soweto, however, witchcraft is only rarely subject to forms of "publicly sanctioned counter-action" outside the private sphere of healing activities. Allegations and accusations may be hurled at particular suspected witches, but only in the most unusual cases is public action taken. More commonly, these matters circulate within the realms of gossip.

The psychological essence of gossip is the desire for secret knowledge about other people, especially their vices and failings. The coin of gossip is authentic "inside information," indiscreetly revealed. The confidence betrayed is gossip's gold-bearing lode. Max Gluckman pointed out in his famous essay on gossip and scandal that "gossip does not have isolated roles in community life, but is part of the very blood and tissue of that life" (1963, 308). The right to gossip is the "hallmark of membership" of a group, re-fusal to gossip is the denial of membership, and the practice of gossip over time serves to "unite a group within a larger society, or against another group" (Gluckman 1963, 313). For social analysis, the interest of gossip de-rives from its evanescent character, the accidental way in which it reveals truths of social life that are seemingly uncorrupted by the imposition of an analyst's interests. That same fleeting nature, however, makes gossip diffi-cult to study or to use as the means for studying something else—such as the ways in which people live with witches. Gossip can be studied only in retrospect, reflexively, for if it is an object of study in itself as a researcher is gossiping, it is no longer real gossip (P. Wilson 1974). Yet, if we are to get anywhere close to understanding what it is like to live in a world with witches, gossip is where we must start.

I had been living in Soweto, off and on, for several years before I was sufficiently integrated into the circuits of gossip in the neighborhood to grasp the basics of how discussions pertaining to matters of witchcraft work. To know who the witches are is to be part of the community. Being part of that community means being able to talk of witches without mentioning names at all. My right to gossip was circumscribed, as everyone's is, within a particular domain of people who considered me part of their family, one of their friends, and a member of the community. The lesson of gossip was that life must be lived in terms of a presumption of malice: unless you have good reason to believe otherwise, and only for so long as those reasons remain plausible, everyone must be presumed able and willing to cause you harm.

Circuits of gossip within a community are identical to the pathways of suspicion regarding witchcraft because gossip is only meaningful when it refers to someone who is known personally to the gossipers or who could become so known. Indeed, even when gossip is about celebrities in the public sphere, it takes the form of a virtual face-to-face relation mediated in ways that mimic real intimacy. Talk of witchcraft similarly involves suppositions about forms of personal power operating within identical face-to-face networks. Of course, there is an inevitable circularity about this: we gossip about those whom we suspect of malice and we suspect of malice those about whom we feel the need to gossip. The key elements are envy and jealousy. Witchcraft is said to be motivated by envy and jealousy, and the networks within which those emotions can plausibly circulate are identical to those of gossip. Witchcraft, then, has a necessary connection to gossip by virtue of the dynamics of intimacy and secrecy. Gossip marks the boundaries of networks of personal relations within which talk driven by "secrets" may be shared and revealed. And "witchcraft," for people living in a world with witches, is a term referring to forms of personal power premised upon secrecy.

The circuits of gossip within social networks are the same as those of witchcraft suspicions, with parallel intensity and prevalence, because they both engage the same personal connections and emotions. The closer the emotional connection between gossipers (the more exclusive the group), the more intense the gossip will be, as will be the dangers inherent in perversion of the aims, purposes, and character of the group. Thus, in close kin groups, perversion of the love, trust, and openness that ought to prevail is both a product of witchcraft and a source of the motive to perpetrate witchcraft. As Madumo's granny cried after witnessing the hatred that subsisted between him and his siblings: "this really is witchcraft" (Ashforth 2000a, 224). Kinship relations, however, form but one set of possible "gossip cells." In contemporary Soweto, it seems to me, the connection between understandings of familial relations and witchcraft suspicions has less to do with ideologies of kinship as such and more to do with expectations and resentments about reciprocity and redistribution, which are organized in terms of the ideology of family.

Gossip is also the primary medium within which invidious everyday comparisons are made between members of social networks and within which sexual indiscretions are revealed. These comparisons and revelations feed the secret envy and jealousy that are the motive forces of witchcraft. Francis Bacon could have been speaking of Soweto when he wrote in 1597: "There be none of the affections which have been noted to fascinate or bewitch, but love and envy. They both have vehement wishes; they frame themselves readily into imaginations and suggestions; and they come easily into the eye, especially upon the presence of the objects; which are the points that conduce to fascination [witchcraft], if any such thing there be" (Bacon 1955, 23). Why this might be so neither Bacon nor anyone I have ever discussed these issues with in Soweto considered it necessary to explain. That it is so is an axiom of social life.

Comparisons of relative status, from which envy is bred through gossip, are not only comparisons of material well-being. Virtue itself can also be a focus of resentment, particularly among women, for whom the values specifying motherhood and family life are supposed to be predominant. The woman who has a responsible husband and healthy, well-behaved, and dutiful children, who attends church, and who is hardworking and attentive to her familial and community duties is also a woman at risk of being envied and considered proud. For although virtually everyone endorses such an ideal of motherhood and family, few are in a position to achieve it. For this reason, weddings are the occasion of intense gossip and danger, because when a woman gets married, especially if it is in the style of the "white wedding," which is much beloved by females in these parts, her less fortunate friends, neighbors, and relatives may be "happy" for her in a way that can be relieved only by her suffering serious future misfortune.

The feedback loop of gossip—through which you learn, through gossip, that others are gossiping about you—is a crucial element of witchcraft suspicions. For if people are sufficiently motivated to gossip, particularly if the gossip is malicious, they must also be presumed motivated to act in the form of witchcraft. In practice, in Soweto, it is wise to presume that the desire for harm may be fulfilled. That is, knowing that someone is jealous of you is enough to arouse worry about their willingness to cause serious harm. And if you know that someone is gossiping about you, you can be assured they are making invidious comparisons and are most likely jealous.

The challenge of breaking through the secrecy that surrounds every aspect of witchcraft poses a slew of epistemological problems in the course of everyday life in places like Soweto and affects the character of social life profoundly. Yet while witchcraft is an endeavor predicated upon secrecy, the powers and possibilities imagined as its currency are also experienced as commonplace accompaniments of everyday life. Times of crisis bearing signs of witchcraft can strike terror into individuals and their families— very occasionally sweeping though whole communities in a hysteria of accusation with direful consequences for the families of those accused for generations to come. Yet talk of witches is mostly a matter for idle gossip, laughter, and the sort of quotidian philosophizing that follows what Sowetans call "after-tears beers," that time when, after returning in buses from a neighbor's burial and having enjoyed a good meal at the neighbor's relatives' expense, people enjoy idle speculation about other people's problems. This is not exactly the stuff that is preached by the people who seek believers, like the ministers and healers and prophets that abound in this place. But this is the stuff that people bring to bear on their problems when the pleasurable speculation and joke-filled gossip turns to dread. And this is the stuff they take to their preachers, prophets, and healers when seeking succor. It is also the stuff that I shall take as the raw material for my inquiry.

Understanding the significance of occult powers in everyday life in Soweto requires taking seriously the ways people talk about witches and witchcraft. It also means taking seriously the way people do *not* talk about such things and learning why they do not. Something like a public secret hangs over every discussion of these matters in turn-of-the-millennium South Africa. Moreover, public discourse about witchcraft, especially between black people and white, is so perverted by the history of racism and oppression in these parts that some will do their best to prevent any talk about it at all. Yet the matters of which people speak when they talk of witchcraft are of the first importance for their sense of security in everyday life.

Gossip, Jealousy, and the Presumption of Malice in Community Life

Life in a world with witches must be lived in the light of a presumption of malice: one must assume that anyone with the motive to harm has access to the means and that people *will* cause harm because they can. If the supposition that harm *can* be caused by mysterious means must be taken seriously, then it is dangerous to assume that an instance of suffering might be accidental or a product of purely impersonal forces devoid of connection with human or spiritual agency. When the possibility that the real cause of suffering can be deliberately obscured and made secret by the perpetrators has to be countenanced, as is the case when witchcraft is taken as a plausible hypothesis, it is difficult, if not impossible, to prove the counterfactual: that witchcraft was *not* the cause of suffering in any particular instance. Thus, it is wise, when living in a world of witches, to seek protection against suffering being so caused. And it is also wise, when misfortune does occur, to inquire into *who* might be responsible, if for no other reason than to afford protection against further mishap.

Now, if harm and death must be presumed capable of being caused by malicious others using secret means of deploying "evil forces," the question arises as to the motives that might induce these others to act.[1] In every instance, the answer to the question "Why would they do witchcraft?" is "Because of jealousy." In everyday usage in Soweto, the commonplace English word "jealousy" encompasses envy of others' goods and good fortune as well as fear of rivals' obtaining what one already has. Local African languages make no distinction between "envy" and "jealousy": *fufa* serves in Sotho and Tswana and *umona* in Zulu for both types of emotion and all types of object. "Jealousy" serves as the name of the primary motive for witchcraft. It is premised upon hatred, which itself is taken as a free-flowing accompaniment of everyday life (as omnipresent as its opposites: love, comradeship, and fellow feeling) that flares into rage on account of jealousy. Particularly dangerous are the hatred that cannot be openly expressed and the desire for revenge that, for reasons of impotence, cannot be acted upon. The emotional state most feared approximates that of ressentiment as described by Max Scheler in elaboration of Nietzsche's critique of Christian morality, where not only is the feeling of envy experienced as a nonfulfillment of a desire for something but the "owner is falsely considered the *cause* of our privation" (Scheler 1998, 35). The jealousy that is most dangerous is thus connected with a deluded sense of righteousness that allows an attack to be construed as defense.

When does an unfortunate event become an act of witchcraft, a deliberate malicious assault perpetrated by some other person? People worry about acts of witchcraft mostly in connection with events surrounding premature death and serious illness and events that could have resulted in death, such as accidents or assault. While there are many ways of dying before the biblical allotment is complete, three predominate: illness, murder, and motor vehicle accidents. Death in old age is a privilege accorded few. Any death, or foretaste of death, is an occasion for speculation about witchcraft. The character and intensity of such speculation will depend primarily upon the relations of the interlocutors with the victims. Regarding deceased neighbors, strangers, and distant acquaintances, the tone might be one of idle speculation; for close relatives and loved ones, the matter can be so serious that it might not be spoken of at all. Construing a death or unfortu-

1. I draw my treatment of motives primarily from Kenneth Burke's exposition of "dramatism" in *A Grammar of Motives*, wherein he identifies the five "basic forms of thought . . . exemplified in the attribution of motive," which he summarizes under the rubrics Act, Scene, Agent, Agency, and Purpose, elements that are always involved whenever "we say what people are doing and why they are doing it" (1969, xv). I am also influenced by C. Wright Mills's classic essay (1940) drawing on Burke's earlier work.

nate event as an act of witchcraft implies the imputation of agency to a perpetrator or perpetrators who might plausibly be considered motivated to harm the victim or those connected with the victim.

A general sense of possibility—"they can do *anything* . . ."—is all that is required to lend plausibility to a suspicion of witchcraft, and in an ordinary narrative of misfortune, no one expects his or her interlocutor to be able to specify exactly how the misfortune was achieved. Professional healers who specialize in treating instances of occult harm will be expected to provide more detailed explanations. Typically they do so in the form of narratives positing the illicit use of *muthi*. The scene, or background situation, within which events interpreted as witchcraft are invariably played out in Soweto, as elsewhere, is the household. Whether the main protagonists in the drama are relatives in the same family or not, the stage upon which most events play out is the home. Visits to healers, churches, clinics, and hospitals can play an important part in the affair, but the heart of the drama, the reckoning of motives and culprits, is focused upon the home. The range of possible assailants and their motives will be assessed by analyzing relations between suspects and the household as a whole. When a family is intact, an unfortunate event interpreted as an act of witchcraft will be seen as an attack upon the family as a whole. Other players in the drama are usually situated within intimate networks of relatives, friends, neighbors, schoolmates, fellow church congregants, workmates, and so on—anyone who can plausibly be reckoned to possess a motive of jealousy. Acts of witchcraft are not usually perpetrated by strangers, although a great many harms can originate from impersonal forces acting through strangers, particularly forms of pollution. Because the effects of witchcraft are felt inside a household, and because the work of healing is dependent upon the support of household and family (both living and dead), such troubles should not be spoken of to outsiders. Mostly, they are not.

Anyone can be a witch. Everybody, being human, is presumed to possess the potential for the motive of jealousy and thus the desire to perform witchcraft. It is also assumed in these parts that anyone who has the desire—the "bitterness in the heart" as MaMfete terms it—can gain access to the means. The means of deploying evil forces consist of special skills and knowledge, innate capacities, or relations with invisible evil beings. Even if maliciously motivated persons lack the abilities, skills, knowledge, or access to demons themselves, the presumption is that specialists abound who are willing to sell their deadly services. Even bona fide healers are presumed to have the ability to harm as well as heal. Judging by the number of healers who have described clients approaching them in search of *muthi* to kill, the market for such services must be considered significant. I have no doubt that there are many *inyangas* who will cheerfully dispense *muthi* that they guarantee will kill, though I seriously doubt its efficacy. In addition, sufficient numbers of mutilated corpses are found regularly, with even an occasional prosecution of an *inyanga* for "*muthi* murder," to indicate that an underground market in occult services is reasonably widespread. Most people have an impression of this market for illicit occult services that resembles the popular image of the illicit narcotics market in American cities, where citizens know such a market exists, imagine it to be more extensive than it probably is, imagine everyone else, including their own children, has ready access to it, but nonetheless would not be able to participate in it—say, to buy a kilogram of cocaine—even if they wanted to. The desire to perpetrate witchcraft is both hidden in the manner in which all innermost desires are obscure and deliberately kept secret because it is a murderous and illegitimate impulse.

A Sociology of Jealousy

In a world where witches must be taken seriously, safety can never be guaranteed. Ultimately, security depends upon the beneficence of invisible beings such as the triune Christian God and the ancestors. Legions of preachers, prophets, and healers in Soweto promise their clients safety by virtue of their special connections with these beings. Even people with unshakable faith, however, can never be completely confident that they do not deserve punishment for some lapse or sin. Nor can they be confident that a misfortune that might be construed as resulting from contact with pollutants is not in fact an attack by witchcraft. So the wise know better than to attract unnecessary attention from malicious people who would do them harm. They try not to arouse the jealousy of others. And they try to be discreet. In a world of witches, loose talk costs lives. Let me illustrate.

In May 1994, at the time of the ANC's historic election victory, my "sister" Seipati was preparing to give birth to her first child. I drove her to the clinic when her labor pains began, returning home to find the street in a state of joyous uproar celebrating Mandela's announcement of victory. "Free at last!" he had said. "Free at last." Seipati's mother, MaMfete, was standing in the street with a neighbor, a woman of about my own age who had been close to the family since she and Seipati were children. I had come to know her as something like another sister. After returning my greeting, this neighbor asked, "Where's Seipati?" An innocent question. Indeed, in the Sotho language, which we were speaking at the time, the standard greeting translates as "Where are you?"—to which one answers, "I am here"—and ordinary politeness requires following up an initial greeting with inquiries into the whereabouts, and thereby the well-being, of relatives and mutual friends. So when the neighbor inquired, "Where's Seipati?" I replied with the simple, stupid, truth: "In the hospital having her baby."

Almost before I could finish the sentence I was drawn up short by an alarmed glare from MaMfete. I knew then that I had committed more than a gaffe. I had been around long enough by then to know I should have known better. After several days of celebrating the ANC's historic victory, I found an opportunity to inquire about how grave my mistake had been, to learn how dangerous these times of birth and death can be. Yet even then, after MaMfete had fully explained the situation and the dangers, I refused to believe that the woman with whom I had spoken so freely, whom I knew as a friend, a sister, would want to cause harm to the extent of killing her own good friend's child. "*She* may not," was MaMfete's response. "But she's a gossip. She might give the ammunition to someone who will." MaMfete, who was by no means paranoid and was well liked and respected in the neighborhood, had no doubt that there were people around prepared to kill the new child and perhaps her mother, too, despite all appearances to the contrary. "Why would they do that?" I asked. "Because they are jealous," she replied.

The moments of birth and death, when persons are in the process of transition from one form of being to another, are particularly vulnerable to attack by malicious agents using invisible forces. Discretion is of the utmost importance at such times in order to secure the mother and child from hostile interference or to allow safe passage for the deceased into the afterlife. Discretion at times of childbirth is also more generally important in order to prevent the circulation of information that might give rise to jealousy. If gossip is the medium within which witchcraft grows, discretion is the first line of defense. The circuits of gossip through which MaMfete feared the news of her daughter's vulnerability could spread were almost exclusively female. The dangerous people in this case, too, were all women. Later that night, under the cover of victory celebrations, a young man was gunned down at the end of the street. Although his killers vanished into the darkness and no one was arrested for the crime, no one doubted that the killers were male. Similarly, if anything had happened to Seipati or her baby during the period of confinement, no one would have doubted that the assailant was female.

An elementary gender distinction underpins the folk sociology of witchcraft in these parts: conflicts among men are more likely to result in violence; conflicts among women are more likely to result in witchcraft. This is not an absolute rule. Everybody knows that men can use witchcraft and women can be violent. Generally, however, the gender rule applies. Men are presumed to be more likely to resort to witchcraft the less powerful they are physically or the less capable of mobilizing physical violence—that is, the less manly they are—just as physically strong women may resort to violence in their conflicts with others, men included. Because witchcraft engages secret means for causing harm, it resembles the ambush and the assassination as uses of violence. Men will resort to it—or so it is said—when they fight from a position of weakness or know their ends are illegitimate.

Certain relationships are considered more prone to jealousy than others and thus more susceptible to both witchcraft and violence. Relations between lovers and spouses are fraught with jealousy. When a man beats his woman for no apparent reason, when he is said to have no good cause to "discipline" her, he will be said to be motivated by jealousy. When a man dies, his wife will automatically be suspected of killing him. The motive, again, will be jealousy. In 1993, a neighbor named Mahlatsi died in a car accident late one night after leaving a party in a town some forty miles away on the other side of Johannesburg. He was thirty-three years old. In accounting for his death nobody seemed to think it particularly relevant that he was an alcoholic who probably was quite drunk before trying to drive home. On hearing of his death, I went to his home to pay my respects to his family. "They say his wife is to blame," I was told by another neighbor, a young man, visiting for the same reason. Because neither of us was particularly close to the deceased, we could speculate freely. "Why would she want to do that?" I asked. "Jealousy," the neighbor said. "She knew Mahlatsi was having girlfriends." I could have pontificated about drinking and driving if I had cared to, but only a fool or a naive outsider could fail to see the connection between the death and the wife. After all, he had been driving drunk for years. Similarly, when my friend Mr. Dladla was shot by young men at Merafe Hostel, his neighbors at home in Snake Park on the other side of Soweto blamed his common-law wife, Thoko, despite the fact that, as far as I could see, she had the least motive for killing him of anyone. She stood to lose all by his death. And she did. After the funeral, Mr. Dladla's relatives chased her away from the home and business she and Mr. Dladla had built together.

Relations between co-wives have always been said to be fraught with suspicions of witchcraft. These days, although formal polygamy is rare in

places like Soweto, men (providing they have the wherewithal to have anyone at all) typically have several "girlfriends" at a time even if they have
a wife. Where two or more women have children with the same man, the
presumption is that one or both of them will be tempted to use witchcraft
against the other. They might also be tempted to deploy *korobela*, a species
of love medicine, against the man to keep him faithful. Relations between
mothers-in-law and daughters-in-law are similarly prone to tension, particularly when the mother is dependent upon her son for financial support.
When my friend Martha married her colleague, a fellow schoolteacher, she
refused to follow the "tradition" that stipulated she should move into her
mother-in-law's home and serve her. Instead, she insisted that she and her
husband buy their own home in the suburbs, thereby depriving her mother-
in-law of the extension to the family home that she had long expected from
her successful son, as well as the unpaid servitude of his new bride. When
the mother-in-law fell sick and died a few years later, Martha was held responsible. She knew this, not because anyone leveled a formal accusation
or because she heard open allegations of her complicity, but because she
was forbidden to attend her mother-in-law's funeral by her husband, who
subsequently divorced her. The husband's family probably consulted a diviner who identified Martha as the culprit—Martha never knew—but they
could just as easily have come to the same conclusion unaided.

In the same way that certain relationships are deemed prone to jealousy,
everyday interpretations of the patterns of individual propensities for causing harm produce, and are produced by, definite stereotypes. Just as young
men are considered the social category with the greatest propensity for using violence, so older women are said to be the persons most likely to perpetrate witchcraft. Older women are presumed more susceptible to dangerous feelings of jealousy because after years of working to raise their
families (mostly without much help from men), their status is dependent
upon the success of their children and grandchildren, which, in turn, is
measured in comparison with other families. As one older woman, Ma-
Buthelezi, once explained to me: "Others who are down are wanting to hurt
the people. Others who are coming good are trying to stop people from progressing to their level." I asked why older men were not so motivated: "No,
those ones are useless. They are too busy drinking. They don't care."

Though they lack the capacity for physical violence, their age lends
plausibility to the supposition that older women have greater access to the
knowledge of how to deploy evil forces. The fact that older women predominate in the ranks of healers and prophets, adepts in the use of mysterious forces, also lends substance to the imputation of unusual spiritual

capacities to them as a class. Outsiders usually find this attribution of power to older women perverse. The Boy Scout helping the little old lady across the street where I grew up was not encouraged to think of her as a weapon of mass destruction. In Soweto, on the occasions—rare occasions—when collective action is taken against the perpetrators of witchcraft, it usually takes the form of violence committed by young men against older women. They do not think they are killing weak and marginal members of society.

As well as being patterned according to age and gender, the propensities for jealousy, violence, and witchcraft are also said to be patterned along lines of race, ethnicity, and class. "Whites," as old Mr. Mashile told me, "*are* having witchcraft. Many are using *inyangas* in town. But we blacks are too jealous. That is why it is worse this side." Some white people have indeed been initiated as healers.[2] Many people also stereotype those with dark complexions as particularly prone to witchcraft (Ashforth 2000a, 83). Particular ethnic groups, most notably the Zulus, are said to be predisposed to violence, just as others (typically those from far away, such as the Venda) are known as dangerous witches. When I have asked healers why this is so, they have said it is because the herbs of far-off places are unfamiliar to local healers and thus more difficult to counter. By a similar logic, healers hailing from distant parts are generally reputed to possess greater powers than locals. Poor communities are reputed to be more prone to both violence and witchcraft. Urban people, such as most of those who live in Soweto, tend to view rural areas as hotbeds of witchcraft. Rural people tend to view cities as especially violent and dangerous because of uncontrollable witchcraft—a "cesspool of sorcery" in James Kiernan's phrase (1984). Just as one learns to identify and avoid as best one can people prone to violence and the places where they prowl, so one strives to minimize exposure to people who might be prone to jealousy and witchcraft. And just as the worst scourge of violence is often found inside the home or close to home, so the dangers of witchcraft are never entirely avoidable.

Relations among neighbors are often fraught with feelings of jealous resentment and fears of witchcraft. Schoolmates, co-workers, fellow churchgoers, relatives, and anyone else who might have cause to make an invidious comparison are also deemed prone to jealousy and may thus be motivated to perpetrate witchcraft. The literature on witchcraft in Africa has been well served by studies of the sociology of witchcraft accusations in villages and the politics of resolving conflicts expressed in the idiom of

2. For an example of a white *sangoma*'s career, see the memoir by a former city councilor of Johannesburg: McCallum 1993.

witchcraft (Douglas 1970b). The relationship between witchcraft accusation and social tension is well documented across much of the continent (Max Marwick 1982). Not surprisingly, this literature shows that witchcraft accusations predominate where social relations are deemed by the people living them to be prone to emotions of jealousy. Less well studied in this literature have been the procedures by which families and communities manage jealousy and resentment in community relations in order to reduce the dangers of witchcraft and obviate the emergence of accusations.

The Paradox of Confession

Discretion can afford a modicum of protection against the dangers of gossip, and a modicum is as much as can be had in that domain, but nothing can avail against the jealousy of those presumed likely to be consumed by such an emotion except their own voluntary confession—for jealousy is an emotion that is most powerful when hidden or disguised. The more powerful the feeling is, the more the jealous person will be driven to deny and hide it. No amount of disavowal from a person suspected of being jealous will suffice as proof that his or her jealousy does not exist. Yet, when jealousy is taken as the motive of the most heinous crimes that can be committed (harm and death inflicted through mysterious secret means: witchcraft), then the detection of its presence in community relations is of the utmost importance. The actual existence of the emotion and the dangers of the malice that it can motivate can be fully revealed only through positive confession by the person or persons presumed likely to be subject to the emotion. A person who voluntarily confesses feelings of jealousy toward another, and whose confession is taken as a genuine renunciation of malice, can be forgiven or punished *before* any crime is committed. That person can also be exempted from suspicion in the event of a subsequent mishap. In the absence of confession, occasions of harm and death become evidence of crimes having been committed, and the usual suspects, the persons presumed likely to have been jealous of the victims, will be suspected.

In order for the usual suspects in matters of witchcraft to preserve their innocence, full confession of their jealousy and resentment—preferably before any event for which they might be blamed—is the only valid defense. Only by confession can the motives that everybody presumes they have be revealed and renounced. Axel-Ivar Berglund is one of the few anthropologists of Africa who have made a detailed study of the dynamics of confession. Focusing on the dynamics of ritual confession, Berglund has shown how it serves as a way of "speaking out grievances, grudges, envy, etc. which lead to anger and subsequent expression of witchcraft and sorcery" (1976, 313). In his description of family and community relationships in 1960s Zululand, Berglund revealed the lengths that people would go—and sometimes be forced to go by the application of physical and psychological pressure tantamount to torture—to confess the dangerous emotion of jealousy. These confessions were thought particularly important for women during the period of confinement and childbirth, for the one about to give birth as well as all others intimately connected with her. By confessing everything that might be construed as a motive for witchcraft, a person engages in a process Berglund described as the "emptying of evil in oneself" (1976, 319). If anything were to go wrong in the birth, those who had confessed and emptied themselves of evil could perhaps escape suspicion of witchcraft. Berglund also emphasized how the people he knew saw the act of confession as material to the process of curing illness and restoring health as well as preventing future mishaps (1976, 315).

The mode of confession described by Berglund, interpreted as an act of emptying or purifying, seems to me to be less about the acknowledgment of a past sin, as it is in Christianity and criminal law, than a procedure for neutralizing motives for future evils. The object of this kind of confession is not justice or redemption but security.[3] It serves to prevent people from causing future harm and to protect the community from the disruptive forces of suspicion. Such confessions can be far more effective than a mere denial of resentment or disavowal of malicious intent, for these can never be complete or completely convincing—especially when fears of witchcraft involve motives and means that are assumed to be secret and when "objective" evidence, therefore, other than the evident fact of the injury, is unobtainable.

But what if a person has nothing to confess? What if a confession is not true? If the act of confession is performed as a practical demonstration of the absence of malice with a view to the future rather than the past, the factual content of the confession becomes less important than the evident authenticity of the desire to come clean. Often the confessions that Berglund witnessed in Zulu families were not factual from what he referred to as the point of view of "Western concepts of truth and reality" (1976, 318). These confessions were frequently recanted, at least in their factual specifics, after the occasion necessitating them had passed, such as a difficult labor and birth. In each of the examples cited by Berglund, the authenticity of the act

---

3. For a discussion of the history of confession in religion, literature, and law as an authoritative but deeply problematic mode of speaking truth, see P. Brooks 2000.

of purification is attested by the risks incurred in the act of confessing. The logic seems to be that by confessing my jealousy and resentment to you, and thereby my desire to cause you harm, I am not only renouncing these desires but am publicly placing myself in the position of holding myself responsible for any misfortune that may in future befall you and thus reducing the risk that I will so act. Once I have acknowledged that I want to cause you harm, you can sleep soundly knowing that I won't, because you know that I know that if anything untoward happens, I will be blamed. If something does go wrong, however, since I am one who would ordinarily fall under suspicion, my prior confession—assuming it was convincingly sincere —may cause people to think twice before accusing me. This, then, is the paradox of confession: a suspected witch can best prove that he or she is innocent of future witchcraft by confessing to past crimes and present motivation. Absent confession, there is no reason not to suspect the usual suspects.

In contemporary Soweto, no forums exist wherein neighbors can demonstrate themselves to be free of the jealousy and resentments that are taken as a motive for witchcraft; few occasions arise where hostile feelings and ill intent can be revealed and renounced while community harmony is embraced. This would matter less if people were more secure. When witchcraft is suspected, or when healers divine the work of evil forces, more often than not they point to some generic jealous "neighbor" as responsible. The difficulty of defusing jealousy within residential communities, whether by means of confession or some other device, is a major impediment to the management of witchcraft in contemporary urban life. Some families use rituals surrounding feasts for ancestors as occasions for reaffirming familial unity and laying hostilities to rest, but confessions of the sort described by Berglund are rare. The drive to confess and to hear others confess their jealousy and malice, however, is by no means absent. Churches concerned with the struggle against witchcraft, such as the so-called Apostolic and Zionist congregations, which abound in Soweto, practice forms of public confession as central parts of their liturgical ritual; these serve the dual purpose of promising the penitent individual redemption from sins while cleansing the congregation of motives that are deemed dangerous to the harmony of the group and the health of its members.[4] These confessions take place in relatively small forums. The congregations of these churches are typically small bands numbering twenty or fewer members. Unfortu-

4. For discussion of the centrality of confession in these churches, see Oosthuizen 1992, 141.

nately, while confession may help to keep the peace within these bands, members of these churches tend to see themselves as under siege from sorcery and evil spirits at large in the world outside their own band, so their preoccupation with witchcraft does nothing for the peace of mind of those outside.

In the absence of occasions when confession or other means can be assumed to reduce the dangers of witchcraft by revealing and removing malicious motives from persons in relationships deemed prone to jealousy, life in a world of witches entails a continual presumption of malice. People must be constantly vigilant against occult attack. This is a fact of life both of no particular significance in everyday affairs and of profound importance for the quality of life as a whole, a fact of life akin to the habits of security that become second nature to those accustomed to living in a world of criminals, such as locking one's doors and not strolling the streets at night. It is wise to presume malice, even despite appearances to the contrary, when community life is subject to the risk of occult attack. Such wisdom, however, makes trust inordinately difficult.

Speaking of the Dead

Reports of death and summonses to funerals are prime occasions for speculation about witchcraft. In this age of AIDS, hardly a week passes without word of the "passing away" of another neighbor, colleague, relative, schoolmate, fellow congregant, friend, or acquaintance. When the event of the person's death is not too painful, when the connection with the deceased is not too close, idle speculation and gossip about the cause of death inevitably arise. Premature deaths are almost always presumed to result from some sort of malicious human action classified under the general rubric of witchcraft. This is not to say that nobody recognizes the possibility of death from "natural causes" or illnesses they refer to as "natural." They do. But when a person dies, the cause of death is always of interest. And when a person dies before his allotment of three-score years and ten, as most do, somebody, if not everybody, connected with the deceased is going to wonder why. Wondering why someone died is tantamount to wondering who might have killed him. As my friend Simon said when I asked, "What happened?" while he was recovering from a gunshot wound after surviving what seemed to me a random act of violence by strangers: "There's no such thing as an accident in this place."

In a world of witches, people usually speak about deaths in three distinct registers of interpretation, each with different protocols of discourse, though the participants in conversations may overlap. Before the funeral, a cause of death will be publicly announced, often with a notice in the *Sowetan*, and publicly acknowledged with all the grief and hypocrisy bereavement commonly arouses everywhere. It will be made by senior relatives of the deceased, usually shrouded in euphemism: "he died after a long illness"; "she died after a short illness." Everyone will pray for rest in peace, whatever caused the death. To publicly dispute this story would be a grave insult to the family of the deceased. Private accounts of the death will circulate, nonetheless, and gossipers—particularly those mourners little afflicted by grief—will unpick the public pronouncements with scant regard for the wishes or feelings of the family. These accounts will be shared in intimate conversations by relatives and friends close to the deceased. In these conversations the medical name of a disease might be mentioned and the suffering of the deceased recalled. Mourners might also comment on efforts to seek a cure, the consequences of various forms of treatment, and the powers of particular healers. These days, since HIV/AIDS has become the major cause of death, friends and relatives sometimes debate whether HIV was a factor in the illness and whether it should be spoken of publicly. Most families, however, bitterly resist publicly acknowledging the disease as a cause of death. Information from these intimate conversations inevitably spreads into wider networks of gossip through the age-old mechanism of the confidence betrayed. Generally speaking, the causes of death cited in public pronouncements and private conversations will be stated in an idiom expressing illnesses, accidents, and violence as afflictions of the body named in medical terms.

As they gossip and speculate about the real cause of death, however, these people will know that there is another dimension of explanation for which they grasp mostly in vain, a secret meaning of the whole event that only those intimately connected with the deceased can have access to and will rarely be willing to share. This is the register within which witchcraft is the key. Let me illustrate.

In 1991, I attended the funeral of a young woman in her early thirties. Her family announced during the funeral that she had died of an "illness" and explained to those who inquired that it was *isifuba,* which can be anything relating to the chest, such as asthma, tuberculosis, pneumonia, or the flu (Conco 1972). Those who claimed to really know why she died, however, such as my friend Refilwe, whose neighbor she was and who had heard her story from a mutual friend who knew the dead woman's sister, spoke confidentially about a botched illegal abortion. This was in the years before abortion was legalized. It was also before AIDS was well known in the townships; by the end of the decade, a death such as this would also have aroused speculation about HIV/AIDS. A botched abortion, however, was more than sufficient reason for secrecy concerning the cause of death, as such procedures were generally abhorred in the townships.

The full story of that young woman's death, however, was much more complicated. I heard it some months later from Mary, a friend of mine who had known the deceased since she was a child. Mary, a grandmother in her mid-fifties, had lived in the neighborhood for thirty-five years, ever since it was first settled with families evicted from Sophiatown, when the houses of that "black spot" in the White suburb were bulldozed to make way for Whites and a new suburb named Triomf (Triumph) was built over the rubble. Mary told me the story of the young woman's death on an afternoon when I called in to visit and found her feeling seriously ill. Her health was failing and she was worried that she was becoming a victim of the rampant witchcraft in these parts.

Her fears had been inflamed the previous evening when she visited her next-door neighbors, the family home of the deceased woman, to watch an important television announcement that was to be made by President de Klerk. While she was watching the television, an *inyanga* entered the house and greeted her by asking her if she knew him. She did not.

"Why would he ask me that?" she asked me, not waiting for a reply. The *inyanga* repeated his question several times: "Do you know me?" Each time she answered, "No. I've never seen you before!" The *inyanga* just stared at her and said nothing more.

That night, after returning home from her encounter with the *inyanga*, she suffered acute pains in her stomach and spent a sleepless night pondering the meaning of his visit to the neighbors and his insistent questions. The next day when I called, she seemed seriously ill. Not so ill, however, that she could not sit up in bed and narrate the history of her family's conflicts with the family next door, going back thirty years to the days when her brothers were young and were made mentally ill—"not normal," as they say—by the witchcraft of the grandfather of that house. Obviously, she surmised, if an *inyanga* was visiting the house after dark, they must be up to something, probably retaliating for the death of the young woman. But why, my friend wondered, should they target her? She had done nothing. I could see that she was ailing as she told me this story, so I offered to drive her to the hospital. She declined. "No one gets out of there alive," she said.

Mary was certain that the young woman's death, which she did not doubt followed from an illegal abortion, really resulted from a conflict between two grandmothers living on either side of Mary's house: Mrs. Nkadimeng, the one with the dead daughter, and Mrs. Mudau. Here is the story:

A year or so before the death of Mrs. Nkadimeng's daughter, the son of Mrs. Mudau died. He had been working at a good job and had life insurance. After the funeral, his mother was told to come to the "office" to collect on the insurance. Mrs. Mudau, however, did not know how to read or write, so she asked Mrs. Nkadimeng to accompany her to town to help with the papers. When they collected the check, Mrs. Nkadimeng insisted that it should be deposited in the Allied Building Society for safety. So they went to Allied and deposited the check. The teller gave them a passbook for the bank account and told them to return later for the card. Then Mrs. Nkadimeng said to Mrs. Mudau, "You must take the book, and I will look after the card." Then they went home. Mrs. Mudau told Mary all these details a year or so later. By that time she knew that she had been robbed.

Over the next year, Mrs. Nkadimeng began improving her house. She built a high wall outside. She bought a new room divider, a lounge suite, and a television. "She is not working," Mary told me, still indignant. "How can she afford such things? I am working, but I can't afford."

After a year had passed, sufficient to accord the proper respect to the deceased and time to start thinking about erecting a headstone over his grave, Mrs. Mudau's other children went to examine the savings account. They found only three thousand rand in it. Mary speculated that there ought to have been about twenty or thirty thousand rand on deposit, although she confessed she never knew the exact figure. Mrs. Mudau, apparently, knew instantly what had happened. Her children wanted to take action, but she stopped them. She told them not to do anything. Shortly afterward, Mrs. Nkadimeng's daughter died.

In recounting this story Mary mentioned nothing about witches or their craft, though in the course of her story she found it necessary to tell me that Mrs. Nkadimeng was a Pedi and Mrs. Mudau was a Venda. She did not need to remind me that these two ethnic groups ("nations" or "tribes" as they are also sometimes called) are considered in Soweto notorious for their witchcraft. In telling the story, however, it was clear that she considered the coincidence so powerful that no one could doubt but that Mrs. Mudau had killed Mrs. Nkadimeng's daughter in revenge. Mrs. Mudau probably also held Mrs. Nkadimeng responsible for the death of her son. Now it was Mrs. Nkadimeng's turn to retaliate.

Mary was worried that she would become a victim. She could not see any particular reason for herself or her family to be targeted, but with so much hatred in the air and so many evil forces flying back and forth, she reasoned that innocent bystanders could get caught in the crossfire. Besides, the *inyanga* visiting the Nkadimengs might not know the history of the conflict with Mrs. Mudau and could quite easily pinpoint my friend as the culprit responsible for the recent death. Perhaps that was why he kept asking if she knew him, to make some kind of point to the rest of the family.

Mary was a devout Anglican. Her church frowns upon talk of witches such as this. It does, however, recognize the existence of evil in the form of the devil and in recent years has been "progressive" about "inculturation," which involves integrating African reverence for ancestors and healing rituals into church liturgy. Anglican authorities, however, are useless when someone is bewitched, and their church services offer little comfort to someone, like Mary, who finds herself in the middle of an occult war zone. They offer no rituals to heal the effects of witchcraft or protect against occult attack. In the Truth and Reconciliation Commission's hearings on the role of churches under apartheid, Archbishop Ntongana of the Council of African Instituted Churches, after boasting of the Zionist churches' power of healing, could not resist taking a sly dig at the churches represented by the chairman of the commission, the Anglican archbishop Desmond Tutu. "Some of your own members, Mr. Chairperson," he said, "come to us in the dark and they go back to you in daylight, to your church" (Council of African Instituted Churches 1999). Mary was one of these people. She would never have told her Anglican priest she was worried about witchcraft, but she had no compunction about asking me to drive her to visit prophet-healers.

Mary's plight worsened. She went to doctors seeking medicine and to prophet-healers, though she kept clear of *inyangas*. She died within the year. Nobody accused anyone of anything. Many had their suspicions.

Witchcraft and *Ubuntu*

When describing the different ways in which people speak of misfortune, I use the metaphor of "dimension" to suggest that the notion of witchcraft provides an interpretive depth without which the other aspects of events —those representing ordinary social strains and conflicts—lack meaning. None of these dimensions can be reduced to the others without losing a sense of what is actually happening. While sometimes it seems that talk of witchcraft merely serves as an idiom through which other conflicts are expressed, often, especially upon close, nay intimate, inspection, it turns out that talk of other kinds of social conflict is rather the idiom through which struggles in the domain of invisible forces are expressed. It is this secret dimension that is sounded through conjectures about motives and actions surmised from gossip. For family members to speak publicly of the witchcraft dimension of their suffering risks both exposing themselves to further retaliation from the witch and opening themselves to suggestions that they are making accusations. Sometimes, very rarely, the gossip about witchcraft will metastasize into rumor and allegations that may lead to open accusation.[5] Even more rarely, rumor will serve to mobilize people into action and something will be done about the witch or witches: they will be killed. But accusation and action are the exception, not the norm. Like the family of Mrs. Mudau, most families will guard against details of their secret suspicions becoming known. When they seek revenge, and it is generally presumed that they will, they will do so in secret, too.

In recent years in South Africa many African intellectuals, politicians, and religious leaders have proposed reinvigorating what they call the "philosophy of *ubuntu*" as part of the project of the African Renaissance, drawing on the adage "A person is a person through other people." Where this notion goes beyond a restatement of the Christian precept "Love thy neighbor" as a principle guiding individual moral action is in the proposition that personhood is constituted in and through community with others: the person who is supposed to love his neighbor cannot exist as a full person without that neighbor. In one of the earliest discussions of the concept of *ubuntu* as an explicit principle of African identity, Jordan Ngubane stressed its difference from missionary Christianity by emphasizing the humanist basis of African thought. Personhood, in his view, was not something bestowed by God but a gift from other persons in community with one another.[6] *Ubuntu* is often referred to as the foundational principle of African humanism. More recent writers on the subject of *ubuntu* have been less inclined than Ngubane to distinguish it from Christian doctrines, proclaiming it rather as an ethic of harmonious community relations involving duties of care and respect for others and expressing forms of self-love that nurture and sustain all. This is usually represented as diametrically opposed to the "Western" individualist emphases on competition and self-interest, characteristics of capitalism rather than Christianity.

Nobody denies that these virtues of *ubuntu* are valuable and worthy of respect. A skeptic, however, might want to question how easily an ethics of

5. I borrow the cancer metaphor from Luise White, who borrowed it in turn from Edgar Morin (White 2000, 77).

6. See, e.g., Ngubane 1974, 304.

harmony can survive transplantation from face-to-face life in small villages and communities whose inhabitants have been related to each other for generations to large industrial cities where people must scramble for cash. But skeptics are few and far between when *ubuntu* is invoked, as it regularly is by the new African elites, as the essence of "Africanness."

Like many worthy principles, *ubuntu* is mostly praised from the pulpit and ignored in practice. Its inverse, however, is neither praised nor ignored. If *ubuntu* can be described as an ethical principle promoting harmonious community relations, what I shall call "negative *ubuntu*" might be termed the practical reason of community disharmony. To the adage "A person is a person through other people," the negative corollary of *ubuntu* adds: "because they can destroy you." That is, a person can survive only to the extent that others in the community choose *not* to destroy him or her. How they might do so is less important than the fact that they can. And when they do, whether by physical or by occult violence, the demand for justice inevitably arises. The central task of this book is to find a way of framing questions about this dimension of the sense of injustice and its possible implications for African democracy.

Witchcraft, though it is conceived and experienced in many different ways, is above all a form of human action that is driven by the emotion of hate, particularly as that emerges from jealousy and envy. Hatred is a phenomenon that has been poorly served in the literature of the social sciences, unlike the positive emotions that can be subsumed under the general rubric of love in all its multifarious forms, from the erotic to the greater love that no man hath than that he lay down his life for his nation. Perhaps because of the centrality of Christianity to the emergence of the modern state and the consequent emergence of the social sciences within the framework of modern statecraft, few of even the most hardheaded social scientists have difficulty recognizing the power of love in binding people together and creating social solidarities that are greater than the sum of their parts. But raise the question of the power of hate, however, and most of us are stumped about how to begin thinking about it.

Psychologists and psychoanalysts since Freud have studied the destructive effects of emotions such as hate on individuals. But very few have examined the broader social effects of these emotions other than as motives causing individuals to act in antisocial ways. I draw upon Scheler's notion of ressentiment, which is one of the few sources in the available literature for thinking through these issues (Scheler 1998). And I shall merely note in passing that the only time I have found myself seriously wondering whether talk of witchcraft might actually refer to some other sort of reality than those I am familiar with was when I witnessed the extreme hatred between Madumo and his brother described in my book *Madumo* (Ashforth 2000, chap. 18). This experience convinced me that just as people united in feelings of love can seem to generate a force that is external to each of them and that they can experience as acting upon them independent of their wills, so can hate. "Witchcraft" seems as good a name for this phenomenon as any.

4

FREEDOM, DEMOCRACY,

AND WITCHCRAFT:

SOWETO IN THE 1990S

When Witchcraft Increases

Returning to Soweto in the years following the first democratic elections of 1994, I was often struck by the frequency with which people would insist that witchcraft was increasing. A topic of conversation that had previously been a matter of curiosity and amusement was arising more often as a matter of intense concern. Many were even arguing, like Madumo himself, that witchcraft was increasing as a direct consequence of the political changes (Ashforth 2000a, 97–103). The literature on witchcraft is replete with examples of Africans lamenting the proliferation of occult activities at times of dramatic change and social strain.[1] Indeed, witchcraft always seems to be increasing. Nonetheless, the association of freedom and democracy with exposure to occult assault in postapartheid Soweto was striking.

An outsider cannot easily judge whether or not witches are more active than before, for an increasing fear of witches will not necessarily produce objective indicators such as a surge in public accusations, witch killings, or public witch eradication campaigns. Indeed, witch killings, depending upon how they are conducted, may indicate that the threat of witchcraft is being kept under control. Occult malefactors can be more fearsome for a community in the absence of procedures for public punishment. The absence of witch killings, for those who fear the depredations of witches, may in fact indicate that the witches have the upper hand. An increased fear of witch-

---

1. See, for examples, Douglas 1970b; Geschiere 1997; Max Marwick 1982; Moore and Sanders 2001a, 10.

craft attacks would stimulate an upsurge in business for healers and attendance at faith-healing churches, though these responses will not usually be apparent in the public scene. Although it may be impossible to judge the reality of increasing witchcraft, it is certainly possible to examine the changes in social conditions that might lead people to suspect such an increase. It is also possible to examine the availability of resources for managing occult threats.

When Africans invoke "witchcraft" in accounting for their suffering, as many observers have noted since Evans-Pritchard published his famous study of Zandeland (Evans-Pritchard 1937), they are articulating an interpretation of the meaning of misfortune that frames suffering in terms of harm caused by persons motivated by hatred and resentful jealousy using secret occult means. Social change, then, can contribute to perceptions of an increase in witchcraft in four basic ways: when there is manifestly more misfortune to be explained; when conditions conducive to fomenting jealousy and hatred arise; when procedures that previously served to hold jealousy and resentment in check decline in effectiveness; and when alternative interpretations of misfortune lose credibility.

Socioeconomic, political, and biological conditions in postapartheid Soweto are all conducive to interpretations that suggest increasing witchcraft. The rapidly increasing inequality within African communities and families that has marked the past quarter century leaves many feeling left behind and resentful of others' good fortune (or fearful of others' resentment of theirs), everyone is struggling to make sense of the mounting death toll from HIV/AIDS, and the collapse of that structural evil named "apartheid" leaves much misfortune still to be accounted for.

Inequality, Jealousy, and the Meaning of Misfortune

Most people remember the last quarter of the twentieth century in South Africa primarily as the time of antiapartheid struggle and political change. At the same time, however, and largely obscured by the fury of politics, a seismic shift in the social stratification among black South Africans was taking place. New black middle classes were emerging and new African political and economic elites were gaining prominence—at the same time as the fortunes of the poorest sections of African society were declining. This long-term process was driven by increasing demand for skilled labor by urban industries and the consequent relaxation of racial job reservation, which favored long-term urban residents with access to education.[2] In the last quarter of the twentieth century, as Sampie Terreblanche has pointed out, "While the income of the top 20 per cent of African households (involving about 6 million people) increased by more than 60 per cent over this period, that of the bottom 40 per cent (involving about 18 million people) declined by almost 60 per cent" (2002, 132–133). This process of class formation had been taking place over a period of decades but its pace increased in the 1990s, particularly after 1994, when positions for black professionals opened in institutions of government, business, media, culture, and education in the process that came to be known as "transformation."

In the first half of the 1990s, according to calculations based upon the 1991 and 1996 censuses, the number of Africans in the richest 10 percent of the population more than doubled and the number of Africans who qualified as "middle class" rose by nearly 80 percent. During the same period, the income of the poorest 40 percent dropped by 27 percent (Whiteford and Van Seventer 1999). In 1991, the richest 20 percent of African households earned nineteen times more than the poorest 40 percent; by 1996, the top group was earning thirty-one times more (see also S. Terreblanche 2002, 133; Whiteford and McGrath 1994, table 6.3; Whiteford and Van Seventer 1999, table 3.6). By the turn of the century, Terreblanche estimates, the top group of African households enjoyed more than forty times the income of the poorest 40 percent of families (2002, 133). A quarter century earlier, the difference had been a factor of 8, and while the richest 20 percent of African households improved their circumstances enormously within that time, the rest had become significantly poorer (Whiteford and McGrath 1994, 51). Meanwhile, as the Reserve Bank reports, the number of jobs in the formal sectors of the economy shrunk during the 1990s to a level "broadly similar to that of the late 1970s" (South African Reserve Bank 2000).

The rapidity of these developments can hardly be overemphasized. Within the space of one generation, the social landscape of black South Africa changed dramatically. I am not speaking figuratively. Prior to 1991, under the Group Areas Act, Africans were compelled by law to live in segregated townships and rural Homelands (as were other designated "popu-

---

2. The origins of this process of class formation are probably to be found in the massive expansion of "white-collar" jobs in the black public schools and black administration in the Homelands and urban areas in the 1950s and 1960s resulting from the apartheid policies of the National Party government. In the 1970s and 1980s, as the demand for skilled labor in public and private employment outstripped the supply of white workers for whom these jobs had previously been reserved, job reservation laws were relaxed and opportunities for black socioeconomic advancement opened up that favored people with education and experience of city life (Crankshaw and Parnell 2000).

lation groups") in houses built by the authorities according to standard designs. Throughout the 1990s black people with money were free to modify their township homes or move to the suburbs. Although a number of officially designated "White" areas became home to black people before the repeal of the segregation legislation (most notably Hillbrow in inner-city Johannesburg; A. Morris 1999a), the flight of the black middle classes to the suburbs did not begin in earnest until the mid-1990s. Nor has it only been the wealthy who have left the townships. As property values in inner-city suburbs fell in the wake of white flight, opportunities opened for less affluent black investors, who calculated, despite widespread "redlining" by banks, that a rough suburb was less risky than a township.

In a country long known as one of the most unequal places on earth, the disparities of wealth are no longer simply between black and white. Within the African population the Gini coefficient, which measures socioeconomic inequality, is .54, which is almost as great as in that of the country as a whole, which had a Gini coefficient in the late 1990s of .58 (May 1998, chap. 2, sec. 2). One of the most important social aspects of these changes is the continuing high degree of social connection among the African rich, along with their more numerous compatriots who are merely comparatively well-off, and the African poor. It would be hard to find a single family among the 20 percent of African households that the economists tell us have gained in wealth over the past decades who can enjoy their good fortune without knowing they have relatives, friends, and neighbors — or, increasingly, former neighbors — who are poor. And it would be even harder to find one of the newly prosperous Africans who is free of people regularly reminding him or her of financial obligations to less fortunate family and friends. These connections, and the informal practices of redistribution that they enable, are the principal reason that the high levels of poverty and unemployment have not resulted in complete destitution for whole populations. The burden of providing for the permanently indigent is also the source of a great deal of strain, jealousy, and resentment in families and communities. And jealousy can be deadly.

The burden of providing for the indigent is steadily rising and in the coming years will be exacerbated by the AIDS epidemic. By 2010, at least one in every four adults alive in South Africa today will have died of AIDS. Before dying, each victim of the disease will cost his or her family significant sums in healing costs. The amounts will vary in each instance according to factors such as family income, whether the ill person is a bread-winner, whether he or she has health insurance, and the extent to which the family engages the services of traditional healers. Each funeral will cost, if the burial is to be "decent" — and everyone will insist it should be — a sum in the vicinity of a year's income for the family of the deceased. Some 40 percent of these victims will have been working full-time and earning significant incomes, which will be sorely missed in their households, families, and social networks. And they will almost all leave behind children, of whom about half will also die of the disease.[3]

Families that remain more or less intact, where there are grandparents, aunts, and uncles as well as AIDS orphans, will probably be able to accommodate the extra financial burdens, though the increase in stress, depression, and general impoverishment will surely take a toll of its own. Where AIDS deaths break the generational structure of existing families, where survivors, both old and young, have no one upon whom they can depend as of right, orphan children and adults without means of support will find diminishing capacities for sustenance among neighbors, friends, or communities of reciprocity. Such people will increasingly become dependent upon the mercies of strangers in ways that have scant precedence in the history of these parts. Communities, governments, and charitable institutions will be hard-pressed to meet the challenge.

Why Are We Poor?

Given the election slogan of the ANC promising a "better life for all" and a general sense that upward social mobility is the rightful entitlement of all, few people living in places like Soweto can escape noticing that their lives hardly measure up to the good life being enjoyed by some, be they relatives, neighbors, or simply the ubiquitous successful black people on the television. Such comparisons are further complicated by the fact that the historical basis for group comparison, the comparison that has grounded South African politics since the creation of a national state in the south of Africa at the turn of the twentieth century, has been the binary opposition between the categories Black and White. The postapartheid leadership maintains the opposition in its political rhetoric. As Deputy President Thabo Mbeki put it in his opening statement for the 1998 parliamentary debate on reconciliation, "South Africa is a country of two nations," the one black and poor, the other white and rich (Mbeki 1998). The distinction continues to serve the purposes of political debate well enough, particularly when the

3. For a general accounting of the impact of AIDS in South Africa as a whole, see Whiteside and Sunter 2000. On AIDS mortality projections, see Bradshaw et al. 2001.

interlocutor is white and can be reminded of his historic privilege. In everyday discourse among Africans in places like Soweto, however, the question is not "Why are Whites rich and Blacks poor?" but "Why are some Blacks rich and others not?" Nothing in the indigenous political or social traditions of this country offers guidance for interpreting the meaning of economic inequality among black people, particularly now that Africans are politically dominant.[4]

The emergence of the dramatic socioeconomic inequality that now marks African populations in South Africa presents enormous problems of interpretation, particularly for those who find themselves being left behind. When those not enjoying the good life in Soweto ask themselves why, few ready answers present themselves. In the past such questions could always be answered by reference to the oppression suffered by all under apartheid. Since no black person could prosper without the direct support or acquiescence of the hated authorities, it was not unreasonable for those who were not prospering to brand the few who were as "sellouts." Few in Soweto during the decades of the antiapartheid struggle would have agreed with the black entrepreneur Arthur Shipalana when he asserted in 1983: "If I can make it to the top then I believe I am aiding others by showing that it can be done. It is too easy to blame the system for what are often personal failings. . . . So many barriers for blacks today are self-generated" (*Rand Daily Mail,* March 24, 1983, cited in Sarakinski 1987, 53). Far from standing as a shining example for all that black people could achieve despite "the System," people like Shipalana ran a serious risk of being branded sellouts and treated by the comrades of the liberation movements to the equalizing effects of the dreaded "necklace"—a petrol-filled tire draped over the neck and set alight.

---

4. Even the theoreticians within the South African Communist Party (SACP), who might be expected to have much to say about class formation, have been muted in their discussions of the new black bourgeoisie for fear of compromising the gains of what they like to call the "National Democratic Revolution"—a joint project of the Tri-partite Alliance, of which they are a member along with the ANC and the Congress of Trade Unions. SACP leader and poet Jeremy Cronin has perhaps been the most vocal in raising questions about Black Economic Empowerment and the direction of ANC economic policy in producing a new class of black privilege (see his many articles in the party journal *Umsebenzi* (available online at http://www.sacp.org.za/umsebenzi/). Cronin's qualms about ANC economic policy and social inequality, however, did not find a wide audience until he voiced criticism of the government's program in an interview with an Irish journalist. The ANC leadership quickly forced him to retract.

At the time the new black middle classes began to consolidate in the late 1970s and early 1980s, the National Party government embarked upon a program of reform that, among other things, aimed to ease the plight of black business and encourage them to support the reformist programs of the state. Members of the National African Federated Chambers of Commerce (NAFCOC) greeted this program cautiously, articulating throughout the 1980s a moderate brand of probusiness black consciousness. Meanwhile, the theorists of revolution engaged in earnest debates in theoretical journals about the revolutionary potential, or lack of it, of the black bourgeoisie. Communist Party chief Joe Slovo summed up the orthodox view: "insofar as we can speak of an African bourgeoisie at all, it is pathetically small and has arrived too late on the historical scene to play a classic class role either as a leading element in the national struggle or as the main beneficiary of mass revolutionary sacrifice" (1976, 142).[5] In 1999, by contrast, Gauteng minister of finance and former South African Communist Party central committee member Jabu Moleketi announced that the "agenda of the ANC [was] to create a patriotic bourgeoisie" (Justice Malala 1999). For the most part, black business leaders during the apartheid years were viewed with skepticism or hostility in places like Soweto. And although new suburbs were built in Soweto in the 1980s to house the middle classes in a greater degree of comfort than their compatriots enjoyed in the publicly owned matchbox houses, the principles of equality and solidarity were primary not only in political ideology but in the practice of everyday life.

This, however, was before everyone was supposed to be "progressing" toward the "better life for all" promised by the ANC in their election slogans of 1994. Despite the fact that many in the ANC still clung to communist and socialist doctrines and everyone continued to invoke the mantra of "serving the needs of the poorest of the poor" as the purpose of policy, the regime that came to power in 1994 seemed more invested in serving the interests of the wealthier parts of the black population. Thus, while the majority of black people remained poor in the new era, they were faced with the problem of explaining how some black people were managing to become wealthy and powerful. The task of explaining black inequality in the postapartheid era was not helped by the attitudes of the fortunate few, such as the ANC economic adviser and periodically disgraced oil baron Don Mkhwanazi: "I want every black person to feel that he or she has the opportunity to become rich and only has himself to blame if he fails. The more black millionaires, the better for the country" (Justice Malala 1999). After

5. For an account of the NAFCOC view of the world, see Sarakinski 1987.

1994 the business of politics also changed. What had once been a path to personal privation and family hardship through selfless devotion to liberation opened in the new era into a field of lucrative opportunities both in highly paid government jobs and in private-sector "Black Economic Empowerment" programs. When the general secretary of the ANC, Cyril Ramaphosa, resigned from politics after being passed over by Mandela in the choice of his successor, for example, he went into business and instantly became, with the assistance of white capitalists, a rich man and a symbol of black potential. During the latter half of the 1990s, the sense that those who failed to become rich had failed in life more generally became palpable in Soweto, even when "rich" was construed at a level considerably below Mkhwanazi's "millionaire."

As the 1990s wore on, the legal, political, and ideological infrastructure of racial domination in South Africa was steadily dismantled. The apartheid system came to an end and with it the emotional resonance of that harsh word signifying shared oppression for all black people. No one in Soweto lamented its passing, though I did hear an occasional mordant cynic foretelling doom ahead. In the years following the demise of apartheid, however, as life for most remained difficult and for many became steadily harder, the meaning in misfortune had to be reckoned in the absence of the comparative solace of knowing everyone was enduring their part of the collective suffering imposed upon black people by white racism. Nor could comfort be found in the hope of a collective redemption from the burdens of apartheid, a redemption for which some had paid the ultimate price. The greatly desired "progress" that was once generally assumed to be the inevitable accompaniment of liberation proved elusive. The certainty of an eventual end to suffering began to prove elusive as well. None of the people I know in Soweto who failed to become rich—which is virtually everyone—would take Mkhwanazi's words to heart and agree that he "only has himself to blame." They had to find other ways to make sense of their misfortune.

The ending of apartheid brought not just the experience of freedom for masses of people who had known themselves as oppressed but also a slow transition from a widespread consciousness of collective power to a pervasive recognition of individual and collective powerlessness. In the postapartheid period, the organizing rhetoric of politics changed from the old emphasis on collective struggle and resistance as a means of ensuring collective redemption to language emphasizing "progress," "development," and a "better life for all." Meanwhile, "the masses" who had previously been at the "forefront of struggle" lapsed into widespread apathy, awaiting what came to be known as "service delivery." The first generation of postapartheid political leaders, veterans of those years of passion and action, clung to the old verities of popular struggle and mass action even while forging policies designed to demonstrate fiscal discipline for the benefit of global financial markets. Yet they clearly found the subsequent apathy and dejection frustrating. Thabo Mbeki warned of the dangers of apathy in his speech opening the African Renaissance conference of 1998 when he said, "it is critically important that we not allow the revolutionary energies built up in the struggle against apartheid to dissipate, with the masses of the people disempowered and demobilized to a situation where they become passive recipients of the good things of life from their rulers — objects rather than subjects of change" (1999, xix). His words fell on deaf ears.

When those not enjoying the good life in postapartheid Soweto ask themselves why, nothing serves to answer their question in the same way that "apartheid" once did. When people find themselves forced to ask, "Why are relatives, friends, colleagues, or neighbors prospering while we are not?" no ready answer is available that can go unchallenged. Neither the experience of antiapartheid struggle, already a dimming historical memory, nor the evidence of postapartheid policy offers any satisfactory answer to the question of why some people should be thriving while others are not. It may be the case that some, as Mkhwanazi advised, can look upon their lives of daily struggle and disappointment and agree that they can hold no one else to blame but themselves. It is even possible that, looking back at a history where all black people suffered together under a manifestly evil regime, they might conclude that simple bad luck explains why they are not, to twist the words of Joe Slovo, among "the main beneficiar[ies] of mass revolutionary sacrifice." Perhaps, like a sanguine development economist, they accept that the rewards of freedom are inevitably distributed with less-than-perfect equality and thus blame no one for their inability to find a sure footing amid the seismic shifts of the social structure that marked the end of apartheid. They might simply reflect that the world is made up of winners and losers and that someone has to be on the losing team.

If anyone reasons like this, however, I have yet to meet him or her in Soweto. I have yet to encounter anyone who accepts that his own poverty is inherently meaningless, that it represents nothing more significant than his own personal misery. Fortunately, or unfortunately, to questions like the above about the inequitable distribution of good and bad fortunes, other answers are readily available. Suppositions informed by the witchcraft paradigm offer one of the most emotionally satisfying: "We are being held back and are suffering because of other people's malice."

A Tale of "Progress," Jealousy, and Witchcraft

Consider this story of hard work, success, upward mobility, and witch-craft that was written at my request in April 2001 by Moleboheng, a young woman from a family in a shack settlement on the outskirts of Soweto whom I have known since 1991. I asked Moleboheng to write an account to use in this book after I visited her family in their new home and was told by her parents of the neighbors' jealousy and the problems it was causing.

One never realizes the power of jealousy until you experience it in the first degree. I come from a poor family background. All my life I've always worked hard with the hope that some day my family will have a comfortable life. I've always had hope for a brighter future. Luckily I did well at school, most probably from the extra effort I always contributed.

For many years my family was staying in a shack in somebody else's back yard in Soweto. It wasn't comfortable for us as children as we were not allowed to play in the yard and were limited in our water usage. Luckily, in 1991 a new squatter camp was opened near Soweto and my mum got her name down for a stand. We then moved to what we proudly considered our own home. We were happy for the freedom of being in our home, even though it was still the same shack we had lived in before and we had to ad-just to life without electricity. But it wasn't too bad. My sister and I were at-tending school and doing temporary work at OK Bazaars on weekends and holidays. My mother was working in factories, although at a low income.

In 1992 I passed my Matric but life was shuttered for me as we had no money for further studies. I tried to apply for bursaries [scholarships], but had no luck. I was stuck at home for a whole year. Then I was saved by my dad's friend. He organized a bursary for my college fees. The night I received that good news I couldn't sleep from happiness. I had to decide on a course that would help me get a job, so I went to Tech to study business, majoring in Production Planning. I worked so hard at Tech that after my first year I was rewarded with another sponsor, Premier Milling Company. Till today I'm happy with the choice I made.

So I graduated. For a year after I graduated I could not find a job. [Pre-mier Milling went out of business, so the job she had been promised disap-peared.] My mother wanted to take me to an *inyanga* as she was thinking that someone might have bewitched us to keep me from getting a job. But I didn't accept that and eventually found a job on my own. I moved to stay with my aunt as I needed access to a phone which we didn't have at home and I also wanted to be independent and far from family pressures.

After getting my job I slowly became unpopular among friends and neighbors at home. Some thought I had become too proud after getting a job. They all had different views. Some started calling my sister and me "Choice Assorted" after the biscuits. They said that to insult my mum because they had discovered that we were not our father's biological children. I told myself I will not take them seriously.

Still, our house was always full of people. My mum was receiving some few Rands from me her working daughter, so she could buy liquor for her friends. Sometimes she was selling beers from home too. My parents were popular, with regular friends who would come by every day. If they had money they would pop it out and send the children to buy beers. They would sit in the house laughing, drinking and having fun.

Finally, after working for some three years, I was in a position financially to help my parents build a real house. They were still living in the same shack we had moved from the other side of Soweto. I decided to surprise my mum by just buying a load of bricks and having them delivered. She already had the plans for some years but had never been able to raise the money to build.

So for some months we were building the house. During that time things became sour with the neighbors. My mum was insulted as being a witch. They said that she had used her powers of witchcraft to get that money as they didn't believe that I could have paid for the house, a "little thing" like me. One of them even said that my mum had used witchcraft to take the money that was supposed to go to her. Our house that had always had people in it became deserted. No one came to visit. Jealousy grew worse day by day. Then another neighbor from down the street accused my mum of killing her sister's family. That whole family, seven people, died in a car crash last year on their way to the Transkei. She confronted my mum right in the street. She said that my mum was the witch who made that accident to happen. After that my mother started attending church again.

Well, as for me I'm proud of what I have done for my family. That house is finished and it is beautiful. It never worries me to be blamed or hated for having achieved something in life. Luckily those people never tried anything serious against my family and now my parents are making new friends amongst others who have built houses of their own.

Although the author of this story is a remarkable young woman, her tale is not unusual. When I retell it to other friends in Soweto, they simply remark that such jealousy is "typical." The general understanding is that whenever anyone tries to "progress," others will be jealous. And when people are jealous, they can do anything.

Although Moleboheng is one of the few people I know in Soweto who is thoroughly skeptical about the powers of witchcraft, her mother, MaNdlovu, was terrified by the turn of events. The danger of witchcraft was heightened by the fact that once rumors that MaNdlovu was a witch were abroad, neighbors might now consider themselves justified in "using *muthi*" to avenge what they decided in retrospect, mulling over their misfortunes, to be this witch's previous assaults. Moreover, if anything untoward happened in the neighborhood after she had been singled out as a dangerous source of evil, she knew she could be blamed. She started attending church again. Church offered some respite from the neighbors' antagonism. It also offered a chance of gaining access to a higher power capable of resisting any witchcraft that the neighbors might launch against her or her family.

Moleboheng's mother was particularly concerned about the neighbor who, in Moleboheng's words, accused her of using "witchcraft to take the money that was supposed to go to her." I should elaborate a little on this conflict, as it centers on me. I am the father's friend of whom Moleboheng speaks when she says someone organized a bursary for her. At the time, her father and I were playing music together in shebeens around Soweto. A well-known Zulu musician, he was teaching me how to play the style of Zulu music known as *mbaqanga;* we were two noisy violins together. One of the places we used to play was the house of a Sotho record producer (whom I only ever knew by his nickname "Skwama," meaning "bag"),[6] whose wife it was who subsequently accused MaNdlovu of stealing the white man from her. She claimed that MaNdlovu had used witchcraft to lure this white man to her house, where MaNdlovu had several young attractive daughters, and subsequently to make him build a house for her. The major flaw with her theory, as far as I can tell, was that the white man did not build the house. The "little thing" of a daughter did.

MaNdlovu's immediate response to the talk of witchcraft was to head for church. The Catholic Church, however, affords little protection in such matters. Some months after the house was completed, Moleboheng's father was injured in a road accident. The minivan taxi in which he was riding home ploughed into a car. Several people died. He broke both legs and spent four and a half months languishing in Baragwanath Hospital receiving cursory medical attention and no physical therapy. When he was dis-

6. According to the local gossip, "he must have got that nickname from always carrying bags moving from one woman's house to the other, as he has always been a womanizer with no house of his own but looking for ones with their own homes."

charged, he could no longer walk and suffered a persistent infection in the wound where his femur had been repaired. He consulted an *inyanga*. According to the *inyanga*, someone in the neighborhood was bewitching the family. Their house was surrounded by invisible snakes, some of which were coming into the house at night and entering his wound. The whole family would have to be treated to protect them from this assault. Moleboheng, however, refused to be part of this, arguing that since she did not believe in *inyangas*, her participation would undermine the power of the treatment, and besides, they should not be wasting the money she gave them for groceries on treatments that would not work. A year later, her father was still languishing in bed with a suppurating wound, which he had taken to syringing with a patent herbal cough medicine in an attempt, painful and futile, to clean out the "poison." His femur was infected, but even if he had had access to the expensive surgery and drugs that were required to treat the infection, he would have insisted on treating the witchcraft, too.

Meanwhile, the relative of the family that was killed in a car accident persisted in her accusations that MaNdlovu was a witch. She took to standing in the street and loudly proclaiming to her friends that the witch had a *tokoloshe* (familiar) who was helping with her evil work. To make matters worse, the woman leveling the witchcraft accusations was thought by neighbors to be suffering from AIDS. MaNdlovu took the dispute to the Street Committee, but they could not stop the accusations. Eventually she went to the police and "opened a docket" against her accuser. Under the Suppression of Witchcraft Act it is illegal to level accusations of witchcraft. The police visited the woman and informed her of the charges and the date set for the court hearing. Rather than inhibiting the accusations, however, the charges made her even more persistent in her abuse of MaNdlovu. One afternoon, a few days before Christmas, MaNdlovu was watering her garden when the accuser confronted her again and began harassing her. MaNdlovu was a strong healthy woman in her midfifties with none of the chronic health conditions such as hypertension that afflict so many of her generation. When confronted in her garden that afternoon and denounced yet again as a witch, she collapsed to the ground. Before any of her family had time to find transport to take her to the clinic, she died. No postmortem was performed, but from eyewitness accounts it seems to me likely she died from a seizure brought on, most probably, by the rage and fear and stress of the accusations.

Community Life at the End of the Struggle

Over the course of the 1990s one of the most significant changes I witnessed in Soweto was the steady dissipation of the community fellow feeling that had been a hallmark of the struggle years when people united in resistance to the apartheid authorities. The coming to power of a regime celebrating "the community" as the rhetorical touchstone of democratic governance ironically coincided in the Soweto neighborhoods I knew best with the erosion of the social connections of friendship and neighborly regard that make the term more than an empty catchword. As MaMfete puts it, ruefully, "people here are very much independent, now of late." This erosion of community spirit was accompanied by a collapse of the local political "structures" that marked the era of struggle. As if reacting to the vacuum of social energy created by the end of politics, an upsurge of religious activity occurred, primarily within evangelical Pentecostalist churches preaching a gospel of prosperity. Tent crusades sprang up all over Soweto, with preachers promising health and wealth through the power of the Holy Spirit for the price of a monthly tithe.

The neighborhood where I have lived the longest while in Soweto, Mapetla Extension, is fairly typical of the townships that make up what is sometimes called Greater Soweto. Built by the Non-European Affairs Department of the Johannesburg City Council in 1964, Mapetla Extension is home to predominantly Tswana- and Sotho-speaking families. In the street where I lived, there are thirty houses. All but seven, by the end of the 1990s, were still occupied by the families of the original tenants. The other seven had all been occupied for at least twenty years by the same families. Restrictions on the movement of black people, enforced under laws that were at the heart of the apartheid system, meant that in places like Mapetla Extension local communities grew up together and knew each other over generations. The children playing in my street in 1999 were the grandchildren and great-grandchildren of the original tenants. Though Soweto was large enough to seem like a city in itself, with major thoroughfares and transportation hubs thronged with strangers, its residential streets were also like a network of villages—with all the dense sociability, mutual aid, and undying enmities of village life. On top of this "organic" solidarity, the years of struggle against a repressive state followed by the war with the Inkatha Freedom Party enhanced the sense of unity and steadfastness.

In the latter half of the nineties social life in Mapetla Extension underwent subtle changes, as if the barometer registering community solidarity and fellow feeling was steadily falling. An index of this could be seen in the fashion for building high perimeter walls around houses that spread through the townships after 1994. Although high walls had long been a feature of white suburbs, in Soweto such gestures were extremely rare before the middle of the nineties. People generally considered their security better served by having their property open to the view of neighbors, whose intervention they would expect were anyone seen disturbing their property. During the era when authorities maintained a tight control over the state-owned properties, permission would not be granted to tenants to build such walls even if they wanted to. They would not have wanted to. A fence, usually topped with barbed wire, and a lockable gate were adequate and legitimate security measures. These were only really necessary for households in possession of a car.

In the past, obscuring a house with high walls, even with hedges and trees, would have been considered an antisocial affront to the rest of the community. A house hidden like this would, moreover, likely have aroused suspicion as a place where witches might be presumed to work without hindrance. The ideal of privacy was virtually unknown. Households were usually so crowded that private space was a luxury few could enjoy. By the late 1990s, however, high brick walls with heavy steel gates had become commonplace in Soweto. Expensive to build, they helped to mark status with another adoption of suburban style. But they also signified that household security was a matter no longer just of protecting oneself from strangers but also of exclusion of neighbors. When I asked MaMfete in 1997, after I had been away from Soweto for nearly a year, why she had gone to the trouble and expense of building such walls, she answered with one word: "Privacy."

In the political struggles of the late 1970s and 1980s, the heavy-handed response of the state's security forces solidified the sense of community among people living in Soweto. Although many of the older generation of residents were disturbed by the unruliness of the youth in their political struggles during those years—especially when comrades turned against suspected informers, imposed "stayaways" and boycotts on hard-pressed workers and consumers, or spurred conflicts with the migrant workers from rural areas living in hostels—virtually no one in Soweto doubted the justice of their cause or the necessity of standing together against the hated and brutal "System." Even the "necklacing" of informers (*izimpimpi*) with petrol-filled tires, though appalling to most people, was understood as an unfortunate but necessary community defense against the secret agents of the evil system of apartheid.

The whole of Soweto was united in opposition to apartheid. Local communities organized themselves in defense. Activists imagined "people power" as both the key to liberation from apartheid and the foundation of democratic community self-government. Grassroots activists organized streets and neighborhoods and townships into larger networks of Street Committees and Civic Associations, bolstered by the industrial muscle of the trade union movement, that ultimately linked most of the country into what became known in the late 1980s as the Mass Democratic Movement (MDM) (Mayekiso 1996). When negotiations began for a new constitution in 1990, most activists were convinced that it was a direct result of the struggles of the MDM acting as a proxy for the outlawed ANC.

As I roamed around Soweto in the early 1990s, I was struck by a strange paradox in people's attitudes to state power. On the one hand, every encounter with public authorities, from the pass office (until 1986) and the pensions office to the police—never mind the hospitals, clinics, and schools—was marked by bureaucratic incompetence and corruption. Confusion was endemic. My "grandmother" Buba for example, had her pension applications denied for years and suffered through countless trips to the "Office" because her "I.D. Book" listed a date of birth four years after the birth of her first daughter. My "brother" Thabo drove an unregistered car without a driver's license for years until he bought one from corrupt officers of a former Homeland. When stopped by the police it was never difficult to "make a plan" (as the local parlance denominates bribery), rarely costing more than the price of a couple of bottles of beer, which could be bought virtually everywhere from shebeens, private houses where residents illegally sell liquor. Ordinary people had extensive and intimate experience of public authorities' inability to enforce law or perform necessary services and had few illusions about their capacities.

At the same time, however, everyday conversation conveyed a powerful sense of the government as the evil organizing intelligence behind the "System" that was oppressing everyone. When war broke out between township residents and hostel dwellers near where I was staying in 1990, no one doubted that the whole conflagration had been "masterminded" by "the government." The ANC leadership was also convinced that the violence was being choreographed by a mysterious "Third Force," the "hidden hand" of the state. This sense of the supreme efficacy of state power both enabled a sort of messianic faith to emerge concerning the potential of a postapartheid government to rectify social ills and, at the same time, fostered a conviction that there remains a widespread subterranean conspiracy of evil powers seeking to derail democracy (see chapter 11).

After 1994, when the ANC took power at national, provincial, and local levels, the political organizations of community life that had been forged in the antiapartheid struggle—the network of Street Committees and Civic Associations—fell into desuetude. Some local activists retained the mantle of "the Civic," and Street Committees periodically convened in some areas, particularly shack settlements where local notables could gain control of land allocation or where insecurity of tenure created a need for collective vigilance, but in general political organization in local communities collapsed. Few activists in Sowetan communities had the energy to commit to such forums. Some national Civic leaders tried to promote an independent role for the Civics in the name of a vibrant democratic civil society, but the movement collapsed into a mess of bitter factionalism and accusations of corruption and mismanagement (Soggot 1997). Meanwhile, the ANC branches in Soweto, as elsewhere throughout the country, were afflicted by the ordinary apathy of normal political life. Their sense of purpose was not enhanced by the fact that the constitutional arrangements of the new regime centered power in the executive branch at all levels of government and left little direct local role for elected officials.

In the early 1990s, shortly after Mandela and the other leaders were released from prison, the political movements unbanned, and the exiles allowed to return, a war started between residents of Soweto and the supporters of the Inkatha Freedom Party, mostly Zulu-speaking migrant workers living in hostels in their midst (Ashforth 1991a). At first, the community solidarity that had developed in struggle against the state carried over into this battle, with young men mobilizing to "defend the community" as they had in the old days. But the nature of the conflict between the ANC and Inkatha in the early 1990s was different from anything that had gone before. The enemy was not so clearly defined as when the battle raged between young black men and the security forces of the white regime. Soon, the fact that the Inkatha Freedom Party, generally perceived by Sowetans as the cause of the violence and the enemy of their peace, was composed of black men who for the most part looked similar to Sowetan men sowed a harvest of fear and suspicion throughout the whole community. (There were subtle distinguishing marks of the "typical" Zulu, but even he might be an ANC supporter and not necessarily a Zulu nationalist of the Inkatha Freedom Party.) The political euphoria that had previously served to cement community ties now had to be suppressed for fear of falling prey to attack by enemies within. Whether the war with Inkatha was the death knell for community fellow feeling in Soweto, I cannot say. I am certain, however, that community life after 1994 (when that conflict finally ceased) was never the same.

In the late 1990s, with apathy replacing action as the normal state of politics, and distrust of neighbors permeating community life, the church business boomed—at least that part of it that could promise material, as well
as spiritual, rewards for the faithful. Protestant evangelical Pentecostalist
congregations sprang up around the townships, mostly housed in large
tents with booming sound systems. Most of these churches derived inspiration and organizational backing from American ministries such as those
of Jimmy Swaggart and Bennie Hinn, though the largest and most rapidly
growing of these churches, the Universal Church, originated in Brazil. Despite differences of liturgy, ritual, and theology, the principal message of
these churches is the same: illness, poverty, and unhappiness are products
of demonic action that can only be undone through being "born again" in
Jesus. The power of the Holy Spirit can be directed to heal and bring prosperity to those who are "saved." Those who are not saved, those who, denying the power of Jesus in their lives, remain contaminated with the demons
of Satan, are a dangerous threat to those who have been born again and
should be avoided if they cannot be saved.[7] Health and wealth are the rightful property of all and have been stolen from humans by Satan. All that is
needed to regain them is prayer and the repentance of sin, along with tithes
paid to the church leaders—which will be rewarded many times over by
the Lord, with real money. The message was summed up for me once by a
preacher who insisted: "If God had the power to create the world in seven
days, you think he can't help a person buy a car?"

Death and Dying in an Era of AIDS

While the people of Soweto were waiting for freedom in the early 1990s, an
invisible threat was gaining strength in the form of the HIV/AIDS epidemic. Few public institutions in the early 1990s were capable of addressing black South Africans in a way that was readily granted the authority of
truth such that statements about this strange disease could be accepted as
facts. Agencies of the government were certainly not among them. By 1988
the National Party government had begun to realize the potential for the
epidemic to spread in the general population and initiated rudimentary
awareness and prevention programs (Grundlingh 2001). They began dispensing free condoms at public clinics. Young men in Soweto laughed at
these displays and derided the program as a ruse by the "regime" to re-

---

7. For an account of the theology of these churches, see Gifford 1998. For an account of
Pentecostalist debates regarding demonic possession, see Möller 1987.

duce the black birthrate, yet another instance of their intention to eliminate Blacks. Churches were, and are, widely respected as institutions devoted to the pursuit of truth. But the people at risk of contracting and transmitting HIV were already running afoul of the same doctrines that precluded most clerics from advocating *safer* sex, so the churches were mostly silent. Even the private authority of well-meaning people trying to educate their friends was limited—judging by the number of unplanned pregnancies that occurred among my own circle at that time. My friends knew better than to contradict my preaching about the dangers of HIV but were less than completely persuaded of the need to always use condoms. Then the dying began.

By the end of the 1990s, virtually everyone in Soweto had buried someone who they suspected had died of AIDS. No one doubted the existence of a disease afflicting young people—the very people who ought not to be dying now that they were no longer at war with the apartheid regime. Acknowledging the presence of AIDS in any particular case, however, remained extremely problematic. Neighbors, distant relatives, and casual acquaintances might be quick to speculate that a sick person's condition was AIDS, but denial remained the norm among people close to the sufferer. To be told that a person had been diagnosed HIV positive was to be given possession of a terrible secret. Intense stigma surrounded the very name AIDS. Few Sowetans in the 1990s were aware of their HIV status. The Abt Associates book *The Impending Catastrophe: A Resource Book on the Emerging HIV/AIDS Epidemic in South Africa,* published in 2000, cited a study that found that "fewer than one in ten people who were caring for an HIV-infected patient at home acknowledged that their relative was suffering from AIDS. Patients were only slightly more likely to acknowledge their status" (Abt Associates 2000, 23). Mourners at funerals of people who died too young, where no injury or violence could be named as the cause, were typically addressed with euphemisms such as "she passed away after a long [or short] illness," without the particular illness being named.

Perhaps the most egregious example of the stigma and hypocrisy surrounding death by HIV/AIDS was the official prevarication over the death, in his late thirties, of ANC presidential spokesperson Parks Mankahlana in November 2000. The official pronouncement that the young man had died "after a long illness" provoked a wave of public speculation about AIDS as the cause of death, prompting bitter denials from his family and former colleagues, including President Mbeki (Harvey 2000). Despite their denials of AIDS, however, neither the Mankahlana family nor the young man's former political colleagues offered any other diagnosis of the cause of death. Mankahlana's case is sadly ironic, as he was in the forefront of defending President Mbeki when the latter made headlines by denying the connection between HIV and AIDS. Two years later, a discussion paper circulated throughout ANC "structures," reputedly authored by the "AIDS dissident" Peter Mokaba, Mankahlana's close friend and old comrade from the South African Youth Congress, claiming that Mankahlana was "vanquished by the anti-retroviral drugs he was wrongly persuaded to consume" (Kindra 2002). A few months later, Mokaba also died "after a long illness," and the ANC leadership remained silent except to denounce rumors of AIDS. When the Inkatha leader Themba Khosa died in June 2000, however, no chorus of disapproval arose over media reports of rumors that his death was AIDS related (Cullinan 2001).

When the history of this plague comes to be written, the first democratic governments of South Africa will almost certainly be found to have failed in their duties.[8] By the late 1990s, the conjoining of the ANC's AIDS policies, or lack of them, with apartheid as equivalent crimes against humanity had already become a commonplace of political rhetoric. Mbeki's willingness to entertain doubts about the connection between HIV and AIDS will similarly tarnish assessments of his presidency for decades to come—perhaps rightly so. Despite the failures and shortcomings of political leadership, however, and because of the efforts of a great many people working in public and private institutions, by the turn of the millennium the vast majority of people in the country were aware of the dangers of HIV/AIDS. This in itself was an extraordinary achievement. The effort to persuade people in this part of the world about the dangers of a retrovirus named HIV also constitutes one of the greatest cultural impositions in the history of these parts.

Awareness of AIDS, of the incurable disease brought on by an invisible virus, rarely suffices to make sense of the suffering and death it occasions. When people suffering the devastation of HIV/AIDS face the questions "Why me? Why now?" they are rarely permitted—neither by themselves nor by those who love them—to entertain an answer based on the sheer mischance of "catching" a virus. Consider the sad tale of Themba, written for me by his relative, my friend Jombolo, after we visited him in Soweto in the year 2000. Distinctive in its details, it is not untypical of reactions to the disease at the time:

8. For an account of these political failures regarding AIDS in the 1990s, see H. Schneider 2002.

Themba was at some stage a successful businessman. He owned two hair salons in downtown Johannesburg and was a shareholder in a small company manufacturing hair products. He drove an expensive red BMW and had a townhouse in Mondeor, a white suburb. He was very supportive of his family and was seen as the pillar of the family's strength.

Themba started to slowly deteriorate. He was constantly ill with different illnesses—flu that would take longer to heal, exhaustion, headaches and tension. What was clear from the onset was that the family was worried about his illness. He also started to lose his possessions. Firstly he lost the car and never told his family what actually happened to it. Secondly he started staying at his parents' home, raising the suspicion that he also lost his townhouse, not to mention the furniture. Finally, he was desperately cash strapped.

As his illness continued, the family decided that the doctors could not help. As Christians, his family decided they must consult a prophet. The prophet prayed for Themba and gave him some water to drink. Still, his health did not improve. Then they decided to consult an *inyanga*. He could not help. They went to another *inyanga*. Then another. Three *inyangas* and one medical specialist later, Themba's health started showing signs of improvement. What was disclosed by all the *inyangas* was that a neighbour —they didn't say who—was responsible for his illness and was wanting to kill him using *muthi*. What the medical specialist started advising was that Themba should tell the whole family about his life and accept he had AIDS.

Finally, he confessed that he was HIV positive. His family just did not accept any of this. They believed Themba was deranged. Someone must have bewitched him to tell these lies. When they went to doctors they demanded miracles or else they would move to another doctor. They would change doctors after every three to four consultations. Then they reverted back to the *inyanga* again to use his divine powers to get rid of this witchcraft. As the months passed by Themba's health never improved. When he finally succumbed to the virus almost 40 000 Rands had been wasted seeking a cure.

The money spent was a fortune by Sowetan standards, sufficient to buy a small four-room matchbox house like the one Themba's mother lived in and watched her son die in. Had they more money to spend, they would have wasted that, too. When Themba died, they were not sure they had done enough for him—or for themselves, for when Themba became sick and died, they lost their only source of income other than his mother's meager pension.

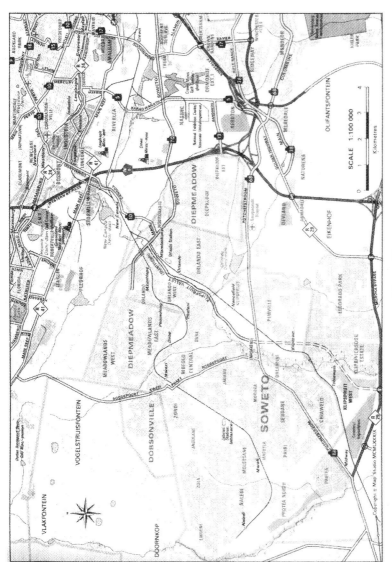

1. Map of Soweto.

MWING-NJHA KENYA

Asim K, Kalongha
705 Rock Ville
Vundla Drive
P.O. Kwaxhuma
Soweto
Johannesburg
Tel: 9847524

Ukugula koku khohlola abakubiza T.B. Siya kwelapha. Nokugula koku pufumula masithi iphika ugaphefumuli kahle, ASMA siyakwelapha.

Wezase mazweni mhlobo wami, woza wena siqu sakho, u ngezwa ngoko tshelwa a bantu. woza e nge ka hambilo mnumzane wase mazweni o so bonana naye lani babile nje.

SINE MITHI E LANDELAYO

Umuthi woku thandwa ngabelungu.
Umuthi woko khipha isinyama ngoku ngena e bavine nge   xuphela.
Umbhulelo ngi ya we lapha.
Iqonto ngiya yiqeda.
Umuthi oko thwala ube rich. Iza wena.
Abangathole abantwana siba siza babe nabo. Iza wena.
Umuthi wa mabande obunduna sinawo.
Umuthi woko thandwa yizintombi u khona .
Umuthi woko lapha induku uma I wile.   omncane . . . .

0.   Umuthi wa bafazi wokuthi uma e hlangana ne ndoda azwakale . .
1.   Umuthi wa mabande okuvimkela izingonzi   amuncane
2.   Umuthi omkhu wokuphalaza wase mazwene
3.   A ba gula lu kufa koku phambana (Hlanya)
4.   Abana mafufunyana siya wa khipha a buyele kumnikazi.
5.   Kwaba gula ngo kufa ko kuwa (Fitts)
6.   Umuthi woka bamba aba thakathi u babone . . .
7.   Umuthi waka bamba amahashi D . . .   . Umukhulu

Moriyana wabatu babebedi molilapeng batumane tabo mauna limusadi uteng walihlohonolo gwana

Ukuqinisa imoto kubantu abanomona abangafuni kuhlalanabanye kahle abatsatsela abanye ebusuku belele, kufuneka azisole elisela abone ukuti kubinjani ukweba qinisa ndoda.

Okuphepha kuisikali esitana nesinje madoda izigebengu sezizinengi, kuwena ozwisisayo lesisigodo sabakona nasemandulweni

Nomuzi wako siyawubethelela, ofisa ukwenza okubi kuphindele kumnikazi, lemiti yase mwingunjha kenya, izulu lingangeni abatakati bahiuleke ikaya lako likokelwe u nkulunkulu kuphela, amandlozi ako aze ajabule umdeni wo muziwakho, inhlanhla yakho ize ziswabe isitha

Uma uzimisele ini ouiendza yo uyayizuza umuti ukona si norla idiozi

ASIM KALOGHA
Umnumzane olanda imithi yasemazweni ngapandle iza ukhulume okufunayo naye

2. Front of Dr. Kalongha's flier, 1994.

MWING-NJHA KENYA

Asim K, Kalongha
705 Rock Ville
Vundla Drive
P.O. Kwaxhuma
Soweto
Johannesburg
Tel: 984 7869
984-7524

NA KQALE O BATLA THUSO

Moriana o hlahang mafatsheng a ka ntle, tlo ho oponela ka mahlo a
Basotho bare: Pela ene e hloke mohatla ka ho romeletsa. Tloho ngweneso
o tlilo kopana le monghadi enwa ya tia o senolela diphiritsohle mooo le leng ba bedi feela.
Bulwetsi bakgukgohlola T.B. Rea Ualafa Kgufele. Lebulwetsi Bakuhema Bubitsa ASMA Boyalodiswa

RENALE MERIANA E LATELANG:

1. Moriana wa ho ratwa ke makgowa.
2. Moriana wa ho ntsha senyama ka ho kena bateng le ho futha ka
3. Tokoloshi re ya tebela.
4. Ho phephethwa re ya ho ntsha.
5. Boloi re ya bo fedisa.
6. Moriana wa ho ratwa ke banana
7. Moriana wa ho ratwa ke bahlankana re nale ona. le wa ho kgutlisa mohlankana wa hao ha tsamaile.
8. Moriana wa mabanta a bontona re nale ona.
9. Moriana wa ho tsosa thupa ha e wele (banneng)   Omunyane
10. Moriana wa ho lokisa basadi hore ba utlwahale ha ba kopane le banna
11. Renale moriana o moholo o siko mona wa mafatsheng wa ho Hlatsa
12. Re alafa lefu le bowe (bohlanya).
13. Ba naleng mafofonyana re a kgutlisetsa ho mong a wona.
14. Ba naleng lefu la howa reya ba alafa (Fitts)
    Se lebale ho hlahisa pampiri ena ha o lahlehile o botse ka yon. monghadi enwa.
15. Re nale moriana wa ho tshwara dipere. D.R. omukulu
16. Re nale meriana ya dipapad tse dileng teng kaofela.
17. Re nale moriana wa ho botsha motho / ho tshwara motho o ho loyang, o bone hore ontse a etsang ha
    le robetse. Ke   :ela.
    Sitopo, reyasesebetsa. Lemabetla red sebetsa.

Utliyisa Koloi Miliko Yabatu Isikakena Limashodi Ahlulehe. Muriyana o
uteng.

Mutsi wahao riyaoriyisa obathlang kwetsasibi
simufetuheele miriiyana yena hule kenya
MWINGUNJHA Mutsi wahao uduie unali tabo basiniyi
bamoyambi bahlulehe, umtsware umfumane ayemi
alimaswabi

Dira Dingata Reshible
Butata mositsa beng,
miriyana yakutibela nto
etswana li yena, etswang
mafatsing walu lukiswa.

Ndate Olatang miriana mafatsing
MWINGUNJA KENYA

3. Back of Dr. Kalongha's flier, 1994.

4. Madumo (*left*) and Mr. Zondi.

5. Madumo's family home, 1991.

6. Madumo's family home, 1997. Madumo at right.

7. Typical four-room matchbox house in Soweto.

8. *Ukuthwasa* at Klip River.

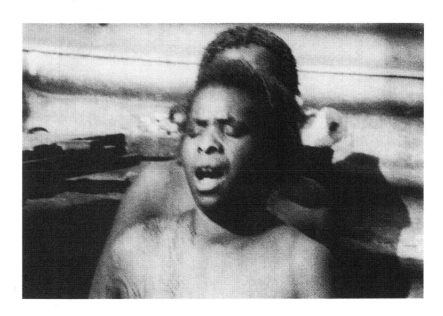

9. *Ukuthwasa* initiates.

To kill someone "using *muthi*" is to kill him with witchcraft. We shall see in detail later what this might mean, what people like Themba and his family have to worry about when they worry about witchcraft. To suspect that someone's suffering is a product of witchcraft is to wonder *who* is responsible. The *inyangas* that Themba's family consulted told them, in the way that *inyangas* usually do, that a "neighbor" was responsible. Themba's death was thus also a case of murder. I cannot say for certain what his mother made of the *inyangas'* diagnoses, though I suspect she believed they were true—true enough to spend a fortune on the strength of them. Some members of Themba's family, such as my friend Jombolo—who was called upon to provide financial support after Themba's savings were exhausted— thought the imputation of witchcraft was ridiculous. He does not entirely discount the reality of supernatural powers, but he knew Themba well enough to know that he was a prime candidate for infection with this sexually transmitted virus for which there is no cure. The fear of witchcraft, however, dominated this family at the time of Themba's death. No one could ignore the hypothesis that *someone* was killing him. Themba's admission that he was suffering from HIV/AIDS was taken by some in the family to be itself the result of witchcraft. And even if it was AIDS, *someone* must have sent it.

In this part of the world, AIDS awareness, which, unfortunately, was not coterminous with the spread of the disease, has brought with it the largest and most sustained intervention by state power and medical science into popular understandings and practices relating to health, illness, and healing in history. The AIDS-awareness message is comparatively simple and by most accounts has been heard by virtually everyone in the region capable of hearing. It runs something like this: There is a disease that kills and it is known as AIDS (or HIV/AIDS). It is transmitted by a virus that attacks the body's immune system, the natural protection against disease, and lowers its defenses. The virus is spread primarily through sex. The way to protect against infection is to either abstain from sex, be faithful to one partner (in the hope that partner is faithful to you), or use condoms for every sexual encounter. This message has been broadcast far and wide through all media and in all manner of campaigns. At the time of writing it had not succeeded in stemming the tide of new infections. If the idea of a retrovirus is complicated for virologists, how much more difficult must it be for people not accustomed to thinking of themselves as living with microorganisms such as those described by biomedical science?

Few African families afflicted by HIV/AIDS are able to ignore the sorts of issues Themba's family had to grapple with in their quest for a cure. Life is lived amid a plethora of invisible agencies: viruses, spirits, God, and the ancestors, to name but a few. Making sense of a bad situation requires drawing from resources of interpretation provided by conflicting authorities in the traditions of biomedicine, Christianity, and indigenous healing, among others. Making sense of misfortune is not an end in itself. Managing the dangers posed by these agencies requires correctly assessing their nature and capacity. These are matters of life and death.

5

ON BELIEVING, AND NOT BELIEVING,
IN WITCHCRAFT

The Two Big Questions: Rationality and Modernity

Two questions inevitably arise whenever people who live in worlds devoid of witches hear African accounts of witchcraft. The first we can call the rationality question: Are people who believe in witches and witchcraft rational? (Or, though it is not quite the same question: Can it be rational to believe in witchcraft?) The second is the modernity question: Why do people *still* believe in witches?

For more than a century, because of the long shadow cast over Western social thought by the concepts of enlightenment, reason, and modernity, writers treating of witchcraft, sorcery, magic, and religion in Africa have been preoccupied with one or another version of these questions of rationality and modernity. These questions still shape considerations of witchcraft, both in scholarly literature and in popular discourse. I cannot hope to resolve all aspects of these questions here and I shall not try. Nor have I space and time sufficient to describe the enormous volume of literature relevant to the subject.[1] I shall, however, outline some of the ways these questions of rationality and modernity inflect thinking on the subject of witchcraft and how these preoccupations are unhelpful for understanding the character of spiritual insecurity in contemporary South Africa. Then I shall describe how many people in Soweto struggle *against* believing in witchcraft while knowing full well that they live in a world with witches.

Though millions of ordinary South Africans refer daily to "witches" and "witchcraft" in every kind of linguistic configuration, few South Africans,

---

1. For a good general survey of ideas pertaining to magic, science, religion, and rationality, see Tambiah 1990.

black or white, are comfortable discussing these issues in public. Many African intellectuals object to the terms, arguing that they are both derogatory and misleading. This is undoubtedly so. In English usage it is almost impossible to escape the connotations in the word "witchcraft" that cast a disdainful backward-looking glance to a premodern history which Europeans and people of European descent or influence, having long since forgotten the terrors of those times, like to think of themselves as having progressed beyond. In the folk wisdom of the moderns, the progress of which we are so proud is typically figured as a progress of reason and enlightenment over superstition, enabling scientific mastery over the natural world and rational management of the social.[2] The rational subject of modern times, the individual bearing rights, exercising preferences, and making decisions—including the democratic rights and duties of collective self-government—is not supposed to be someone grappling with those forces of evil named as "witchcraft."

The fact that the history of European modernism is also the history of colonialism in Africa (leaving aside the small question of whether or not "we" have ever been "modern"; Latour 1993) compounds the difficulties of using the word "witchcraft" in an African context and thinking about what such practices might mean for the building of a new African democracy in the twenty-first century. Being able to say Africans believed, or "still believe," in witches served as a handy device for colonial regimes to justify their exclusion of Africans from the right to vote. Until late in the colonial enterprise, African involvement with matters spoken of as witchcraft was taken as proof that Natives, as they were known at the time, were not sufficiently rational to be able to govern themselves. Thus, like children and imbeciles—and, for a long time, women—Natives were considered by the ruling orders to be subjects who could be excluded from the rights and liberties of full political citizenship. Prior to the Second World War, few imperialists would have disagreed with John Stuart Mill that principles of liberty apply only to "human beings in the maturity of their faculties," thus precluding self-government for people in "those backward states of society in which the race itself may be considered in its nonage" (Mill 1859, 15).

In the present postcolonial era, to suggest that matters spoken of as witchcraft are still relevant in African life risks exciting the prejudice—or stimulating the anxiety that such prejudice will resurface—that people who

---

2. The classic exposition of what became established wisdom on this question in the modern West was the great Whig historian Lecky's celebration of the triumph of rationalism over superstition (Lecky 1891).

believe in witches are irrational and "backward" and thus not capable of governing themselves. Given the long and bitter struggle for freedom in South Africa, even mentioning these issues can seem like a willingness to compromise the fruits of victory over racism and oppression. If these matters were only of academic interest, such risks would not be worth taking. But the burden of suffering in contemporary Africa is so enormous that any effort to understand or alleviate it must also take account of these dimensions of life.

The Rationality Question

Against the background of the ready conjunction of racism and rationalism that would write off large parts of humankind as irredeemably irrational, most of the more sophisticated thinkers about questions of reason and witchcraft in Africa have sought to demonstrate that believing in witchcraft does not necessarily mean a person is irrational. Most of these thinkers have distinguished between the "belief" in witches and witchcraft, which they consider to be obviously absurd, and the otherwise rational behavior of people who seem to believe misfortunes can be caused by witches. "Witches, as the Azande conceive them," Evans-Pritchard famously observed, "cannot exist" (1937, 63). However, "Zande belief in witchcraft in no way contradicts empirical knowledge of cause and effect" (1937, 73).

Two basic modes of squaring the circle of rationality and witchcraft—allowing rational people to have irrational beliefs—were deployed by Evans-Pritchard and have remained standard in scholarly approaches to this subject ever since. The first is to demonstrate that the logical framework of propositions regarding witchcraft can be internally consistent and rational in its own context, even though it may not be in others. The second is to show how statements about witchcraft that might seem irrational if taken as literally applying to the material world actually apply to different kinds of objects—such as morality, the nature of evil, or the meaning of misfortune—and are thus of a different order of discourse from "empirical knowledge" (Evans-Pritchard 1937). Evans-Pritchard's great contribution to the understanding of African witchcraft was to elucidate an internal logic within the patterns of Zande talk about witchcraft while demonstrating that when a Zande invoked witchcraft as an explanation for misfortune, he or she was not practicing bad science or mistaking the facts of empirical reality but rather asking the questions "Why me? Why now?" and attributing responsibility to another person (1937, 69–70). Evans-Pritchard interpreted Zande talk of witchcraft as providing a framework of moral agency that could make sense of what would otherwise seem to be random coincidences in space and time. In the Zande world as Evans-Pritchard portrays it, the invocation of witchcraft in regard to undeserved misfortune —that is, suffering that cannot be satisfactorily construed as either justified punishment or self-inflicted wound—provides ways of answering the questions "Why me? Why now?" with attributions of moral responsibility.

Since it is always anchored in concrete social situations, talk about witchcraft can thus be interpreted as an idiom through which other kinds of social realities are expressed. The idea of witchcraft discourse as an idiom expressing other realities—usually "social and psychological strains" (Mayer 1970, 55)—has proved remarkably flexible in the hands of anthropologists and remains the predominant emphasis in the literature on witchcraft in Africa. During the middle decades of the twentieth century, as the colonial enterprise began to give way to independence, anthropologists studying witchcraft in Africa concentrated on the relationship between witchcraft beliefs and social structures, examining the strains introduced by "culture contact," "modernization," and "development," especially as they were evidenced through accusations and witch-finding movements (Max Marwick 1982; Middleton and Winter 1963). The study of witchcraft came to focus almost exclusively upon witchcraft accusations and the microsociology of conflict at the village level, an emphasis that remains to the present (Andersson 2002; Niehaus 2001). Witchcraft accusations were seen as an index of social conflict, a mechanism for managing conflict, and an idiom in which conflict was expressed. The key task of the anthropologist was to figure out who accuses whom of witchcraft and why (Gluckman 1955). In the later decades of the century, the interpretation of witchcraft talk as idiom focused more on aspects of modernity, such as colonialism, capitalism, and globalization (Comaroff and Comaroff 1993; Geschiere 1997; R. Shaw 2002). While this literature has revealed much about African social life, it suffers from the singular defect—as Robin Horton has pointed out on numerous occasions (Horton 1993)—of treating statements that Africans clearly intend as literal, or factual, as if they were meant to be metaphorical or figurative. One of the principal challenges facing the writer on African witchcraft today is that of building upon the insights of these earlier writers while treating the statements of African interlocutors as literal—without thereby reverting to prejudices about African irrationality.

Evans-Pritchard's work stimulated an industry of philosophical inquiry into questions of rationality, relativism, and the philosophy of social science (Polanyi 1995; B. Wilson 1970; Winch 1970; Hollis and Lukes 1982; Geertz

2000). Questions of African rationality and the logics of African "belief systems" also became a staple of African philosophy (Mudimbe 1988, 1994; Karp and Masolo 2000; Masolo 1994). When not preoccupied with the question of whether an *African* philosophy as such can exist at all, African philosophers, as Masolo points out (1994, chap. 1), have been obsessed with the "rationality debate"—arguments over the nature of "African" thought and its relation to the ways in which Western thinkers have drawn the divide between peoples possessed of reason, and thus admitted to the ranks of the civilized, and those without. Although this so-called rationality debate has helped elucidate problems of explanation and epistemology in the social sciences and the history of Western denigration of Africa, it offers little guidance for understanding how people live in a world with witches and manage problems of spiritual insecurity in places like contemporary Soweto. This is so because the category of "society" or "culture" as a relatively homogeneous, discrete, and bounded social entity no longer applies in such places, if it ever did. The frames of reference for translation of categories between human groups are no longer stable in the manner necessary for such comparisons of rationality.

If Evans-Pritchard and those who followed him had not been able to make statements of the kind "among the Azande . . . ," neither of his strategies of interpretation would have worked to recuperate the presumption of African rationality. For if the people talking about witchcraft are not in fact part of some distinct cultural unit, if, rather, they have to be considered part of the same "modern" world as those who, like Evans-Pritchard, know that witches cannot exist, then it is difficult not to conclude that they are merely ignorant and superstitious. At the turn of the twenty-first century, it is not always possible to make statements of the form "among the Azande . . . ," and it is pointless to speculate upon the putative logic of a closed system of belief belonging to such people. As Clifford Geertz noted of life in a "world in pieces" at millennium's end, "rather than being sorted into framed units, social spaces with definite edges to them, seriously disparate approaches to life are becoming scrambled together in ill-defined expanses, social spaces whose edges are unfixed, irregular, and difficult to locate" (2000, 85). To get some sense of these "ill-defined expanses," we have to dispense with those comforting claims, so common in African ethnography, of the "among the Azande . . ." variety, wherein the peculiarities of a whole people can be handily summarized in a single sentence. It may be the case that in some secluded parts of the continent such statements are not yet completely meaningless. But they are in South Africa, especially in the big cities of Johannesburg and Soweto. Better, then, to simply set aside these conundrums of rationality. Despite the impossibility of reasonable answers to the rationality question, however, witchcraft remains a major problem.

The Modernity Question

To the second question that, I have suggested, usually accompanies inquiries into witchcraft—Why do people still believe in witches?—three basic types of answer have been offered over the past century or so. The first is the straightforwardly modernist assertion that the persistence of witchcraft beliefs is evidence that the proper course of modernization has been thwarted. Although this attitude still holds considerable sway in popular discourse, few scholars take seriously the central tenets of what is termed the "secularization thesis" of modernization theory or the underlying presumption of linear progress in human history.

A second, and far more persuasive, approach requires a less linear view of progress while still taking the concept of "modernity" seriously. In the decades since classic modernization theories fell out of favor in the social sciences, many writers have argued that change, even progress, need not entail a single common cultural outcome (i.e., modernity) for all. Indeed, a multiplicity of modernities is conceivable in this view—the parallel outcomes of multiple local histories. If the possibility of many forms of modernity is conceded, witchcraft today need not necessarily be the same as in the past, nor need the fact that some people still worry about witches necessarily indicate an absence of modernity. The reason people *still* believe in witchcraft, then, can be posited as resulting from the fact that discourses of witchcraft still work in making sense of their worlds, including the changes that modernization and globalization have wrought. Of course, it would be difficult for even the most dedicated relativist to assert that the idiom of witchcraft is the *best* way of making sense of the world and of acting upon the global structures of what Jean Comaroff and John Comaroff (1999a) have called "millennial capitalism." But the fact that these "occult economies" exist (Comaroff and Comaroff 1999b) suggests they are serving some useful purpose.

Scholars, mostly anthropologists, intent on redressing notions of witchcraft as atavistic, premodern, or antimodern tendencies in African societies have recently been dubbed the "modernity of witchcraft school" (Comaroff and Comaroff 1993; Geschiere 1997; Moore and Sanders 2001b). Underpinning their approach is the conviction that talk of witchcraft should be interpreted metaphorically as an idiom through which other matters of pressing social reality are expressed, particularly those relating to the marginalizing of Africa in the era of globalization. A major problem with talk of modernity and witchcraft in this literature, however, is that writers in the modernity of witchcraft school often seem to want to have it both ways: on the one hand, they acknowledge the fallacies embodied in the old ways of distinguishing tradition and modernity, the ideological project of celebrating modernization as the eradication of "non-Western" cultural difference in the name of "enlightenment," while, on the other hand, they invoke the notion of progress in the guise of a multiplicity of "modernities," each arrived at down its own distinctive "path." Indeed, some have even suggested that there are "modernities" past, present, and future (R. Shaw 2002, 265).[3]

If this multiplication of modernities through space and time has occurred, and if the specific combination of cultural, economic, social, and political features of a particular era of European history can no longer be taken seriously as the universal destination of humankind, then the term "modernity" has surely outlived its analytic usefulness when applied to places like turn-of-the-millennium Africa. As Bruno Latour has suggested in his book *We Have Never Been Modern* (1993), it is better to proceed from the recognition expressed in his title and thus stop looking for modernity in every corner of the globe and wondering why the modernities to be found there are not what they are supposed to be. I am not suggesting that ideologies of modernism, projects of modernization, experiences of change, and celebrations of "modernity" are not everywhere to be found. But the fact that people all over the world constantly talk about things being "modern" while experiencing dislocating changes in their modes of living does not mean they are referring to something called "modernity," certainly not in the form that term took in the hoary old annals of "modern" social theory. All it means is that they see fit to deploy ideological categories of modernist discourses in making and making sense of their worlds. Why they do so is, sometimes, interesting but is no reason to suppose there is such a thing as modernity out there in the world. By the same token, although there are countless traditions, invented as well as timeless, there is no such thing as *the* traditional or tradition. These points would hardly be worth making—in this day and age—were it not for the fact that anxieties about tradition and modernity still confound thinking about witchcraft in Africa.

The third type of answer to the question of why people still believe in witchcraft insists they do so because, unlike in the countries of the West, witches remain a problem in Africa. While the modern secular rationalist

---

3. For criticism of the "modernity of witchcraft" approach, see Englund 1996.

might find this view absurd, it is widespread in Africa, not so much among ordinary people for whom the realities of witchcraft are simply given, but among members of elites who are aware of the "Western" predilection for seeing witchcraft as a backward belief yet who find themselves living in a world where the dangers of occult forces are manifold. A version of the argument was a central contention of the *Report of the Commission of Inquiry into Witchcraft Violence and Ritual Murders* (Ralushai Commission) published in South Africa by the government of the Northern Province in 1996. Witchcraft is no longer a problem in the West, according to this report, because the West dealt with the witches long ago. Evidence for this, they suggest, can be found in such documents as Shakespeare's *Macbeth*, where it is clear that, at the time it was written, witches were still around and still a nuisance (Ralushai Commission 1996, 13). Witchcraft, in this view, will remain a problem in Africa until the witches are dealt with. The main issue is whether they should be punished and killed or reconciled with the community. The Ralushai Commission advocated the latter strategy, proposing procedures akin to those of the Truth and Reconciliation Commission as a way of restoring community harmony.

A related version of this argument is also professed by theologians and practitioners of most world religions. In Christianity, the dominant religion of southern Africa, the authority of the Scriptures is replete with references to witchcraft and the importance of exorcizing demons. In 1999 the Vatican updated its policy on exorcism, warning priests to consult physicians and psychiatrists before proceeding with the liturgy of exorcism. The church did not deny the dangers of demonic possession and of human interactions with demonic forces of varieties that Africans would have no difficulty in recognizing as witchcraft.[4] Pentecostalism, which is the most dynamic of the global religious movements active in Africa today, is engaged in a continual and massive struggle against rapacious demons and their human allies. Until the Second Coming, witchcraft and its relative, Satanism, will surely remain problems for these faiths.

One of the most puzzling features of talk relating to witchcraft for Westerners in Africa is the attribution of agency and intention to substances in ways that seem to defy universal principles governing the nature of the material world. Most commonly, these agencies are posited either as possessed by invisible beings and analogous to the agency of human persons or as in-

---

4. The Vatican, however, has rarely been comfortable with the activities of priests (such as the Zambian archbishop Milingo) who engage too vigorously in the struggles of the African spirit world (Milingo 1984).

herent in substances, objects, and images. Agencies of the latter type may, or may not, be represented as analogous to the agency of human persons. This emphasis on interrelations among forms of human and nonhuman agency is the general feature of witchcraft discourses that came to seem particularly implausible to people for whom mechanical metaphors governed interpretation of the possibilities of action and reaction—human and nonhuman; natural and supernatural. As a child of the machine age, I find myself unable to grant credence to the stories I have heard about the miracles of *muthi*. A child of the digital era, however, such as the children of Soweto, would have less reason to doubt the possibility of invisible forces extending from a person to activate and communicate with agencies inherent in substances or other entities. The same thing happens every time a cell phone rings. Much of the talk about the potentialities of *muthi* I have heard over the years seems to me to operate within a paradigm of communication rather than one of mechanism, the exchange of information between various kinds of agents rather than the action and reaction of forces motivating material bodies. These attributions of agency are usually coupled with much broader interpretations of the abilities of humans to interact with substances, objects, and images than anything Westerners imbued with a "modern" sensibility would normally consider reasonable.

In the literature on witchcraft in Africa, the ready and apparently wholehearted orientation of indubitably reasonable people to everyday interrelations with mysterious aspects of material reality has always proved most problematic for those who would treat matters of seeming "superstition" with sympathy. Unlike talk of ancestors, deities, and spirits—which can be subsumed within the category of "religious belief" and treated therein with as much respect or contempt as any other form of faith—talk about material substances acting in mysterious ways or human bodies acting in ways that transcend the laws of nature to wreak havoc on others seems simply absurd. In the middle decades of the twentieth century writers seeking to interpret the meaning of "witchcraft" and "magic" in Africa could confidently assert that African claims regarding the uses of substances and the abilities of persons to cause harm were simply implausible and could assume that readers would readily agree, even if neither author nor reader was a specialist in the natural sciences. The proliferation of popular discourses about scientific fields such as genetic engineering, cloning, telecommunications, robotics, artificial life, and digital imaging is reconfiguring the public imagination at the turn of the twenty-first century with each new broadcast day. The convergence of information and communication technologies, biotechnologies, and nanotechnologies is opening new frontiers of apocalyptic dread. And it is not so easy to dismiss African imaginings of the mysteries of witchcraft as physically impossible and likely to be rendered implausible by exposure to science.

Indeed, recent advances in science and technology over the past two or three decades, particularly as these are presented in popular discourses and everyday experience, tend to make suppositions about human abilities to interact with the material world such as those commonly expressed in narratives of witchcraft seem more, rather than less, plausible. Some African intellectuals have also started exploring consonances between new forms of science and old African traditions. Arguing the case for African indigenous knowledge systems to form the basis of an African Renaissance, Pikita Ntuli has argued that "the world view of traditional Africa, and indeed of all traditional people of the world, bear[s] striking similarities with some aspects of quantum physics." "Whereas Newtonian physics saw dichotomies, quantum physics perceives interconnections" (2002, 54, 57). Although such arguments are more persuasive to those seeking the verities of identity rather than a theory of everything, they nonetheless reflect the ways in which discourses about science have become cultural resources that can be set to work in quite different contexts. Commonplace objects such as the cell phone and the remote control also afford ordinary people an everyday experience of action that extends and transcends human physical ability in the manner once thought the sole province of witches and sorcerers. Media reports about cloning and genetic engineering, as ubiquitous in Africa as everywhere else, make it seem that anything is possible at the frontiers of science.

Experience of these technologies, then, lends new plausibility to suppositions regarding the powers of both witches and their opponents, healers. Science has become the primary frame of reference for interpreting these capacities in Soweto. By postulating a secret "African science" analogous to the science producing the everyday miracles of late capitalist technology, Africans are able to reconcile suppositions about the extraordinary powers of witches and the lived realities that are the fears of witchcraft without compromising their own, or anyone else's, putative rationality or presuming their cultural inferiority. When the powers of witches and healers to interact with substances, objects, and images in ways that transcend the ordinary limitations of space and time are figured in terms of "African science," the only way to categorically deny these abilities, to assert "this they cannot do," is to deny that Africans are capable of matching the scientific powers of "Whites." This is not easy to accept.

To understand why people can "still" believe in witchcraft despite no longer living in a world that remotely resembles anything "traditional," it is first necessary to understand how claims about the forms of agency embodied in material substances, objects, and images can be made to seem plausible. And if it is true that the people of whom I write in Soweto are living in a world with witches while also, and at the same time, living in the same world as people like me and the people who are reading this book, then the conditions of this plausibility should be describable without having to be translated from one culture to another or one putative scheme of rationality to another. That is to say, the project is no longer one of making African assertions about forms of power seem reasonable in their own terms within the bounded confines of a particular worldview or system of belief, but rather of explicating how questions, *doubts*—entertained not only by Africans but by all of us—about the possibilities of power and action in the world can both seem plausible and be reasonable. As Wittgenstein wrote, in his acerbic annotations of Fraser's *Golden Bough,* "too little is made of the fact that we include the words 'soul' and 'spirit' in our own civilized vocabulary. Compared with this, the fact that we do not believe our soul eats and drinks is a minor detail" (1979, 10e).

Since it is pointless to speculate upon some putative "African" metaphysics or system of belief—or ethnic subset thereof—that supplies comprehensive answers to questions regarding the essential nature of the material world, and since the task of examining how people construct such understandings in general would be far too much to attempt here, I shall proceed by examining some of the elementary questions about the *dangers* posed by invisible forces that emerge from everyday life in Soweto. I shall presume that these questions are not exclusively resolved in explicit discourses regarding the nature of the world but that the various modes of professional "healing" practice, everyday routines of health maintenance, and rituals of one sort and another also provide plausible answers to them.

Witchcraft and the Conundrums of Belief in Contemporary Soweto

Every family in Soweto is intimately acquainted with sorrows wrought by disease, violence, and accidents resulting in untimely death. Most are familiar, too, with poverty and hunger. None of the families I have known in Soweto survived the decade of the 1990s without someone in the not-too-extended family dying of a preventable illness, in a crime of violence, or on the roads. Since the late 1990s, every family has also been touched by the steadily rising death toll of HIV/AIDS. At the start of the twenty-first century, few families in Soweto can unambiguously declare themselves financially secure, safe, healthy, and free from suffering. And I know none that in recent years has not had to grapple seriously with questions of how to manage crises of witchcraft.

Most of the people in Soweto whom I know well and with whom I have discussed matters of spiritual insecurity recognize the existence of a field of human activity they are happy enough to describe as "witchcraft," translating the local terms *ubuthakathi* (Zulu) and *bomoloi* (Sotho). Nonetheless, in the course of these discussions over the years virtually every one of them asserted that, for a variety of reasons, one ought not to believe in witches. In 1997, for example, while gossiping one morning in MaMfete's kitchen, Modiehe, a neighbor and old friend of MaMfete, told me that "witchcraft . . . it partly exists. That's true. But me, I don't believe" (Ashforth 2000a, 73). I was perplexed. Did she mean to say that sometimes witchcraft exists and sometimes it does not? Or was she saying that sometimes she believes and sometimes she does not?

In the course of our conversation it became clear that Modiehe had no doubt about the general possibility of witchcraft and indeed had heard many of the local rumors about another neighbor who was reputed to be a witch. However, because she had not been afflicted personally by that woman, particularly in the time since she had built a new house and was thus susceptible to witchcraft attack because of the increased jealousy such a project usually provokes, she was prepared to suspend her judgment. For Modiehe, witchcraft was real, but she tried to live by the precept that it is better not to believe the worst about people. When her house was hit by lightning some years previously, she had been worried that a lightning bird had been dispatched to kill her by an enemy and was persuaded by friends to seek protection from a local prophet. She also followed the common procedure of placing an old car tire on her roof to protect the house from future lightning strikes. Everybody knows that electricity cannot flow through rubber.

Modiehe's attitude to believing in witches and witchcraft is by no means unusual. The recognition of the reality of witchcraft and the axiomatic acceptance of the general possibility of occult action causing real harm are almost universal in these parts. At times of crisis, this recognition can produce profound anxieties in the lives of individuals, families, and communities. Recognition of the general possibilities of occult action, however, is often coupled with a resistance to belief. To say that people "believe in witches" is about as meaningless in this context as to say they "believe in God." The point is not *that* they believe but what they believe, how they believe it, and with what consequences for the conduct of their lives. It is necessary, I believe, to be circumspect when making statements about other people's beliefs. As Rodney Needham (1972) has pointed out, the concept of belief is extremely problematic as used in ethnography. Often statements about belief serve to mask two sleights of hand: on the one hand, they imply that the propositional content of some putative "belief" said to be a common feature of a culture is in fact held with some degree of commitment by the persons who constitute that culture; on the other hand, they imply that the particular proposition classified as a "belief" is part of a putative "system of belief" within which it relates to other propositions in some sort of logical way. These two things might indeed be true of statements reported as "beliefs," but they are rarely demonstrated and it is extremely difficult to do so.

In chapters to follow I shall generally eschew claims about beliefs. Rather, I shall outline some of the reasons that people accept as plausible the general possibility of occult action, along with other forms of danger emanating from invisible forces. Often I shall reconstruct these frameworks of plausibility from practices and discourses related to the seeking of spiritual security. I shall also devote many pages to exploring the social and political consequences of spiritual insecurity. Here, however, I want to emphasize a dimension of commonplace attitudes to believing in witchcraft, a second order of "belief" regarding witchcraft—beliefs about beliefs. In this domain, most Africans I know are engaged—not all the time and not always with the same urgency and intensity—in a struggle to refuse belief, an effort to resist believing that others desire and possess the ability to cause them harm. This struggle against belief sometimes confounds outsiders seeking to understand witchcraft in contemporary Africa.

Some people strive to resist believing misfortunes are products of witchcraft by embracing identities celebrating modernist assertions of the primacy of science. Sometimes they are successful. But denying the possibility of witchcraft is akin to denying the existence of God. It is easier to do when life is good. Marxism, as the most rigorous of the twentieth-century ideologies of liberation, the "science" of socialism, has been the main driving force among Africans who embrace varieties of modernism—far more important than formal education, which was always limited for Africans and never strong in the sciences. Even for those who feel no need to express themselves in the languages of modernism, however, "science"—the name of the force behind a myriad of miraculous everyday objects and the industrial technologies that produced them—is everywhere. Particularly as it is embodied in individuals and institutions of what is known here as "White" or "Western" medicine, science inexorably shapes the experience of misfortunes that had long been registered as witchcraft. Sometimes the evident power of Western science serves to diminish fears of witchcraft. A visit to the clinic that results in a clear medical diagnosis coupled with swift and effective treatment of an illness, for example, usually trumps suspicions of witchcraft and strengthens the conviction among the latterly afflicted that it is better not to search for occult causes of evident distress. Ailments for which Western medicine can provide no decisive diagnosis and cure, however, exacerbate fears of witchcraft. Bear in mind, too, that most black people in South Africa do not have access to world-class medical facilities. "Science" also serves as analogy—"African science"—for the name for the secret knowledge informing both healing and witchcraft. In this guise, science becomes the point of reference for imagining enormous capacities for occult evil.

Many strive to resist the pull of worrying about witchcraft by embracing a Christian insistence on the power and love of Jesus to keep a person safe. They say one should simply pray. Although everyone knows that the Bible teaches about the evils of witchcraft ("Thou shalt not suffer a witch to live"; Exodus 22:18), and although many Christians have a vivid sense of demonic powers at work in the world, the professed Christian also knows that one should love one's neighbor and not accuse them of witchcraft. Christian missionaries of the churches commonly referred to as "mainline" have long preached that witchcraft does not exist, although they acknowledge the power of Satan to foment evil in the world. Members of these churches, however, as we shall see in more detail in later chapters, tend to have ambivalent attitudes to the subject of occult forces. They know they ought not to believe in witches and need not take steps to protect themselves from evil forces beyond offering prayers. Yet, surrounded on all sides by signs that are commonly taken to be evidence of witches' work, at times of crisis few Christians will refuse to seek additional forms of protection from their neighbors' and relatives' witchcraft. The most dynamic Christian churches, those that have emerged under African leadership over the past century, devote enormous energies to combating witchcraft.

Sometimes, a deliberate reluctance to believe in witchcraft or to countenance the possibility that a particular misfortune is a sign of evil forces at work is part of a practical strategy of self-defense, a means of avoiding the psychological snares that await the person who becomes preoccupied with seeking signs of occult assault. As my friend Thabo once told me after we had debated the meaning of a smear of dirt we had found on the front wall of the house: "once you start thinking about that shit, you're finished. Then witchcraft is everywhere." The year was 1993. We found that brown smear after a party to which the neighbors were not invited. It might have been mud. It might have been *makaka* (shit). Or it might have been *muthi* and, therefore, evidence of an occult assault. No one could say for certain. We all made a conscious decision to resist the temptation to think that it contained *muthi,* preferring instead to think of the act as vandalism rather than witchcraft. Perhaps it was the work of naughty children, perhaps someone annoyed by the sounds of merriment inside, to which they had not been invited. Fortunately, our discovery of the smear was not accompanied by any serious mishap in the house, so it was not difficult to discount the threat of occult attack. Had something awful happened while the memory of that mud lasted, resisting the pull of witchcraft explanations would have been difficult. In any event, as we all knew, the house had been protected from such attack by a pair of traditional healers some months earlier, so we did not have too much to worry about.

Another reason for resisting the pull of witchcraft explanations for misfortunes invokes the "power of the mind." It is a commonplace of traditional healing ideologies that medicinal *muthi* will not work if the patient does not believe in its powers. The corollary of this is also taken to be true: if a person believes strongly that he is being bewitched, the powers of the poisonous *muthi* that has been sent to harm and kill will be enhanced. Witches are also commonly thought to be able to use their targets' own minds as weapons of self-destruction. One of the most terrifying aspects of life in a world of witches, it seems to me, arises from the widespread conviction that witches can hijack people's innermost desires and will in such a way as to cause them to engineer their own doom. Witches are said to be able to act upon and through their victims' minds, just as they can act upon bodies. The core of witchcraft is a putative ability to interfere with the ordinary arrangements of agency inherent in persons, substances, and spirits. People who become obsessively frightened of witchcraft, then, make themselves vulnerable by weakening their mental defenses against occult action.

When a person succumbs to an excessive fear of witchcraft, not only does her life become miserable with worry, but the "psychological" weakness that ensues affords witches greater opportunity to cause actual harm. Thus, Madumo, when he found himself bewitched, believed that "Westernizing" his mind so as to banish thoughts of witchcraft could help in reducing the actual power of the real witches seeking to destroy him. Denying fears of witchcraft, as Madumo struggled to do, did not result in the witches disappearing into those realms of nothingness known as the "imagination," as a good Westerner might imagine would have been the case, but merely rendered his occult enemies less effective than they might otherwise have been. In the end, as we shall see in greater detail in chapter 10, these interactions of evil forces with the inner realms of personhood are most perilous for those without access to healers or spiritual guides in whom they can place their trust.

Living in a world of witches in a place like Soweto in the late twentieth century, then, almost always involves a struggle *against* believing in witches. Attitudes to witchcraft are dynamic, changing with circumstances, mixing belief and unbelief. Virtually everyone accepts the general possibility of occult action. Yet they know that they do not know the nature of that action and no one can say of witches without fear of contradiction: this they cannot do. Nor can anyone be sure of the identities of potential perpetrators, since the primary motives driving occult assaults, hatred and jealousy, are emotions common to all. When circumstances of untoward misfortune demand that a person confront the possibility of witchcraft, the struggle against belief typically results in a form of *akrasia,* or failure of the will to refuse belief.[5] During ordinary times, when the forces of misfortune seem manageable, this failure of the will to refuse belief is of little import. A person can calmly say, like my former neighbor, "I partly believe." When calamity strikes, however, the struggle against belief can be hard to maintain.

Consider the sad case of Simon. Simon is a young man with advanced degrees from good universities, a professional who was well respected and envied in his community. In the late 1990s, after his mother died, he became locked in a dispute with an estranged aunt over possession of the family home. After several years of lawsuits, Simon won the case and evicted the aunt. After she left, Simon's daughter found a suspicious powder on the kitchen floor as she was sweeping up one morning. Terrified, she called her parents. Everyone knew what the dust signified: the witchcraft known in Zulu as *umeqo,* where the witch sprinkles *muthi* in the path of the victim. Simon was unperturbed. He swept up the powder and danced atop its remnants. He laughed at the stupidity of his poor aunt and the gullibility of his family. For five years he laughed whenever he told the story, happy in his victory over the malicious aunt. Then his life fell to pieces.

Over the course of a year or so Simon's troubles mounted. His wife left him. He was shot by thugs. His business went broke. Lawsuits were threatened. His flat was burgled. He was hijacked and his car stolen. His girl-

---

5. The phenomenon is akin to that described by Aristotle in his *Ethics* as *akrasia* (Aristotle 1953, bk. 7, chap. 1) and by Amelie Rorty in relation to the act of believing as when "a person believes that *p,* being implicitly aware that *p* conflicts with the preponderance of serious evidence or with a range of principles to which he is committed" (1983, 175).

friends disappeared, too. Try as he might, he could not help seeing connections among his misfortunes. Obviously, some were his own fault. He was never one to shirk blame for his own irresponsibility. His wife had tolerated his infidelities far beyond the bounds of human endurance. He knew that. Others were plain bad luck. Anyone can be hijacked in Johannesburg. Some misfortunes, he admitted, would not have occurred had he not found himself driven by urges he could identify in the language of psychology as "self-destructive." Why else would he seek out girlfriends in dangerous neighborhoods and place himself in danger by visiting them late at night? He recognized also that he was depressed, possibly suffering "post-traumatic stress disorder," and took advantage of the treatment and medications available under his Medical Aid plan. But he could not stop himself from wondering whether something else was behind the concatenation of events that brought his charmed life to an end. He could not stop worrying that perhaps his aunt or one of his many abandoned lovers, a business partner, or even a jealous neighbor was orchestrating his demise. He could not escape the possibility that he had been bewitched.

People suspecting that their illnesses, misfortunes, or bad luck result from—to adopt the felicitous phrase of the Portfolio Committee on Arts, Culture, Science, and Technology—"the involvement of evil forces" are confronted with a bustling marketplace of specialists offering to set matters aright. Traditional healers, faith healers, prophets, prayer circles, preachers, teachers, and doctors abound, all professing powers indispensable to the afflicted. People facing crises indicating witchcraft, such as Simon, a comfortably agnostic member of his local Anglican church, often find themselves alienated from their normal sources of social support and spiritual security. Why would they be in a crisis if their normal practices sufficed? The necessity of seeking, and paying for, new sources of spiritual succor and security at such times, however, can produce further anxiety. For not only do most of these specialists assert their own particularity as skilled practitioners, but they are divided by fundamentally contradictory assumptions. The sacrifice to the ancestors that rectifies the root causes of bad luck by mollifying their anger and enlisting their renewed support can result in a salutary lifting of mood, as it did for another friend of mine, sufficient to warrant discontinuing the Prozac. The same sacrifice, however, as the born-again Christians in her family did not hesitate to tell her, is also tantamount to trucking with demons. When the bad luck returned, she did not know who or what to blame. This is what I call epistemic anxiety, a sense of unease arising from the condition of knowing that invisible forces are acting upon one's life but not knowing what they are or how to relate to them.

The Predicament of Not Knowing

In the cities of South Africa, custodians of African tradition have long been both too few and too many: too few because too many families have been unable to reproduce the traditions of their ancestors; too many because few communities have formed around a shared sense of local cultural continuity, which has allowed space for numerous contending authorities to emerge. Parents and other elders have struggled to transmit authoritative interpretations of custom and tradition to their children, often regretting that they were not properly taught the ways of old by their own parents. Young people have struggled to graduate to life-cycle statuses where they become custodians of the old ways, but life in the city is hard on families, and those statuses premised upon marriage, especially that of father and household head, are for too many impossible to achieve. Transformations of family life after more than a century of urbanization, exacerbated by the impositions of apartheid, have disrupted traditions that solidified relations between the living and the dead, a primary source of spiritual security. The ethnic diversity of the city also encompasses many different traditions and customary practices, producing an abundance of competing self-proclaimed experts and established authorities. Where father is a Zulu and mother a Tswana, there is little doubt about the procedures to be followed in honoring the ancestors. But if father is a drunkard and ignorant of what people here call "culture," mother will be left to sort out relations with the ancestors. Should her improvisations become the foundation of her children's notions of tradition, they will surely find themselves challenged by others who denounce them as ignorant. Add to this the fact that for several decades in the latter part of the twentieth century many Africans actively resisted the ethnic identities imposed upon them in the name of apartheid and rebelled against their elders, whom they saw as quiescent in the face of oppression. No wonder then that Madumo, when confronted by the need to ingratiate himself with his ancestors, lamented:

> In a true sense, I don't know these things. Not at all. You know, Adam, our tradition is really dead. To tell you the honest truth, it's dead. Dead. Because with this thing of feasts for our ancestors, we are talking about tradition. And tradition, really, we don't know it. Say if I take ten elders and tell them that I've made a feast, and I've given people a chicken, two out of ten will support me. The other eight will say I've done a wrong thing. So what am I supposed to do? All I know is that I am supposed to do *something*. (Ashforth 2000a, 24)

Madumo eventually managed to find someone to give him confidence to do what needed to be done despite the knowledge that eight in ten elders would disapprove, though it was no easy matter for him to achieve this.

A person finding himself worried about witchcraft in Soweto at the turn of the twenty-first century, someone needing remedies for unwarranted suffering and misfortune, would be most unlikely to claim adequate knowledge of the true nature of the forces that might be acting upon him. Everyone knows stories about witches and their craft. Rumors of miracles accomplished by healers are also widespread, often propagated by the popular press and magazines such as *Bona* and *Drum*. But a man bewitched, or a woman for that matter, will be acutely aware that he or she does not know the whole truth about these matters. That such a truth exists, however, is a conviction universally upheld. *Someone* must really know about these things, someone to whom the afflicted can turn for the African wisdom and secret knowledge that will remedy the situation and provide protection against further affliction. In practice, however, there are too many such authorities—and too much disagreement among them.

Hence, when the Portfolio Committee on Arts, Culture, Science, and Technology concluded its investigations into indigenous knowledge systems and traditional healing, it could only produce the following somewhat plaintive recommendation: "the concept of witchcraft must be debated and clarified further" (Portfolio Committee on Arts 2000, para. 24.3). The predicament that this committee found itself in—of knowing that something called "witchcraft" exists, yet not knowing precisely what it is and not being able to find out, even after consultation with experts—is emblematic of the predicament of a great many people in contemporary South Africa. This sense of ignorance and uncertainty, coupled with the conviction that witchcraft is real, does little to allay fears of witches in everyday life.

For outsiders to begin to imagine what it might be like to live in a world with witches in a place like Soweto at the turn of the twenty-first century, we must approach these issues of spiritual insecurity, not from the point of view of cultural authorities, but from the perspective of those who are ignorant of tradition, torn between conflicting interpretations, or simply confused—the perspective Murray Last has characterized, in his work on "medical culture" in Hausaland, as that of "not knowing" (Last 1992). Far too often writers on these matters invoke the term "system"—systems of belief, medical systems, cultural systems, and so on—in ways that conjure into being images of stability and regularity in worlds where confusion is more often the norm. In places like Soweto, a profusion of confusions is the reality of everyday life. Empirical understanding of these worlds cannot be predicated upon presumed systematicity. Knowing about not knowing, however, as Last also pointed out, is extremely difficult, requiring a sociology of ignorance and the imaginary that not only poses abstract problems of representation (How can one represent the "beliefs" of people who do not know what to believe? How can one represent the "culture" of people who are ignorant of "their" culture?) but can also run afoul of locals with vested interests in their own claims to authority regarding representations of cultural realities and social identities. Nonetheless, we must try.

Part Two

SOURCES OF SPIRITUAL INSECURITY

$$\Rightarrow \quad 6 \quad \Leftarrow$$

POISON, MEDICINE, AND THE POWER

OF SECRET KNOWLEDGE

The Dialectics of *Muthi*

When people worry about "witchcraft" in Soweto, they almost always have in mind the possibility that malicious persons are using harmful substances known generically, in the Zulu lingua franca of these parts, as *muthi*. When traditional healers administer aid to patients in distress, they almost always dispense substances also known generically as *muthi*. The term *muthi* (spelled *muti* in Xhosa transliterations) derives from the Nguni root *-thi,* signifying "tree." Usually translated into English as either "medicine" or "poison," with the anodyne "herbs" used in ambiguous instances, *muthi* refers to substances fabricated by an expert hand, substances designed by persons possessing secret knowledge to achieve either positive ends of healing, involving cleansing, strengthening, and protecting persons from evil forces, or negative ends of witchcraft, bringing illness, misfortune, and death to others or illicit wealth and power to the witch.

If the context of conversation leaves unclear whether medicine or poison is suggested, the valence of the term can be specified by reference to the colors black and white: in Zulu, *umuthi omnyama* (black *muthi*) is the harmful poison, and *umuthi omhlope* (white *muthi*) is the healing medicine. The color of the actual substances—which are mostly shades of brown —is less important than the moral distinction between legitimate and illegitimate uses of powerful substances, although healers do place great significance upon particular colors as having healing properties (H. Ngubane 1977, chap. 7). To understand the sorts of things people worry about when they worry about exposure to invisible evil forces in places like Soweto, it is essential to understand the various ways in which people interpret the agency inherent in substances categorized as *muthi* and the ways in which both human persons and invisible beings interact with them.

The distinction between healing and its antithesis, witchcraft, is an essentially moral one, based on interpretations of the motives of persons deploying *muthi* and the ends to which these forces are directed. Witches seeking to cause harm work with *muthi* as poison; healers seeking well-being work with *muthi* as medicine. Though directed toward health and well-being—a general condition of bodily health, spiritual ease, and social harmony referred to as *impilo* (in Zulu; *phela,* Sotho)—the *muthi* of healers also brings death. When a healer sets out to cure a person afflicted by witchcraft, he or she will typically promise that their *muthi* will return the evil forces deployed by the witch to their source, thereby killing the witch. Such violence, however, is legitimate, for it is executed in the name of defense. Witches, by definition, are engaged in illegitimate uses of the powers of *muthi.* In everyday discourse when Sowetans refer to witchcraft, they do not usually trouble themselves with distinctions between people enjoying innate capacities to direct evil forces, people with secret knowledge about the evil uses of *muthi,* and people purchasing *muthi* from professionals for their own nefarious purposes. Each and every person deploying *muthi* for malicious or illegitimate ends—such as, say, accumulating excessive wealth or power—is spoken of as a "witch."

There are no limits to the possible uses of *muthi* other than the skill and supernatural connections of the person making and using it. Witches using *muthi* are said to be able to cause every disease and misfortune under the sun. Healers claim to be able to cure every disease (including AIDS, though many know better than to mention this to outsiders now) and to remedy every misfortune ever suffered.[1] A typical healer will advertise abilities to supply *muthi* to protect your house against burglars and your car against hijackers, to keep your husband faithful, to help your children pass their exams, and to keep your boss at work happy. He will also have *muthi* to cure your high blood pressure, diabetes, swollen ankles, and whatever

1. A flier advertising the services of a *"dokotela"* (doctor) named Maama Asha Maraka (a woman from Uganda) that I picked up on the main street of the Zululand town Mtubatuba in November 2003 included the statement, in English, "People with AIDS/HIV can be helped on symptoms." The rest of the pamphlet was in Zulu and offered cures for all the symptoms of AIDS, plus everything else besides. Since Mtubatuba is home to many English-speaking medical researchers attached to the Hblabisa Hospital and the Africa Centre for Health and Population Studies, Maama Asha was wise to deflect inquiries about her capacities to treat AIDS.

else ails you. Such a healer will also know how to protect clients from police and criminals alike, though legions of the dead must be regretting the day they gave money to healers claiming to be able to turn bullets into water.[2] *Muthi,* then, is a category of substances that act both *on* persons and *with* persons—and not only human persons as ordinarily understood. *Muthi* also plays a part in communications between humans and spirits. Spirits both activate the powers inherent in *muthi* and empower these substances with new force. These propositions are treated as axiomatic by most people, including those such as born-again Christians who find the whole enterprise of traditional healing anathema and see *muthi* as a means of engaging with demonic forces.

Dangerous substances deployed as *muthi* can enter the body through the mouth in the form of food or drink, through the lungs, through contact with the skin, through sexual intercourse, and through the anus—so anyone who eats, drinks, breathes, or puts their body in contact with other persons or substances needs to be careful. The most feared mode of deployment is that of *muthi* in food or drink, referred to as *idliso* (Zulu) and *sejeso* (Sotho) after the verb "to eat": *ukudlisa* in Zulu and *ho jesa* in Sotho. Other conventionally recognized modes of deploying *muthi* to cause harm include blowing a powder from the palm of the hand toward a victim (a gesture that also serves in everyday conversation to signify witchcraft), laying the *muthi* where the victim will walk over it, and placing it near the victim such as in her bed, on the roof of her house, or buried in her backyard. Burning *muthi* can also activate its powers. While one can protect oneself, to a certain extent, from *idliso* by being careful about what one consumes and avoiding offers of food or drink from untrustworthy sources, the other modes of deployment are more problematic, as the *muthi* is mostly invisible to its victim. Protection from witchcraft generally requires supernatural prophylaxis activated by a healer's *muthi* or a prophet's treatments.

The forces operating in *muthi* are said to be operative over long distances, even without any direct contact between witch and victim. *Muthi* can also work as a material force through the medium of a dream. A person can dream he is eating something without being aware that a witch has poisoned the food in his dream. When he awakes, the *muthi* will cause af-

2. Rian Malan has an account of an incident during a miners' strike when African workers treated with *muthi* designed to turn bullets into water encountered management's new riot control technology: the water cannon. The strikers' jubilation was short-lived when management returned to its old method of using live ammunition (Malan 1990, 209).

flictions just as real as if the food had been consumed while awake. The ethnographic record is silent about indigenous notions of contamination through insect vectors, although in January 2000 the *Sunday Times* reported a story of a mob in a village in Mpumalanga attacking a traditional healer who was "accused of bewitching mosquitoes and making them infect a client's business rivals" (Lubisi 2000), and there is considerable lore about the use of animals and mystical creatures by witches. Nor has contamination through the eyes in the manner of the "evil eye" so prevalent in Europe and the Mediterranean figured as a major source of harm in this region. As an active agency, *muthi* can produce effects of a wide variety limited only by the skill of the person making and deploying it.

The defining capacity of both the witch and the healer is the ability to interact with the invisible agency inherent in certain substances to create *muthi* so as to effect specific desired ends in concert with these forces. The term *muthi* has botanical roots. A contemporary traditional healer's apothecary, however, though dominated by natural products harvested and marketed in a multimillion-rand industry with an increasing burden on the natural environment (Mander 1998, chap. 9, sec. 2), is by no means limited to a folkloric pharmacopeia of roots, leaves, barks, and animal products. The popular image of the traditional healer is one of a highly skilled sage dispensing secret recipes of natural herbs, recipes that have been handed down through generations and that embody the collective wisdom of indigenous knowledge. Healers, however, commonly use synthetic animal "fats" (especially the much prized fat of the lion, imported from India) over-the-counter pharmaceuticals, and patent medicines in their healing practice (Cocks and Moller 2002). Many also find uses for a range of industrial chemicals such as mercury, chromium, potassium permanganate, copper sulfate, and other colorful metal salts, a practice that has contributed to making South Africa, in the words of a leading toxicologist, a "toxicologist's goldmine" (Stewart 2002). Nor is the healer's nemesis, the witch, limited to the herbs available to the ancestors of old. The quest for powerful substances to both cause and alleviate misfortune cannot be limited to old recipes because in many instances the misfortunes to be caused and the sicknesses to be healed are new.

Witchcraft and healing are endeavors that privilege innovation. The key to both is knowledge. Healers and witches alike draw their powers from three possible sources: inheritance of abilities from ancestors; training by skilled masters; and direct communication with higher powers such as the ancestors, spirits (evil ones in the case of witches, of course), or the Holy

Spirit. Most healers claim a little of all three in accounting for their powers. The same is presumed true of witches. But the witch's art is predicated on secrecy. The knowledge of witchcraft is known only to the witches. They may share it in secret among themselves, but it cannot be made public. If a witch were to confess to his art and make public the nature of his techniques, he would no longer be a witch and the techniques would no longer work.

The antithetical relationship between the witch and the healer in this context of secrecy places enormous significance upon the ability of the healer to demonstrate legitimate sources and purposes of his or her knowledge—which, like witchcraft, must also be of a character unobtainable by the ordinary person—though the suspicion that always clings to healers that they may, despite protestations to the contrary, be capable of dark arts rarely hurts their business. In everyday Sowetan life at the turn of the twenty-first century, both the evil arts of witchcraft and the sources of healing knowledge are commonly spoken of in terms of "African science." The scientific basis of healing is also an article of faith in government circles. In 1998, for example, the *Report of the Select Committee on Social Services on Traditional Healers* of the National Council of Provinces recommended that "this *science* [my emphasis] should also be developed through research and technology without necessarily westernising it" (Select Committee on Social Services 1998, 1.1). Before we examine the character of this "science," we should examine the enormous endeavor that is commonly referred to as "traditional healing" and that carries the secret knowledge of the powers of *muthi* at its heart. Since the arts of witchcraft are secret, the practices and procedures of witches are generally inferred through analogy with their antitheses: the healers.

When specifying the abilities of "African scientists" and identifying the kinds of interactions between the intentions of malicious persons and the capacities of substances to cause harm or the corollary capacities of healers and their herbs to cure, the field of possibility is so wide that it is virtually impossible for someone to say, "This they cannot do" without fear of contradiction. Who can say that the foreign witch does not have access to *muthi* unheard of by the local healer? Who knows how the "modern" witch is adapting new technologies to the pursuit of old evils? Nobody. Ordinary people do not possess the means of distinguishing among the agency inherent in the *muthi* (whether it be harmful or healthful), the agency of the human principal, and the agency of the victim or patient. For this they must rely upon experts, healers. And the healers, they are many.

Witches and Witch Doctors

African healers of all stripes must constantly be on guard against being suspected as a witch. For this reason, many are extremely sensitive about being called "witch doctors," a term they interpret as meaning they are both witch and doctor, when they insist that in fact they are doctors struggling against the evil work of witches.[3] The Sowetan healer Sarah Mashele, for example, insists she is a "doctor," not a "witch doctor," though the ambiguity inherent in her profession is clear:

> An *inyanga* is a doctor. . . . The witchdoctor is the person that kills . . . [Ellipses in original.] He is the *"Moloi"* [a Sotho word usually translated as "witch"]. You go to him when you want a person to die; when you want somebody to crash in his car, and when you want to hit somebody with lightning. You go to that *"Moloi"* and he will give you something bad. The *inyanga* is different. He is only the person to help—to heal. The witchdoctor can heal also but the *inyanga* doesn't do bad things. I don't kill, I only help. If you want to do a bad thing, you mustn't come to me. The *inyanga* fights the witchdoctor if he does something bad. I am an *inyanga;* it means that I am fighting with the witchdoctors. (L. Simon 1993, 34)

Despite "Dr." Mashele's insistence, however, most people presume that most healers can in fact cause harm if they so desire, and several healers have told me that they constantly have clients seeking their aid in causing harm. Moreover, just as it can be advantageous in a dangerous place to have the most dangerous criminal as an ally, suspecting that a healer knows how to cause harm can give a client confidence in the healer's powers to heal and protect. Since witchcraft is premised upon secrecy, no amount of denial such as that of Sarah Mashele can suffice to eliminate the possibility of nefarious activity behind a screen of respectability. The fact that news media periodically report the arrest of a "traditional healer" in connection with "*muthi* murder" (also known as "ritual murder"), in which a victim has been killed for body parts to use in *muthi,* confirms the possibility of evil healers, that is, witches.

Most healers within the *ngoma* cult justify their occult capacities by celebrating their own survival of serious illness, which is interpreted as a

3. See, for example, the testimony of healers before the Portfolio Committee on Arts, Culture, Science, and Technology in September 2000 (Portfolio Committee on Arts 2000, para. 24.5).

call from the ancestors. As Ria Reis argues, this "ideology of the wounded healer" serves a handy legitimation function:

> For those who consult diviners as patients, a history of ancestor illness testifies to the true calling and legitimacy of these healers. Such a history testifies to the involuntariness of divinership. It clears healers of selfish motives, such as greed for power or money. It is necessary to have suffered a serious illness to be able to claim that one's healing power originates from the ancestors. Suffering certainly is a lived reality for diviners, but as a sign of a calling it is also an ideology. (2000, 73)

Suffering illness as a qualification for healing also serves in distinguishing the healer from the witch. Nonetheless, healers are always open to suspicion.

Deploying *Muthi* to Kill and to Cure

Although both poison and medicine, the dual aspects of *muthi,* are defined in relation to human actions and intentions—the healer's *muthi* cures while the witch's *muthi* kills—an essential ambiguity inheres in the substances themselves. Medicines can be poisonous; poisons can serve to cure. Since these are substances with *inherent* agency, capacities for independent action, persons who seek to create particular mixtures of substances designed to achieve particular sorts of ends, whether geared toward health and well-being or destruction, must know how to interact with this agency. For example, the acid that burns a person's skin does so without regard to human intention. The person who deliberately places acid on another's skin exploits the capacity inherent in the substance for his own malicious ends. But the person who can harness the acid's *capacity* for burning, who can direct that potential for causing harm toward particular ends at will—so that it will burn you but not me, for example—exercises another form of power altogether. It is this latter form of interaction that is feared as the work of witchcraft and embraced as the work of healing.

At the heart of discourse about *muthi* is what might be termed a "communicative" model of interaction with substances—or, more accurately, the agencies inherent in substances. For example, in 1997 when Madumo, who, as I have already mentioned, was suffering severe depression and social ostracism after the death of his mother, finally found a healer in whom he could trust, a local *inyanga* named Mr. Zondi, he was offered a comprehensive account of his problems that identified the root causes as human jealousy. Madumo was told he had been attacked by witchcraft. Mr. Zondi, in consultation with the ancestors, discovered that Madumo's misfortunes were the result of a jealous relative removing a small amount of soil from the grave of Madumo's mother shortly after she was buried and mixing the soil with *muthi,* herbs obtained from an unscrupulous *inyanga.* This mixture, Mr. Zondi reported, had been secreted in the backyard of Madumo's family home, sowing discord among all in the house and heaping miseries upon my friend.

This tale of graveyard dirt and poisonous *muthi* as the instrument of a man's misfortunes represents a typical example of the dangers that people like Madumo have to worry about when reckoning with the forces that can cause harm in life. When I first heard Mr. Zondi's story I thought it ridiculous. My schooling in natural science, limited as it was, coupled with a few decades' experience of being in the world, made it impossible for me to imagine that physical substances could act in the way Mr. Zondi was describing. Madumo, however, had no such difficulty accepting Mr. Zondi's analysis. For him, the account made perfect sense; it resonated with his understanding of how the world works—that it is a place rife with invisible agencies—as well as his everyday experience of the dangers of noxious substances, and it confirmed his suspicions about the malice and hostility of people around him. Mr. Zondi's story provided him with a serviceable interpretation of his unhappiness that accorded not so much with some putative "traditional system of belief" but with Madumo's own experience of being in the world—the "modern" world of science and technology as well as that of the ancestors, spirits, and God. Mr. Zondi's treatments, which involved a grueling regime of cleansing and fortifying Madumo's body, served, ultimately, to relieve Madumo of much of what ailed him—though not before nearly killing him first.

When a healer suspects that an affliction is the result of *muthi* being deployed against his client, three basic strategies are available to him: cleansing the offending substance physically from the body; countering the intentionality and direction of the poisonous agent given to it by its human principal; and protecting and strengthening the victim against further assault. Cleansing as a mode of treating *muthi* is in principle no different from cleansing the body of other impurities and pollutants, although the work may be more difficult and physically taxing. Identifying and administering cleansing substances is similarly a matter of skill, knowledge, and experience. When a healer identifies a client as a victim of attack by *muthi,* he or she will typically prescribe a course of cleansing that may include bathing or steaming the body and cleansing the "stomach" and "blood" with purgatives, emetics, and enemas. Mere cleansing alone, however, is unlikely to achieve a full restoration of health in the case of a man-made disease, for the *muthi* possesses agency of its own and that agency is invisible, hidden within the visible substance. Once it has taken hold of a victim, *muthi* can move and transmute itself within the victim's body, resisting efforts to expel it and thereby confounding efforts to counteract it by means of cleansing.

When a healer engages with the force that is the motivating power of harmful *muthi,* serious obstacles arise that cannot be overcome without superhuman assistance. Counteracting the effects of *muthi* involves more than merely acting against the material substance. The healer and his client must struggle against the will and intention of the evildoer directing the assault, as well as whatever evil spiritual entities are assisting him or her. Hence, the work of healing is commonly thought of as "defense." Protection involves a strengthening of the inherent powers of the person and the lining up of support from relevant spiritual entities such as the ancestors, Jesus, and the Holy Spirit. In most instances when *muthi* is at issue, the practice of healing is also a form of defensive retaliation, an assault against the witch that is usually presumed to be fatal. Hence, if a person suspected of witchcraft should suddenly die, the death will be taken as evidence of guilt and vindication of the healer's powers. When treatment has been successful, healers will move to protect their clients (again, through specific varieties of *muthi*) against further assaults. Integral to this work is the strengthening of the patient to resist and overcome occult assault.

The mixture of graveyard soil and *muthi* that Mr. Zondi told Madumo had been secreted in the yard of his family's home brought into being forces directed by the witch to cause death and dissension. Mr. Zondi's *muthi,* which he administered to Madumo to counteract the work of the witch, was programmed to turn the curse upon the person who dispatched it. In activating the power of this *muthi,* Mr. Zondi called upon his own and his client's ancestors to set up a complex alliance of forces—an alliance that ultimately had to be cemented with a feast and rituals for the ancestors.

Older and unschooled people tend to assume that the physical substance of *muthi* embodies agencies akin to invisible beings that hear and obey the witch or healer in the manner of command and obedience within human societies or between humans and animals. The principal commands the substance, usually by means of words, though other objects and substances can also be used. In classic ethnographic accounts of *muthi* used in witchcraft, witches speak to their concoctions and direct them to their evil ends by direct commands.[4] A well-known procedure of healers, and thus also widely presumed to be a weapon in the witch's arsenal, is known as *ukuphehla* (Zulu) or *ho fêhlêla* (Sotho). In this procedure, the healer or witch churns a decoction of *muthi* in a pot into a foam while speaking the name of the patient or victim. Some say this is how witches direct lightning to strike their victims. *Muthi* is also directed toward targeted victims by mixing in various bodily effluxions and clippings, personal items, or articles of clothing.

Younger people tend to have a broader conception of the ability of healers and witches to direct the agencies inherent in substances than their elders. These days the direction of *muthi* can be achieved more effectively by what my friends call "technological" means than by the old direct command of the master. Principal among these are the computer program and the remote control. These are the two most persuasive analogies currently available for thinking about the ability of persons to direct the action of *muthi*. References to these devices inflect much of the discourse of young Sowetans concerning occult power and *muthi*. While few Sowetans have experience in writing computer code, all younger adults are familiar with computers (many, indeed, dream of careers in "IT," information technology), robots, and all the myriad programmable devices that are now ubiquitous the world over.

Consider the analogy of the program applied to the making of *muthi:* no one knows for sure how the witches achieve their evil ends, so who is to say that *muthi* cannot be created with programmable capacities? To doubt this would be to doubt African abilities. *Muthi* thus programmed could be directed toward a particular victim just as surely as *muthi* directed by the spoken commands of the witch. Consider, further, the analogy of the electronic remote control. Everyone is familiar with the action at a distance effected by the electronic remote control, a device embodying the magic of "White" science. Who will deny that an "African scientist" could not create analogous devices? Perhaps the effects will be achieved with "spiritual" powers instead of the equally mysterious powers of electronics, but the capacities will be the same, allowing for a continuous adjustment of the ill effects of *muthi* from a distance just like turning up the volume on a television set. If the abilities of witches are inferred from analogies to these kinds of devices, programmable *muthi* would be just the tip of the iceberg.

4. For an excellent example, see Hunter 1961, 290–291.

When Madumo, for example, was told by the prophet in the Zion Christian Church that he was suffering from *isidliso* (poisoning), he immediately assumed that a witch was directing the creature (sent to him through *muthi*) by means of the program and the remote control. The witch was receiving a regular "printout": "they can get a printout from this thing [the creature they have set into the person's stomach]. That is how they control it. Remote control" (Ashforth 2000, 177). Mr. Zondi, however, denied this interpretation. As an older man from rural Zululand, the technological analogy was less immediate for him. He could countenance witches from different regions possessing different kinds of herbs that were unknown to healers from other parts, but not these printouts and remote controls. The experience of the *idliso* poison for someone like Madumo still feels like an invasion by a small creature rather than, say, acid reflux disease. That is to say, he has to distinguish between mere indigestion and *isidliso*. And when he suspects *isidliso*, he assumes that interaction between the witch or healer and substances involves some form of communication. But the ways of understanding how inanimate substances can be made to act in the cause of evil are radically different in these "technological" analogies from the models available to the old Zulu traditionalist Mr. Zondi. The march of scientific progress, then, can make the powers of witches more dreadful than ever.

From whatever perspective the issue is approached, a person worried about witchcraft or hoping for health is faced with two central questions: What sort of relation is there between the victim/patient and the substances working on his or her person, and how does this relation connect with the human principal behind the *muthi*? In everyday life, for most people, such questions remain open until misfortune creates a pressing need to resolve them. And although evidence for the power and effectiveness of healers and their *muthi* is scarce—evidence that would be manifest in abundant health and prosperity among their clients—anyone who cares to look about them in a place like Soweto for evidence of others' capacities to cause harm will be overwhelmed by proof positive evident in the hardship and suffering that abound in this place.

In the Shadow of the Pharmacy

People in places like turn-of-the-millennium Soweto live in a cultural context shaped by biomedical, pharmacological, and toxicological discourses regarding the properties of drugs and poisons, institutions of health and healing governed by scientific medical principles, multinational corporations producing chemicals and pharmaceuticals, and the partly forgotten traditions of the ancestors. For most people worrying about dangerous substances these days, a notion of "poison" serves as a basic building block for interpreting the dangers arising from the domain of "witchcraft"; the notion of "medicine" serves similarly as the foundation of security against such dangers. In the contemporary South African context, the ambiguity inherent in the use of the English words "poison" and "medicine"—both translated in everyday parlance and public discourse as *muthi*—offers substantially different connotations for African and white audiences, allowing African users to switch between what might be termed natural properties of substances and supernatural capacities of persons while avoiding the stigma of irrationality conveyed by the term "witchcraft." This is of the utmost importance at a time when the population is suffering a devastating assault from a mystifying form of agency known as a retrovirus, the popular media are preoccupied with debates over the toxicity and efficacy of pharmaceuticals for treating HIV/AIDS, and political leaders denounce plots by international pharmaceutical companies to poison the African people with toxic AIDS drugs (Anonymous 2002).

Sowetans are as familiar with industrial poisons, commercial pharmaceuticals, and ordinary household poisons as anyone else in this late capitalist world. Bleach, pesticides, paraffin, pills, and other harmful products are kept out of reach of children.[5] Common knowledge, mostly derived from soap operas on television, teaches that consuming large quantities of pharmaceutical pills is a good way to commit suicide. Common experience teaches that for every ailment there is a medicine: either a pill (or, better, an injection) from the clinic or *muthi* from the *inyanga*. Some workers even have experience in industries producing and using dangerous chemicals.[6] So, although few Sowetans are formally educated in principles of toxicology and pharmacology, a wide variety of information sources and educative

5. Paraffin is perhaps the most dangerous substance encountered in everyday life. The widespread use of paraffin as a heat source makes it the most common cause of poisoning, both when drunk by children or in adulterated alcoholic drinks (or, in the absence of other suitably intoxicating drinks, by desperate drunkards) and as carbon monoxide poisoning from poorly functioning heaters. Paraffin accounts for almost half of hospital admissions for poisoning (Stewart et al. 2000, 417).

6. Most poisoning with toxic chemicals in South Africa occurs through the misuse, deliberate and accidental, of agricultural herbicides and pesticides on farms; there are comparatively few cases in other industries (Stewart et al. 2000, 418).

life experiences teach of the dangers of household and industrial poisons and the powers of medicinal drugs. Interpretations of the power of *muthi* are shaped by this toxicological and pharmacological landscape as much as by traditions of medication or stories of witchcraft and the miraculous powers of *inyangas*. Few people in Soweto, however, would accept the proposition that the same approach to understanding household chemicals and pharmaceuticals constitutes an adequate way of reckoning the powers of *muthi,* either in its destructive or in its healing dimensions.

Despite a widespread concern about the malicious use of *muthi,* the forensic toxicology evidence suggests that when people want to poison themselves or others they generally use commercially available poisons such as Robertson's Rattex, a commonplace domestic rodenticide, rather than varieties of *muthi* (Stewart et al. 2000). Malicious individuals in South Africa no doubt attempt to achieve their ends by means of *muthi.* Yet, while there is no shortage of evidence in the form of suffering and misfortune to make their imaginings of *muthi*'s efficacy seem plausible, very little actual poisoning with varieties of *muthi* occurs other than through the inept ministrations of healers and efforts at self-medication gone awry—a major cause of hospitalization.[7] In one recent and widely publicized attempt to use *muthi* to kill an enemy, for example, the failure of the herbs to work effectively resulted in the consulting "*sangoma*" having to beat the victim to death with a blunt instrument.[8] A significant and growing body of literature documents the efficacy and toxicity of "traditional medicine." I have been unable to find, however, any references to what might be termed "indigenous toxicology" or the art of making poisons other than passing references in ethnographic texts to healers' awareness of various plants' toxicity (Bryant 1970, 21) and colonial-era references to the poison-tipped arrows used by "Bushmen" (Bunn 1996). Yet, just as the scientific basis for the medicinal properties of traditional healers' *muthi* akin to biomedical pharmaceuticals has become an article of faith in postapartheid South Africa, so

7. There is some debate over the incidence of poisoning from "traditional medicines" in South Africa. Recent studies have suggested that it is far less than the "50% of deaths among black South Africans" that was previously cited in toxicology textbooks (du Plooy et al. 2001).

8. On January 14, 2003, "Pretoria housewife" Bettie Lotter and two accomplices were convicted of murdering her husband and sentenced to life imprisonment. One of the accomplices was a "Mozambican sangoma" from whom the housewife had purchased *muthi* with which to kill her husband. When his *muthi* failed to have the desired effect, Mrs. Lotter evidently employed the *sangoma*'s services to beat the husband to death (SAPA 2003b).

no one I know in Soweto doubts that the malicious arts of manufacturing *muthi* are underpinned by a body of "scientific" knowledge akin to that informing the manufacture of industrial toxins.

"African Science" and Witchcraft

In everyday talk about witchcraft and healing, "African science" serves as a basic reference point for reckonings of the potentials of secret African knowledge and skills. "African science" in everyday talk occupies a place alongside the miracles of Scripture and the magic of what is usually referred to as Western or White science in its ability to transform the world in mysterious ways. African science and White science constitute two distinct aspects of human power to understand and shape the world. Living in a world where the miracles of computers, the remote control, and mobile telephones are everyday realities, and where images of nuclear explosions and space travel are commonplace, no one doubts the power of science to effect action at a distance and transform the world and all who live in it. Nor would many doubt the power of God and the devil to transcend the ordinary laws of physics in performing their miracles.

The fact that no one seems to know for certain how any of this is achieved is of little consequence. As a young high school student once told me: "To my personal point of view, I think physical science, or physics, goes hand in hand with African physical science. Why I'm saying that is that physical science, well it is approved, and it is done by different nations, like Greeks, Americans. But it is in a modern way. There are labs, there are laboratories. With us, we don't have laboratories. It is done in an olden way. But it goes hand in hand." By "hand in hand" he meant they are equal partners in explaining and shaping the world.

Commodities embodying Western science, classes in physical science taught in schools, the prevailing imagery of industrial and technological power and the people responsible for it, and the doctors staffing clinics and hospitals have an irreducibly alien feel in this context. They are not indigenous, not African. They are "things of Whites," in the local parlance. Even when the scientists or doctors are black and African, they are not thought of as practicing *African* science.[9] Most people have only the vaguest appre-

9. There is no reason to presume that Africans working within the medical system as doctors, nurses, and technicians are completely severed from all cultural forms and practices of the world in which they live, nor that their professional practice and personal lives conform seamlessly with the ideological stipulations of "scientific" medicine such that they would automatically treat all popular understandings of suffering and illness as "supersti-

ciation of what scientific inquiry entails. Pitifully few high school students graduate with adequate mastery of mathematics and science to proceed to university-level studies. Of the more than 400,000 African candidates taking the national matriculation examinations in the year 2000, only 20,243 attempted the "higher grade" of mathematics required for university-level science studies, and only 3,128 passed (Republic of South Africa 2001, 13). Though the objects of "modern technology" are ubiquitous, scientific theories and methods remain a mystery for most.

African science, that body of knowledge my young friend imagined as walking hand in hand with Western science, is equally mysterious, though for a different reason. African science is secret knowledge. This secrecy is its essential core. Some have argued that secrecy has been necessary to protect indigenous knowledge from exploitation and denigration by Whites. Participants in discussions with the Portfolio Committee on Arts, Culture, Science, and Technology on indigenous knowledge systems, for example, "argued that the reason why indigenous people originally introduced secrecy and sacredness, was to protect indigenous knowledge from misappropriation and scrutiny by missionaries" (Portfolio Committee on Arts 2000, para. 11.2). Be that as it may, however, secrecy is also consonant with a great many features of ritual knowledge in which mysterious powers are mobilized. The fact that African science, with its "olden ways," is practiced in secret broadens the field of imagination in which the potential powers of *muthi* and the people who deploy it play out.

Even the most passionate advocate of the power of secret African science will concede that it is less effective than Western science in building industrial technologies and national prosperity and in making wars and conquering peoples. Yet Western science seems irrelevant to the everyday misery and suffering of individuals and their families. As the young man quoted above put it, "science can't prove anything about my self. It's got to do with the planets, the whole universe." The healer who can throw the

tion"—a superstition that they, as medical practitioners, are supposed to be above. A survey of black medical students' attitudes to witchcraft in the early 1980s at the Medical University of South Africa, Medunsa, found that the majority of them did not doubt the powers of witches (Elliot 1984). Many important questions concerning African medical practice in South Africa remain unexamined in the literature of medical anthropology, such as: How are meaningful diagnoses made and communicated to patients living in a world of witches? How are treatment options and drug-prescribing practices influenced by expectations deriving from "traditional" medical experiences of doctors and patients? How are practices of self-medication among African patients shaped by lessons learned in consultations with Western and with traditional practitioners?

bones to divine the nature of a person's problems, problems created by a witch using *muthi,* is far more powerful when it comes to proving things about the "self." In speculation about the powers of witchcraft, no one will admit to having mastered African science or publicly pronounce upon its precepts or demonstrate its techniques to public scrutiny and empirical testing. To doubt that it is every bit as powerful as White science, however, is tantamount to betraying a lack of faith in Africa and Africans. When one must worry about the ability of others to cause harm with dangerous substances in contemporary Soweto, more often than not African science represents the source of the powers that must be reckoned with. Obviously, however, because the witchcraft that consists of "poisoning" by *muthi* is practiced in secrecy, little can be publicly known about it—not so the properties of its diametric opposite: medicinal *muthi.*

Faith in the power of African science can best be seen in talk about the scientific status of traditional healing and indigenous medicine. When substances categorized as *muthi* are considered as medicine, their powers are universally assumed by black South Africans to be open to scientific confirmation. A great many black South Africans and sympathetic white people consider proving the pharmacological effectiveness of *muthi* part of the project of restoring the respect that should be accorded "African culture" as an "indigenous knowledge system" long denigrated by the West and Whites through centuries of colonization (Serote 1998). Although some critics argue that this research is really part of a "biopiracy" conspiracy organized in tandem with international pharmaceutical corporations to make "indigenous medicine knowledge" more amenable to exploitation by drug manufacturers (Rees 1999), the press regularly carries stories with headlines such as "*Muti* Passes the Science Test" (Bishop 1997), usually quoting a traditional healer uttering words to the effect of "we told you so."

"African Science" and "Indigenous Knowledge Systems"

In 1987, the eminent Sowetan medical practitioner, community leader during the 1976 Soweto Uprising, and businessman Ntatho Motlana gave an address to the graduating class of medical students at the University of the Witwatersrand. In his address, Motlana launched what has since become a much quoted denunciation of traditional healing. Motlana remains one of the few prominent Africans in South Africa willing to take a public stand skeptical of the wisdom of traditional healing. His argument in this speech is worth considering in some detail because it expresses a radically modernist perspective on traditional healing that, though still widespread (particularly among white doctors), is politically difficult, if not impossible, to articulate in these times.

Motlana argued that "the scientific basis for traditional medicine has not been established, that most of it was based on superstition and meaningless pseudo psychological mumbo jumbo that was often positively harmful" (1988, 17). His attack on traditional healing was launched in the aftermath of World Health Organization (WHO) policies advocating official recognition of these healers. According to Motlana, "African health professionals trained in scientific medicine" had opposed the efforts of well-meaning but misguided Europeans and Americans to promote the so-called indigenous doctor in framing WHO policy. He began his address by praising the European missionaries who worked to eradicate "superstition" and by denouncing those well-intentioned liberals "who want to take us back into the Dark Ages of Medicine by romanticizing the half naked drummer of the night." These latter, he insisted, "choose to forget that the so-called advanced nations of the West also passed through an age when they believed that diseases were caused by mists arising from marshes; they too believed in witchcraft, and it took centuries of turmoil, conflict, of rejecting scientific discoveries (and even executing innovators) to eradicate it" (1988, 17). People who insisted that in order to cure the "whole person" of the "Black African" it was necessary to "pander to his nonsensical superstitious concerns" were attempting to "lock the Black man permanently into the 12th century." Traditional healers, in Motlana's view, were "dangerous people" who should be locked up under the provisions of anti-witchcraft legislation, and he noted approvingly Samora Machel's policy of incarcerating them in reeducation camps. "Above all," he argued, "health care professionals—including psychologists—must stop romanticizing the evil depredations of the sangoma" in order to "wean our Black (and White) patients from the tyranny of superstition" (1988, 18).

Most of Motlana's address to the graduating doctors was taken up with this strident attack upon superstition, as well as its white liberal supporters. Toward the end of the speech, however, he changed the focus of his remarks somewhat and set out a project that seems remarkably prescient in the light of postapartheid experience: "One often gets the feeling that some of my comrades in the struggle and in the professions, thrashing around for some meaningful contribution to the total sum of human achievement by Blacks, mistakenly latch onto indigenous medicine as part of that contribution. If so, let us first subject indigenous medicine to rigorous scientific examination before there is the beating of drums in the Great Hall of our University" (1988, 18). In the postapartheid era, when Motlana's former "comrades" gained office in the national state (Motlana was Mandela's personal physician), they proceeded to foster efforts at "scientific examination" of indigenous medicines. Progress in the enterprise to date has been modest. The conviction that there is a scientific basis to traditional medicine waiting to be recovered, however, remains an article of faith.

The effort to reveal the scientific foundations of traditional medicine is part of a larger cultural politics in South Africa. Beginning in the late 1990s, African intellectuals and political leaders in South Africa began efforts, under the general rubric of the "African Renaissance," to foster the development of systematic knowledge about traditional medicine in terms of "indigenous knowledge systems" (IKS). The concept of IKS owes its genesis to a confluence of intellectual and political movements in the last quarter of the twentieth century emerging in the aftermath of decolonization out of the ecological movement's concern for sustainable environmental management, dissatisfaction with prevailing models of economic development for the Third World, and concerns with the cultural "survival" and rights of minority indigenous peoples within larger national states. In the 1990s, the rapid development of biotechnology industries and research into scientific medical uses of traditional remedies from different parts of the globe spawned debates over questions of intellectual property and the appropriate remuneration of indigenous peoples for biological materials and knowledge exploited from their territories.

By the early twenty-first century, while much of the discussion of IKS remained inflected with countercultural romanticism about the essential unity of native peoples with nature, the acronym IKS had become part of the ready coin of international organizations and a focus of the World Intellectual Property Organization (WIPO), a United Nations intergovernmental agency, which in 1998 and 1999 sent out fact-finding missions to Asia, Africa, and Latin America. And while the origins of the idea of indigenous knowledge lay in a concern with local people's particular and culturally embedded understandings of themselves and their place in the world, "IKS" now serves as a convenient shorthand for categorizing aspects of local cultures in terms of global schemes. The World Bank, for example, issues "Knowledge Packs" as part of its "Indigenous Knowledge Program for Development" to "provide users with quick access to synthesized information by country or selected thematic area" (World Bank, Sub-Saharan Africa, 2001).[10] There is considerable debate in development

10. As of July 2001, the World Bank's Indigenous Knowledge Pack for South Africa contained little other than a summary of an article from the *Sowetan* reporting research

circles over whether indigenous knowledge, which by definition is context specific, can be generalized in the manner of science, which, though it may have emerged in particular cultural contexts, is by definition independent of context.[11]

The South African discussion of IKS has been stimulated by the Portfolio Committee on Arts, Culture, Science, and Technology, chaired by the ANC poet and novelist Mongane Wally Serote. Serote is an enthusiast of the idea of IKS. In a paper presented in 1998 to a roundtable on intellectual property and indigenous peoples organized by the WIPO, Serote argued: "Indigenous knowledge and technologies that were denied, destroyed and suppressed in the past will form the basis of our rebirth. . . . Indigenous knowledge, folklore and technologies have the potential to assist in the rebirth of our nation" (1998). Serote reported to the WIPO meeting that "a programme is currently under way to harness this potential [of IKS for nation building], and the very institutions that were created to maintain apartheid—the Science Councils and the black universities—have been brought into the process in a massive, visionary exercise of transformation whose outcome will be the economic empowerment of South Africa's rural poor" (1998).

To this end, the National Research Foundation was chartered in 1998 to "support and promote research, in order to facilitate the creation of knowledge, innovation and development in all fields of science and technology, including indigenous knowledge." In the financial year 2000/2001 R 10 million was set aside for IKS projects, although only R 5.4 million was actually allocated to fifty-four successful projects.[12] The use of the term "IKS" in postapartheid South Africa is more than a little ironic. Not only does the

---

from Stellenbosch University on the use of the "African potato" in the treatment of HIV and other viral infections, with the following appended: "*Lesson:* Combining Western and traditional medicines in treating terminal illnesses may help developing [*sic*] efficient treatments" (World Bank, Sub-Saharan Africa, 2001, emphasis in original). The African potato, *Hypoxis hemerocallidea*, has been hailed in the popular press as a "miracle *muthi*" after tumor-suppressing and immune-system-stimulating properties of its phenolic chemical constituents were isolated and tested, although as the chemist who initially identified them has noted: "with the present fragmentary knowledge regarding the effects on the human body of the complex mixture of compounds present in the whole extract of the *Hypoxis* plant, we would advise caution in hurriedly 'taking to the bottle'" (Drewes and Horn 2002, 4).

11. For surveys of debates on IKS, see Ellen and Harris 1996, 2000; Rouse 1999. For examples of attempts to make the notion of IKS relevant to South Africa, see Odora Hoppers 2002c.

12. George Mukuka, IKS manager, National Research Foundation, July 19, 2001, personal communication.

program postulate notions of cultural distinctiveness that the architects of apartheid would have found most agreeable, but the programs are advocated by African intellectuals and political leaders who consider themselves indigenous while representing (or being representative of) the majority of the population. On the one hand, these intellectuals experience aspects of the well-attested derogation of African culture by Whites and express the need to restore respect and dignity to their own traditions and culture. On the other hand, they are mostly city-dwelling educated professionals who operate in their professional lives for the most part in cultural milieus that are indistinguishable from those of their white peers but that are worlds away from the life of the rural village.

Since the late 1990s, research into the health benefits of traditional medicines has become more of a priority for the Medical Research Council of South Africa and university departments of pharmacy. In 1997, for example, a "traditional medicines" (TRAMED) research project was established by the Universities of Cape Town and the Western Cape with the support of the Medical Research Council to, among other things, create a database of traditional medicines for eastern and southern Africa; conduct laboratory screening of traditional medicines for malaria and tuberculosis; and develop systems for scientific understanding of the action and uses of "essential" traditional medicines in the prevention and treatment of disease.[13]

Although certain plants may have beneficial bioactive properties, identifying medicinal properties of *muthi* is complicated because different plants are often combined in making *muthi,* they are prepared in infusions and decoctions with little regard to standardized dosage, and they are administered according to methods such as drinking and regurgitating, all of which makes it virtually impossible to determine their health-giving effects with any sort of scientific rigor. Recipes for particular remedies are usually treated as trade secrets by healers and often incorporate animal products and industrial chemicals (Stewart, Steenkamp, and Zuckerman 1998). *Isihlambezo,* for example, a variety of *muthi* prescribed for pregnant women, is widely used by African women, has some beneficial effects, but is potentially harmful to both fetus and mother (Varga and Veale 1997). A literature review on plants used during pregnancy found that "at least 57 different plants are used by black South African women either as antenatal remedies or, more specifically, to induce or augment labor. Among these, 16 have been reported to be toxic. The uterotonic effects of only a few of these plants have been studied" (Veale, Furman, and Oliver 1992). A later study

13. See the Web site http://www.uct.ac.za/depts/pha/satmerg.htm.

by Veale et al. assessed some of the plants specifically used as oxytocic remedies (to "induce or augment labor or control postpartum bleeding") and found positive effects on the uteri of laboratory rats, but the researchers remained cautious about the dangers inherent in the difficulty of controlling dosages in practice as well as possible toxic interactions with other ingredients in the *muthi* (Veale et al. 1998).

The vast majority of black South Africans would applaud this endeavor to verify the scientific basis of traditional healing. In everyday parlance, such as I have heard over the years in Soweto, what the political elite call "indigenous knowledge systems" pertaining to "indigenous medical systems" are referred to as "African science." African science in everyday talk, however, is postulated not only as the scientific foundation of healing but also as the witchcraft against which healers must fight. In common talk, witches as well as healers are referred to as "African scientists." As we have seen, the dialectical nature of *muthi* means that for every powerful healing substance or technique an opposing evil power is presumed. The new investment in uncovering the scientific bases of traditional healing, then, also contributes to the plausibility of suppositions about the abilities of persons to cause harm to others by means of powers—"evil forces"—categorized under the rubric of healing's antithesis: witchcraft.

7

DEATH, POLLUTION,
AND THE DANGERS OF DIRT

A Polluted President?

On the eve of his eighty-fifth birthday in July 2003, former president Nelson Mandela made a speech in the Johannesburg Planetarium announcing a new satellite television network for schools that had been launched in his honor. In the course of the speech, in which he dedicated himself to spending "the rest of my days trying to help secure a more educated and healthier South Africa," he reiterated his oft-repeated plea for people to overcome the stigma associated with AIDS. A local press report of the speech included the following account:

> Dressed in a black trademark Madiba shirt, Mandela told a story about the stigma surrounding HIV/Aids.
>
> He said one day he was in a province run by a "progressive premier" when he was shown a family of three young children whose parents had died of Aids-related diseases, and were forced to fend for themselves.
>
> According to Mandela, the premier and officials of that province invited him to accompany them to provide the children with food parcels. But when they got to the house, they called the children out and threw the food parcels at them without venturing any closer.
>
> "I was disappointed and I went inside the house and spent half an hour with those children. When I came out nobody wanted to come near me," he said.
>
> Mandela said the crowd were singing songs about him outside when he came out of the house, but when he attempted to approach them, they all kept their distance.
>
> "I had to go back to my car," he said. (SAPA 2003a, 1)

The available press reports of the speech offer no commentary on this story, nor do they report Mandela as commenting upon the meaning of the story or suggesting it was anything other than an example of prejudice. The scene it describes, however, is extraordinary.

Mandela is a legendary figure in South Africa, a person whom almost everyone treats with the utmost devotion, indeed reverence. For the neighbors of those three young AIDS orphans to pass up an opportunity to be close to Mandela, to touch him and bask in his aura, for them to back away from him when he approached them even though they were singing songs in his praise, suggests they must have had very powerful motives. I cannot pretend to know exactly what those motives were, especially since Mandela was careful not to mention where this incident occurred. And I wonder how many of these people would have been able to give a convincing account of their fears to Mandela himself. I doubt they feared catching AIDS from him. Virtually everyone in South Africa knows how HIV/AIDS is transmitted. And I doubt their behavior can be understood as a product of stigma associating AIDS with sexual immorality since they surely would not have suspected Mandela was up to anything improper with the children and the children themselves are merely victims of their parents' illness. Nor, I am sure, would anyone have feared witchcraft in this instance. Yet Mandela was clearly being viewed as the bearer of some invisible and dangerous force. He was contaminated by contact with these children, but with what?

The incident Mandela recalled in his speech did not occur in Soweto. If he had visited orphans in Soweto, though there may have been neighbors who felt as those in his story did, more would have been ignorant or disdainful of whatever it was that was holding the others in thrall. Yet in Soweto, too, people live with a lively sense of the dangers of contamination, particularly from invisible forces associated with death. When people return from the cemetery for a funeral feast, for example, they are greeted at the home of the deceased with basins of water containing a slice of aloe to wash their hands in. Were such basins not to be provided, mourners would be affronted not so much by the breach of protocol or by the inconvenience of having to eat without having washed their hands, which is not such a problem in any case as cutlery is always provided at such feasts. Rather, they would be outraged by the threat to public safety posed by the negligent family, who were putting the community as a whole at risk by exposing them to the dangers of pollution without offering the means of cleansing.

These fears are not the same as those relating to witchcraft. They are, however, related to the general phenomenon I am calling spiritual insecurity, which involves the sense of exposure to invisible forces. The principal difference is that the invisible forces active in the case of witchcraft, those involving *muthi,* possess agency, agency that malefactors and healers alike interact with. The invisible forces operative in the case of pollution, however, are inert. They are dangerous nonetheless. The best way to understand fears arising from pollution is to consider everyday practices relating to cleaning and dirt. From there we can begin to speculate upon the dangers connected with invisible pollutants such as might have been clinging to the person of Nelson Mandela that day.

Everyday Dirt and the Necessities of Cleansing

Of all the forces that cause harm, those embodied in dirt are the most plentiful. Dirt is ubiquitous. Anything can become polluting merely by being in the wrong place at the wrong time. As Mary Douglas put it: "uncleanness is matter out of place" (1966, 41). Legions of Sowetan women with their brooms and washcloths would agree. Dirt disturbs domestic order and symbolic order alike, taints food, soils clothes, and interferes with the proper functioning of machines and other systems. Dirt in your carburetor will cause your engine to run poorly. Dirt in your stomach will surely have a similar effect upon you. The ordinary functioning of bodies, and everything else, creates filth: *makaka,* "shit." The untoward accident also makes a mess. Dirt has to be dealt with. Just as the sources of pollution are everywhere, so the work of cleansing is constant. As Keitumetse used to say when I teased her about the futility of constantly cleaning the house and washing the painted concrete stoop, which would soon be soiled: "I can't avoid it. I can't prevent it. I'll clean it again tomorrow" (Ashforth 2000a, 136). To begin to understand the forces acting on life to cause harm, then, we should start by thinking about dirt.

Dirt comes in a multitude of forms. In winter, the dust of Soweto blows into everything and is cleaned out endlessly. In summer, when the dust turns to mud, the work of cleaning continues. Though the burdens of this labor fall heaviest upon women and girls, everyone knows the importance of cleanliness. Children are scrubbed daily for school, weekly for church. Young men lovingly shine cars—even polishing the tires before they plough through the dust. Dirt and the battle against it are the inescapable accompaniments of life. And the labor of cleaning is a serious matter. Women who neglect to keep their houses clean, whose front stoops are not regularly polished, and whose yards and street frontages are not regularly swept are guilty of a moral lapse more serious than mere slovenliness. One of the worst insults that can be leveled, one woman against another, is the charge: "She's a dirty somebody."

The battle against dirt is unceasing. The power of dirt to cause harm, however, though serious, is limited. For dirt is inert. It lacks agency. Dirt cannot act autonomously, nor can it work in concert with other agents toward a common end or execute orders at the behest of a principal. Substances that can act in such ways, substances that fall into the categories of poison and medicine under the general rubric of *muthi,* are far more problematic than dirt. Polluting substances can, of course, be placed deliberately where they will cause harm. Once so placed, however, they do not act of their own accord. Mere presence is the effective factor in dirt's fouling things up. The presence of dirt, however, is not always apparent. Not all dirt is visible. It may be microscopic. It may be hidden. It may, indeed, be immaterial—such as the "filthy" thoughts that are believed by some to be able to pollute a mind or the invisible pollution emanating from the dead. But dirt harms none the less for its invisibility. Indeed, the invisible sources of pollution are the most dangerous since they are the most difficult to rectify.

Popular understandings of pollution, contamination, and infection in southern Africa have been shaped for many generations by a powerful confluence of ideas, practices, habits, commodities, institutions, and rituals that converge to stimulate diverse understandings and practices regarding the dangers posed by material substances. These derive from, among other sources, local traditions (H. Ngubane 1977, chap. 5; E. Green 1999; Hammond-Tooke 1989b, chap. 6), Christian missionary teachings (Moffat 1842, 506; Comaroff and Comaroff 1997), biomedical notions and institutions (Manganyi 1974; Department of Health 1997), multinational corporations in the business of producing and marketing cleaning products and toiletries (T. Burke 1996), as well as, more recently, the welter of talk about viruses, immune systems, and genetics in popular media during a time of plague —not to mention the global trade in "alternative" therapies. Multitudes of specialists claim expertise in interpreting the dangers people face from harmful polluting substances, offering—usually for a fee—diverse strategies for managing the risk of harm, repairing the damage caused, and protecting against future suffering. Dealing with dirt is big business.

Bodies and Spirits and the Work of Cleaning

The relationship of persons to dirt in Soweto as elsewhere is experienced primarily as one of labor—the work of cleaning. This work is aided by substances—cleaning agents—possessing properties serving to remove dirt.

Just as dirt comes in different forms, so cleansers take different forms to secure the removal of different kinds of dirt in different ways. For most ordinary cleaning work, commercially produced soap and related detergents have driven most older indigenous cleansers and cleaning practices from the domestic scene. Soap is the paradigmatic cleanser. Multinational corporations have been advertising the power of soap in these parts for more than a century. Sunlight Soap is the most common cleanser. Used in even the poorest homes, Sunlight is ubiquitous.[1] In their embrace of soap, however, Africans have found a multitude of uses for commercial cleaning products which the manufacturers could never have imagined, and they have incorporated older practices of purification into schemes consonant with the properties of soap. Sunlight serves in washing bodies—inside, as well as out—clothes, dishes, cars, and anything else that might need scrubbing. Prophet-healers of the independent churches use Sunlight, fortified by prayer, to cleanse people of evil spirits. After washing with Sunlight—whether to clean a body of ordinary dirt, invisible pollutants, or evil spirits—people smear themselves with Vaseline. It protects the skin and prevents chapping. It also holds off evil spirits a while longer and ensures good luck.

For many generations, traditional healers have emphasized the importance of bodily purification, plying their patients with purgatives, emetics, and enemas for a wide variety of ailments and indispositions (Bryant 1970, 23). Most of the healing procedures that are today spoken of as "traditional," whether self-administered or directed by a professional healer such as an *inyanga,* involve, among other things, one or another of these purification methods in order to remove harmful pollutants and invisible agents from the body. Conventional techniques of traditional healing focus on the work of purifying the body, strengthening the person in all aspects of his or her being (bodily, spiritual, and social), and protecting against further contamination or attack (Conco 1972; Gumede 1990; Hammond-Tooke 1989b; du Toit 1998, 146). The techniques of purification are similar whether the object of the exertions is removing pollution, poison, or evil spirits. In the latter cases, however, purification is only part of a broader struggle against

---

1. Sunlight is still packaged in large green blocks wrapped in distinctive yellow wrappers in a manner reminiscent of William Lever's 1885 original, which he used to build one of the world's largest industrial empires (and which in this archaic form is now marketed only in places like India and Africa). For an account of the cultural transformations wrought by soap and other cleaning commodities, supported by the webs of commerce, doctrines of cleanliness, and banners of advertisers in this region during colonial times, see T. Burke 1996.

invisible agencies operating through material substances and spiritual beings. In struggles against evil spirits, prophet-healers in Christian churches
engage in analogous purifying, strengthening, and protective practices, deploying water purified by prayer and a variety of sanctified cleaning agents
known generically as *isiwasho* (a Zuluized version of the English word
"wash"), of which water mixed with ash is the most common, followed by
Sunlight soap.[2]

Everyday practices devoted to preserving good health as well as self-
medication in remedy of minor bodily ailments make bodily cleansing,
inside as well as out, a priority. Few people doubt that internal organs
must be regularly cleaned, particularly the "stomach," by which term is
commonly meant the entire digestive system. Regular vomiting to keep the
stomach "clean," induced either with saltwater or *muthi* purchased from an
inyanga or an "African chemist," is widely assumed to be an essential part
of a sound health regimen in these parts. Bile is said by many to be particularly noxious and important to cleanse from the system.[3] Familiarity with
this substance, with which I had previously had only an abstract acquaintance before living in Soweto, is doubtless heightened by the practice of extracting the gallbladders from animals slaughtered for ancestors. Ancestors
are said to be fond of the taste of gall.[4] Suzanne Leclerc-Madlala reports
that the concept of bile in popular Zulu conceptions of the body encompasses far more than merely a liquid secreted by the liver and stored in the
gallbladder. People she knew in KwaZulu-Natal in the early 1990s spoke of
the stuff as a "bad, dirty and potentially toxic" substance flowing through
the body, manifesting its presence in pus, sores, phlegm, mucus, and discharges, and needing to be controlled through regular and thorough cleansing of the digestive system (Leclerc-Madlala 1994, 4).

People lacking an elaborate theory of the nature of bile are nonetheless aware of the need to clean the stomach and other organs. Constipation,
diarrhea, or other digestive upsets suggest a pressing need for cleansing. Commercial laxatives are sold at every *spaza* (tuck) shop and grocery
store, along with aspirins and antacids, all of which are said to serve cleans-

2. For discussion of purification practices within these churches, see Oosthuizen 1992.

3. A survey of 380 patients attending a Natal primary health care clinic in the early
1990s, for example, found that 14.5 percent "spontaneously developed a hypothesis about
their illness . . . that 'bile' was the cause," particularly when gastrointestinal symptoms were
present (although four of the thirty-three women who felt afflicted by "bile" turned out to
be pregnant) (Pillay and Akoo 1993).

4. The gallbladder is also used by *ngoma* initiates, who inflate and attach one or more
to their hair (Berglund 1976, 130).

ing purposes. Enemas are also a regular feature of many health maintenance and self-medication regimes. Most enemas, apparently, are made
with soapy or salty water, though varieties of *muthi* are also used, as are, occasionally, commercial antiseptics like Dettol or Jeyes Fluid. Sometimes,
according to the medical literature on bowel disorders, enemas are pow-
ered by an array of alarming substances, including caustics, bleach, vinegar,
potassium dichromate, copper sulfate, and potassium permanganate (Dunn
et al. 1991; I. Segal et al. 1979; I. Segal and Tim 1979).[5] Vaginal discharges
are also commonly taken as a sign of a body in need of internal cleaning.[6]
In the past, menstruation was surrounded by extensive prohibitions and
taboos.[7] Few younger women these days would find the old taboos about
menstruation anything other than absurd, although their mothers might
still be disturbed to see menstruating daughters handling food or passing
through a vegetable garden.

"Dirty blood" is often invoked as the cause of ill health and indisposition, being at the root of a host of everyday complaints, notably headaches,
as well as more serious illnesses such as HIV. Blood, however, is difficult
to clean. *Inyangas* prick, incise, and cup their patients to remove impurities from and strengthen the blood (Gumede 1990, 89). Sweating over an
herbal steam bath cleanses impurities that may have lodged in the skin, and
steam inhaled into the lungs is also said to purify the blood. Many people
consume pharmaceuticals, such as the antibiotics that are routinely prescribed by clinics and are readily available through informal channels,
in the expectation that they are cleaning blood and other internal organs
(Leclerc-Madlala 1994).[8] Injections, however, are generally considered

5. A 1978 survey of patients at Soweto's Baragwanath Hospital found that 62.8 percent of patients not suffering gastrointestinal diseases admitted the regular use of enemas
(I. Segal et al. 1979, 195). The authors of this study concluded that "there are relatively few
complications associated with these enemas, but those that do occur can be extremely serious, and at times even fatal" (1979, 195). Enemas are also often administered to infants and
children (Booyens 1989; Lusu, Buhlungu, and Grant 2001; Moore and Moore 1998).

6. Several studies stimulated by the AIDS epidemic report that most commercial sex
workers understand their genital health in terms of vaginal cleanliness and regularly engage
in vaginal douching, often with cleaning agents such as Dettol or bleach (Morar and Abdool
Karim 1998), particularly when they suffer malodorous discharges (Josephine Malala 2001).

7. For an account of Zulu attitudes to menstruating women from the 1970s, see H. Ngubane 1977, 79. For an account dating from the first decade of the twentieth century, see
Junod 1910, 142.

8. South Africans have a healthy appetite for Western medicines. According to figures
from medical insurance providers, South Africans consume twice as many pharmaceuticals
as the international average (B. Jordan 2002).

most effective for blood cleaning, as they get directly to the blood (Gumede 1990, 40). Many a white doctor has been mystified by African patients who seem never as fully satisfied with medical treatment as after a painful injection (Fernandes 1970).

Sex is an activity that excites fears of dirt and pollution everywhere. The literature on "traditional" ideas about sexuality in this part of the world makes much of African accounts of the dangers inherent in pollution from acts of sexual congress. Schapera, for example, reports that among the Ba-Kgatla in the 1930s the sex act was surrounded by numerous taboos and restrictions, particularly concerning the dangers of "heat" produced by sex (hot people are dangerous to others) and "blood" being exchanged during sex (semen being conceptualized as a form of blood) (Schapera 1950, 194–201; Verryn 1981). Bryant describes Zulu fears in the late nineteenth century of contracting "a mysterious malady accompanied by a pertinacious cough, shortness of breath and other troubles" if men have sex with menstruating women (Bryant 1949). A century later Harriet Ngubane noticed similar ideas in KwaZulu as well as the general notion that "men, as well as women, are considered polluted during the day following sexual intercourse" (Ngubane 1977, 79). Berglund has a long discussion of the ways certain Zulu men interpreted the dangers of bewitched semen (Berglund 1976, 332). Prior to the explosion of HIV/AIDS and the spread of AIDS awareness at the end of the 1990s, I never noticed that the young people I was with in Soweto were worrying much about the mystical dangers of the sex act or the possibility that the bodily fluids exchanged therein might be a dangerous source of pollution. They were hardly even careful enough about avoiding the risk of unwanted pregnancy. Indeed, the teenage girls in my street used to joke with each other that the best cure for pimples was "Cerebos," by which they meant—playing on the brand name of a table salt packaged in a large, white, phallus-shaped bottle—semen. Since the advent of AIDS awareness, however, sex has become deadly again.

Environmental contaminants are not generally regarded by Sowetans as a particularly dangerous source of harm. Townships were not built so that their residents could revel in the beauty and majesty of nature. By laws restricting their movements and residence, generations of township residents were also denied the sort of relationship to urban places that would enhance regard for the environmental health of public space. While most private homes and yards are kept immaculately clean in Soweto, household detritus will be dumped at the street corner or in the nearest vacant lot, whether or not the authorities plan on collecting it. Young boys love warming themselves at night around a bonfire of burning tires, adding plumes of toxic smoke to the general atmosphere of coal-fired smog. Few think twice about tossing a can out of a car's window or draining their sump oil into the dust. Smokers know they are chancing their health, though for most the risk of lung cancer seems slight compared with the other dangers threatening life.

Invisible contaminants are for many a far more dangerous form of environmental pollution. Some people worry about accidental contamination from contact with invisible forces present in *muthi* discarded by others. Members of healing churches, notably those known as "Apostolic" and "Zionist," fear inadvertently accumulating evil spirits about them in the course of their daily lives and are usually cleansed thereof with copious quantities of holy water when entering church grounds. Evil spirits cleansed from their human hosts in the course of rituals at rivers and streams pose problems for members of these churches in their regular baptismal visits to water, so they devote much energy to cleansing themselves of such pollution. Dangerous places are feared because of the presence of potentially dangerous substances or agencies. Bodies of water where traditional healers and members of African Initiated Churches (AIC) perform rituals, for example, are potentially dangerous because of the presence of spirits and discarded *muthi,* as well as creatures such as the mystical snakes known as MaMlambo and iNkosi ya Manzi (Ashforth 1998a; Green 1997). All of these potential dangers underline the necessity of regular purification in the ordinary health maintenance routines of everyday life in order to secure well-being and good fortune.

The battle against dirt demands a combination of skill and effort, like everything else in life: skill in knowing how to clean and what cleansers to use, and work in doing it. Professional assistance is rarely sought in the work of cleaning, whether for washing a car or to remedy illness.[9] The implicit premise of the work of cleaning is that when impurities are removed, the article cleansed will be "as new." Whether scrubbing an old shirt or removing invisible impurities from the blood, the results should be the same: renovation. These results, moreover, should be achieved without undue delay. Things and people get old and die, of course, but they should still be

9. There is very little literature on the theory and practice of self-medication in South Africa despite the fact that, as a study of "African chemists" by Michele Cocks and Anthony Dold discovered, most people "purchase their own medicines without seeking advice," suggesting that they know what they need, how to use it, and what they need it for (Cocks and Dold 2000, 1511). Most of the medical literature touching on this subject focuses on cases where self-medication or "traditional" treatments go wrong (Stewart, Steenkamp, and Zuckerman 1998).

kept clean. If cleansing fails to achieve a restorative result, despite repeated applications of the cleanser, then the problem must be other than
one caused by the mere presence of an inert pollutant. In cases of illness
and bodily indisposition, the failure of cleansing to relieve malaise raises
the possibility of action by an agent or agents intent on causing deliberate
harm. Such agency—whether it be directed by human or spiritual powers
to malicious or beneficent ends (and we shall see in future chapters how
ancestors can cause their descendants harm as a punishment designed to
secure their ultimate welfare)—requires a different kind of struggle from
mere cleansing.

The widespread awareness of the risks inherent in exposure to invisible
pollutants in Soweto is not a product of complicated cultural taboos or traditions regarding ritual pollution or symbolic defilements. In the literature
relating to these matters, the ordinariness of cleansing is sometimes over-
looked in the search for "symbolic" or "ritual" significance, ignoring the
fact that everyday acts of cleansing such as washing the dishes and ritual
practices engaging the dangerous potentials of invisible pollutants can be
—and in my experience are—encompassed within the same conceptual
scheme without reference to ontological differences. As Gabriel Setiloane
pointed out: "Anthropologists make much about rituals that are performed
in connection with the birth of the child. . . . But this kind of fumigation of
people and the hut is normal procedure in cleansing and purification. It can
be compared to hospital use of Dettol and other disinfectants; however, impurities, germs and infections causing disease in the African context extend
far beyond the physical" (1988, 44). That anthropologists are usually more
comfortable in reducing this extension "beyond the physical" to the ontological status of the "symbolic" should not let us lose sight of the fact that
such an imposition may mislead as much as it enlightens.

Death, Dying, and Pollution

Death presents the most pressing questions about dirt and contamination
because the survivors have to deal with the decaying body. The potential
danger posed by the presence of dead bodies is self-evidently extreme—
more death—but the nature of the pollution they embody is, paradoxically,
both obvious and mysterious. In death, the living person is transformed
into a vile rotting mess while at the same time becoming an invisible spiritual being. Few younger Sowetans are well informed about the meaning and
purpose of the complex rules of ritual procedure that used to govern the
process of dying, the handling of corpses, mourning, and burials in African

villages and homesteads such as are reported in the old ethnographies.[10] Older people, particularly those who grew up in rural areas, tend to have more extensive understandings of ritual procedure and the related risks of pollution from death. Virtually every death in the city, as well as most in rural areas, is now a matter that is routinely handled by paid professionals employed by hospitals, emergency medical services, police, and undertakers governed by laws and regulations founded upon biomedical principles of public health and sanitation. The obvious dangers of contamination by decomposing bodies are taken care of. Mysterious dangers, however, remain. Although many people readily acknowledge less-than-perfect command of "culture" relating to death and dying, everyone is conscious of danger at that time.

Funerals and associated rites and rituals are generally presided over by family elders, professional undertakers, and Christian clergy. Burials take place in public cemeteries. Like most of urban life, township funerals mix indigenous traditions of various ethnic origins with European missionary and African Christian traditions shaped during the decades of oppressive White rule. They are also influenced, like the rest of life, by passing fads and fashions. Funerals are expensive. Families invest great importance in giving their loved ones a "decent" funeral and are prepared to pay substantial amounts to do so. A variant of the rotating saving and credit associations known as the Burial Society helps family members offset funeral expenses (Lukhele 1990). The form of the ceremonies and rituals are fairly constant across ethnic groups and religious denominations. A funeral will typically involve prayers for the soul of the departed—bound, most mourners hope and pray, for the Christian heaven—as well as rituals devoted to securing the place of the departed among the ranks of ancestors, remaining thereby, most are convinced, present in the lives of the living. Some mourners might also beseech the deceased in their prayers to intervene with the ancestors and God on their behalf. Funerals also involve rituals to cleanse and protect those remaining behind from any harm that might be incurred by their association with death.

10. For a compendious account of these practices, see Willoughby 1928. When our neighbors' mother died in Soweto in 1997, her daughters (then in their late twenties and early thirties) had only the vaguest ideas about how to proceed with the mourning and were berated by neighbors for not doing things "properly." Only after an elderly aunt arrived from the rural areas did anyone in the house have sufficient authority to decide how the myriad observances were to be handled. Even so, the daughters were scolded by numerous visitors for their "mistakes."

Writing of the "mental philosophy" of the Bantu in 1920, in one of the first ethnographic accounts of life in southern Africa by an African author, Samuel Modiri Molema (the Tswana scholar, medical doctor, Methodist minister, and ANC leader) noted a "peculiar dread" of "natural death and the dead":

> So far as possible they avoided introducing into their conversation anything connected with death, and the word itself was studiously avoided. Usually, too, in some tribes, when a person was dying, he was taken outside the house so that he might die outside. . . . Such personal belongings as the dead person used in life were generally buried with him, as nobody would dare use them. The whole underlying idea seems to have been a supposed infectivity of death, especially as death was always supposed to be due to witchcraft, unless it could be proved to be due to some force or violence external to the body. (1920, 174–175)

Despite the fact that the business of death and dying has been medicalized, sanitized, and commercialized, an intense, if vague, aura of danger ("infectivity")—quite distinct from the sadness and grief—still surrounds it. When mourners at a funeral return to the deceased's home from the cemetery for the customary feast—and, if they are lucky, "after-tears beers"—they wash their hands in basins of cold water in which a few slices of aloe (known as *intelezi*) soak. People close to the deceased, particularly the mother, widow, or senior female relative who presides over the mourning, are subjected to more thorough cleansing rituals. Special procedures are also observed for the washing of the shovels used to bury the deceased. A young woman I once asked about funeral washing procedures told me that the *intelezi* serves as a "special soap, a traditional cleanser to wash away bad luck." She had no idea what would happen were one to attend a funeral and not be cleansed afterward. To be in the presence of death, no matter that the body has been prepared in a funeral parlor and is housed in a coffin, is to risk being polluted.

Though no one would deny the dangers connected with the dead, explanations of the precautions vary widely. Some say there is something in the air at the graveyard that comes from dead bodies, something like a gas. Others worry about being in the presence of spirits and the souls of the deceased. Everyone agrees, however, that washing is wise after being exposed to such risks, and I have never heard of nor seen anyone defying the practice of washing hands after the burial. A woman who suffers a miscarriage should also be cleansed, both for her own good and for the protection of others. When I have asked what would happen if these cleansings were not performed, I have received different kinds of answers. Mostly people are not dogmatic about particular consequences of hygienic neglect, other than the generic "bad things," although some people are insistent that particular illnesses will result.[11]

When a person dies, healers and relatives tend to speak of the person as being called by the ancestors or God, thereby reaffirming their faith in these powers despite the failure of efforts to cure invoking their assistance. Healing is a matter of struggling against the forces seeking death as long as possible until the final moment comes and the dying person begins the transition to the status of ancestor. To pronounce before a person dies that a particular disease manifest in certain symptoms cannot ever be cured no matter what the sources of power the healer draws upon is tantamount to saying that the forces of God, the ancestors, and the medicines of the healers are inadequate to overcome the malice of the evil forces wishing harm upon a person and his or her family. Few would dare utter such a blasphemy. To name a disease as "terminal," then, to proclaim of a patient that his death is inevitable, particularly if the prognosis includes a definite prediction of the time the end will come, is as good as saying that the person suffering the disease is dead already and has either been claimed or abandoned by the forces of God and the ancestors. Never has the inevitability of death as a consequence of particular symptoms been as widely recognized in these parts as in this age of plague with HIV/AIDS, a terminal disease that has irrevocably imprinted its image as a death foretold upon the public imagination.[12] That being the case, difficult questions arise about the potential for dangerous pollution emanating from the living dead person

11. Young Shangaans-speaking schoolteachers I discussed this issue with while doing research in rural villages in the Lowveld of Limpopo Province in 2002 were adamant that people who were exposed to death, even inadvertently and unknowingly, and who were not cleansed risked contracting a particular kind of lung disease very similar to TB. They were unable to specify, however, exactly how this pollution-induced cough differed from TB. What they knew was that TB was caused by an infection and was treatable at the clinic, whereas the pollution-related illness required the intervention of a traditional healer to effect a thorough cleansing.

12. Until recently, when AIDS mortality began to be experienced on a large scale, cancer was the disease most commonly confronted as terminal. Studies of black cancer patients in South Africa suggest that the disease is highly stigmatized (Bezwoda, Colvin, and Lehoka 1997; Steyn and Muller 2000; Wright 1997). I am not aware of any studies investigating connections between the stigma surrounding terminal illness and perceptions about the possibilities of pollution emanating from the presence of the already dead.

such as the person named as suffering from HIV/AIDS. These are questions that neither biomedicine nor traditional and spiritual healing is well placed to answer since biomedicine has limited appreciation of the dangers of pollution and nonmedical healers acknowledge only a limited conception of terminal disease.

The idea of death as mysteriously polluting captures imaginations even in the absence of well-defined rules of ritual purity and pollution. Everyone knows that dirt is not always visible to the naked eye. Dust, grit, grime, and feces are but some of the manifest forms of dirt; vapors, odors, and stenches are similarly tangible. The most pernicious pollution, however, is often the least evident. Invisible forms of pollution can be the grime that accumulates through imperceptible accretion or the hidden dirt whose presence can be inferred only from its deleterious effects upon working systems, such as the dirt that causes diarrhea. Dirt can even be immaterial. When the possibility of invisible forms of pollution is conceded, however, distinguishing between the harmful effects of mere dirt and harm caused by forms of deliberate agency—such as results from contact with poisonous substances or evil spirits—becomes inherently problematic. Consequently, the same ritual act—washing after a funeral, for instance—can be interpreted by different people in radically different ways: cleaning an invisible, yet inert, form of dirt or removing evil spirits. Most people trouble themselves little about the metaphysical implications of these acts, practicing them rather with a confidence, born of long habituation, that what is effective for dirt will work for spirits and other evil forces, too.

Dirt and Agency

The necessity of dealing with dirt in everyday life serves as a useful analogy for understanding a wide variety of actions relating to interferences, disruptions, and disorders of the ordinary functioning of life in Soweto. The analogy of dirt can also serve to make everyday understandings of illness consonant with notions of contagion and infection as propagated by Western medical practitioners with the germ theory of disease (Green 1999). However, the key feature of talk about dirt and cleansing such as I have heard in Soweto is the fundamental premise that dirt, however dangerous it might be, is inert. Dirt consists of material substances and immaterial traces with no autonomous agency of their own. The biomedical notion of the "germ"—whether microscopic algae, bacteria, fungi, protozoa, or viruses —embodies definite notions of agency. The forms of agency commonly expressed in biomedical talk of germs is limited to action programmed by

DNA bequeathed by evolution, although popular accounts of germs and infections tend to anthropomorphize their subjects with talk of such things as "the secret life of germs" (Tierno 2001), and scientists in their less rigorous moments tend also to speak of germs as if they were sentient beings with intentions and motives informing their actions. Biomedicine restricts its interpretation of the agency of germs to a limited, quasi-mechanistic model of systems and functions. Popular African imaginings are less constrained.

In the ethnographic record of southern Africa I have not been able to discover traditions of specifying the nature of the distinction between the visible and invisible in conceptions of scale such as the notion of the microscopic as a category of invisibility. Most accounts of the invisibility of invisible forces seem to draw either upon analogies of internality—the little man inside the man (Tempels 1959, 51)—or the breath, a normally invisible wind that can become apparent under certain conditions (Berglund 1976, 84), such as on a cold misty morning. The history of encounters with European technologies of image making and reproduction reveals a complex of epistemological problems relating to the nature of visible and invisible realities that hinge on issues other than dimension. Everyday talk about the dangers of pollution emanating from things such as corpses does not typically invoke concepts of the microscopic to explain the nature of the problem. And as countless writers have repeated: "African custom, tradition and usage does not know the germ theory" (Gumede 1990, 38). Nevertheless, the notions of the invisible as microscopic —such as inform the germ theory of disease—are readily assimilable with understandings of the invisible as secret, hidden, and spiritual or immaterial that have long informed "African custom, tradition and usage." But even when the notion of the "germ" is introduced into this context, the question of the nature of its agency remains: what is it capable of and to whom does it answer?

When people in Soweto worry about substances that might cause them harm, they generally conceive of possibilities of action less in mechanistic terms than in terms of power relations between competing or cooperating agencies inherent in persons, spirits, and substances framed in a paradigm of communication. That they speak of these possibilities of agency in terms of "witchcraft" does not mean they are being irrational or unreasonable. Rather, it seems to me that when my friends in Soweto worry more than me about the possibilities of danger emerging from their relationships with polluting substances, they are operating within a richer imaginative field of action and interaction than mine, one less constrained by mechanical metaphors inscribed into every aspect of life in ways that limit the apprehension of powers and forces to possibilities that accord with a model of the universe as fashioned in the likeness of a clock. An imagination less fettered, perhaps one shaped by understandings of the material world as a manifestation of various forms of communicable information, would probably have less difficulty accepting African witchcraft discourse as pertaining to reality.

Paradigms of pollution that, in Setiloane's words, "go far beyond the physical" in no way require any systematically "magical," "irrational," or even "religious" orientation to the material world. Nor need they be opposed to "rational" or "materialistic" dispositions—even when the modes of engaging with pollutants deploy what appear to be mystical, ritual, or symbolic procedures for the detection and cleansing of invisible forms of dirt. Nor, for that matter, do they preclude ignorant and erroneous understandings of the world. Dirt is encountered in the ordinary course of life and is unavoidable. Bodies produce dirt in being born, in living, and in death. Children play in the dirt. Work is dirty. The wind blows. We clean up. And we will clean again tomorrow. Living with dirt affords people a straightforward and entirely plausible analogy for comprehending the possibilities of invisible sources of harm that accords with all available teachings of the authorities prevailing in places like Soweto—whether they be ancestral, religious, educational, or medical—without requiring any great effort of study or gifts of imagination to grasp. It is an analogy as widely used as Sunlight soap and the scrubbing brush. Therein lies its power.

8

A BRIEF HISTORY OF THE SPIRIT WORLD

Living in the Spirits' World

In the previous two chapters we explored some of the ways people interpret relations with physical substances, particularly in the ways they worry about sources of danger arising from the inert pollution inherent in dirt and the forms of human interaction with the agency of substances that can act as poison and medicine. We now must turn to the realm of those invisible agents devoid of material substance usually known as spirits. Spiritual agencies are considered the ultimate source of security. They can also be a source of serious danger. Managing relations with these entities can be very time-consuming. For some—including the tens of thousands of healers, prophets, and preachers—it is a full-time job. And the spirit world itself, judging from what I have heard of the activities of its denizens, must be a tumultuous place.

The spirit world of Soweto is crowded with hosts of invisible beings. For the spiritually aware, humans are but transient bodily forms attached to immortal and eternal spiritual essences, temporary residents in a world dominated by spirits, a world whose deepest realities are spiritual mysteries. As Paul Makhubu, one of the few published theologians of the African Initiated Church movement, puts it: "African religious life is notable for its awareness, and recognition of, the active world of the Spirits. Most religious life is concerned with defining and establishing one's relationship with such spirits" (1988, 85). Relationships with invisible beings can be either hostile or friendly, supportive or antagonistic. What they cannot be is neutral or disinterested.

In the first of a series of lectures on Christianity in late antiquity that traced the impact of the new religion on the old Roman deities, the histo-

rian Peter Brown urged his audience to make an imaginative leap to approach an understanding of the Roman spirit world. "It is not easy to do
so," he warned. "Living in a bleakly sub-monotheistic age, we tend to look
up into the sky and find it empty. We no longer see there a *mundus,* a physical universe as heavy as a swollen cloud (for good or ill) with the presence
of invisible beings" (1995, 8). Brown's characterization of the spirit world of
late antiquity is apposite for turn-of-the-millennium South Africa. There,
the image of a well-ordered cosmos ruled by a single almighty deity that
came to dominate Western Christianity has incomplete purchase on the
imaginations of people struggling to manage relations with hosts of invisible beings wielding forces that are experienced as shaping the lives of the
living in every detail.[1] Managing relations with these beings is the central
part of life.

The immanence of invisible beings in the physical universe and the inevitability of human interactions with them, for good and for ill, is an everyday fact of life in Africa which newcomers struggle to comprehend—especially those of us enjoying "bleakly sub-monotheistic" lives. The pallid
doctrines of personhood and power that allow such lives to be led make it
difficult to appreciate the standpoint that the spirits have made the world,
and we only live in it. Outsiders with imaginations more sensitized to the activities of invisible forces, or stronger commitments to the reality of spirits
and demons—American evangelicals, for example—find the African spirit
world in places like Soweto both galling and enthralling. One such evangelist, Dean Carlson of Global Harvest Ministries (headquartered in Colo-
rado), produced in 1998 a report entitled *Towards the Spiritual Mapping of
Dobsonville, Soweto,* in which he attempted an accounting of the spiritual
forces battling for the souls of Sowetans. Under the subheading "Levels of
Demonic Activity," Carlson concluded: "It is clear that in Dobsonville there
is plenty of ground level demonic activity. People suffer greatly under the
influence of demonic spirits." Nor was the problem only at ground level:
"We have also noted that there is significant occult-level activity. This is evidenced by the presence of sangomas, nyangas, witches and Satanists in the
community" (1998, 23). Many Sowetans would be appalled to hear Carlson's assessment of demonic activity in their community and his character-

1. Gerhardus Oosthuizen has suggested that the similarities between the condition of
Christianity in late Roman antiquity and late-twentieth-century South Africa arise because
"Afro-Christianity" is still in its first and second centuries of existence, as was the Christianity in the Roman world of which Brown wrote (Oosthuizen 1992, xxii–xxvii). Oosthuizen's own Christian faith prompts him to consider twentieth-century Afro-Christianity as
being in an "early" stage of development.

ization of cherished cultural traditions as Satanic, especially the *sangomas* and *inyangas* who see themselves as healers battling the invisible forces of evil—the very antithesis of witches and Satanists. Many other Sowetans, however, having been "born again" themselves and joined the ranks of Christians known in these parts as Bazalwane, would emphatically agree with the evangelist. Yet despite disagreement over the ethical character of the spiritual beings prevalent in the world, few would consider absurd the effort to identify and "map"—as a first step toward countering—the invisible beings responsible for hardship and suffering in their communities.

The strong consensus here is that the world is a dangerous place rife with invisible forces and powers. Evil spirits must be fended off and protected against; spiritual forces upholding the good must be supplicated and revered. Virtually no one doubts that the safety and security of the living, the conditions under which their health, well-being, and prosperity can be assured, depend upon relationships with these invisible forces. Hardly a soul alive in Soweto today—certainly no one that I have met—would dare claim indifference to the possibilities of action by spirits, though they may argue vehemently about the nature, character, and capacities of particular entities. One person's beneficent ancestor can be another's demonic power; one person's beloved healer through whom she communes with her ancestors can be another's benighted Satanist. Invisible beings, indeed, are such a vital presence in everyday life that it makes little sense to bracket a single dimension of life as a specifically "religious" domain.

In the interests of scholarly detachment, I shall categorize all deities and other spiritual beings, agents, and entities—of all varieties and ethical inclinations—as generically "invisible." Despite myriad differences, these beings share the general characteristics of not being amenable to ordinary human perception while enjoying some degree of autonomous agency in relation to human life. People who live with these beings tend to be emphatic that they belong to the physical universe, albeit in mysterious ways, and speak of experiencing their presence and communicating with them in a variety of tangible ways. Specialists of various sorts, persons gifted with capacities for communicating with these beings beyond those normally available to ordinary persons, ply their trade in a bustling marketplace of healers, prophets, and priests. Ensconced in every variety of organized cult, established church, secret sect, prayer group, and private practice, these specialists are constantly striving to engage spiritual powers in efforts to resolve problems of human life in this world—many of which they insist are produced by the actions of invisible beings—as well as securing redemption in the next. The scale of their enterprises, ranging from the poorest of backyard shacks to multimillion-rand megachurches, is directly related to perceptions of how successful they are at addressing these problems.

Such a capacious category of "invisible beings" as I am using here—with due deference to Peter Brown—may strike people who experience meaningful relations with one or another subset of them as fundamentally mistaken, not to say blasphemous and perverse. For the category encompasses beings of radically different ethical character (God and the devil, for example) and treats those who some believe objectively exist alongside others they are convinced do not (Jesus and the *tokoloshe,* for example). It might also be objected that these issues are simply matters of "religion" and "religious belief" concerning human institutions and personal faith or the "inner life," and that it is a mistake to insist on referring to bilateral "relations with invisible beings" as if such things really exist and can be treated analytically as occupying the same terrain as relations among persons. However, in order to examine the varieties of ways in which people seek security through managing relations with perceived sources of both harm and safety, it matters little whether or not these beings exist or whether we can adequately discover how people experience their encounters with them in the deepest reaches of their souls. What does matter are the ways in which people live with these beings and the implications of these relations for the ways they live with each other. A person facing a crisis of spiritual security, someone feeling exposed to invisible forces intent on causing harm, has to find a way of engaging the power of invisible beings in his or her support. That there is much more to religious experience and spiritual life than this goes without saying.

When discussing questions of theology and cosmology in a place like Soweto, it is not wise to be dogmatic about what people believe (or say they believe) or say others ought to believe. There is no unanimity of opinion. Even within particular congregations of churchgoers where matters of belief are propounded with some degree of rigor, divergences of opinion about spiritual matters abound, both among the congregants and between congregants and church officials. Questions concerning relationships among ancestors, the Christian God, the hosts of invisible entities and powers, and the lives of ordinary living persons are matters of intense concern for enormous numbers of people, for whom the issues at stake go to the heart of questions of life and death—*eternal* life and death. We cannot hope to cover all of these issues here with any hope of doing justice to the intricacies either of theological disputation or lived faith. Rather than trying to sketch orthodoxies or summarize actual beliefs, then, I shall endeavor to outline some of the questions arising from everyday experiences of relations with invisible beings and the sorts of answers that religious and other specialists provide that are deemed plausible by those who must live by them. I shall do this by sketching the broad parameters within which statements about invisible beings can plausibly be made and indicate some of the main lines of debate in available interpretations of their nature, ethical character, agency, and power. I shall also sketch the elements of disputes about legitimate modes of human access and interaction with these powers, focusing particularly on questions of security.

Colonizing the Ancestors

The invisible beings with whom we are concerned exist in a world whose history has been shaped in recent centuries by, among other things, European colonization and market capitalism, the subordination of African polities (first to colonial rule and subsequently to varieties of national state power), urbanization, Christian evangelization, and the spread of indigenous religious movements. It is impossible to do justice to the full complexity of the ways in which these processes have transformed both human and spirit populations in these parts, so I shall briefly sketch the general outlines of some of these changes and then concentrate on the question of how they affect the powers ordinary people have access to in places like Soweto when seeking security in everyday life. The primary spiritual powers that Africans, through the course of this history, have had access to, and have been forced to accommodate into new schemes of interpreting the nature of the spirit world, have been known under the general rubric of "the ancestors"—*badimo* (Sotho) and *amadlozi* (Zulu). All of the large-scale processes of social change that have transformed human social life in these parts have been registered over the course of the past century or more—in different ways and at different times throughout the region—in profound transformations of African family and community life, and it is through these changes that the powers of ancestors and other invisible beings have been most affected.

Some observers, following Monica Wilson (1951), have argued that the English term "ancestor" is a misrepresentation of the ontological status of the invisible beings known locally by such names as *amadlozi* and have preferred the word "shades" instead (Martin West 1975b). Axel-Ivar Berglund has perhaps made the strongest case against calling these entities "ancestors," arguing that the term implies too strongly a Western notion of death and fails to accord sufficient presence to the invisible beings who, though dead, remain among the living only in a different form. Berglund has suggested that the difference between the living and dead in this context is analogous to the difference between a fetus and a newborn baby (1976, 29–30). While it is undoubtedly true that the ontological status of these dead relatives is difficult for outsiders to grasp, it is not clear to me that the word "shades" makes the task any easier than calling them "ancestors." Considering that everyday usage in South African English favors "ancestor," I shall use that term. Berglund's point, however, is important: "ancestors" should be treated more as a stage in the life cycle of the person than as an altogether different kind of being. Relations with them are every bit as complicated as relationships among the living, and then some. Ancestors are, nevertheless, invisible—though they are said to be able to make themselves known through dreams, visions, and tangible signs, most notably bodily ailments and unfortunate events.

Colonial conquest and the subordination of African polities to European domination, followed by their incorporation as subordinate suzerainties within the apartheid state and their anomalous semiautonomy in the postapartheid constitutional structure, not only transformed the powers of indigenous kings, chiefs, and other local political authorities in southern Africa but dispersed and reduced the powers of their ancestors, those tutelary spirits who, in much the same way that a father was deemed responsible for the welfare and security of his family, were responsible for the general welfare and security of the collectivities over which their descendants ruled.[2] By the end of the twentieth century, relatively few people in this part of the world could participate in meaningful relations with ancestors beyond those of their immediate family. Even in rural communities, the number of people in a neighborhood who could invoke common ancestors in the cause of social harmony and collective prosperity was small compared to the whole population of the community. And although many traditional leaders still claimed the spiritual connections grounding their political status, the number of people who could engage with the idea of a king's or chief's ancestor as a potential protector of them and their community was diminishing. Ironically, the largest group of people who do claim to have ready access to structures of ancestral power greater than those of ordinary kinship groups, analogous to the king's ancestors in precolonial polities, are members of the Zion Christian Church (ZCC). The ZCC is explicitly modeled upon the structure of the Pedi polity, and the spirit of the founder, Engenas Lekganyane, is regularly invoked in the work of healing, protecting,

2. For discussion of the spiritual dimensions of African political power, see Hammond-Tooke 1975; Packard 1981; Pettersson 1953; I. Schapera 1970.

and strengthening that takes place in the church. The establishment of a new African polity in the 1990s, with a universally acknowledged "Father of the Nation" in the person of Nelson Mandela (a figure whom many already consider saintly, not to mention a secular messiah), in decades to come may open access to a communal structure of spiritual power that has been diminished since conquest.

Labor migration and urbanization, coupled with the wholesale disruption of rural life through forced removals and confinement of Africans to "Native Reserves," particularly during the middle decades of the twentieth century, when apartheid "influx control" policies made life difficult for people who wished to move permanently to towns, broke apart families and fragmented the organized kinship relations underpinning the "ancestor cult" as a system of religious ritual. By the late twentieth century, few young urban-born people participated in relationships with kin extending much beyond their immediate family. The ancestral powers associated with clans and lineages were thus unavailable to them. Moreover, while the outlines of what is usually referred to as "African traditional religion" or "ancestral religion" are broadly similar across the region, there are and always have been significant differences in details of ritual practice among different communities. In the course of urban life these differences have become blurred, not to say confused. Since ancestors are by definition guardians of tradition, and as traditions teach that ancestors are very particular about their descendants observing rules and rituals correctly, the mingling of traditions and the forgetting of rules and prohibitions in urban life has undermined the sense of ancestral efficacy. These days, then, "the ancestors" is the name for a domain of spiritual power that resonates within a smaller sphere of social life than was the case in the past. Moreover, parental authority of the sort enshrined in ancestor veneration has diminished markedly within families in recent generations, giving rise to questions not only about how to manage relations with ancestors but also about the power of ancestors themselves and the efficacy of rituals seeking their aid.

Evangelical Invasions and Invisible Powers

In the history of the spirit world in this part of Africa, nothing has been more dramatic than the transformations wrought by the arrival of Christianity. The old rituals and routines governing relations with ancestors offered people access to a more or less extensive hierarchy of spiritual power extending from their own deceased relatives to the spirits of the founders of their society, putative ancestors of the present rulers. Christianity, however, offered access—even for the lowliest of believers, even for women and children—to the Supreme Being, the Creator, the Almighty himself. Africans, by most accounts, spoke of such a being long before the missionaries came. Missionaries in southern Africa, as in other parts of Africa, adopted local names for this being as their name for "God" when translating the Bible into local languages. Many Africans, following conversion to Christianity, have insisted that the God of the missionaries was always known in Africa. As Mpho put it one afternoon when we were sitting at home amusing ourselves with theology: "even in the past people used to believe in God, but they gave him different names. Like in Zulu they call him uMvelinqangi. Even in the past."[3]

Not everyone agrees with this blithe assertion of indigenous monotheism. Madumo, for example, took issue with Mpho's claim for the God of the Zulus being one and the same as that of the Christians: "I think people misunderstood that point. They pray God. And in those gods there is one who is the head of the gods. They call him uMvelinqangi. Of which if they pray for that god he's more powerful than the other gods. That's what I know." Madumo was less troubled about the ontological status of the deities. Ultimate creator of the world, or original ancestor of the people, they were all the same to him.

Even those who insist God has always been with Africans will not always agree about how connected he was to his creations in the old days before the missionaries brought the gospel, nor do they agree on how best to connect with him today. African ritual practice in the past, as it remains for many today, was focused more on engaging spiritual powers and beings closer to home than the Creator, namely the ancestors of families and other social collectivities such as those known as clans, lineages, tribes, and nations. As Samuel Modiri Molema explained of the African Creator: "This god ... was more of an absent god; he lived retired on high, took no concern in what was going on, and although the author of Nature and more powerful than the spirits, he was inactive" (1920, 166). Ancestors, in Molema's account, occupied the space between the living person and the distant Creator, shaping the fortunes of daily life and sharing its joys and hardships as

---

3. The Kenyan theologian John Mbiti would have applauded Mpho. In his view: "The missionaries who introduced the gospel to Africa in the past 200 years did not bring God to our continent. Instead, God brought them. They proclaimed the name of Jesus Christ. But they used the names of the God who was and is already known by African peoples—such as Mungu, Mulungu, Katonda, Ngai, Olodumare, Asis, Ruwa, Ruhanga, Jok, Modimo, Unkulunkulu and thousands more. These were not empty names. They were names of one and the same God, the creator of the world, the father of our Lord Jesus Christ" (1980, 818).

full members of the community. For many, they still do. For many African Christians, the figure of Jesus has been incorporated into this intermediary position between the human person and the almighty God.

In the nineteenth century, southern Africa was one of the most intensely evangelized territories on earth. African conversions to the churches of the missionaries in the early decades of this endeavor, however, were relatively few and mostly confined to people at the margins of indigenous polities, particularly women and refugees spawned by colonial conquest (Etherington 1978, 67; Comaroff and Comaroff 1991, 261). Efforts at conversion by early missionaries were contingent upon the success of colonization and were largely determined by the character of relations between African polities and European powers. As Eugene Casalis, one of the first missionaries to the BaSotho in the time of the great nation-builder Moshoeshoe, wrote of his labors in the mid–nineteenth century, "all the success which attends the Africans in their struggles with Europeans, is followed by a reaction fatal to the cause of Christianity and civilisation" (1861, 260). Norman Etherington (1978) has shown that few Zulus were interested in the word of God until the British defeated the armies of the Zulu kingdom and subjected Zulus to colonial rule.[4] Only in the course of the twentieth century, when European political domination became firmly entrenched, did the wholesale adoption of Christian faith(s) take place. Richard Elphick has described this adoption of Christianity as "one of the most dramatic cultural transformations in human history" (Elphick 1995, 19). Central to this transformation has been a reconstitution of the place of ancestors in both the visible and the invisible worlds (Kiernan 1990b).

Throughout the nineteenth century, European Christian missionaries to southern Africa sought to describe the people among whom they settled with a view to both stimulating support for the mission at home and providing future missionaries and colonial administrators with handbooks of "native custom" to aid the labors of saving souls and governing conquered people. The earliest accounts of life in these parts were written by European travelers and adventurers. These accounts, being based on short periods of interaction between people of very different backgrounds, are of uneven quality. In the words of one recent editor who compared the description of the Tlaping, a southern Tswana people, by the English explorer William Sommerville with the standard ethnographic work by Isaac Scha-

---

4. The role of missionaries as agents of cultural imperialism has provoked lively debate, for examples and accounts of which, see Beidelman 1974; Comaroff and Comaroff 1991; Dachs 1972; Etherington 1983; Sanneh 1993.

pera (1953), the best are "by no means contemptible" (Sommerville 1979, 21). Some of the books written by missionaries in the late nineteenth and early twentieth centuries, who lived many years with the people about whom they wrote, remain classics of their type and offer important glimpses of the character of life before European colonization and the impact of colonialism on indigenous peoples.[5] As Henri Junod, perhaps the most perceptive observer of African life among European missionaries to southern Africa, noted, missionaries and colonists "are apt to make the most dangerous mistakes from mere ignorance of the true nature of rites or superstitions which they do not understand" (1962a, 8). The "rites and superstitions" with which Junod and other missionaries were most concerned were those relating to the management of evil forces and understood, in the missionaries' translations, as "witchcraft"—a term which often conflated antisorcery action with activities relating to fears of pollution.

Among nineteenth- and twentieth-century missionaries, opinions about the place of "witchcraft" in African social life seem to have been determined by more general perceptions of what they took to be "African religion" (or the lack of it, since they found neither buildings, bishops, nor books consecrated to the worship of deities), especially the place of ancestors in religious and social life. When missionaries adopted a sympathetic view of the ancestors, seeing reverence for them as evidence of an African spiritual life that would be amenable to Christian teachings, witchcraft as such was treated as a secondary, albeit not minor, matter. When missionaries viewed African ritual practices as demonic, witchcraft and the procedures associated with its management were demonized as anathema to the Christian way. These attitudes were not merely a product of theological disputation between Catholic and Protestant, as one might expect given the history of Protestant objections to reverence of saints. One of the most articulate exponents of the "sympathetic" view of ancestors was the American Protestant missionary William Charles Willoughby. In his *Soul of the Bantu* (1928) he surveys Bantu religious practices and notions so that Christian missionaries in Africa could better master their craft and present

5. I am thinking particularly of J. Tom Brown 1926; Bryant 1929, 1949; Callaway 1970; Casalis 1861; Junod 1962a, 1962b; Wessman 1908; and Willoughby 1928, 1932. The missionary and traveler literature, along with associated unpublished archival sources, has been masterfully interpreted by Jean Comaroff and John Comaroff in their historical anthropology of colonialism and Christianity on the frontier of the Cape Colony and the southern Tswana kingdom (1991, 1997). These works (along with Comaroff and Comaroff 1993, 1999), though not uncontroversial, lay the foundations for a fruitful new approach to long-term processes of cultural formation in the region.

to their African flocks the "religion of Jesus . . . as the full expression of that
for which their fathers groped" (1928, xxiii). In Willoughby's view, magic
and witchcraft in Africa constituted "a slavery of the mind which is much
more terrible in its consequences than any slavery of the body ever was
(1923, 61). African reverence for ancestors, however, Willoughby saw as
the building block for liberating minds through the power of the gospel. He
reserved his scorn, not for the African who consults a diviner to communicate with ancestors in times of trouble, but for "those disdainful people
who dilate so readily upon his pitiable 'superstition,' without taking the
trouble to understand either it or the word with which they label it" (1923,
62). Willoughby treated witchcraft as part of a broader religious, moral,
and ethical system, albeit of a "childish" variety, as "the Bantu are a child
race" (1923, 61).

When missionaries were less sympathetic to African cosmologies, as
many, perhaps most, were, they tended to see the influence of witchcraft
and the related ancestor cult as a demonic, pervasive, and dominating phenomenon in social life and as the principal factor retarding progress and
upliftment in the present world as well as precluding salvation in the next.
The Transkeian missionary J. R. L. Kingon, for example, in a presidential
address to the South African Association for the Advancement of Science
in 1919, argued that tribalism was the main impediment to Africans' progressing to a higher stage of civilization, that such progress was predicated
upon a transition from "communalism" to "individualism," and that witchcraft was the "binding force of tribalism" and thus the key to the whole civi-
lizing mission (1919, 123). Thus, he advocated "resolutely facing and dealing
directly and wisely with belief in witchcraft, and the associated superstition concerning the ancestral spirits" (1919, 129). For Kingon, the belief in
witchcraft kept the population in a permanent "state of disturbance" (1919,
129). The fear of being accused of witchcraft restrained people from accumulating wealth and improving their circumstances. Moreover, because of
this danger, it fostered the practice of polygamy (a self-evidently evil practice for the Christian missionary of the time), for it was safer for a man
to exchange cattle for wives than to hold large herds and risk their im-
poundment by the chief after accusations of witchcraft (1919, 130). Chiefs
also traded upon the terrors of witchcraft to maintain their power. "Witchdoctors" aided chiefs by smelling out witches from among his subjects,
thereby allowing the chief to increase his wealth by impounding the property of the unfortunate "witch."

Despite differences of opinion and emphasis regarding witchcraft, invisible pollutants, and ancestors, all European missionaries and the churches

they founded sought to convince their followers that the powers they feared as "witchcraft" had no basis in reality. Recognizing the reality of evil, personified in the devil, they denied the reality of local understandings of harmful invisible forces while prohibiting their followers from practicing ancestral rituals associated, among other things, with witchcraft management and spiritual purification. African Christians, most of whom remained worried about the dangers of witchcraft, pollution, and the importance of relations with invisible beings other than those endorsed by the missionaries, were forced to seek remedies outside their churches. This they did either in private while remaining active in the mission church (Setiloane 1976, chap. 10) or by establishing new kinds of churches to address their problems directly (Makhubu 1988).

From time to time in the missionary narratives an image emerges of the everyday implications in African life of what might be called the colonization of the spirit world, a sense of how Africans perceived power struggles between their own spiritual forces and those represented by the European missionaries. Eugene Casalis, the French Protestant missionary to the Ba-Sotho in the mid–nineteenth century, noted in his memoir of life with the people of Moshoeshoe: "The idea that exterior and material means are capable of acting on the soul, and changing its tendencies, is so deeply enrooted among them, that the first conversions to Christianity that they witnessed were all attributed to the influence of some mysterious specific, which those who frequented the society of the missionaries had unconsciously received from their hands" (1861, 259). Conversions to Christianity, that is to say, which the missionaries proclaimed as the result of their earthly labors empowered by their Christian God, were often seen by the locals as a product of sorcery or other mystical forces.

In the course of the nineteenth century, as it became clear that European power in the region would remain a force to be reckoned with, Africans lost little time in seeking to gain access to these spiritual forces. It was not only the converts, who tended to be people from the margins of African societies, who sought these powers. In 1829, for example, the English missionary Robert Moffat was summoned by the Ndebele chief Mzilikazi in a manner described by Setiloane as akin to "the employment of the services of a Great Ngaka [traditional healer] by a Great Chief" (1976, 135). Perhaps the most significant public struggle between the old and new spiritual forces was fought out over the power to bring rain. Jean Comaroff and John Comaroff describe in exquisite detail how the English missionaries to the Tswana in the early nineteenth century became "obsessed" with eradicating rituals connected with rainmaking. The missionaries' own work with meteorological instruments to predict weather, coupled with prayer to the God they insisted "had ultimate authority over the elements," from the point of view of the Tswana "seemed to confirm that they were really rain-makers of competing power" (Comaroff and Comaroff 1991, 208–209).

While Casalis and other missionaries wrote of these matters as a way of providing evidence of African superstition for European readers—and, hence, the need for Christian conversion and education—it is clear from Casalis's remarks that the missionary enterprise was embroiled in a complex politics of spiritual power whose long-term outcome for much of the nineteenth century was by no means certain. Africans rapidly appreciated the possibilities afforded by the new order of spiritual power presented by the missionaries and devised ways of harnessing that power to all manner of ends never dreamt of by the Europeans. Among the principal purposes of African engagement with this power represented by the triune Christian God, particularly in the person of the Holy Spirit, has been the struggle against witchcraft. Christianity, rather than banishing "superstitions" concerning the invisible agency of substances and capacious conceptions of invisible pollutants, became a resource of power for individuals, families, and communities seeking to manage these dangers. The history of Christianity in South Africa, while much else besides, is also the story of an African struggle for spiritual security in a world of witches.

African Access to Almighty Power

For ordinary Africans, Christian missionaries (representing every extant version of modern Christian theology) brought the promise of access to the ultimate power in the world, Almighty God. This was a promise of far greater power than the ancestors alone could offer. Along with access to supreme powers of good, however, the Christians also brought exposure to an organized hierarchy of evil forces dedicated to seducing God's creatures from the path of righteousness: legions of demons presided over by Satan. This image of a monolithic structure of evil power was new to this part of the world (Willoughby 1932, 113).[6] Since the arrival of God and the devil, African spirituality has been dominated by concerns over the nature of relations between these entities and the ancestors. Though conversions to the new religion were slow at first, soon after they embraced Christianity

6. For an account of the impact of the figure of the devil on indigenous ideas of evil in Ghana, see B. Meyer 1999.

Africans began engaging divine power to address the problems of everyday life that previously had been the preserve of ancestors and attributing to Satan and evil spirits the source of dangers manifest in the human activity of witchcraft and the omnipresent risk of pollution. The work of healing illnesses, remedying misfortune, securing prosperity, and gaining protection from occult assault by witches became integrally connected with managing relations with the spiritual powers of the Christian heaven. The ancestors, however, despite the teachings of white missionaries, who denounced "ancestor worship" as idolatry, did not disappear. The history of the spirit world over the past century and a half, then, has been one of ancestors being integrated into, subordinated to, or rejected by the powers represented in the Christian Bible. The history of Christian churches has turned upon the way reverence for ancestors has been assimilated into, and rejected by, the manifold modes of Christian worship.

Every denomination of missionary found a home in South Africa during the nineteenth and twentieth centuries. Before they had been at work long, however, African converts—particularly those men who were recruited as lay preachers within the missionary endeavor—began noticing the contradictions between the message of brotherly love and human equality found in the Gospels and the racially stratified character of colonial mission life and the racist attitudes of white Christians. They began to organize their own Christian churches. African initiatives in establishing and controlling their own independent Christian churches began in the late nineteenth century. During the twentieth century, African initiatives in Christianity came to dominate the religious scene throughout the continent. These churches were profoundly important in shaping the early generations of African political leaders in South Africa. In his address during the centenary celebrations of the Free Ethiopian Church of South Africa in 1992, Nelson Mandela traced the "seeds of the formation of our organisation to the Ethiopian Movement of the 1890s" and noted that it was not only the thwarting of black theological ambitions in white churches that produced the demand for independent churches but also the fact that Africans noticed that white missionaries were complicit in the dispossession of Africans from their land (Mandela 1992). The emergence of these churches also aroused the interest of the white political authorities, who found themselves captives of the same contradiction. Unable to oppose the conversion of Africans to Christianity, they worried about the proliferation of African churches calling themselves "Christian" but living beyond the control of Whites. The South African Native Affairs Commission of 1903–1905, for example, was charged with inquiring into these "Native separatist churches." After making a few snide comments about the "relaxed strictness in the moral standard maintained" by these churches, the commission reported that "so long as it remains unassociated with mischievous political tendencies, members [of the commission] unite in advising that any measure capable of being represented as religious persecution should be avoided" (South African Native Affairs Commission 1905, para. 320). Government efforts at regulating these churches as they proliferated throughout the twentieth century proved futile.[7]

Varieties of African Christianity

At the conclusion of *Bantu Prophets in South Africa*, the foundational text in the study of these religious movements (first published in 1948 and revised in 1961), the Swedish missionary to Zululand Bengt Sundkler suggested that the main reasons for the emergence of independent churches was the "colour-bar of White South Africa," coupled with the "fissiparous influence on Bantu church life of Protestant denominationalism" (Sundkler 1948, 295). This emphasis on racism as the source of African indigenous Christianity has been a recurrent theme throughout the literature on these churches (Kiernan 1990a, 16). Though the impact of racism on African Christians should not be underestimated, racism alone was by no means the whole of the story of the African adaptation of Christianity.

Although the original "separatist" or "Ethiopian" churches owe their existence to the reaction against racism, scholars now generally acknowledge that the spirituality and religious practice of African Christian churches cannot be reduced to a merely reactive phenomenon of racial politics. This is particularly true of those churches known as "Zionist" and "Apostolic" (or Zion/Apostolic), which have produced distinctive forms of organization and worship, as well as being true of the Neo-Pentecostalist churches that have arisen in recent decades as part of a global religious movement (Corten and Marshal-Fratani 2000; B. Meyer 1999). These churches emphasize healing, security, and prosperity in their activities.

7. Sundkler notes that after 1925, following the tragic Bulhoek massacre, the government instituted a registration procedure for separatist churches but officially recognized fewer than 1 percent. Church leaders, nonetheless, religiously submitted application forms for registration and in many cases used the receipt of application notice in lieu of a recognition certificate (Sundkler 1948, 74).

Their theology and ritual practice emphasize the struggle against demons, witches, and sorcerers, and they thrive by virtue of being able to provide for their members a sense of security and well-being they cannot obtain elsewhere. Without doubt, these churches are now the most significant expression of Christianity in southern Africa, and the fact that they have been growing so fast is testament to their success not only in meeting what Allan Anderson calls "the spiritual hunger that needed to be assuaged in a truly African expression of Christianity" (2000b, 30) but also in responding to efforts to manage the dangers, doubts, and fears about the unseen forces acting upon people and causing harm, particularly in the cities.

Sundkler established the basic analytical framework for studying African churches (variously denominated "Independent," "Indigenous," or "Initiated" and known collectively by the initialism AIC) by distinguishing between three types of churches.[8] The first he categorized as "Ethiopian" after the name of the first independent African church, founded by Nehemiah Tile in 1892. Led by mission-educated African clergy, these churches broke from established European mission churches in reaction to white overlordship. The use of the biblical term "Ethiopia" in the naming of these churches by their founder "prophets" was interpreted by Sundkler as an attempt to reclaim the antiquity of African Christianity as well as a more specific reference to the African country, ruled by a black king, that had never been under European domination (Sundkler 1948, 56; Sundkler and Steed 2000, 426).

Sundkler characterized the second group of independent churches as "Zionist" because these churches arose from the interactions of African religious traditions and Christian faith healing and owed their inspiration either directly to the teachings of John Alexander Dowie, founder of Zion City, Illinois, and the Christian Catholic Apostolic Church in Zion, or to the biblical narratives of John the Baptist (Sundkler 1948, 54). The fountainhead of Zionism in South Africa was a nineteenth-century Scottish-born Australian faith healer resident in Chicago named John Alexander Dowie. Dowie styled himself "First Apostle and Prophet of the Restoration" (Sundkler 1976, 34) and published a magazine called *Leaves of Healing,* which spread his gospel of faith healing around the world. In 1897, in-

8. For reviews of the literature on AICs, see Kiernan's introduction to his collected papers (1990a); Tinyiko Sam Maluleke's foreword to Allan Anderson 2000b; and H. L. Pretorius 1995. For discussion of classifications of these churches and the problems of typologies, see Hodgson 1990.

spired by Dowie's message, a missionary of the Dutch Reformed Church named Petrus Louis Le Roux began preaching to the Zulus at Wakkerstroom (Sundkler 1976, 19). In 1903, Le Roux left the Dutch Reformed Church, whose members were less than thrilled about his work with the "Natives," and, assisted by an emissary from Dowie, established the first Zionist congregation among Zulus. Although Dowie's mission of faith healing to South Africa was originally targeted at white people, particularly white immigrants, it was among Africans, who were long accustomed to drawing on spiritual powers to meet earthly needs, that the possibilities of harnessing the Holy Spirit in the cause of healing were fully explored. In the course of the twentieth century, African "Zionism" and its related "Apostolic" variant became the most significant local varieties of Christianity.[9]

These churches are typically organized in the form of small "bands" of one or two dozen members, some linked to other congregations of likeminded believers, others completely independent, although a handful have become large, highly organized institutions. The largest of these churches is the Zion Christian Church (ZCC). Founded in 1924 by Engenas Lekganyane and now presided over by his grandson, the ZCC claims a membership of eight million and is generally considered the largest church in the region (Lukhaimane 1980, 23).[10] Typically founded by a charismatic individual—who may be a "bishop" (primarily a religious leader and teacher) or a "prophet" (primarily a healer)—who experiences a call from the Holy Spirit and, sometimes, his or her ancestors to found a church, these organizations grow primarily through the reputations of their prophet-healers for effectiveness in healing.[11] By the end of the twentieth century there were between five and ten thousand of these churches, counting between 33 and 40 percent of black South Africans as their members (Allan Ander-

9. The designations "Zionist" and "Apostolic" that are found in the names of thousands of churches throughout South Africa have, in Sundkler and Steed's interpretation of their naming practices, a "technical meaning": "With this name the prophet defines his organization as a New Testament Church which in detail carries out the religious programme supposedly developed by a central figure in the Zionists' Bible, John the Baptist. Thereby, the prophet links his baptisms with that apostolic succession which flows from Jordan, the River of life. 'Zionists,' *amaZioni,* is the term used by these leaders themselves" (Sundkler and Steed 2000, 427).

10. For a history of the ZCC, see Lukhaimane 1980, and for discussion of ZCC theology, see Naude 1995.

11. For a general description of the work of these churches in Soweto during the 1970s, see Martin West 1975a.

son 2001a; Kritzinger 1993). Most of the recruitment of new members in these churches comes through success in healing work, and much of their healing efforts are directed to spiritual purification and counteracting the work of witches and sorcerers in the communities within which church members live (Kiernan 1987; Oosthuizen 1992, 122). The vast majority of members of these churches have been the poorest of the African poor.

A third variety of AICs share with Zionists their emphasis on healing and reliance on the Holy Spirit in the struggle against demons, witches, and sorcerers but are dominated by a far more charismatic prophet-leader than the ordinary Zionist and Apostolic congregations. Sundkler hesitatingly suggested that these churches might be called "messianic." Because of the distress such a designation causes Christians, Sundkler was tentative about suggesting it, usually adding a question mark whenever he used the term in this way (see Sundkler 1976, 308ff.). The largest and most famous of these churches are the amaNazaretha, founded by Isaiah Shembe in 1911 (Vilakazi 1985), and the International Pentecost Church of Frederick Modise (Anderson 1992b). These churches also direct a great deal of their energy toward combating the evil forces of witchcraft and the dangers of pollution. In 1921, devotees of one of these churches, the "Israelites" of Enoch Mgijima, established a settlement at Bulhoek, near Queenstown in the Eastern Cape, squatting on Crown land in defiance of the white authorities while awaiting the Second Coming. The authorities, reluctant to allow "Natives" to be seen to defy them, even in pursuit of millenarian ends, sent the army and police. At least 183 Israelites were massacred (Edgar 1988, 33).

Sundkler always insisted that these typologies were not definitive (Sundkler 1948), and his categories have been criticized for identifying a wide range of religious communities according to their relation to a Western interpretation of Christian orthodoxy (Etherington 1979). Nevertheless, the three categories remain a useful device for grouping African churches as forms of human social organization. They do not, however, adequately account for the varieties of religious experience among African Christians or for the complex dynamics of relations with the worlds of invisible beings that religious specialists offer ordinary believers.

A recent, and somewhat contentious, categorization of indigenous and independently initiated African Christian churches has grouped them with churches affiliated with the Pentecostal movement into a single broad category on the grounds of their common emphases on a theology of the "Spirit." Allan Anderson, who was himself a missionary in a white Pentecostalist church before becoming a member of an African "Apostolic" (Pentecostalist) congregation and a scholar, has argued that indigenous African Christianity has much more in common with the theology and rituals of Pentecostalism that emerged from the black American revivalists of Azuza Street in early-twentieth-century Los Angeles than is usually granted (Anderson 1992a). In South African church historiography, this is somewhat unorthodox, as the established Pentecostalist churches in South Africa, until recently, have tended to be exclusively white, predominantly Afrikaans, and decidedly separatist, if not completely racist (Anderson and Pillay 1997). Anderson's categorization, while perhaps problematic for the conventional sociology of South African churches, has the salutary virtue of emphasizing the connection between the theology of the Spirit, the search for spiritual power among impoverished populations, and the explosion of global religious movements such as Pentecostalism in the twentieth century. It also serves to highlight the increasingly important role of an aspect of the triune Christian deity in the spirit world of Africa, both reinforcing and supplanting other spiritual powers.

Considering the vast numbers of people belonging to independent churches and the amount of time and energy they commit to their devotions pursuing healing and prosperity in the everyday work of their religious life, the AICs are seriously underrepresented both in the literature on African social life and in public forums of "civil society." They hardly figure in the scholarly literatures relating to black South African society outside the disciplines of church history and missiology.[12] Nor have they ever produced a public figure of the stature of Desmond Tutu or an associational presence in public life equivalent to the South African Council of Churches. During the apartheid years, these churches were studiously apolitical, sometimes earning the resentment of more politically active Christians for their quiescence. Their principal focus has been on matters of spiritual security. As Kiernan has argued, "they provided intimate and supportive communities, they gave concentrated attention to healing, and they mobilized spiritual reserves to counter the aggression of sorcery. In all of these ways—organizational, supportive, therapeutic and protective— they formed coping institutions which aimed at the delivery of benefits in the here and now" (1995a, 124).

White Christian scholars have written most of the literature on these

---

12. Some notable exceptions are exemplary works by Jean Comaroff (1985), Kiernan (1990b), and Martin West (1975a).

churches. Their works, while providing an enormously valuable insight into the religious life of these movements, have been obsessively concerned with varieties of a single question: Are these genuine Christian churches — or, as many Christians would frame it, genuine parts of *the* Christian Church? The early literature on Zionist/Apostolic AICs, preoccupied with issues of doctrinal clarity, tended to treat them as syncretic cults reacting against white mission churches, "indigenous" religious sects mixing half-baked Christian teachings with indigenous religious practices to create a new hybrid form of syncretic spirituality to the detriment of true Christianity. In the first edition of *Bantu Prophets,* for example, Sundkler, expressing a common worry of white missionaries, posited in an unfortunate locution that came to haunt him long after he removed it from the revised edition fifteen years later, that Zionism served as a "bridge" back to paganism from Christianity: *"The syncretistic sect becomes the bridge over which Africans are brought back to heathenism* [emphasis in original]. . . . It can be shown how individuals and groups have passed step by step from a Mission church to an Ethiopian church, and from the Ethiopians to the Zionists, and how at last via the bridge of nativistic Zionism they have returned to the African animism from where they once started" (Sundkler 1948, 297). From the outside, these churches seem remarkably similar in ritual and practice to "traditional" African religion—in Sundkler's phrase again: "New wine in old wineskins" (Sundkler 1948, chap. 7). From the inside, however, as Allan Anderson, the Pentecostalist missionary and scholar, has demonstrated in a large body of work over the past decade, these churches exhibit a "radical discontinuity between the new Christian faith and the old traditional beliefs" (Anderson 2000b, 217). Among other things, members of these churches tend to view the old practices as demonic.

Attitudes of white Christian church leaders to these religious groups throughout the twentieth century have ranged from disdainful indifference to contempt, viewing AIC members, in the words of C. M. Pauw, "as misled and sectarian people who jeopardise the work of God through syncretism or neo-paganism" (Pauw 1995, 9). Gerhardus Oosthuizen, one of the most dedicated students of these churches in the missiological vein, initially regarded them as forms of African "post-Christianity" (Oosthuizen 1968). In his later work, however, he embraced them as epitomizing the spirit of Christ at work in Africa, albeit in a manner reminiscent of Christians in the third and forth centuries (Oosthuizen 1992, xxii). Recent writers on AICs, most of whom study them from the perspective of Christian missiology (and happen to be white),[13] have generally preferred to acknowledge the character of these groups as genuine Christian churches "independent" of white missionary Christianity (Daneel 1971; Makhubu 1988; Oosthuizen and Hexham 1991). These writers mostly celebrate the African contribution to the universal church by stressing how the AIC churches have "initiated" a genuine Christian mission in Africa from which white people could learn much (Allan Anderson 2000b).

Despite the tendency in recent years of liberal white theologians to embrace these forms of African Christianity, the obsession of AIC congregations with combating witchcraft and pollution prompts observers to wonder whether these churches liberate people from their fears of witchcraft or enslave them to a heightened sense of exposure to evil forces (Daneel 1990; Lagerwerf 1987). Christian theologians themselves engage in struggles with "evil forces," recognizing them as spiritual and social realities. Their consideration of African practices of managing evil is thus not entirely academic. Some writers, notably Marthinus Daneel, emphasize the positive value African Christians discover in their struggle against spiritual evils by belonging to a religious community such as a Zionist church. Others have shown how the practice and ritual of these congregations, who without exception abhor sorcery, paradoxically heighten the sense of being exposed to these forces: "the more vigorously they resist it, the more surely do they support it" (Kiernan 1987, 5). Kiernan has shown in his work with Zionists in Kwa Mashu how people sensitive to the dangers of sorcery come to see themselves as "encircled by sorcery" and find in their church a constant battle against sorcerers, forming in the process "closed communities of the saved, bounded by a protective barrier or mystical *cordon sanitaire*" (1995a, 127). This sense of embattlement and hostility to outsiders constitutes a rather different form of community than that typically invoked under the currently faddish rubric of "faith-based communities."

The preoccupation of AICs with healing and their obsessions with the dangers of witchcraft and pollution have been something of an embarrassment to black theologians of the mainline churches. Most black theologians and clerical activists—practitioners of "contextual theology," "black theology," and "liberation theology" alike—have belonged to mainline congregations. Although these theologians have been happy to recognize the

13. Very little has been written about these churches by black theologians, although there is a useful introduction to them by an Apostolic minister, Paul Makhubu (Makhubu 1988), and Absalom Vilakazi has written an account of Shembe's amaNazaretha (Vilakazi 1985).

AICs as constituting a genuinely African religious movement, they have tended to focus their "contextual" concerns more intently on the context of white racism and political oppression than on the black-on-black occult violence that preoccupies the AICs. Black ministers in the mainline churches and their Ethiopian offshoots have tended to be similarly dismissive, particularly regarding the AIC preoccupation with issues of witchcraft, which, in Oosthuizen's assessment, they see as "below the dignity of advanced people" (Oosthuizen 1992). This division remains. Black theological disdain for the AICs of the Zionist and Apostolic variety was particularly intense during the years of the antiapartheid struggle, when the AICs seemed acquiescent, if not actually collaborationist, in the face of apartheid (Maimela 1987; Mosala and Tlhagale 1986; P. De Villiers 1987; Petersen 1995).[14]

During the era of antiapartheid struggle, the AICs were mostly quiescent. The ZCC, for example, South Africa's largest single Christian denomination, remained studiously disengaged from the political struggle. The ZCC was viewed by many activists as particularly suspect after its leader, Bishop Lekganyane, invited State President P. W. Botha to attend the church's annual pilgrimage at their headquarters in Moria in the middle of the turmoil of 1985. This quiescence remains a point of contention on the part of political activists from that time, though members of the ZCC have insisted to me that Bishop Lekganyane was in fact the force that brought about negotiations in the first place—a view that strikes me as more revealing about their sense of his significance than an accurate reflection of history. At the Truth and Reconciliation Commission's hearings on the role of the churches under apartheid in 1999, the ZCC's spokesperson, Rev. Emmanuel Motola, was challenged to defend the church's role during apartheid. Motola replied: "as a church, the Zion Christian Church did not lead people into a mode of resistance against apartheid. But as a church the ZCC taught its people to love themselves more than ever, to stand upright and face the future, to defy the laws of apartheid. And that all these teachings are not known in the press, in the general public at large can hardly be the problem of the Zion Christian Church" (Zion Christian Church 1999). Motola's account confirms the thesis first proposed by Jean Comaroff, who set the terms of academic debate regarding implicit patterns of resistance

14. In the 1980s, when everyone concerned with South African issues was fixated with resistance, a number of writers investigated the political inclinations of Zionist and Apostolic churches. Mathew Schoffeleers (1991) decisively reviewed the AIC doctrines and practices for evidence of explicit political resistance and found little. See also Anderson 1997.

in Zionist ritual by arguing that they constituted a "radical form of cultural resistance" to colonialism and white domination (Comaroff 1985, 166). In the postapartheid era, although the vast majority of AIC members actively supported the liberation struggle and the ANC, the churches have remained quiet. While church leaders like the Anglican archbishop Njongonkulu Ndungane have been outspoken on a range of political issues, most notably AIDS, the AIC churches have not spoken out.

Postapartheid Spirituality

It remains to be seen whether the end of white domination in the state will lead to transformations in the structure of the spirit world on a par with those that accompanied the conquest of African polities in the colonial era. Early signs, however, suggest that some changes are taking place. The most significant of these has been the steady emergence, noted in the proliferation of "Spirit-type" churches discussed above, of the Holy Spirit as the primary spiritual agency responsible for the fortunes of human life. The Christian trinitarian conception of God is a notoriously tricky concept, even for the most sophisticated of theologians and church officials, who have struggled mightily through the ages to control divergences in interpretation. In this part of the world the concept of God as a father with a son who was once among the living resonates with the hierarchical logic of ancestral reverence as well as customs of respect for age and principles of political order. The concept of the Holy Spirit as a generalized force infusing all life is similarly resonant with many local traditions. What the Spirit-type churches offer their members are modes of direct personal engagement with this force to secure relief from suffering and well-being in the here and now. These churches are booming.

In recent years the African Pentecostalist AICs have been competing for members with a burgeoning global network of evangelical "Neo-Pentecostalist" churches originating in the United States and Brazil (Corten and Marshal-Fratani 2000). These Neo-Pentecostalist churches practice varieties of "Faith Gospel" or "Prosperity Gospel" promising "a right to the health and wealth won by Christ" by his victory over sin (Gifford 1998, 39). All of these churches, global Neo-Pentecostalist and AIC alike, though differing widely in ritual practice, emphasize connection with the Holy Spirit and share practices such as adult immersion baptism, divine healing, exorcism, prophecy, revelation, and speaking in tongues (Anderson and Pillay 1997, 227). While the AICs still draw their members from the poorest of the poor, the Neo-Pentecostalists are proving popular among the new black middle classes and are building multiracial congregations. As these congregations have gained in strength, membership of mainline Protestant denominations has declined dramatically; the number of Roman Catholics has remained more or less steady (Goodhew 2000, 365).[15] Within this profusion of churches, a wide variety of attitudes to ancestors flourish.

15. In the years between the 1980 and 1991 censuses, the fastest growing church in South Africa was the ZCC, whose membership was second only to the Catholic Church (Kritzinger 1993).

9

INVISIBLE BEINGS IN EVERYDAY LIFE

A Visit to an Ancestor

On the day I was to leave Soweto to return to work in New York in late August 1994, we rose early to go to Avalon Cemetery to clean Grandfather's grave. We were five: Thabo, the firstborn, his sisters Seipati and Keitumetse, their father, Hendry, and me, the adoptive brother. Seipati and Keitumetse were also leaving home that weekend, returning to their schools.

Avalon Cemetery was already busy though the sun had scarcely risen. We followed a convoy of buses and cars filled with singing Sowetans on their way to the graves for the unveiling of a tombstone. Scattered throughout that huge cemetery—dry, brown, and dusty in the midwinter chill— were smaller groups, families, like us, come to talk to their ancestors, to tell of the changes in their lives, of misfortunes visited upon them by persons known and unknown, seeking solace, enlisting aid and protection from those who had gone before in facing the trials of this world. Straggling behind the buses, slowing our passage, a driver struggled with the gears of his battered old Peugeot while trying to document the procession with his video camera held out of the window.

Grandfather, Hendry's father, died in 1978. Thabo found the grave and parked in the rutted track nearby. Keitumetse took a bucket off in search of a tap. I carried the pot of *mqomboti,* sorghum beer. Thabo carried five small stones from the backyard and a spade. Seipati had the old newspapers.

We gathered at the head of the north-facing grave. Chiseled into the sloping granite stone sitting like a pillow atop the granite slab were the words "Amos Mfete 14-8-1882 11-10-1978 *Robala ka Kagiso.* [Rest in Peace.]" He would have been a very young man, I thought to myself, when my own father's grandfather marched through these parts with the Lancashire Fusiliers to fight the Boers in 1899. Footprints in the dust on the granite of Grandfather's gravestone pointed toward a fresh grave nearby.

Keitumetse returned with the water. She covered her head with the hood of her jacket. Seipati adjusted her scarf. Thabo began. He took a draught of the *mqomboti* and squirted it onto the dusty grave in three milky jets. He prayed to Jesus and called out to Grandfather. He told Grandfather why we had come. "Seipati, Keitumetse, and Adam are leaving home today," he said. "Please, Grandfather, look after them." He also asked for help for himself in finding a job since he had been unemployed for more than two years. At the end of his speech, Thabo wet one of the stones we had brought from home with spittle and placed it upon the grave. Hendry followed his son. He again called upon his father to look after the family and protect us all. Seipati followed. She spoke of her new baby and how she would be returning to work, asking for strength and assistance. She also concluded by spitting on a stone and placing it on the grave. Keitumetse followed her older sister, telling Grandfather of her impending return to college, asking for help in the coming term, her last before graduating as a technical teacher, and appealing for protection for the new baby and also for Adam, who, she said, was traveling to New York to return to his job at the university. She placed her dampened stone on the grave. I was last to speak. I took the *mqomboti* into my mouth—gritty, sour, milky, delicious— spitting just as the others had done. "Ntate Moholo," I said, using the Sotho idiom, "I am Adam. I don't know if you know me. I am the new son. I am thankful. For four years I have been living here. Living here with your family. I came as a visitor from overseas, and they made me one of their own. Thank you." Then I ran out of things to say. I was beginning to feel foolish. I paused. It was one of those eternal moments. "Grandfather . . ." I continued in English, fumbling for words. "They have looked after me so well, made me part of your family. They have made me safe. I am leaving today for America, for New York. I don't know when I will be able to come back. Please look after everyone when I am away so that . . . so that when I come back I can find them all living . . . living well. So that I can find them all well and happy." Again I fell silent. I could not think of anything else to say. I could not find words to express my gratitude to the people with whom I was standing by the grave of their ancestor on a Soweto winter's morning. I could not say anything sensible to that slab of granite, so I dribbled on the stone and placed it on the grave. It was a blue stone, the sort they use in reinforcing concrete. Father had lifted a load of them from a building site down the street from us. Keitumetse began washing the tomb, wiping the dust away with water and newsprint. Thabo scraped away the weeds from the edges with a bright pink spade. Father stood back, pensive, hands in pockets. We finished up and went home for breakfast.

Jesus and the Ancestors

Ancestors remain a vital presence in African life. Even to be indifferent toward them requires effort. Anyone with a reasonably wide circle of friends in Soweto can find a feast for ancestors most weekends where they can enjoy free food and drink. After we returned from the cemetery that morning, MaMfete served the chicken she had slaughtered for the ancestors. Money was short, or we would have slaughtered a sheep. We drank the *mqomboti* she had brewed for the ancestors and shared what little there was with whoever happened to drop by. Ancestors must be fed with the meat of a freshly slaughtered beast and freshly brewed beer lest they become angry with their descendants and punish them or allow misfortunes to befall them. Many people pursue relations with ancestors in a manner not unlike that described in old accounts of life written by early missionaries, such as those elaborated in Willoughby's "sympathetic" account of "ancestor religion" *The Soul of the Bantu* (Willoughby 1928). Accounts of life in southern Africa from previous centuries, however, suggest that the ancestors imposed far more extensive sets of laws and rules upon their descendants than seems to be the case today.

Although the missionary churches were generally hostile to rituals relating to ancestors throughout most of the nineteenth and twentieth centuries, African Christians continued to revere them. MaMfete is the most devout of Methodists, yet it was she who motivated that trip to the cemetery. Within the missionary churches the African faithful typically adopted the practice of publicly adhering to the rituals and theology of the church, which disdained ancestral reverence, while performing the necessary ancestral rituals privately within their families—particularly at times of crisis and life-cycle events such as births, weddings, and funerals (Setiloane 1976). Not infrequently, this produced, and in many instances still creates, in African Christians a sense of loyalties divided between church and ancestors: a "divided soul" in the words of one observer (Partain 1986). Even South Africa's most famous black Christian, Archbishop and Nobel Laureate Desmond Tutu, speaks of experiencing tensions between reverence for ancestors and the teachings of the church: "I, though a third-generation Christian, knowing only urban life with a father who was headmaster of an Anglican primary school, feel this division within my own soul" (1969, 103). Were this problem of the divided soul merely a matter of conflicted identity—a matter of the struggle to integrate the identity of "Christian" with that of "African"—it would be complex enough. But since the ancestors are also postulated as being able to harm and to help in ways most commonly manifested in matters of bodily sickness, physical injury, and material prosperity, the issue is also one of security, managing threats to health, welfare, and prosperity that can result in poverty, violence, illness, and, death.

Most members of "mainline" mission churches, along with their independent black "Ethiopian" offshoots, have achieved accommodations between Christian teaching and ancestral reverence that allow them to live with the sort of divided soul of which Tutu complained; according to Gabriel Setiloane, reverence for the ancestors helps compensate for "the felt deficiencies of a western form of Christianity already secularized at the coming of the first missionaries" (1976, 224). If pressed to justify their continued veneration of ancestors, such Christians will usually speak of them as agents of God: intrinsically virtuous beings who serve as intermediaries between God and the living, informing God of the needs of their descendants and helping their descendants with powers granted by God. As Seipati once explained to me when I questioned the purpose of ancestors for Christians such as she: "God is more powerful than the ancestors. Ancestors are getting their power from God and they give this power to the people." Among Christians who have achieved an accommodation between ancestral relations and faith in the Christian God, attitudes to ancestors are supposed to be a matter of respect but not worship. Seipati also explained: "a person should not *pray* to their ancestors. They must pray to God only. And to Jesus. But they can talk to their ancestors and those ancestors will pray to God for them, too. So then everything will come good."

African Christians have long debated whether the proper attitude of the living toward their ancestors should be described as worship, veneration, or reverence. The implications of these English descriptions have taxed and infuriated generations of African Christians, particularly those who have sought accommodation between ancestral practices and Christian teachings and who vehemently deny the charge that they are practicing the sin of idolatry or trafficking with demons. By the latter part of the twentieth century, the consensus among African theologians within mainline churches in South Africa and other parts of the continent was that so long as relations with ancestors were conducted in terms of a model of community premised upon respect for elders, the authority of age, and an understanding of death as a transition to a state of being closer to the divine, reverence for ancestors and respect of rituals acknowledging them need not be thought of as idolatry or worship of deities in conflict with essentials of Christian teaching (Fashole-Luke 1976). Anthropologists have also debated the appropriate terms for describing African relationships with ancestors. Some have insisted, despite the objections of African Christians, that ancestors were in fact "worshiped" in the manner of deities, not "revered" in the manner of elders (Kopytoff 1971). Some have argued that ancestors were not always treated in the same way throughout the continent, with some societies worshiping them while others merely revering them (Hammond-Tooke 1978). And some have argued that some types of ancestral spirits have been worshiped while others have been revered (Kuckertz 1984, 12). My own experience in Soweto suggests that while "reverence" is the best term to describe what might be called the official ideology of "ancestorship" (a term I borrow from Madumo), neither reverence nor worship adequately describes the relationship with ancestors, particularly as it becomes invested with hope and dread in times of crisis, when people desperately need to connect with some sort of effective power, power which the ancestors may, or may not, possess. Whatever the scholarly or theological niceties, however, the fact of communication between spiritual beings and humans continues to present substantial problems for African Christians in places like contemporary Soweto.

Despite being ordinarily invisible, ancestors can make their presence felt in the lives of the living. Few doubt the objective reality of ancestors or of evil spirits such as those that some Christians insist disguise themselves as ancestors in order to mislead the living. Experiences suggesting connection with the dead such as dreams and visions are accorded a kind of "external" objectivity, too. Conventional wisdom has it that ancestors can speak directly to their descendants through the media of dreams and visions or indirectly through speech mediated by healers possessing spiritual gifts (i.e., being gifted with possession by spirits). Here is how Madumo describes the process of interaction with ancestors:

> My mother's not a *sangoma*. She's not a witch doctor. But she can dream something of which it can happen days after. Because once she told me: "Madube, I dreamed about you that someone will stab you." The following day I went to school and I was nearly stabbed. But I was aware of this, so I was okay. Then I came and told her: "No, it's true." So you see that power is a certain spirit from ancestors. And if that spirit is within you, you must do what the spirit tells you, otherwise you go mad or you are mentally disturbed. So to cure that mental disturbance, you must do what the spirit tells you. Even me, I've got a certain spirit whereby if I'm walking alone I might have the fear that if I go that direction maybe something will happen, so I

change the direction. And it is true. After turning to right, I'll hear somebody screaming *Hhhhhhhheeeeeeee!* You see that? With us Africans it is
like that. We've got that ancestor spirit, and there are those people who
are rich because of these ancestors. Ancestors just come to you and tell you
what to do.

Ancestors can also signify their feelings, wishes, and intentions by means
of omens, particularly by appearing in the shape of creatures such as
snakes, although few Sowetans are familiar with the detailed mythologies
of these matters that were once known to particular clans and described in
A. C. Jordan's novel *The Wrath of the Ancestors* (1980). Omens can portend
both blessings and misfortunes.

Signs of ancestral action are usually read retrospectively in the remem-
brance of blessings or misfortunes. Yet signs of ancestral displeasure are
not always clear, since the ancestors are but one of many forces that could
be operating to cause suffering. Specialist assistance by diviners who can
communicate directly with the spirits of the dead is usually needed for confidence in interpreting the message. When Madumo's mother died and he
was accused of killing her with witchcraft and chased away from home, he
assumed he was being punished by the ancestors for his neglect of them.
Later, however, he consulted the *inyanga* Mr. Zondi and discovered that his
ancestors were actually very protective of him, but he had been bewitched.
In everyday routines, the living can communicate with their ancestors by
means of gestures such as tipping a drop of beer to the ground, acts of fealty
such as tending their graves and speaking to them, or rituals such as slaughtering a beast, brewing beer, and preparing a feast.[1] Diviners can also facilitate direct communication of needs and desires to ancestors. This can be
particularly important for people who are not in a position to draw upon
the resources of their family to consult with ancestors in the way the Mfetes
did in their visit to the cemetery described at the beginning of this chapter.

The central experiential domain of human relations with ancestors is
the dream. While dreams convey an immediate and intense experience of
connection with ancestors, they pose definite problems of interpretation.
Ancestors are said to appear in dreams, particularly vivid dreams or dreams
from which the sleeper wakes with bodily aches and pains, but they do not
necessarily appear in the image of their living bodies nor speak with the
same voice they had while living (Berglund 1976, 98). I once interviewed a

1. For an extended discussion of the dynamics of Zulu ancestral feasting, see H. White
2001.

man named Nkonyana who claimed to have been commanded by an ancestor who appeared to him in a dream to warn members of his community in the shack settlement of Snake Park to dismantle their shacks and move or else the monster iNkosi ya Manzi (Lord of the Water), an enormous snake manifesting itself in the form of a whirlwind or tornado and whose home in the nearby creek was being disturbed, would sweep up their homes and dump them on the border of Swaziland. The man was convinced of the veracity of the warning because the message had been repeated in four different dreams. The first time he was aware only of a voice passing on the message from iNkosi ya Manzi. In the second dream the ancestor appeared in the form of a creature that was half horse and half man. In the third, he was spoken to by a creature that was half man and half ox. Finally, he was spoken to by a voice embodied in a bright light.[2]

Other times the ancestors communicate by means of symbols that can have more or less conventional interpretations, such as snakes (a common ancestral symbol for Zulus), water, or eating meat in the dream (Bryant 1949, 624; Berglund 1976, 100). The most intense form of ancestral intervention comes in the form of dreams associated with illnesses that are interpreted as a call to become a healer. Both *sangomas* and prophet-healers of AICs typically experience such dreams (Oosthuizen 1992, 22). As Seipati explained it:

> A prophet can heal you just the way a *sangoma* can heal you. But the only difference is that the prophet gives the water. She will just give you water to drink. That's all. And the *sangoma* will give you all this kind of *muthi* that he has done. So I think they go hand in glove, because they are nearly doing the same thing, you see. Helping people, you see. Even in witchcraft they help people if they have that spirit. Maybe that spirit always comes as if you are ill. As if you are ill, say you are having a stroke or whatever. So they will take you and send you to a *sangoma*'s place and train you to be a *sangoma*. Then you get healed. The same way happens on the Christianity. It can just happen that way. You are ill; they'll take you to a prophet. He'll train you to be a prophet. Then you are healed. And again, in your turn, you'll heal other people. So I think they go hand in glove.

For those who have embraced the born-again forms of Christian faith and rejected the possibility of meaningful relationships with ancestors, dreams

2. For a fuller account of the events surrounding this warning, see Ashforth 1998a.

that would otherwise lend themselves to interpretation as ancestral communications seem like assaults by evil spirits.

When a senior diviner identifies a patient as having an affliction that is a call to become a healer, the afflicted person is typically required to move in with the diviner, undergo training in ritual and instruction in healing, and devote months to establishing a relationship with the troubling spirits by means, among other things, of drumming and dancing, culminating in a feast where beasts are slaughtered both for the senior healer's and the patient/acolyte's ancestors. Such treatments are expensive, and most people will say they dread the prospect of being so diagnosed, particularly as it is said that when a person refuses such a call, not only will their own ailments persist but the ancestors will also trouble others in their family. However, as James Kiernan has astutely noted, the "call" is less mysterious than it sounds. Consulting diviners carefully select the people who seem likely candidates: "It is in fact the consulting diviner who pronounces on the suitability of the candidate to go forward for training; it is simply a form of professional recruitment. The mystical 'call' is no more than the symbolic idiom in which this human selection is expressed" (1995b, 8).

Or, as John Janzen has argued: "It is not appropriate to assume that the *twasa* diagnosis, or call, corresponds to Western psychoanalytic or therapeutic labels. In fact, there may be better reason to suspect that this diagnosis singles out individuals for recruitment to ritual leadership roles on the basis of characteristics of greater sensitivity, ego strength, and cultural receptivity in a time or situation of stress" (1992, 55). Among those who are diagnosed as being called, few will complete the rigorous, inconvenient, and expensive process of *ukuthwasa* (i.e., the process of becoming a healer, a *sangoma*). Among those who complete the training, few will accede to the position of full-time professional healer. More will participate in the *ngoma* cult on a temporary or part-time basis. The work of these specialists in communicating with ancestors, however, is of the first importance in maintaining among the population the more general sense of the possibility of interacting with ancestors and drawing upon their power. In a context where traditions are ill taught and families fall apart, the *sangomas,* by virtue of their purported capacity to speak directly with ancestors, are able, at times, to convince people about the nature of ancestral displeasure that is being manifested in present misfortune and the steps necessary for appeasing the invisible powers. That is, not only do adepts of the *ngoma* cult perpetuate tradition, but they also serve as specialists enabling people to maintain relations with ancestors in the absence of, or their ignorance of, tradition.

Ancestors make their presence felt in the affairs of their descendants in the form of both misfortune and prosperity. Yet, although good fortune as well as ill is properly attributed to the ancestors, people definitely turn to their ancestors more often in time of need than of plenty. As Madumo put it when his own miseries were many: "the problem with this ancestorship business is that we Africans, myself included, when life picks up and things are going smooth for us, we normally forget about ancestors" (Ashforth 2000a, 24). Times of suffering, particularly when prolonged or intense, are occasions not only for reflection on ancestral wishes and intentions but for supplication in search of aid. Given that ancestors are generally presumed, by those who revere them, to have the true interests of their descendants at heart, any suffering they inflict must be presumed to be driven by important reasons, reasons related to the ancestors' project of protection. In all accounts of ancestors, the primary reasons given for their inflicting of harm, or allowing harm to be caused, consist of righteous anger: anger at descendants' infractions of rules or neglect of obligations. After prolonged neglect, this anger is said to wither into indifference, with the neglected ancestors unwilling and, finally, unable to intervene on their descendants' behalf, since ancestors themselves are dependent upon the living for support.

When the Ancestors Are Angered

Ancestors, being family, are not usually thought inclined to kill, though their punishments might at times be severe. In times of trouble, most people find it difficult to avoid wondering whether they are being punished by their ancestors. When my friend Khanyile was injured in a road accident, his family wondered what role had been played by ancestors. He had been traveling from Soweto to town in a *combi* taxi when someone in a Mercedes turned in front of them and wrecked both vehicles. Obviously, Khanyile's ancestors had been with him at the time, for he had not died in the crash with the driver of the *combi* and two other passengers. Equally obviously, however, the ancestors must have been angry for some reason—otherwise, he would not have broken both legs and fractured his jaw. When the family consulted an *inyanga*, they learned that the accident had been caused by witchcraft. Someone was using *muthi* against them. Although ancestral displeasure in this instance was not the sole problem, it remained necessary to appease them with a feast to thank them for their assistance and to enlist their aid in helping Khanyile recover from his injuries and in protecting him from further assault by the witches. Ancestors are most commonly thought to allow harm or cause suffering to befall their descendants as a way of reminding them to fulfill their obligations to the dead. Principal among these is the requirement of tending their graves and honoring them with feasts.

When suffering is interpreted as being caused by ancestral displeasure, one of three possible motives is usually invoked: punishment for infringement of rules of custom; anger at neglect of ritual duties; or, more rarely, a call to a descendant to establish a more intense relationship with the spirits and become a healer. Two other possibilities also exist, though they are rarely specified in what might be termed "official" ideologies of ancestorship. One is that the ancestors, through prolonged neglect, have become impotent and powerless to protect the descendants they hardly know. The other is that the ancestor himself or herself is inherently malicious and is intent upon perpetrating forms of abuse from beyond the grave. As very few people can honestly claim to have accorded their ancestors the respect, honor, and sustenance they deserve, while even fewer can account themselves blameless in upholding all the rules, customs, and traditions of their forefathers, the possibility of ancestral anger is always a plausible suggestion at times of trouble. An element of wishful thinking also inheres in such interpretations of misfortunes. After all, however angry and obnoxious ancestors may be, they are family. Their punishments are interpreted as efforts to secure the respect and sustenance they themselves need in order to perform their own special duties of protecting their kin. Relationships between ancestors and their kin are symbiotic.

The old ethnographies are replete with accounts of "taboos" proscribing a wide range of actions in infringement of which supernatural sanctions could be expected, but present-day Sowetans, especially the young, have a limited sense of such things. The Mfetes' paternal grandfather, whom we visited at his grave in 1994, for example, was a Tswana. In the late nineteenth century, when he was growing up, he would have been subjected to an elaborate code of rules known as *moila*, some of which, in Isaac Schapera's terms, were "trifling," while others were backed with supernatural sanctions—such as drought or storms—that affected the whole community and whose infringement could also result in punishment from the chief (Schapera 1938, 39). Historically, these rules were taught to young people in households at appropriate points in their social development and in initiation schools (also known as circumcision schools) attended, separately, by cohorts of boys and girls of similar ages under the stewardship of local political authorities (Setiloane 1976, 36). Most young Sowetans, however, have been taught only a very limited set of such customs and rules within their families. None of my friends attended initiation schools. There are no formal institutions devoted to the teaching of custom or tradition in urban areas. Although some families in urban areas do send their boys to initiation schools, the young men I know who felt the need to lose their foreskins had them removed in a clinic without any instruction in customs, law, or lore whatsoever.

Although the laws of the ancestors have lost much of their purchase in contemporary everyday life, new systems of rules have arisen to take their place, mostly articulated in the language of biblical injunction and institutionalized within the multitudes of Christian churches. Each has its own particular schemes and emphases. Indigenous churches have been particularly rigorous in their emphasis upon extensive rules of conduct analogous to the "taboos" of old. Apostolic and Zionist churches, for example, generally prescribe distinctive uniforms and proscribe the consumption of alcohol, tobacco, and pork—with due reference to biblical authority. As well as guiding the spiritual subjection of their members to the laws of God, these rules have the salutary effect of isolating communities of believers from social and spiritual contamination by others in the community as well as limiting their exposure to *muthi* and spiritual pollution from their unpurified neighbors (Allan Anderson 2000b, 137). Within "mainline" churches, the women's *manyano* prayer groups (associations of married women, who in many respects are the dynamic heart of the whole religious enterprise) are also characterized, in the words of Mia Brandel-Syrier, by "an extreme preoccupation with laws and rules" (1962, 53). Both AICs and *manyanos* place great store upon the wearing of correct attire, including uniforms and badges identifying themselves as members of particular congregations. All churches insist upon timely payment of dues, including tithes, as required by the constitution of the church. In his survey of AICs in Shoshanguve, Allan Anderson found that many respondents cited the existence of these rules as a primary reason for their joining a particular church, although more were drawn in by their experience of healing (Anderson 1997).

The customs and rules that do exist tend to be seen as applicable only in the limited domains of particular families. One of the difficulties in maintaining a sense of ancestral authority in urban life is that the rules particular ancestors are said to insist upon are always specific: these ancestors require adherence to these rules and procedures. Incorrect performance of rituals or ignorance of rules is supposed to be backed by particular ancestral sanctions. But it is more difficult to follow the old rules in towns, because urban areas bring together people—often in multiethnic families —practicing a multiplicity of particular procedures within the general field of ancestral reverence. Consequently, a great deal of the particularity has dropped from contemporary rituals, and a good deal of collective innovation has taken place. Before Madumo's mother died, for example, she instructed her family not to slaughter any animals for her funeral but only to serve "ready-made" food and drinks. Her family would not have dared displease her, although most of their neighbors thought the arrangement peculiar. In a context such as a big multiethnic city, ancestral rules and prohibitions are constantly being broken on all sides. Fear of the efficacy of sanctions for particular infractions seems to have diminished.

Worse than the active anger of ancestors is their indifference. After years of inattention, even the most long-suffering guardian can give up on his or her charges and lose interest in their fate. Because the duties of maintaining proper relations with ancestors can be onerous and expensive, few feel confident that their ancestors are well satisfied. When ancestors neglect their descendants, as opposed to actively punishing them, the living become vulnerable to attack by malicious forces, human and invisible, and all sorts of evils can befall them. And while the punishments meted out by ancestors seeking attention are relatively minor, the ancestors who have forgotten their descendants are inattentive when the forces seeking to kill are at work. Hence, the turning away of neglected ancestors has been a common theme throughout the history of European colonization in this part of the world, along with millenarian proposals to ensure their return.[3] The problem of ancestral neglect is exacerbated by the fact of fractured families. For the propitiation of ancestors requires participation from family members, particularly elders, and if elders are unavailable the rituals are incomplete. Furthermore, if the ancestors are unknown, or have never been properly introduced to those whom they are supposed to protect, how can they do so?

When suffering seems clearly undeserved, yet must still be accounted for as either imposed or allowed by the higher power of invisible beings, it can also be interpreted as some kind of test of faith, loyalty, or trustworthiness, an ordeal. If successfully endured, this suffering will be followed by bountiful reward. Exemplified by the biblical story of Job, this notion of the test is often invoked in efforts to make suffering sufferable, particularly among those grieving for lost loved ones. The test of faith is also the prom-

3. The most dramatic of these movements was that surrounding the Xhosa "cattle-killing" in 1856, when, in response to a young woman's prophecies that the ancestors would return with new cattle and restore the land lost to British control, tens of thousands of people were persuaded to kill their cattle and burn their crops, with dire results. See Peires 1989.

ise of redemption, the guarantee of reward in either this life or the life to come. For those whose lives are otherwise insufferable, the life to come sometimes can seem like the only life worth living and this one on earth an extended test of faith. The idea of suffering as a test, an idea that makes little sense except in relation to the promise of relief, if not full redemption, is deployed in much healing work by all varieties of healers. Traditional healers and faith healers make much of having endured suffering themselves as a "call" from the spirit world for them to become healers and, thereby, vehicles for ancestral and spiritual power in the world.[4] Healers play the central role in interpreting the interests and desires of ancestors for ordinary people, perpetuating thereby a sense of the ancestors' vitality.

Most people profess a general sense of the efficacy of ancestral power, but when the forces of their available ancestors are arrayed against the sources of evil apparent in all the misfortunes of the world, the balance of power is not in the ancestors' favor. These days, when generations of city dwellers have lived beyond the purview of chiefs and other authorities who can claim access to powerful ancestors whose authority extends over wide social terrains such as nations, tribes, clans, and lineages, the ancestors are generally restricted to caring about their own immediate descendants. Most people in places like Soweto do not have access to ancestral forces powerful enough to meet the challenges of large-scale suffering in the form of scourges like apartheid, unemployment, poverty, and AIDS. No institution outside the Christian churches akin to the rainmaker of old exists today to supplicate invisible powers for the benefit of the community as a whole. Large-scale evil powers such as can be mobilized by the devil are generally too much for the ancestors of a single family alone to counteract. Moreover, in the fractured families of South Africa today, many families have no memories of fathers, let alone ancestors, to look over them. Mothers find themselves, contrary to tradition, managing their families' relationships with the deceased. And many people, younger people especially, are spurning ancestors as never before.

The New Assault on Ancestors

Despite the practical accommodation between ancestral reverence and Christian faith that Africans have managed to sustain over generations and

4. For examples of autobiographical narratives of healers describing these illnesses, see Broster and Bourn 1981; Bührmann 1986; Eiselen 1932a, 1932b; Farrand 1980; J. Hall 1995; Janzen 1992; Kohler 1941; H. Ngubane 1981; Sachs 1947.

despite the increasingly favorable attitude of mainline churches to these aspects of African spirituality, expressed in recent decades in terms of notions of "inculturation" and "contextual theology" (Bate 1995), many Africans have rejected ancestors entirely. This rejection takes two basic forms. For some, ancestors have simply fallen into irrelevance. My friend Palesa, a nurse in her early forties and a grandmother, tells me that she does not believe in ancestors at all "because here in my church we are having the Holy Spirit and with the power of the Spirit you can do miracles. Even cure AIDS." Palesa had migrated through a variety of Pentecostal churches, including the Rhema Bible (mega-)Church of Pastor Ray MacAuley, before finding satisfaction in her present "Apostolic" congregation. Her mother, however, is deeply attached both to her Anglican church and to her ancestors—a reverence Palesa treats with tolerant bemusement though she refuses to participate in any ancestral rituals. Xoliswa, a Catholic Information Technology specialist in her late twenties, is less enthusiastically connected to the Holy Spirit than Palesa but is equally dismissive of ancestors: "these people are stupid if they think that dead people can help them with their problems. Only God can help a person." Her father is a Zulu traditionalist of the old school who turns first to his ancestors in times of need —which only partially explains why his daughter rejects them. The fact that her unemployed father, while extolling the virtues of his ancestors and insisting upon the honor due to a Zulu father, begs her without shame for money to buy cigarettes and liquor tends to undermine her ability to believe.

Many African Christians, particularly those who have embraced varieties of evangelical fundamentalism and refer to themselves as Bazalwane, or Born Agains, as well as many who belong to AICs, consider the beings referred to as "ancestors" to be intrinsically evil phenomena. In their view, ancestors are either evil spirits masquerading in the form of deceased relatives in order to seduce their descendants from the path of righteousness or else idols, false gods, the worship of whom, the Bible teaches, is a sin. No Christian will deny that human life continues after death. Many, however, will vehemently deny that the dead can interact with the living. Of course, the dead will be remembered—the more recently deceased and the most dearly loved will be remembered the most vividly. This offers Satan, in his ceaseless struggle to seduce humans from the path of righteousness, a fruitful opening to use the image of the departed—call them "ancestors" if you will—to tempt and mislead people. By appearing in the guise of beloved ancestors, the devil can trick people into worshiping him instead of God. These demons must be rejected and fought against by all means avail-

able. Churches of the "Spirit" type, whether African initiated such as the
Zion and Apostolic congregations or those of the international evangelical
Pentecostal varieties of Born Agains, devote enormous efforts to battling
these demons (Allan Anderson 1992a). Since these churches constitute the
largest and fastest growing sector of South African Christianity, it appears
that increasing numbers of black South Africans are being exposed to, if
not adopting, hostile attitudes toward the category of beings known as ancestors. At the same time, they are participating in a vast collective struggle
against the devil and evil spirits—albeit one riven by countless denomina-
tional fissures—through rituals of baptism, exorcism, and "deliverance crusades" all "in the name of Jesus."

Others, however, are neither sanguine about the harmlessness of the
beings known as ancestors nor positive that they are agents of the devil.
A good example of the complexity of modes of rejecting ancestors can be
seen in the response of a member of the Apostolic Faith Mission, a born-
again church, quoted in Allan Anderson's study of Pentecostal churches in
Shoshanguve:

> I personally do not venerate the ancestors, but I believe that ancestors are
> there. Ancestors do exist; they are people who have fallen asleep. Before I
> was saved I used to venerate them; and I know what they can do in the life
> of a person. You really can become a slave of the ancestors. Even the Bible
> acknowledges that there are "gods" and that we should not worship any
> other gods but our Father in heaven. They do have the power to help or harm
> you—that I saw when I was not yet saved . . . when I did what I was instructed,
> such as slaughtering a goat, then I saw things definitely improving. They have
> the power to harm you if you do not follow their instructions; and they have
> the power to help you if you follow them. . . . I believe that if people knew
> the power of the gospel they would not have anything to do with the ances-
> tors. But because they are bound by the devil they are still in darkness. They
> go up and down buying goats, slaughtering cows—and nothing seems to
> come right. So if only people could know the power of the gospel and believe
> in Jesus Christ, they could be set free. Now that they are still in darkness they
> must do as the devil commands them. (Anderson 1997)

This disquisition exemplifies many of the elemental theological issues involved in all speculation about the powers of ancestors, their ontological
status, their degree of autonomy, and their relation to the powers of God,
Jesus Christ, the Holy Spirit, and, of course, Satan. Anderson's respondent
accords the ancestors a degree of autonomy but only limited power. An-

cestors in this person's view do have their own power to help or to harm a person. They also have the power to make people their slaves. This power is nothing, however, compared with the power of Jesus and the gospel.

The ethical character of ancestors in Anderson's respondent's view appears to be indeterminate. They are neither intrinsically good nor intrinsically evil, "merely people who have fallen asleep." They can be as good or bad as the people they were in life. A commonplace assertion in these parts is that sleeping ancestors can be woken, either deliberately by means of invocation through slaughtering a beast in their honor or inadvertently, such as when someone unknown to the ancestors slaughters a beast at their home place or someone who is not initiated into *ngoma* rituals beats a *sangoma*'s drum. Ancestors thus awakened without sustenance being provided will be angry and will punish their neglectful descendants. People who venerate ancestors, in the view of Anderson's respondent, do so because they are kept in darkness by the devil and do not realize the vastly superior power available to them should they become "saved." This superior power is in no sense abstract, a mystery to be contemplated with awe, such as the miracle of Creation, but a force accessible in everyday life necessary for the very material ends of prosperity, health, and happiness.

Though superhuman in their powers, ancestors are still human in origin and take with them their human characteristics into the otherworld. Debates about the character and capacities of ancestors revolve around two polar positions. On the one hand, people who observe their commitments to ancestors religiously, so to speak, tend to argue that the ancestors are the primary force responsible for a family's security and welfare. Their confidence in these beings derives from the knowledge that these beings have a particular interest in and deep commitment to them because they are members of the same family. This view is not necessarily incompatible with Christian faith. It merely accords ancestors a special role among spiritual beings. On the other hand, ancestral powers can be disparaged by the argument that if the ancestors carry into the afterlife the same limitations and negative human qualities they had as living members of families—absent, abusive, jealous, unreliable, tyrannical, or even just plain evil—then their descendants are sorely in need of other spiritual powers to guard their security and prosperity.

Ancestors and Kinship in Troubled Families

While details of customs and traditions pertaining to ancestors have varied across the communities of the region and have changed over time, particularly under the influence of Christianity and urban life, ancestral rituals seem in all instances to have at least two features in common: they celebrate ties of kinship between the living and dead within families, clans, villages, or nations and are presided over by persons possessing both ritual knowledge and social authority within the relevant communal milieu.[5] Ancestral rituals both require such collectivities and help to create them, just as they require such authority and help create it (Kuckertz 1990). When people serve their ancestors well, they strengthen the power of ancestors to help them. Even when ancestors communicate with specific individuals through dreams or afflictions, it is always within a group, especially the family, that ritual communication is organized. In the absence of an appropriate authority, such as a family elder, or in the absence of persons with appropriate ritual knowledge, ancestral rituals are difficult to organize and will be futile, if not actually counterproductive. For the ancestors are nothing if not jealous guardians of the ways of the past. And an ancestor roused to anger by mistaken or inappropriate ritual performance is worse than no ancestor at all. Individuals who are alienated from their families find that the possibilities of connecting with ancestors are severely limited.

Perhaps the most important changes in African family life over the past century in Soweto have been those associated with the diminution of paternal capacity and authority within families, arousing a corresponding disappointment within families over the men who are supposed to fulfill the role of father. In the past in this part of the world, law and custom ordained that a father was master over his wife and children. Particular details regarding the role and status of fathers differed slightly in the various social groupings across the region, but the general story was the same. The father was king, the primary guardian—in theory—of a family's physical and spiritual security. A man, as Isaac Schapera explained in his *Handbook of Tswana Law and Custom,* "once he sets up his own household, . . . is for all practical purposes his own master. The woman, on the other hand, passes from the legal control of her parents into that of her husband, who now becomes her guardian and as such responsible for her actions" (1938, 150). The father, Schapera also noted, "is the founder and legal head of his family" (1938, 176). He must recognize and name his children, make sure all rituals and "doctorings" are performed for them, and "see to it that their mother is in a position to rear and feed them" (1938, 176). He is responsible for his children's education and must see that they are provided with the

5. The ethnographic literature of southern Africa contains many descriptions of rituals pertaining to ancestors. For a classic example, see Hunter 1961, 235ff.

necessaries to make a start in life as adults, either with cattle for bride-wealth for boys or with domestic utensils for girls. In sum: "As head of the family, the father must keep order and maintain discipline over his children" (1938, 177).

In the assessment of Gabriel Setiloane (a Tswana father himself, as well as a Methodist minister, political activist, and scholar), a father in a Sotho-Tswana family is head of household, "protector and judge, provider of their needs, their security against the outside world, representing them at 'kgotla' [court and administrative center], responsible for all their misdeeds. He exerts discipline and is regarded with the respect due to one who, to his children at least, is the direct and only link with the 'badimo' [ancestors] of the patriline" (1976, 28). Not only does this model of father-protector-ruler lend plausibility to the notion of ancestral powers supporting the welfare and security of the family, but the reverence for ancestors grounds respect for the father-protector as the nodal point through which ancestral power flows for the benefit of all the family. The father, supported by the ancestors, is supposed to provide physical and spiritual security for all family members. Where precolonial political structures extended over broader terrain, they were founded in similar interpretations of kinship and patriarchy (Schapera 1956, 68). In postcolonial Africa, too, as Michael Schatzberg has shown (2001), political rhetoric often emphasizes the role of leader as "father."

Even in the 1930s, however, this image of paternal power was less than comprehensive (Schapera 1938, 182). In the cities and townships it was always more of a fantasy than a reality. After all, most of the people who migrated permanently to the cities and towns were young and seeking, among other things, escape from the yoke of paternal rule. As permanent migrants became settled in cities in the early decades of the twentieth century, raising families of their own, the problem of youthful disobedience arose in new forms (Hellmann 1940), frequently in the guise of gangsterism (or "*tsotsi*-ism," as it is locally known; Glaser 2000). Each generation of urban-born youths has been denounced by their elders as beyond discipline and out of control. Urban communities have struggled to produce institutions capable of meeting the challenge of socializing the masses of children and youths. In theory, the father provides for the security of his family not only by establishing a safe and comfortable home but by managing relations with neighbors in such a way as to defuse potential hostilities and ensure support in times of crisis. Central to his role in providing security for his family is the responsibility to discipline family members and prevent them, especially the boys, from causing disruption and hostility in relation to neighbors. In the event that such disruptions do occur, as they inevitably do, it is the father's responsibility to preside over the discussion wherein amends are made and recompense for damages is determined. In the extreme case, the father is also the one who should organize violence to protect his family and property or to punish offenses against them. In the absence of fathers, each of these roles is compromised: boys and young men cannot be disciplined, legitimate organized violence cannot be effectively directed, and neighborhood convocations (*indaba,* Zulu; *pitso,* Sotho) flounder.

This diminution of paternal authority has occurred in tandem with a shrinking of the general domain of relationships that are actively maintained in the name of "family," although kinship terms remain powerful as metaphors for interpreting and marking relationships of friendship, reciprocity, and solidarity that extend far beyond the familial household. The prevailing ideology of family life, despite complex transformations in family structure and the achievement of equal legal status for women, remains strongly patriarchal. Fathers generally still claim the right to govern women and children absolutely. Mr. Khanyile was echoing a commonplace masculinist claim when he shouted in frustration at his rebellious daughters: "I am the government in this house." And, when everyone ignored him, he experienced the common fate of fathers. Nor could he really complain, for not only were his daughters not really misbehaving, but they were the ones working for meager wages in a supermarket so as to be able to put food on the table. They were simply not prepared to be subservient in the way a "typical Zulu"—as they describe their father—expects of his daughters.

Where men succeed in fulfilling the expectations women and children have of them as fathers, these rights of rule are granted willingly enough, albeit with the usual troubles and tensions of family life. Success in fatherhood, however, is not easily achieved or maintained. Not one of the families I have known intimately in Soweto over the past decade deems their father entirely satisfactory as an example of fatherhood. Mamphela Ramphele, echoing the observations of Raymond Smith in his classic description of the "matrifocal" family in the Caribbean, has described the state of black South African masculinity as a "role reversal between strong women and weak men" (Ramphele 2000, 113–114). Given the scarcity of cash in this place and the absence of other resources upon which to found respect for their manhood, it is extremely difficult for most men to live up to the ideals of masculinity that have been bequeathed to them down the generations and that are based upon the capacity to support, protect, and dominate women and children. Ramphele has argued that black manhood in

South Africa has been undermined by, among other things, the history of white racist domination that named African men "boys" and placed them on a rung below white women and children in the general status hierarchy of a racially segregated society. Apartheid policies disabled men's capacity to protect their families at the same time as women and children were drawn into conflict with the state. Poor education and scanty job opportunities have further undermined their role as "breadwinner" within families, while an unwillingness to engage in menial work viewed as beneath their dignity has increased their dependence upon women (Ramphele 2000).

A wide variety of household family configurations has emerged in Soweto as in other African communities in South Africa over the past century or so, driven by a history of urbanization marked by large-scale cyclical labor migration of men between rural homes and urban workplaces coupled with efforts to prevent the permanent urbanization of women, the impositions of racist "influx control" measures making urban residency for Africans insecure, township planning policies favoring families that resembled "nuclear" models (stimulating applicants for public housing to imitate the model whether it suited them or not), wages insufficient for financing adequate shelter for working families, periodic cycles of unemployment, and all the other constraints on the good life in a hard city, as well as the struggle to reproduce family structures consonant with "tradition" (particularly in relation to patriarchal authority and masculine sexual dominance enshrined in polygynous ideals) and "respectability" (as taught by the monogamously inclined Christian mission churches). Despite the variety of actual family life, however, virtually everyone I have ever met in Soweto insists that the ideal family and household consists of two married parents—with a male "head" and "breadwinner"—living with their own children in their own home (with as few additional relatives as possible).

The realities are otherwise. If the "nuclear" type of family is the ideal, then about six in every ten Sowetans live in households with some sort of family configuration that they probably consider suboptimal to some degree. The most common forms arise from adult children living with their parents as well as their own children long after they are supposed to be independent (21 percent of the population) or mothers making homes without the fathers of their children to help (by the Wits Survey's reckoning, 23.4 percent of households had a female "head"; A. Morris 1999b, table 5.1). Other families include relatives who have outstayed their welcome. Virtually no one in Soweto (outside the hostels) shares accommodation with people who are not family, although sometimes the kinship is of a fictive or virtual variety (such as the kind that I experience as a member of the Mfete family). But, most of the time, life goes on happily enough in families as they actually are, and nobody pays much attention to how they wish it were otherwise—unless something untoward happens such as calamities that seem uncanny or misfortunes become unbearable or others' successes in meeting the ideal make our own failures intolerable.

Though no one could have grown up in this place at the end of the twentieth century without taking for granted as the reality of life these suboptimal varieties of family, virtually every young person dreams of achieving nuclear bliss. Their efforts to beat the odds and meet the ideal, more often than not, are heartbreaking. Shebeens and churches overflow with their loss. Considering the obstacles to achieving even the most elementary foundation of the ideal type of family life, primarily the difficulty of achieving financial independence, the fact that some 35 percent of the population live in families at least outwardly consistent with the nuclear norm is remarkable (A. Morris 1999b, table 5.1).[6] Within the "nuclear" ideal, as it has been internalized here and elsewhere, the general presumption is that children are supposed to be financially dependent upon their parents only until they finish school and reach adulthood at the magical age of twenty-one.[7] Twenty-first-birthday parties are still celebrated, finances permitting, as the main coming-of-age ritual. According to the standard model of family life, offspring are "children" for so long as they remain in their parents' home. By rights, they should leave home when they get married, at which point they should establish their own families and homes. Until that time, however, they remain subject, in theory, to the authority of their parents and should contribute to the finances and upkeep of their home.

For the generations that came of age in the 1950s through the midsixties, such a model was reasonably practicable, for jobs and houses were generally available. From the late sixties through the nineties, however, housing

6. I have derived this figure of 35 percent of the population living in nuclear-family arrangements by calculating the numbers of such families in each housing domain using figures provided for "Family Type by Domain Type" and "Population by Housing Type" in A. Morris 1999b. The Wits Survey estimated that 45.7 percent of households were occupied by nuclear families. However, most of the population live in households in the older public housing sections of the township, where only 20.8 percent of households meet the "nuclear" description. I have excluded hostels from these calculations because these dwelling places are by definition not familial domains, though there have been more "family-type" accommodations provided in hostels in recent years.

7. In the Piazza-Georgi study, of 1,082 household members surveyed under the age of eighteen, only four claimed to be "self-employed" (all from the same family), two claimed to work part-time, and one full-time (Piazza-Georgi 2000, 12).

became increasingly scarce in the townships. More and more families were forced to "double up," with adult children remaining at home with their parents. Since the sixties, too, structural unemployment has steadily increased, leaving more and more "children" unable to find work well into their adulthood. Most families have children living at home through their twenties and thirties, even their forties and fifties. Few think the arrangement is ideal—particularly when the desires of young adults for independence clash with the demands of fathers for authority and respect. Tensions in families with adult children still at home seem to be lower in female-headed households, where the pressure on the family head to maintain dominance over sons and the appearance of controlling daughters' sexual behavior is less intense than in homes where the father is still trying to rule over his adult children.

How might the failings of fathers affect the powers of ancestors? On numerous occasions I have had discussions with Sowetan friends of the sort where, questioning their faith in ancestors, I have asked: "How can you trust your ancestors to help you? You don't even know who your father is. If your own father couldn't even be bothered to hang around long enough to look after his children, how can you believe that some dead relative of his is going to care about you?" This question, or variants of it, usually serves in its crude way to catalyze vigorous discussion, although perhaps not of the sort that David Hammond-Tooke expected when he enjoined scholars of "indigenous religion" to "investigate in depth the relationship between cosmological constructs, on the one hand, and the structures of kinship and descent, on the other" (1985, 47). Very few Sowetans are sacrilegious enough to express the predicament of ancestors in the same way I did, but the question emerges constantly from the relations with ancestors among people whose everyday family life leaves them with much to desire.

Once again, with ancestors as with most aspects of family life here, mothers come to the rescue. Most events where ancestors are invoked and propitiated in Soweto are organized and funded by women. As well as bearing responsibility for the mundane matters of family life, women have taken central roles in ceremonies, rituals, and maintaining the traditions relating to ancestors. Women are now predominantly responsible for managing ancestral relations within their families. Ancestral rituals are mostly motivated by women. Older women lament the development in much the same way they lament the general decline of masculine capacity and authority within families. In the words of MaMfete, changing gender roles relating to ancestors have arisen "because lately the fathers they are useless in homes. The woman would want to do that [rituals for the ancestors] because now she thinks that the home is being in trouble. That's why it's like this. Seventy-five percent of the rituals are done by women. Twenty-five percent by men. And mostly around here the responsibility is too much on the women, and the dads they don't care what is happening with their life at home, so that makes it for the woman to secure her home." Men are still called upon to participate in "traditional functions," as these rituals are called, particularly if there happens to be an elder in residence. The actual killing and butchering of the beast will be carried out by men, though I have seen a mother intervene when a cow refused to die after the son of the house stabbed it in the neck with an "assegai" (Zulu stabbing spear) assembled from a sharpened butter-knife bound into the end of a broom handle.

The "role reversal" in township life "between strong women and weak men" that Ramphele wrote of (2000, 113–114) evidently extends beyond the grave. In the past, most of the work of ancestors was performed by spirits on the male side of the family. Now, however, many families grant maternal ancestors equal importance to those of the paternal line. In Sowetan families, maternal ancestors—both male and female—are receiving more attention than they used to, particularly when the father's people are hard to find. This trend in urban life was first noted in the 1960s when Berthold Pauw wrote that urban-born Africans in the Eastern Cape had more interaction with the ancestors of "non-patrilineal kinsmen" than those of rural areas, attributing the change to the difficulties of maintaining extended patrilineal kinship networks in towns and the emergence of the "matrifocal" family (1974, 106). No doubt many mothers and grandmothers in earlier generations had to find means of their own to provide protection for their children in similarly novel ways.

The extent to which mothers and grandmothers manage relations with ancestors varies across families, and the extent to which such observances depart from tradition varies across the major ethnic groupings of the region. The ethnographic record suggests that some groups traditionally accorded greater significance to maternal ancestors than others (Hammond-Tooke 1989a, 48). Setiloane, for example, suggests that "Sotho-Tswana are related as closely to the 'badimo' [ancestors] of their mother as to those of their father, with the maternal uncle playing the central role in mediating relations" (1976, 22). Nguni-speaking peoples, however, seem to have had less regard for ancestors on the mother's side. Absolom Vilakazi writes that "the ancestral spirits that are important in any family or in any day-to-day situation are the husband's ancestral spirits. . . . The ancestral spirits of the mother's clan are, as a rule, unimportant in her husband's home" (1965,

90). Harriet Ngubane reports that "the place of a [Zulu] wife's ancestors is at her parental home, and not at her marital home. There can be no equal range of ancestors in one home (except in the case of diviners who achieve this by certain sacrifices)" (1977, 53).

After living in rural Zululand in the 1960s, Axel-Ivar Berglund reported that although "a woman becomes a shade [ancestor] to her own children, especially if she dies in ripe old age," patrilineal ancestors were generally considered more influential in the affairs of the living (1976, 122).[8] Henry Callaway found much the same a century earlier (1970, 146). And William Willoughby, in his 1928 survey of "Bantu religion" asserts that generally speaking "the gods [ancestors] of a husband do not help his wife, nor do her gods help him, and the gods of their children are those of that side of the house from which property and status are inherited—though it is true the mother's divinities may demand occasional attention" (1928, 178). Hammond-Tooke distinguishes between Nguni ancestors, who "were conceived of as a vast, undifferentiated category of patrilineal forebears, who were depersonalized and unknown," and the ancestor cults of other South African Bantu-speaking peoples, which were far less patrilineal, populated with ancestors "who had been known personally in life," related to with a "more relaxed attitude," and allowed a greater "ritual importance of women" (2002, 281).

People who revere their ancestors are not infrequently forced to seek ways of accommodating the promise of ancestral protection with the realities of what they recognize as imperfect family affairs that fail to fit the model prescribed by "tradition." For example, when a friend of mine in Soweto recovered from a rancorous divorce in which she gained sole custody of her two young children and her husband refused to pay for child support, she was faced with the problem that her three-year-old son had been named in honor of her ex-husband's deceased father. In accordance with tradition, whenever the child reached a milestone in life or achieved something for which thanks should be given to the ancestors, or at times when the child might need assistance in some matter of illness or misfortune, he and his father ought to visit the grave of the ancestor after whom the boy was named and make offerings. Because of the divorce and the loss of contact with the child's father, however, my friend and her family realized they would never be able to pay satisfactory homage to that paternal

8. Berglund notes that the only two occasions when a Zulu woman is "wholly in the hands of her lineage shades" are when she is called to become a diviner or when she gives birth to an illegitimate child (1976, 120–121).

ancestor. The boy would be left unprotected. Not only did my friend's family not know how to locate the husband's father's grave, but they worried that even if they found the place, there would be no end of trouble if the husband or his family found them performing rituals there. They might even be suspected of witchcraft. To avoid such problems, my friend and her mother decided to rename the child and dedicate his fate to a maternal ancestor instead. They chose a similar-sounding name so as not to confuse the boy too much.

When I was told this story of the name change, I asked whether the biological paternal grandfather remained an "ancestor" of the child regardless of their rearrangement of his name. My friend and her mother agreed that he did. When I asked whether they were not worried that the original ancestor might be angry about being deprived of a grandson whose duty it would be to care and nourish his ancestor in the future, they could only shrug: "Perhaps." And when I suggested that surely the purpose of these ancestor rituals was to maintain good relations within families, including all members—living and dead; divorced as well as married—so that even if the relationship between the child's mother and father sours they can stay on good enough terms to serve the best interests of their child, the grandmother could only nod sadly and say, in memory of another failed marriage, "What could we do?" Their solution to the problem reflects the sorts of accommodations that have to be made to make the best of a bad situation. It also illustrates a more general feature of ancestral reverence: whereas "the ancestors" (always plural) represent an amorphous and capacious category of benevolent power, particular deceased relatives with whom definite relations can be maintained are sometimes hard to find.

Another way in which the "structures of kinship" are related to "cosmological constructs" in everyday life in turn-of-the-millennium Soweto reflects the generous and inclusive understanding of fictive kinship that prevails in that place and, I have no doubt, across the continent. Old ancestors have gained new descendants. Questions of genetics and kinship are every bit as complex in the domain of ancestral connection to the living as they are in every other domain of family life. Setiloane, in his discussion of the relationships that "give to a traditional Sotho-Tswana a secure identity," lists three forms of kinship: "(a) 'ka madi' (by blood), that is by patrilineal relationship; (b) 'ka kgomo' (by cattle), that is by marriage; or (c) by affiliation of individuals or groups who adopt the 'badimo' of their hosts and become putative members of the appropriate patriline" (1976, 24). Setiloane, however, does not discuss this third form of kinship in any detail, so I am unable to say how incorporation into a "traditional Sotho-Tswana" family might take place. I can, however, describe my own incorporation into a family with a Tswana father and a Sotho mother.

When I had been living with the Mfetes for a few years and had come to be regarded as an integral, if peculiar, member of the family, I was introduced to the ancestors. The occasion was unremarkable—a small side-event in another, more important, function. A sheep was being slaughtered on the eve of my sister's wedding. The immediate family—father, mother, brother, two sisters, and me—gathered to address the ancestors. In order of seniority, each member of the family spoke. I was last, for although I was slightly older than the other children, I was the latest addition to the family. We knelt together in a quiet corner of the backyard and I was introduced, along with the sacrificial sheep, in the most straightforward of manners. No one doubted that the ancestors would protect me. There was nothing particularly noteworthy about this introduction to the ancestors, and though I felt honored to be counted a member of this family, I do not recall anyone ever discussing its significance.

Ancestors, Rituals, and Public Power in Urban Life

One of the principal differences between "ancestorship" as it exists in contemporary urban areas and the "ancestor cults" depicted in the ethnographic literature (e.g., Kuckertz 1983) concerns the range of dead relatives who are conventionally memorialized. Most urban Africans in South Africa today have no meaningful connection with ancestral powers representing kinship relations on scales larger than that of their immediate family. This is not new. In the 1960s, during his study of "townsmen and tribesmen" in the Eastern Cape, Berthold Pauw noticed that "tribal and clan rituals" were "unknown" in settled urban communities (1974, 106). Few people in Soweto, other than the occasional Zulu nationalist, maintain active engagements with the ancestral spirits of kings and chiefs responsible for the welfare of whole nations such as surveyed by Olof Pettersson in his study of the divine foundations of chiefship (1953, 307–310). Nor do people ordinarily maintain contact with the ancestors of clans and lineages or even "agnatic clusters" of neighboring families headed by men descended from a common grandfather or great-grandfather in the manner described by Hammond-Tooke in the Transkei of the 1970s (1982, 49), unless they are recent migrants to town and maintain close contact with rural homes.

Although ancestral feasts ("traditional functions" or "cultural functions" as they are called in English) are open to whoever cares to come and are occasions when neighbors and relatives gather to enjoy each other's company, the rituals of invocation and supplication conjoining living family members with their ancestors are private. I have never heard of a public "traditional function" being staged in Soweto of the sort encountered in rural villages (Kuckertz 1990, 232) or those presided over by chiefs and kings, such as the Umkhosi, or First-Fruit Ceremony, of the Zulus (E. Krige 1936, 249) or those connected with rainmaking or the preparation of armies for war. I would not be surprised to learn, however, that public ancestral rituals take place in the Zulu-dominated migrant hostels. In recent years some political leaders in the ANC have sought to integrate aspects of ancestral rituals into political gatherings by having *sangomas* invoke the blessings of ancestors, usually in company with various clerics of sundry religions. In December 2001, Mongane Serote, chair of the Parliament's Portfolio Committee on Arts, Culture, Science, and Technology, promoted an innovative effort at harnessing ancestral forces to nation-building projects in a ceremony of ritual cleansing and animal sacrifice involving about six hundred *sangomas* at the former base of apartheid death squads, called Vlakplaas (Terreblanche 2001). The event was not without controversy, however. An opposition United Democratic Movement spokesperson and former lecturer in African religion, Nokuzola Mndende, complained that "the people planning this . . . ceremony do not understand what purification is about" and were not following correct "cultural" procedures. She denounced the operation as "political opportunism" on the part of the government (Joubert 2001, 1).[9]

What sorts of powers do people in places like Soweto consider it reasonable to imagine ancestors as having? Clearly, they were unable to protect people from the sorts of horrors that occurred in places like Vlakplaas, not to mention the whole oppressive system of apartheid. And it would be hard to find a contemporary Sowetan who would attribute the suffering caused by apartheid to ancestral wrath or endorse the view that the ancestors could have hastened the demise of white domination. But ancestors were not completely absent from the story of the liberation of South Africa. The central role played by Nelson Mandela in the political transformations of the 1990s makes plausible the statement made by one of Allan Anderson's survey respondents in Shoshanguve in 1992: "When Mr. Nelson Mandela was released from prison, he went back to his birth place to tell

9. Shortly after this ceremony, Serote resigned from Parliament to take over the running of Vlakplaas as "Freedom Park," which would be devoted to promoting indigenous knowledge, and announced that he was being initiated as a traditional healer.

the ancestors that he was released from prison, and was now on a mission to liberate our country. All the blessings and the changes which are coming to us with him are because the ancestors are backing him and helping him" (Anderson 1993a, 28). Mandela's connection with the ancestors, however, can be controversial. In late 1993 he appeared at a rally where the blessings of the ancestors were called down upon him by a number of *sangomas* in a procedure that has become commonplace in postapartheid political pageantry. Some people reacted with horror. Edward Cain, president of United Christian Action, dashed off letters to the leading black daily newspaper, the *Sowetan,* and to the right-wing daily favored mostly by white people, the *Citizen.* His argument was simple and he reiterated it in January, after his original letter sparked controversy: "the spirits of the dead do not return to Earth to guide their descendants. Demons pretend to be ancestral spirits in order to deceive people" (*Citizen,* January 4, 1994). The Bible is clear on the point, argued Cain. The spirits of the dead go either to heaven or to hell, and anyone who tries to call them back to earth is trafficking with demons. Mandela should call off the *sangomas.* Some readers responded violently to the *Citizen's* Cain, doubly infuriated by the fact that he spoke as a Christian and was a white man. One, Isaiah Shongwe, wrote in a letter to the *Sowetan* a few days later: "Many South Africans of sober mind, particularly those of African descent, may have been surprised by what this fellow has written. It is unbecoming of him to label the ANC as anti-Christian. All black South Africans believe in their ancestors" (*Sowetan,* January 6, 1994). In the same issue of the newspaper, Vambani Castro Monakali of Vosloorus on the East Rand also attacked Cain: "Mr. Cain must forget about sangomas who surrounded Dr. Mandela and called down the blessing of the ancestors on him and cast away evil spirits. The ancestors of our nation must be called for guidance through sangomas." The debate continues.

Although Mr. Monakali invoked the notion of the "ancestors of the nation," few in South Africa would have a concrete sense of the identity of these spiritual entities other than perhaps as the heroes of past struggles against white rule. It is conceivable, however, that when Mandela dies he will achieve the sort of super-ancestor status usually accorded only to kings and will be invoked as a protector of his people. Generally speaking, however, ancestors today operate on a smaller scale. The sufferings they inflict are private and personal; the evils they prevent and rectify are similarly small scale.

The abilities of ancestors are always reckoned in relation to the perceived sources of harm. Among these, in contemporary Soweto, witchcraft is perhaps the most important. Where "witchcraft" names a concern about harm and misfortune originating in acts that are empowered by secret knowledge and spiritual connections and are perpetrated by people close to the victim, ancestors offer a plausible level of protection not only by virtue of superior power but also by virtue of their social connectedness. Because they belong to the same community as the victim, chances are that the ancestors are connected also to the perpetrators and would thus be well placed to fathom the evil secrets of their hearts. Even without such direct knowledge, however, ancestors will be familiar with the sorts of people who could do such things and be vigilant in thwarting them. Where harm is perpetrated by people either embodying or connecting with evil forces on a larger scale than the merely personal, such as those of Satan, then the capacities of ancestors for protection must be reckoned as limited. And where harm is reckoned as originating from spiritual agents of a lesser potency than the senior devil himself, ancestors may or may not be effective in response.

10

VULNERABILITIES OF THE SOUL

Vulnerability and Power in the Hidden Realms of Being

One afternoon in the winter of 1998, in the shack outside the gates of Mer-afe Hostel that he uses as his consulting rooms in Soweto, I tried to engage Madumo's *inyanga,* Mr. Zondi, in a discussion of the essential elements that compose the human person. I did not get far. He had just finished telling Madumo and me a story that involved a recipe for making a *tikoloshe,* the famous witch's familiar (also known as the *tokoloshe*).[1] His recipe — or, rather, what he had concluded must have been the witches' method of man-ufacture, since he insisted that he had never actually made one himself — involved mixing up a complicated mess of animal fats and herbs, bottling the mixture, and then burying the bottle at a crossroads. After some time, a pregnant woman would pass over the bottle, and the *isithunzi* of the un-born child, the spirit of the fetus, would enter the mixture, bringing the *tikoloshe* to life. Although the woman would be unaffected and her baby born normally, the spirit of the child would enter the bottle and create a "monster" that would do the evil bidding of the witch who created it (Ash-forth 2000a, 189).

I was fascinated by this idea of *isithunzi* as a sort of life force that could be replicated in the making of a monster without cost to its original pos-sessor, the fetus, so I asked Mr. Zondi if this *isithunzi* differed from the "soul" of Christianity.

"No, it's one and the same," he replied. "There's a body and a soul, and when a person dies that spirit of the soul goes to the one who created it."

---

1. For anthropological accounts of the *tokoloshe,* see Hammond-Tooke 1974b; Hunter 1961, 275–278; Niehaus 2001, 50–56.

Despite Mr. Zondi's insistence on the universality of the "soul," however, the notion that a fetus bears some sort of immaterial essence capable of extending to and entering a mixture of substances in a bottle buried beneath the soil of a crossroads so as to animate the mixture and bring to life a monster seems to me somewhat different from the sense of an internal spirit animating the person that inflects Christian conceptions of "soul"— even if this personal essence or soul connects in some way with the universal presence of God. Mr. Zondi, though he prides himself on being deeply "traditional," expresses himself within a thoroughly Christian idiom. Axel-Ivar Berglund, who was working as a Christian missionary and anthropologist (with a philosophical bent) in Zululand at about the time when Mr. Zondi experienced his call to heal there in the 1960s, reported that his "traditionalist" informants distinguished between body, shadow, spirit, breath, and *itongo*—the elemental essence of ancestorhood transmitted down lineages through the generations—while insisting upon the unity and indivisibility of the person. Christian Zulus, he reported, were quite comfortable with a more fundamental division of personhood into visible and invisible dimensions (Berglund 1976, 82). For Mr. Zondi, as for most people here, the seat of life, what in English would be the "spirit" or the "soul," is *umoya*.[2]

Nobody doubts that the part of the person surviving after death is this same element, which is an invisible aspect of the living person. The element of continuity in families and lineages—spoken of these days in Soweto as elsewhere in the language of genetics—is constituted of much the same stuff. While other words also apply to the inner, hidden, invisible domains of personhood—such as *isithunzi* (shadow), *umphefumulo* (breath) —when they are explained theoretically, they are all commonly assimilated, in all regional languages, into a framework of body, mind, spirit, and soul indistinguishable from the varieties of Christian teachings. In both ritual practice and everyday life, however, the situation is often much more complex, particularly since these internal elements can become subject to external attack.

2. The most extensive attempt to reconstruct a distinctive "underlying theology" of "Bantu" notions of the "soul" remains that of the nineteenth- and early-twentieth-century London Mission Society missionary William Charles Willoughby. See Willoughby 1928, 1932. See also Kuckertz 1983; Hammond-Tooke 1985. The term "life force" could also be used to describe this sense of *umoya*, despite being encumbered with much Bergsonian baggage and in the African context being associated with the important, but contentious, writing of Fr. Placide Tempels, the Belgian missionary of Congo (Tempels 1959).

Consider another incident from the annals of Madumo and Mr. Zondi. Toward the end of his course of treatment, Madumo reported to his healer a dream in which his mother—dead for about two years by this time—appeared to him and enjoined him to visit her grave. Tending the graves of departed ancestors is an altogether praiseworthy activity, and dreams such as Madumo's are commonplace among people who grieve, whether they revere their ancestors or not. Often they are taken as reminders from the ancestors to perform necessary duties. When Mr. Zondi heard of Madumo's dream, however, he urged caution. He burned some of the fragrant herb known as *imphepha* and consulted the ancestors, whereupon he discovered that Madumo's dream was in fact part of a plot. The ancestors told him that the dream had been implanted in Madumo's mind by his enemies in order to lure him to the cemetery. Enemies—who at this stage seemed to be mainly Madumo's brother and sister—had secreted dangerous *muthi* in the soil covering his mother's grave. The *muthi* was designed to kill and targeted at Madumo. Mr. Zondi warned his patient to stay clear of the grave, giving him additional *muthi* for extra protection to be on the safe side.

Few people in Soweto doubt that dreams can serve as a medium of communication between ancestors and their descendants, and the interpretation of dreams is a central part of the therapy provided by healers of all varieties. The ordinary work of dream interpretation involves distinguishing genuine ancestral communication from the everyday noise of a mind at rest.[3] Even Christians who reject doctrines of ancestorship do not doubt that dreams can convey information from external entities. Nothing in the ethnographic record of these parts suggests an indigenous concept of the unconscious, and I know no one who would accept the proposition that the images and narratives experienced during sleep are "internally" generated by the dreamer's mind or mere products of brain functions. For people who revere ancestors, dreams in which ancestors, or avatars representing the ancestors, appear are a principal means by which ancestral wishes and instructions are transmitted to the living. Although these communications are not exclusively unidirectional from the ancestor to the descendant (the descendant can express himself or herself within the dream), they constitute a definite form of subjection in the sense that ancestral wishes and commands are supposed to take precedence over the descendant's in-

3. For a discussion of the interpretation of dreams by Xhosa *amagqira* (diviners) and a comparison between their techniques of dream analysis and those propounded by the Viennese healer Carl Jung, see Bührmann 1978, 1986, chap. 5.

terests. The descendant is aware that dire consequences will ensue if the ancestor's wishes are not respected. The sense of subjection to ancestral wishes is intensified if a command issued through a dream is repeated in further dreams. Premonitions sensed in dreams, especially when they subsequently reveal a harm that has been avoided, are also typically interpreted as ancestral in origin. Although dreams can originate with ancestors, not all do. Most people, most of the time, do not attach untoward significance to dreams. People needing guidance and help from invisible beings, however, such as those in crisis or people in need of extra luck, such as gamblers seeking the winning numbers for the Lotto or the daily *fahfee* game, will habitually scrutinize their dreams for signs.[4]

Mr. Zondi's detection of maliciously implanted dreams in Madumo's sleep, then, represents a profoundly unsettling dimension of danger. The dream was all the more dangerous because the desire artificially implanted was entirely praiseworthy. Unlike those situations where a sinner acknowledges guilt but mitigates responsibility by claiming "the devil made me do it," the dreamer in Madumo's situation cannot rely upon an external code of conduct—nor its "internal" representation in the conscience—to judge the risks inherent in his desires. Who can doubt or refuse the desire to do what is right, especially if it is commanded by one to whom you owe obedience? For someone in Madumo's position the risks inherent in following the desire aroused by the dream are not merely moral (the risk of doing wrong) but physical (the risk of encountering dangerous *muthi* that causes harm and death). Only a healer gifted with spiritual capacities to communicate with higher powers can perceive the true dimensions of this danger. In the absence of a healer to reveal the dangers of one's inner drives and desires, any amount of misfortune may fall upon one's head. And when it does, the afflicted person alone cannot say from whence it comes.

4. *Fahfee* is a game in which, for a fifty-cent bet, the gambler picks a number between 1 and 36 in the hope of matching the number selected that day as the winner by the game's organizers. The game was brought to Johannesburg by Chinese immigrants in the early twentieth century and is still organized by Chinese "runners" who service Soweto. The Chinese brought with them an associated set of symbols correlated with each number: an eye is 1, a chicken is 7, and so on. Regular *fahfee* players will scrutinize their dreams in search of these symbols and bet accordingly. If the numbers turn out to be winners, ancestors will be praised.

"Hijacking the Mind" with *Muthi*

Muthi can make people act out of character, so they say. When Bheki and his comrades were deputed to rob a municipal policeman of his shotgun at Merafe Hostel in 1991 during the war with Inkatha, not only did Bheki's pistol misfire but his three accomplices, ordinarily the bravest of comrades, turned on their heels and ran away. "That's why I thought he [the policeman] must be having *muthi,*" Bheki told me after he was released on bail. "Otherwise, they would not have run." Madumo calls this "hijacking the mind."

The possibility that internal drives can be commandeered by external agencies—having one's mind hijacked—is most commonly encountered in the domain of sex. We shall see shortly how, upon presentation of a photograph, an *inyanga* can enlist the aid of the ancestors in persuading an object of desire, unbeknownst to that person, to become a lover. Many *inyangas* also claim the ability to make a species of *muthi,* known commonly as *korobela,* that can fix the affections of that mate and prevent him from wandering. While many women consider *korobela* an unfortunate, though oftentimes necessary, aid in compelling men to perform their familial and erotic responsibilities, most men (when not treating the whole thing as a joke) consider the use of *korobela* to be a serious infringement of their rights and their manhood, an assault upon their freedom and their will. Any man who is seen to be attentive to his woman (especially if that attention involves inattention to his male friends or involvement in domestic activities normally deemed the province of females, such as housecleaning or child-minding) risks being derided as a victim of *korobela.* Women sometimes accuse other women of using *muthi* to steal the affections of their husbands and lovers. Spurned suitors are also feared as capable of exacting revenge in ways that impinge upon the ability of the self to pursue independent action. *Umhayizo,* for example, is a complaint afflicting teenage Zulu girls, who attribute their symptoms of hysterical ranting and raving to the use of *muthi* by the spurned suitor. In the most extreme case, external forces hijack the will and desires of living persons completely and turn them into zombies.

The sense that these are real possibilities is regularly reinforced by the phenomenon of spirit possession. The first time I witnessed spirit possession was when a young friend named Lalah, daughter of a woman undergoing an *ukuthwasa* ceremony, fell into a trance while the *sangomas* were drumming and began shaking and convulsing as if she was having a fit of some sort. My alarm was not felt by others. Instead, the senior *sangoma* merely took her inside the house and made her comfortable. Later she told us that she had several spirits who regularly took possession of her and that the senior *sangoma* knew them all. She also told us of another initiate in the house, a young man named Manyoni, who regularly became possessed by the spirit of a "Boer lady" named Alice who lived more than a hundred years ago. When told of this, my friends Mpho and Thabo, who were accompanying me on this visit, wanted to know more. Lalah introduced us to the new *sangoma* Manyoni, who, after receiving the requisite twenty cents to buy snuff for his ancestors, was happy to answer our questions. "Yes," he told us, "I do have this spirit. And when she comes she makes me to dress in woman's clothes and even to speak Afrikaans. And I am not speaking this language." Mpho asked him if the spirit ever came to him when he was at work or on the bus. Manyoni replied that she had not, but she could. And if she did, he would have to obey. Thabo and Mpho were fascinated by this story, and for the rest of the week the cross-dressing *sangoma* and his Boer called Alice were the subject of constant jokes. They did not doubt, however, that the story might be true.

Dramatic demonstrations of the ability of external forces to gain access to and control over the internal, unseen dimensions of persons are commonplace. During services of the "Spirit-type" Apostolic, Zionist, and Pentecostalist churches, at funerals, and in healing rituals, people are regularly overcome by spirits, and it is not at all uncommon to see a person shaking and sputtering with uncontrollable fit-like symptoms, which are taken to be evidence of the presence within them of spiritual forces. "Speaking in tongues" is also taken as evidence of the Holy Spirit being present in a person. Similar phenomena can be found throughout Africa.[5] These outbursts are specially prized by healers, whose powers are said to rest upon their ability to communicate with and channel the powers of spiritual entities. As Raymond Firth observed, spirit possession involves a temporary occupation of a person by another being, creating a condition of "multiple personality" and leading to the subordination of that person's will and desires to the occupying entity. Firth also elaborated the distinction between spirit mediumship and possession:

5. The field of spirit possession is a major area of study in its own right, and I am unable to do justice to its complexity here, nor even to represent the full variety I have witnessed in contemporary Soweto. For discussion of the general issues involved, see Allan Anderson 1991, 2000b; Beattie and Middleton 1969; Behrend and Luig 1999; Hammond-Tooke 1989a; Honwana 1997; Lee 1969.

In both a person's actions are believed to be dictated by an extra-human entity which has entered his body or otherwise affected him. Both kinds of phenomena may often be regarded as instances of multiple personality, that is the individual concerned assumes another identity, refers to his normal self as "he" and sincerely differentiates this new identity sharply from his everyday self. But in spirit possession his behaviour does not necessarily convey any particular message to other people. It is primarily regarded as his bodily expression of spirit manifestation. In spirit mediumship the emphasis is upon *communication*. The extra-human entity is not merely expressing himself but is regarded as having something to say to an audience. (1969, xi, emphasis in original)

Spirit possession can be perpetrated by both sympathetic and hostile spirits, spirits who seek to strengthen and empower as well as spirits who seek to destroy.

Possession by the Holy Spirit, evidenced by speaking in tongues, is much desired by members of Zionist, Apostolic, and Pentecostalist churches. The same people devote much ritual labor to the exorcism of evil demons (Oosthuizen 1987). The mere fact of being overcome by spiritual forces (*ukuba nomoya* in Zulu) is hardly noticed at events of great spiritual excitation such as funerals or when "church songs" are being sung. Persons who display unusual predispositions to spirit possession, however, will be taken to healers for consultation, especially as it is widely believed that if the spirits who are calling a person to become a healer are denied, they will cause that person serious harm and misfortune. In the central healing rituals of the *ngoma* cult, the *ukuthwasa,* the interactions with spirits calling a person to heal can at first seem hostile until an experienced diviner begins the process of domesticating them and establishing cordial relations between the spirits and the novice. Not everyone is assailed by spirits in the course of his or her life, of course. But no one grows to adulthood without witnessing countless occasions of possession. And virtually everyone recognizes such possession as a general possibility for themselves.

Professional healers, whether of the traditional or Zionist/Apostolic variety, regularly demonstrate signs of spirit possession in the course of their work, such as the appearance of being in a trance, for these allow them to claim extraordinary powers of perceiving and counteracting invisible forces. Oftentimes, however, persons claiming engagement with spirits perform the outward appearances of possession in a manner that can only be described as lethargic — rolling their eyes and sighing a lot. In the ordinary course of a working day, healers I have known tend to be somewhat perfunctory in their performance of possession. No doubt, among those who are "called" by the spirits, many are only too willing to hear. And the language of Western psychology has permeated Soweto to the extent that what some take as indications of spirit possession, a few will see as signs of "nerves." But when ordinary people are overcome with sudden and violent fits—in church services, funerals, or *ngoma* rituals—few doubt they are experiencing a completely involuntary possession by an externally motivated invisible being.

Uniting all who claim experience of these forces and most of those who bear witness to such experiences is a conviction that the will of the person possessed is indeed suspended by actual forces existing outside that person. Phenomena associated with spirit possession, then, indicate a degree of vulnerability in the invisible realms of personhood. Much of the ritual work in the practice of healing and worship (in both Christian and traditional forms) is devoted to protecting against evil spirits' assault upon these vulnerabilities by opening up the person to life-affirming spiritual entities.

Just as external forces can assault or hijack essential components of personhood, such as the spirit, desires, or will, so resistance to these harms can also come from within. As Madumo put it when describing his need for faith in his healer: "it all comes down to the science of that *inyanga*. If he's knowing the right herbs, than those herbs can do miracles. But it depends upon the power of mind, too. My mind. These herbs are helped by my belief, by my faith in Mr. Zondi. I can use millions of herbs, but without any belief, they won't work out" (Ashforth 2000a, 65). The work of believing, then, is a deliberate action of harnessing the mind. And a mind so harnessed is a source of power. In a similar vein, in the middle of his battle with witchcraft, Madumo expressed a desire to "Westernize" his mind and forget about witchcraft (Ashforth 2000, 246). I naively imagined, Westerner that I am, that this statement expressed an acceptance of the standard modernist ontological position regarding witches, to wit: they exist only in the mind. Thus, if I do not believe in them, I need not worry that they can harm me. So I was somewhat surprised to discover that Madumo meant nothing of the sort. His view was that if he could convince himself that witches did not exist, it would minimize their actual power to cause him harm. By Westernizing his mind, then, he would be harnessing its power to resist the witches. Whereas fear, paranoia, and distrust bolster the power of witches to interfere in those inner realms we usually refer to as "mind," so disdain fortifies resistance.

Pictures and Dangers

One afternoon in 1993, while I was sorting through a pile of new photographs in my room in Mapetla Extension, my friend Buthi called by. Pointing to the pictures, he laughed and said: "You know, Adam, if you were a Black I would wonder why you had all these pictures." Despite the laughter, his point was serious. Images can be used for nefarious purposes. They can be used to kill the person pictured. They can be used to enslave people. They can also be used to make a person fall in love, regardless of her own desires. As with the uses of *muthi,* although everyone knows that images of persons can be used to powerful effect, few can say exactly what can and cannot be done with pictures, nor can they specify how.

The images I am referring to are primarily personal photographs, but virtually all forms of still imagery, no matter what the mode of their production, are usually assimilated into the general category "photo." On the wall of my room in Soweto, for example, I used to have a large framed woodcut that was always known as "Adam's photo." The word is usually indigenized with the addition of the prefix *i* and pronounced with an aspirated *t,* as in *ifotho.* When images actually made by cameras and darkrooms are spoken of, they are usually referred to as *izinehpi,* a Zulu-ized version of "snap."

Sangomas and *inyangas* claim to be able to use images to prepare *muthi* designed to secure for lovers the object of their desires. This activity, or so I have been informed by reputable healers, is fundamentally different from the uses of pictures in "witchcraft" to harm a person. For, despite the fact that healers might tell their clients they can secure the desired one's affection regardless of that person's feelings in the matter, the "reality" (as one healer explained it to me) is that the healer merely shows the picture to the client's ancestors. If the ancestors desire a match between their descendant and the person pictured, they will bring it about. The *muthi* will then be the agent of the ancestors' wishes. If the ancestors do not wish such a match, no amount of *muthi* can do anything to effect it. The healer who told me this did not seem to think the love object's own desires were particularly relevant to the issue, and he chuckled when he told me that he would still sell his client *muthi* knowing that the ancestors disapproved of the union and the love match would fail. "What harm is there in that?" he asked.

Knowing that others have access to such powers can be nerve-wracking, especially if you have reason to believe that their ancestors might approve of a love match with you which you do not desire or if a person in possession of your picture has reason to cause you harm. In 1992, a friend of mine pleaded with me to approach his recently dumped ex-girlfriend to retrieve images he referred to as "my photos." He was afraid that she would work on pictures of him to cause him harm—a fear heightened by the fact that her mother was now a *sangoma*. He was prepared to offer his spurned lover "her" photos in exchange. In the event, I was unable to accomplish this mission as the fact of my friendship with the ex-boyfriend was sufficient to make me unwelcome at the ex-girlfriend's house. In the course of attempting to assist my friend, however, we had long discussions about the risks he was seeking to avoid. He was a university graduate with a bachelor of arts degree, a moderately devout Methodist, and neither particularly superstitious nor well versed in what Sowetans refer to as "Culture," or African traditions.

My friend had been only too happy to have his photograph taken and had given his girlfriend his photo so that she could cherish their time together and remember him in his absence. When I asked him if he was worried about having his "soul" stolen if he did not get the pictures back, he laughed heartily at the ridiculous suggestion. I have never come across anyone in Soweto who worries about such theft when their photo is taken, though this is probably a result of people having a definite view, derived from generations of Christian faith, concerning the nature of the immortal soul, not to mention long exposure to the everyday realities of photographic film and the ceaseless flickering of television. Nonetheless, like most people he knows, he realizes that photos can pose serious dangers if they fall into the wrong hands at the wrong time. He was not dogmatic about the nature of the dangers he felt himself exposed to but was adamant that they were real. The fact that he knew I thought his fears ridiculous did not prompt him to keep them to himself. On the contrary, he figured his chances of getting the pictures back were enhanced by using a skeptical white man as an intermediary. When I pressed him for details on how his ex-girlfriend might work on the photographs, however, he confessed ignorance. He could only reply: "Maybe she could be using some *muthi,* or else calling her ancestors or some shit like that." That is, the ex-girlfriend (who had good reasons to feel extremely angry about being dumped) might have access to someone who, armed with a photograph of my friend, would know how to call upon her ancestors or other spirits to inflict punishment or exact revenge—someone like her mother, the *sangoma,* for example. Or she might be able to find someone with the requisite skills to act upon the image itself with *muthi* in some mysterious way so as to bring about misfortune in the life of my friend—or to bring him back to her against his will.

Ancestors, though immaterial, retain their bodily senses and appetites as well as their interest in the lives and welfare of their descendants, so it is not difficult to accept that photographs might serve in communication with them. If you accept the reality of ancestors, there is no reason not to assume that images can serve in communicating with them just as they do with a living person. The use of images to cause harm in conjunction with *muthi*, however, is somewhat more complex. In his effort to retrieve his photos, my friend's greatest worry was that his ex-girlfriend, aided by an unscrupulous *inyanga,* might be able to use his photograph as a means of programming *muthi,* or directing another form of evil agency such as a *tokoloshe,* to attack him in revenge for his betrayal. She might even be able to enlist the help of a legitimate healer, such her mother, who appreciated the justice of her claim. Such a use of *muthi* would be similar to the way a witch uses somebody's hair or nail clippings or clothes—a way of identifying and directing the *muthi* toward the specified victim.

At a typical township funeral, mourners will be presented with a "programme," usually a photocopied sheet with a photograph of the deceased, a brief obituary, and the order of proceedings for the service. At the conclusion of the burial, all the programmes are supposed to be collected by family members and either buried with the coffin or burned. This is done in order to protect the deceased from being interfered with by evil forces, for the spirit of the recently dead is vulnerable in his or her new life just as a newborn babe is vulnerable. In cases where the family is convinced that a death resulted from witchcraft, they will be particularly vigilant in collecting programmes. Indeed, in such cases the family might not print a photograph of the deceased in the programme at all, for fear that the witch could use the information to awaken the ancestors of the recently departed and set them against the person they should be welcoming and protecting. I have also been told that a witch might use *muthi* to directly attack the recently deceased's "shade"—that invisible essence of a person which lives on after death. The person who told me this, however, was unable to say quite how such an attack might be effected. Insisting that she gave no credence to these notions herself (though she was happy enough to elaborate what she thought might be the opinions of those who "believe in witchcraft"), she suggested that a photograph bears a similar relation to a person as their shadow and, therefore, can contain a person's "shade, something like their spirit," she said. A person jealous of another's popularity with supervisors at work, for example, might use *muthi* to work upon that person's photograph in order to steal the other's popularity and attract the supervisors' regard for herself. Similarly, a person covetous of another's lover might use a photograph to appropriate the lover's desire to himself. Similar reasoning governs the dispersal of a dead person's clothes and personal effects, which may be used only by close and trusted family members. Some older people insist that photos of deceased persons should not be kept at all for fear of malicious people using them to attack the persons imaged in the afterlife. When pictures of the dead are not destroyed, they are carefully stowed and accounted for.

The most frightful way of using images is in the making of zombies, persons whose powers of independently motivated action have been removed from them. Dolls and carved images can serve in this work as well as photographs. I have not had personal experience of zombies. In January 1993, however, local newspapers reported that a schoolgirl in the Meadowlands district of Soweto had gossiped to her friends about her grandmother's strange nocturnal behavior. Word reached the daughter of an old lady who had gone missing from home a week earlier after a trip to the city. Neighbors claimed to have seen her visiting the house of the schoolgirl's grandmother. Persuaded that the schoolgirl's grandmother had captured the other lady to make her into a zombie, a mob broke into her house and set about digging up the floor of the bedroom, looking for bodies. In the bedroom they found children's toys. Among the toys were some dolls. Convinced the dolls had been used for nefarious purposes, the crowd commandeered a bulldozer and razed the house, the better to make a thorough search. Another old lady's house was demolished, too. Relatives of other missing persons from around the area converged on the ruins to dig for their loved ones.[6]

Such events are not common in Soweto. The sense of danger and vulnerability that makes them possible, however, is an everyday fact of life. Given the history of labor migrancy in this region and the related tendency of people to disappear from home places in search of work and lose contact with their families (not to mention the appalling numbers of unidentified corpses in public mortuaries, victims of murder and accidents), it is small wonder that talk of zombies can capture imaginations.[7] The image is a type of copy of a person. The question underlying the fear is whether an image can also, somehow, embody an aspect of, or copy of, the invisible essence of that person that can allow malicious persons to create some sort of double that can then be subordinated to the will of the person working

6. See the report in the *Sunday Times* (Johannesburg), Africa edition, January 10, 1993, p. 3X.

7. For discussion of these sorts of stories as idioms within which people make sense of capitalist exploitation, see Comaroff and Comaroff 1999a; Geschiere 1997; Niehaus 2000.

on the image. Such seems to be the case in stories of zombies, where a witch creates a copy of the person and leaves it behind at his home as a corpse while capturing the original to work as a slave. Not everyone believes such stories. When Moleboheng's mother was buried, her sister, after some months of troubling dreams and suspicious misfortunes, visited an *inyanga* in Soweto who told her that their mother was not really dead but had been subjected to *ukuthwebula* and turned into a zombie. Moleboheng refused to believe this "bullshit." Her sister, however, began worrying about how to raise the money to perform the procedures necessary for rescuing her mother.

Images, Objects, and Invisible Realities

The philosophical issues relating to images, representation, and power are too complex to attempt to resolve here, and I have yet to meet anyone in Soweto who has developed a comprehensive theory of these issues that I could report as a distinctive account of the matter. An awareness of the possibilities of harm being caused by action with and on images coexists with ignorance of how this might be done — other than through the mysterious manipulation of *muthi.* When the nineteenth-century missionary-translators began work on their Bibles and lexicons in this part of the world, there were no straightforward equivalents in local African languages for the English word "picture" as that term had come to be understood in the West. Two-dimensional representational images were virtually unknown in precolonial southern African Bantu societies.[8] Although there were no pictures, carvings and statues of molded clay—known in Zulu as *isithombe* (plural, *izithombe*)—were commonplace. Children would make themselves dolls from clay: boys apparently favoring model oxen, girls preferring images of mothers with babies on their backs (Kidd 1969, 161–166). Bishop Colenso, one of the foremost translators of the Zulu language, defined *isithombe* in his 1884 lexicon as "a figure of a man, etc. carved or molded of clay, doll, puppet, idol" (1884, 559). All the references to "idols" and "graven images" in the Zulu Bible today are translated as *izithombe* (Word of Life 1978). The Zulu word *isithombe* derives from a root—*thombe*—which forms the basis of words describing the onset of sexual maturity in girls and female fertility: *thomba* (referring to puberty); *inthombi*

8. The "Bushman" rock paintings in the region, some dating from as early as 12,000 years before the present, seem not to have been replicated by the Bantu peoples, who migrated to southern Africa in later centuries (Dowson and Lewis-Williams 1994).

(an adolescent girl or young woman of marriageable age); and *ithombe* (menstrual discharge). As well as referring to photographs, idols, and graven images, the word *isithombe* is also used to refer to a child that strongly resembles a parent, a doll used in witchcraft, and the zombie created by acting upon an image.

If faithful resemblance to an external object, or accurate representation, were the only issue to contend with, Bible translators could have deployed another Zulu word for image: *umfanakiso*. This word has long been used to refer to the images that appear as reflections in pools of water. When mirrors arrived, along with colonists, *umfanakiso* was the word used to describe the strange apparitions in the glass.[9] The term is not commonly used for photographs in Soweto today, but its usage thus would not be particularly outlandish. As a general term for likeness and similitude, *fana*—the root of *umfanakiso*—bears a striking relation to *isithombe*. Whereas the root of the latter is the same as that in words for sexually mature young women, the *umfana* of *umfanakiso* refers to young boy prior to achieving manhood. And while the onset of sexual maturity renders a girl capable of producing life, a capacity which for all sorts of reasons must be carefully guarded, an *umfana* of the same age in this part of the world is a worthless sort of thing, a categorical nuisance. A young boy has no power and virtually no rights. Until he becomes a man (whereupon he will gain an exalted view of his status), he is at the beck and call of his elders (Pitje 1950a, 1950b, 1950c). The image *umfanakiso*, that fleeting representation found in a pond or a mirror and fixed in a photo, bears a similarly subject relation to its object. The generative capacity embodied in the image *isithombe* is an altogether different species of being.

Witches, Healers, and the Transcendence of the Ordinary

Most of the time, people in Soweto live in their bodies in ordinary sorts of ways and are not unduly perturbed by worries about assaults upon their innermost domains of being. Nor do they seem to experience themselves as living in time and space in ways that I, or any other skeptical Westerner, would find outlandish. The vulnerabilities outlined above are real, nonetheless, and can, on occasion, generate deep anxiety. Yet, while Sowetans usually understand their own way of being in the world as subject to all the usual physical limitations of the flesh, they are also (most of them)

9. For an account of the impact of mirrors in the encounter between English missionaries and southern Tswana people, see Comaroff and Comaroff 1991, 185ff.

convinced that some persons—at least some of the time—are not so constrained. Some persons are thought capable of operating in ways that transcend, or defy, the ordinary laws of physics and biology. Healers, for example, regularly swear that they have spent periods of months or years living beneath the surface of rivers, lakes, or oceans communing with powerful beings.

Consider this account by the healer Sarah Mashele. In a memoir of her career as a healer told to the South African writer Lilian Simon, Mashele recounts how on the morning after being taken as a child to a famous healer in Rhodesia, she awoke and heard the sound of drumming from people who assumed she was intended to become a *sangoma,* a member of the healing cult that drums, sings, and dances. But her ancestor told her she was not supposed to be a *sangoma.* The ancestor told her she was destined to be an *inyanga,* a healer who works without drums. She ran from the drumming of the *sangomas* and found a lake. The following is the account Simon transcribed (and "clarified") from interviews with Mashele:

I looked into the lake and saw a mirror. When I looked in the mirror I saw myself and I wanted to go right inside that mirror. I went into the water. I didn't swim, I just fell in. I can't explain how it happened because it was just like in an accident. You get a shock and you don't know what is happening.

Afterwards I found myself deep inside the lake, right underneath, and there was no water any more, just grass. There were trees also but they were smaller than the ones in the forest. They weren't close together and the sun was shining. It was so light and there were a lot of flowers. I saw three snakes. One snake was green and the other two black—they weren't big and they weren't small. They were like standing up with the heads high and the two black ones were making a noise . . . *Shhhh! Shhhh!* They were spitting at me but the poison didn't touch me. I was very frightened because they looked like they wanted to bite but the green one turned round to look at them and they stopped their noise. They started to lie down and talk, like a person, as we are talking now, and I could understand what they were saying. The green one told me he was going to show me how to use the herbs; he was going to show me everything. (Simon 1993, 39)

The young Sarah Mashele spent what her older self reported to have been "a long time" under the water with those snakes. Everything she learned about healing and divination—and she was evidently quite successful in her career, according to Simon—she learned from that green snake.

Although Sarah Mashele's story contains symbolism sufficient to keep a legion of interpreters busy for months, there is no doubt that she intends her account to be taken literally. Mashele's white interlocutor was somewhat skeptical about the account of time spent under the water and inquired how her parents reacted to their daughter's disappearance into the lake, a seeming drowning witnessed by all. The healer replied that her parents had been distraught but were persuaded not to cry for her. They were told to buy a white goat. When the snake had finished his instruction, he took the girl out of the water and the goat was sacrificed in his honor (Simon 1993, 42). According to Mashele, her disappearance into the water was witnessed by others, so it really happened, but she lived to tell the tale; and her instruction was really at the hands of a green snake. On numerous occasions in Soweto I have heard similar stories, usually from people who have heard the stories at one or two removes. Every time I have been told such things, and I am far less polite and respectful of others' nonsense than Lilian Simon, my interlocutors have insisted that everything they say is literally true. I have no doubt that they really believed such things possible. When a friend's mother was undergoing *ukuthwasa* to become a healer in the early 1990s, for example, Mpho was seriously concerned that our friend, who had to participate in the rituals by the river, would be taken under the water by a giant snake. Mpho was a college student at the time (having taken classes in physical science in high school) and firmly believed that healers could live beneath the waters for months at a time. Fortunately, our friend survived the ordeal at the river with nothing more than a bone-chilling dunking.

As reputable healers boast of experiencing and performing miracles in defiance of the ordinary laws of physics, so their antitheses, the witches, are also presumed to be able to transcend the ordinary physical limitations of the human body. The most fundamental, and perplexing, is the reputed ability of witches to extend through time and space so as to be in two places at the same time—for example, leaving a body behind sleeping peacefully in the bed while performing evil deeds on the other side of town. Witches are also said to be able to pass through walls or locked doors, or send their familiars to do so, to physically harm the persons they seek. An Anglican priest once told me, for example, that he had been accused by an elderly female parishioner of sending a brown dog through her locked door to "make love" to her at night. He denied the charge, though he had no doubt that most of his congregation would agree that such a feat would be possible if indeed he was a witch.

Because the craft of witches is secret, and that of the healer is mastered only after a long apprenticeship, most people do not trouble themselves unduly trying to figure out just how these miracles are performed. If they do bother to inquire of those who claim to know, they will be told (as I have been) some version of the following: "I don't know, but it is so." Doubt at your peril. That some people, otherwise ordinary in their bodily flesh and blood, can perform miracles of healing or harm is not doubted. The only question at issue is whether these miracles serve evil or good ends. And since one can never know who has these capacities or their intentions, living in a world with witches can be difficult.

Part Three

SPIRITUAL INSECURITY AND THE STATE

11

WITCHCRAFT, VIOLENCE, AND JUSTICE

A Thug and His Mother, the Witch

In October 1995 Mpho wrote to me in New York with news of a local Soweto thug, notorious in the neighborhoods surrounding Mpho's home in Senaoane, with whom we had once had an unpleasant encounter:

Chafunya was finally cornered and eight bullets were pumped into his evil head. He was shot in a shootout near Lizobuya Stores. He ran out of ammunition and sheltered in a nearby house to load his guns. In the meantime a Phiri boy was more calculating and ran to the other street to jump into the opposite house where he found Chafunya loading. The Phiri boy then emptied his cartridge into Chafunya's head. During the shootout, Chafunya's colonel was shot dead and a small girl in the nearby house was shot dead too.

They say the cause was a quarrel over a girl. The murderer was her boyfriend. He was arrested the following day. His schoolmates marched to Protea Police Station demanding his release, saying that Chafunya had been terrorizing the community. They were not allowed entrance to the Court yard, so they started stoning police cars and causing havoc at the gate. The police responded with teargas and police dogs.

The following day Chafunya's gang avenged his death by shooting three students at Junior High. The Gang stated that they are going to kill a minimum of twenty students, and that students won't be allowed to sit for their exams.

On Sunday they held Chafunya's funeral. The Boss was on his way to Phelindaba ("end of the story"), i.e. Avalon Cemetery. While the procession was passing Potchefstroom Road on its way to Chiawelo the Shangaanis were waiting for him [residents of this part of Soweto are mostly members of the Shangaans-Tsonga ethnic group]. Chafunya used to terrorize them in a big way they say. They did not want him to pass Chiawelo. They blocked the roads and shots were fired from both sides. Police dispersed the angry crowds from Chiawelo and Dlamini [two adjoining suburbs of Soweto]. Finally the funeral procession reached the place of rest. On their way back, the Gang were threatening people in that area and in Senaoane [the area where Chafunya used to live].

On Monday, the Gang was making threats, so the students organized themselves. The other gang member was identified as a student from Sekano [a neighborhood high school]. He was visited and apprehended, along with his friend. But he broke free and ran away. His friend was unlucky. He was disciplined. Like Stephen in the Bible he was stoned, only to be rescued by the police half dead. He died at Baragwanath Hospital. The mob proceeded to the gang member's home. It was destroyed, although saved by the police before it was burned.

They then proceeded to Chafunya's home. Chafunya's mother was hacked to death and the house destroyed. Chafunya's mother was killed because of a general rumour that she was protecting her son by prescribing *muthi* to make him powerful and feared.

Then the schoolboys went on a manhunt for gang members. They were identified, one by one, and fled. The schoolboys formed an army, and were armed with guns for sure. They camped out and pursued the gang everywhere. And today we don't hear any stories about the Chafunya gang. The students have started their exams without hindrance.

Chafunya, who took the nickname from a Malawian-born soccer star of the early 1990s, was a small-time thug in a country wracked by crime. Along with his gang, he was a dangerous presence for much of the early 1990s in his part of Soweto. His criminal activities were considered particularly illegitimate because he preyed upon people in the local community. In those days, "doing crime in town," where the victims were mostly white, was a less stigmatized occupation than "doing crime eLokshini," in the "Location," the Black Township. Robbing Whites was generally considered by young men at the time—and not only young men—to be a form of forcible redistribution of wealth that was more like a job of work than a morally opprobrious crime. Indeed, the category "crime" itself, since law consisted merely of that which was prohibited by the government, was virtually an ethically neutral construct because the government was an instrument of oppression. Robbing, raping, and assaulting people in the community, as was Chafunya's wont, however, was deeply illegitimate.

Organized youth gangs with distinctive names, identities, and organizations and dedicated to the pursuit of criminal ends or identified with particular neighborhoods were the exception rather than the rule in Soweto in the 1990s. This contrasts strongly with the situation in Coloured Townships, particularly in Cape Town, where large-scale gang organizations are the rule (Pinnock 1997). Highly organized gangs on a national scale are also prevalent in prisons, and virtually everyone who passes through the prison system is forced to owe allegiance to one or another of the gangs, but they do not have a strong presence in everyday life in the townships (Haysom 1981; Keswa 1975; Lotter 1988). More common in Soweto are loose cohorts of young men, friends of similar ages, who combine for fun, security, and, possibly, crime. All young men belong to some such coterie or another. Sometimes these groups are dominated by a charismatic and dangerous individual; usually they are not. Within these coteries, competition for status and respect is similar, whether members are united for crime or merely companionship, and is fundamental to the shape of life throughout the whole city. Nevertheless, given the extent of physical insecurity, if you lack friends who consider you a brother and who are prepared to stand up for you, you will be vulnerable at all times, possibly at peril of your life. Schoolboys have access to the largest number of possible cohorts, occasionally coalescing into legions of warriors when the time comes to retaliate for attack upon one of their number. Political action during the days of the struggle against apartheid drew upon these reservoirs of camaraderie in the schools for the formation of organizations. Since the end of the struggle and the demise of comrade culture, school networks remain the most potent source of retaliatory force in the form of mob justice.

During Chafunya's reign of terror, his name became associated with far more crimes than he and his associates could have comfortably perpetrated. For many his name served as a symbol of the sort of criminality that was seen at the time as running rampant, the violence of young men constrained neither by respect for elders, the discipline of political organizations, a sense of loyalty to their communities, nor the morality of basic human decency. Chafunya, that is to say, was emblematic of a particular sort of home-grown evil at a time when the evil of apartheid was waning.

Killing Chafunya, pumping bullets into his "evil head" as Mpho put it, was applauded by those outside his gang as an act of heroism and justice. The arrest of the young man who killed Chafunya was an affront to everyone who had suffered under his reign of terror and a sign that the police had not changed since the days of apartheid—that they were still in fact enemies of the community. Rampaging mobs of schoolchildren marched on the police station demanding justice. When they were met with tear gas, they turned on their enemies in Chafunya's gang to inflict their own form of justice. These children had learned their methods from their elders, who had known the thrills of similar *umzabalazo* (disruption) in the struggle against apartheid. The schoolboys' quest for justice, however, required more than simply rioting against the police or fighting a criminal gang of young men armed with guns. As well as dealing with the gangsters, they had to root out the source of Chafunya's power and punish the person ultimately responsible: Chafunya's mother.

If Chafunya's mother was in fact providing her son with *muthi,* as the schoolboys alleged, she was doing nothing other than what a mother ought to do: nurturing, supporting, and protecting her child. It was not the fact of *muthi* being used that outraged the youths but the illegitimate ends to which they thought it was being directed and the evident complicity of the mother in her son's crimes—complicity for which no other proof was needed than the fact of his crimes. Mothers are constantly using *muthi* to strengthen and protect their children, to assist them in their passage through life, and to bring them good fortune and happiness. Of the hundreds of schoolboys who swarmed on Chafunya's home to burn it and kill his mother, few would not have been treated with *muthi* by their own mothers at some point in their lives. Using *muthi* in such a manner is entirely unobjectionable and unremarkable. When a friend of mine had trouble finding a job after completing her Technikon Diploma, for example, her mother pressed her to visit an *inyanga* to get *muthi* to aid her search for work. She declined because she did not want her mother claiming credit for the *muthi* when she eventually found a job on her own after years of study and hard work. Also, anyone who knows they are going into battle will be grateful for a dose of *intelezi,* a name for the *muthi* that is supposed to strengthen and protect the warrior.

Because Chafunya's activities were so antisocial, however, his mother's support was presumed to be an essential ingredient of his evil. The boys who killed her, and their friends who told me about the event, did not hesitate to treat her as a witch. I was unable to determine whether the boys who killed her thought she was producing the *muthi* herself or merely supplying medicines procured from an *inyanga.* I doubt it would have mattered to them. As far as I know, she was not a traditional healer or in any way professionally connected with the making of *muthi.* Chafunya's mother was killed in a moment of frenzied rage by a mob of boys and young men desperate for vengeance. Everyone associated with Chafunya was at risk at that time. Whatever the facts of the case may be, whenever I have heard the narrative of Chafunya's death, or repeated it myself to someone in Soweto, the reason for his mother's death is taken for granted as having to do with *muthi.*

Mpho's account of the death of Chafunya illustrates key points of connection between witchcraft and violence. People suspected of operating with occult powers, whether supplying *muthi* for others or using it themselves for illegitimate ends, are sometimes killed as "witches" in the name of justice for using their powers to harm and kill others. This happens infrequently, however, and such killings are not always clearly identifiable as witchcraft related or categorizable solely as such. Illegitimate uses of occult forces may be only one of their crimes. Chafunya was a thug, *muthi* or no *muthi.* His mother was guilty enough just for having given birth to him. The violence perpetrated by people like Chafunya and his gang, as well as that perpetrated by the schoolboys in putting an end to his reign, resulted in a great deal of suffering for many innocent victims. The family of the "small girl" who was killed by a stray bullet in the shootout with Chafunya, for example, no doubt wept over their loss. I did not know this family, but I am sure that this tragedy (particularly if it followed on the heels of other inexplicable sorrows for them, as it very likely did given the ordinary hardships of life in Soweto) left them wondering who had singled them out for such treatment. They would not have had to look far to find an expert in healing their sorrows who would claim to be able to identify the person responsible.

In the everyday retelling of a narrative such as Mpho's account of Chafunya's death, no moral distinction is made between the violence of the son and the "prescribing" of *muthi* by the mother. Both were equally wrong. Using violence and using *muthi* are subject to similar principles of legitimation. Chafunya and his mother, as perpetrators of violence and witchcraft, both occupy a radically different place in the moral universe of everyday discourse from the righteous violence of the schoolboys and the proper use of "traditional medicines." In all the tumult of those times no one was able to stand above the fractious violence of those boys and young men and put an end to their fighting. No power existed that could provide security for the community from the depredations of Chafunya and his gang, nor from the consequences that followed his death. Nor did an authority exist that could have held his mother to account for her use of *muthi* in a way that would have satisfied the community at large as much as her death did. Few whose lives Chafunya had touched mourned his passing. Many considered his mother equally reprehensible. No one would claim that the way the community solved this problem was ideal.

Justice and Witchcraft

When a healer identifies a person's misfortune as resulting from the deliberate use of *muthi* by some other person, the problem of justice immediately arises. While healers of all types regularly identify the evil effects of witchcraft and always claim to know the identity of the perpetrator, they rarely name names or encourage the prosecution of justice or revenge by their clients. Typically, the healer will report the results of a divination wherein witchcraft is revealed by reporting vague identifying characteristics, such as saying, "the person responsible is a neighbor, a woman, short, dark in complexion"—providing thereby sufficient detail for the client to make a positive identification of a malefactor but leaving the description general enough so that it is bound to fit someone in the client's circle of acquaintances. The fact that law prohibits the naming of witches can hardly be the reason for this, as the same Suppression of Witchcraft Act that prohibits naming witches also outlaws the divination that is practiced by virtually every healer. This reticence on the part of healers has been noted by writers on the subject since at least the mid-nineteenth century and is most likely a product of simple prudence (Brownlee 1916). By keeping the identity of the culprit secret—all the while alluding to his or her identity indirectly—a healer maintains an aura of power. As most traditional healing is premised upon the promise that the "evil forces" dispatched by a witch to cause harm and death will be returned to the perpetrator to hoist him with his own petard, the possibility of justice is offered as part of the treatment. This is only a limited promise, however, as it is predicated upon the success of the healing treatment.

Prophet-healers of the Apostolic and Zionist churches tend not to promise such retaliatory punishment in the course of their healing, although some acknowledge that their work can result in harm to others because the evil spirits exorcised in the course of healing have to find somewhere else to go (Oosthuizen 1992, 123). Retaliation would hardly be in keeping with the pacific doctrines of Christianity. Simply because the official ideology of this mode of healing disdains retaliation, however, there is no reason to believe that healers' clients do not presume that such justice is being done when demons and evil spirits are driven out of their victims. Because exorcism of evil spirits is such a central part of the AIC practice, many outsiders have cause to wonder what happens to those spirits after being dispatched from an afflicted person. Perhaps they remain in the rivers and streams after baptismal rituals are completed and lie in wait to pollute innocent passersby. Perhaps they are manipulated by unscrupulous Zionists to attack their enemies outside the band. No one can say for sure. But if you enter a Zionist church compound, expect to be doused with holy water to wash these evil spirits away.

When prophet-healers gain a reputation for great power based on their evident success in driving out evil spirits, their churches tend to flourish. Successful churches, however, raise suspicions that their leaders are engaged in nefarious occult activities to strengthen their powers. When I began researching the activities of the Zion Christian Church in Soweto, I was required to seek permission from "headquarters" in Moria before speaking to local members. A letter was drafted and dispatched up the church hierarchy for consideration by Bishop Barnabas Lekganyane, the spiritual and administrative head of the church and grandson of the founder.[1] The letter took months to wend its way through the offices, finally landing on the general secretary's desk. The general secretary and I negotiated by letter and fax from the Northern Province to New York. For a few months in 1998, it looked like I was going to be invited to visit the headquarters of the church in Moria. Whenever I mentioned this possibility to friends in Soweto, however, I was warned, in deadly earnest, not to go. Stories had been circulating that the church was using human body parts to make *muthi.* How else could their power be explained? Mr. Zondi, an *inyanga,* was particularly emphatic. Mr. Zondi told me that the church kept a special room in the bishop's house stocked with body parts, a room that Mandela had demanded to see when he visited headquarters. When I asked why Mandela had not had the bishop arrested for this, Mr. Zondi said he had been bribed.

Despite the promise of occult revenge in the course of healing, the desire to bring the responsible person to justice remains strong among people finding themselves victims of witchcraft. This desire, however, mostly remains thwarted. Public accusations against witches are sometimes made in Soweto, but they are rare. When accusations are leveled, however, neither the accuser nor the accused stands much chance of seeing justice done, for no institutions exist wherein accusations can be properly tested and those responsible for causing suffering punished. Outside the confinement of those Christian congregations that make a priority of combating witchcraft, such as the Zionist and Apostolic bands, the only institutions available for resolving such conflicts among persons who accuse each other of

---

1. For an account of my negotiations with the ZCC, see Ashforth 2000a, chap. 12.

witchcraft are those that have emerged in the interstices of state power as forums for resolving those other conflicts commonly known as "crime."

In the absence of a legitimate legal order and effective policing, Black urban communities in apartheid's townships such as Soweto struggled throughout the twentieth century to find ways of securing themselves from the perils of city life, seeking to resolve conflicts within families and among neighbors and to control young men's violent impulses. Sometimes, varieties of rural forms of communal authority, such as that of the *kgotla,* or council of elders, were instituted in efforts to assert the authority of older men over disorderly youth (Hund and Kotu-Rammopo 1983). Sometimes, associations linking people from the same ethnic groups or rural-based gangs of migrants such as the Sotho MaRashea in Sotho-speaking districts of Soweto have organized attempts at vigilante justice (Bonner 1993). To defend the community both from the police and from local miscreants, in the 1980s neighborhoods organized a network of Street Committees and Civic Associations. Many of these bodies, however, were dominated by young men, political activists known as Comrades, which older people considered a perversion of the proper order of authority (Seekings 1989). None of these organizations succeeded in creating more than a temporary sense of security from violence and crime.[2] They have been even less effective against the threat of witchcraft or in mediating the conflicts surrounding witchcraft accusations.

When MaNdlovu found herself being continually accused of witchcraft by a neighbor, she turned to the Street Committee for help.[3] Unlike the more established neighborhoods of Soweto, where the Street Committees have mostly fallen into desuetude, these neighborhood organizations were still active in the shack settlement where MaNdlovu's family lived. The accusations of witchcraft became intolerable. Whenever MaNdlovu passed her accuser in the street, the other woman would launch into an obscene tirade. MaNdlovu approached the Street Committee and asked for a hearing. The committee called both women, accused and her accuser, and heard

2. In 1999, the South African Law Commission concluded a study recommending the development of "community dispute resolution forums" as a way of both reducing pressure on the overburdened court system while engaging communities directly in the pursuit of justice and order through forms recognizable from indigenous rural and urban traditions (South African Law Commission 1999). At the time of writing, nothing had come of this.

3. I was not present in Soweto at the time of these events. They were recounted for me by Moleboheng and I have not had the opportunity to speak to others connected with the events. For a fuller description of the circumstances surrounding them, see Moleboheng's letter in chapter 4.

the case. MaNdlovu was a well-respected and long-established neighbor. Her accuser was a young woman who was a drunkard and considered a bit wild in the neighborhood. The committee was not inclined to judge Ma-Ndlovu guilty. They told the young woman making the accusations to desist. If she wanted to make such accusations, they told her, she should bring evidence to back up the case. Had she found MaNdlovu naked in her yard in the middle of the night? Had she caught her in the yard with *muthi?* If so, something could be done. But MaNdlovu's accuser had never found anything like that. So the Street Committee told the young woman to stop making allegations.

The young woman kept quiet for a while after the meeting, but not for long. She soon ignored the Street Committee order. The committee could do nothing. Nor were they particularly interested in trying. As men, they were disinclined to involve themselves in this conflict of women. Ma-Ndlovu's accuser was no doubt persuaded of the truth of her accusations. She had probably consulted an *inyanga* about her troubles and been given a description of the witch who caused the car accident that killed her family that fit MaNdlovu. This same young woman was rumored to be suffering from AIDS, so perhaps she had also consulted healers for her own health problems. In any event, she would not cease her assault nor desist in her accusations. Eventually, MaNdlovu went to the police to lodge a formal complaint. The police opened a docket. Under the terms of the Suppression of Witchcraft Act, anyone accusing someone of practicing witchcraft is guilty of an offense.[4] The courts of African chiefs have also long outlawed such calumnies. MaNdlovu died before I was able to talk with her about these troubles, but I doubt she was familiar with the particularities of laws relating to her situation. She was desperate. She knew that what the young woman was saying was wrong. She was not a witch. That woman had no right to say she was. And remember: she was being accused of murdering a whole family. Unfortunately, involving the police infuriated her accuser. She confronted MaNdlovu again. In the middle of their argument MaNdlovu collapsed and died.

In addition to the grief and anger they felt at her death, MaNdlovu's family had to contend with knowing that her sudden death was probably being taken by neighbors to be proof that she actually was a witch. They knew that anyone who had been aware of the accusations of witchcraft (as

---

4. *Seymour's Customary Law* informs us: "The courts have held that, as a general rule, there is no civil action at customary law for defamation except iro [in regard of] statements imputing witchcraft" (Bekker 1989, 343).

most were since the Street Committee had become involved in the dispute)
would have assumed that the accuser had been treated by an *inyanga* who
bounced the witchcraft back from whence it came. People who did not
know and love MaNdlovu were free to interpret her death as an instance of
justice being done. That did not stop them from enjoying the family's hospitality at the funeral. Her death brought to mind for me an occasion a
couple of years earlier when I had brought a friend visiting from England
to visit the family, along with a good supply of meat and beer for a feast.
After we had eaten, I made a short speech introducing my friend to the
family and thanking them for their hospitality. I was feeling nostalgic and
grateful, as the visitor was the daughter of my professor at Oxford, Gavin
Williams, the man who had introduced me to the study of South Africa
some twenty years earlier. MaNdlovu also made a speech. She thanked me
for bringing food to her house. She welcomed the visitor from overseas,
along with my crew of Thabo, Mpho, and Madumo—all regular visitors
to her house in Snake Park. And she welcomed her neighbors. Then she
startled me. She thanked me again for all I had done for her family, all the
help I had given them. By this stage her audience consisted mainly of the
other women from around the neighborhood, along with her daughters,
me, and my friends. Father and his friends were inside the house. She continued, addressing her neighbors: "Adam was sent to my house by God,"
she said. "So you must not be jealous. I know you people of Snake Park.
You are too jealous. And you can even send *muthi* to my house and bewitch
my family." She went on and on, repeating her theme: Adam was sent by
God; therefore, you have no cause to be jealous. Her daughters were angry
and embarrassed. I was puzzled. Such talk about *muthi* and jealousy is most
unusual—improper, even. MaNdlovu had been drinking, but not too much.
I had no doubt that she was speaking deliberately, but I had no idea at the
time what she meant.

Spiritual Insecurity and Political Power: The Colonial Legacy

In precolonial African polities, management of the dangers facing communities that would now be called "witchcraft," the adjudication of social conflicts expressed in witchcraft accusations, and the management of other
dangers threatening spiritual security were foundational purposes of political power. Political authority was constituted in relations with spiritual
powers as well as in ordinary social relations among men and women, and
governing authorities served as key intermediaries between the mundane
spheres of daily life and the invisible domains of ancestral spirits, where

the ultimate sources of security and welfare were said to be found.[5] Healers, with their putative ability to penetrate the secrecy surrounding acts of witchcraft and to perceive the action of forces ordinarily imperceptible to humans, played a central role in political and judicial affairs within African polities, identifying persons deemed responsible for deploying evil forces against the interests of the community and managing relations between the community of the living and the spirits of the dead.

Political leaders whose legitimacy was questionable were regularly suspected of nefarious dabbling with supernatural powers. Myths surrounding the legendary Zulu king and nation builder Shaka ka Senzangakona, for example, suggest that part of his enormous capacity and appetite for power, a drive that both forged the Zulu nation and destroyed Shaka's kingship, derived from his contact with evil spiritual powers mediated through the sorcerer Isanusi. In Thomas Mofolo's famous retelling of the legend of Shaka, the king became enslaved to the rapacious demands of these spirits, and Shaka's ever increasing sacrifices of human life led, ultimately, to his own demise (Mofolo 1931). Mofolo's account of Shaka was shaped by his desire to fashion Christian morality tales, but the basic principle of judging legitimacy is not limited to the Christians: the good leader derives his power from the spirits guarding the welfare and good fortune of the nation (or, as the Christians would say, God); the illegitimate leader derives his power from evil forces—in a word, witchcraft.

Colonial rulers in Africa suppressed practices of witchcraft management in the public sphere and drove concerns of spiritual insecurity into private realms of healing and the quasi-public domains of indigenous churches, religious sects, and healing cults. During the late nineteenth and early twentieth centuries throughout the British colonies in Africa, of which South Africa was one, laws modeled on the 1736 and 1824 antiwitchcraft legislation of the United Kingdom were introduced outlawing the activities of divination (the central diagnostic technique of traditional healing), witch finding, the making of accusations, and the hearing of witchcraft cases in chiefs' courts (Chanock 2001, 322). Among other things, these colonial witchcraft

5. For discussion of the religious and judicial role of chiefs in this regard, see Packard 1981; Pettersson 1953, 342ff.; Schapera 1938. Some ethnographers have argued that witchcraft management was *not* a judicial function of chiefly authority. In her classic study *The Social System of the Zulus*, for example, Eileen Krige argues that although "witchcraft is looked upon as the most terrible crime . . . [it] cannot be tried by judicial processes" (1936, 252). However, as she makes clear in her description of the "sniffing out" process, the procedures of divination, accusation, and punishment, although motivated by diviners and purported victims, all take place under the auspices of chiefly authority.

suppression acts (more accurately described as "suppression of the suppression of witchcraft" legislation because they aimed at people who claimed to be managing the dangers of witchcraft) provided the colonial authorities with a legal weapon to use against Africans challenging colonial rule in the name of healing.

Although the terms of this legislation outlawed all who claimed powers to divine the agency of witchcraft or who named others as witches, in practice these laws were applied only when popular healers emerged who seemed a danger to colonial order. In the process, as Steven Feierman has argued, the colonizers disrupted the connection between healing, justice, and governance in the public sphere (Feierman 1999). For Africans, however, the dangers of witchcraft did not disappear with the passage of the witchcraft suppression legislation. In the course of seeking safety from the dangers of witchcraft, African communities created parallel spheres of political and judicial action pertaining to the management of spiritual insecurity that were centered in the courts of traditional leaders operating outside the purview of colonial officials. Charismatic individuals and religious movements also emerged in response to the demands for justice in the face of witchcraft, as did large-scale organized witch-finding movements and spontaneous ad hoc community action to punish witches without the sanction of traditional authorities. Most important, however, the quest for justice in this domain became the province of healers.

Few Africans seriously believed that the colonial authorities, or their apartheid-era counterparts in South Africa, were concerned with protecting them from the dangers of witches with their suppression of witchcraft efforts. Consider this letter by Chief Pakati (a.k.a. Pakade) to the British governor of Natal protesting the colony's policy of granting refuge to fugitives from witchcraft accusations: "Pakati begs his English lords not to treat the question lightly. His lords say they do not believe that sorcerers can cause the death of any one. There are certain people who are rejoiced to hear this, and who intend to take advantage of it to execute the most fatal designs. Let government beware lest it protect murderers at the expense of the lives of innocent people" (Casalis 1861, 281).[6] The suppression of witchcraft acts, when they were introduced later in the colonial era, were

6. The letter was cited in the memoirs of Eugene Casalis, the early French missionary to the BaSotho. Pakati (or Pakade, as Bryant called him in his classic account of Zulu history) was the son of Macingwane, leader of the Cunu clan, which was decimated in the early nineteenth century by Shaka. Pakati governed a small community on the coast of Natal north of Durban in the middle decades of the nineteenth century. He died in 1880 (Bryant 1929, 271–273).

seen throughout Africa in similar terms—protection of "murderers at the expense of the lives of innocent people"—part of a general assault upon Africa by the foreign powers of Europe. The sense of injustice suffered by those prosecuted under the witchcraft suppression laws, people who saw themselves as engaged in campaigns for justice and security against murderous malefactors, was often intense (Fields 1982; Melland 1935; Roberts 1935).

A witchcraft suppression act is still in force in South Africa. This legislation is bitterly resented by traditional healers, who complain, among other things, that it confuses their work with that of witches (Portfolio Committee on Arts 2000, para. 23.3a). In the African rural areas of the country, the former Native Reserves and Homelands, many chiefs continue to hear cases relating to witchcraft, as they have throughout the twentieth century despite the official prohibition. The clandestine nature of these hearings over the past century, however, has meant that in the field known as customary law no case law has been developed relating to witchcraft issues other than in matters of libelous accusations or in divorce proceedings where a husband suspects his wife of practicing witchcraft (Bekker 1989, 192). The field of official customary law, as fashioned in the courts of chiefs under the scrutiny of colonial and apartheid authorities, is preoccupied with issues pertaining to marriage, the family, and property. In urban areas, witchcraft cases were sometimes clandestinely adjudicated under the authority of "traditional leaders" in hostels housing migrant workers and occasionally treated by Street Committees or ad hoc convocations of residents, as in MaNdlovu's case. For the most part, however, African urban dwellers in South Africa throughout the twentieth century have had no access to public institutions wherein cases arising from suspicions that persons were using evil forces to harm others in the community could be resolved. They have had no access to justice in this domain, just as they had little justice in other spheres of life.

Policing Witchcraft

Hardly a week passes in South Africa without press reports of witches being killed or of mutilated bodies being found with organs removed for purposes of sorcery. Many more killings, like that of Chafunya's mother, have occult dimensions that do not figure in official reports or statistics. When I interviewed the official spokesman for the police in Soweto, Superintendent Mariemuthu, about the Chafunya case, for example, he was aware of the murders and riots but professed ignorance of—and seemed genuinely unaware of—the occult dimension of the mother's death. In the late 1980s and early 1990s an epidemic of witch killings swept the northern parts of the country (Minaar 1998). Hundreds of people were murdered as witches, many of them killed by the same young men who were fighting for liberation as Comrades of the ANC (Minaar, Wentzel, and Payze 1998; Niehaus 2001; Ritchken 1988). When witch finding takes place outside the purview of a country's political system, the challenge to political authority is direct. The history of colonial and postcolonial Africa is replete with instances of documented witch-finding movements forcing both "traditional" and "modern" political leaders to scramble to maintain their authority in the face of competition from charismatic diviners sniffing out witches in their communities.[7] In South Africa, witch-finding movements in the 1980s challenged both traditional leaders and the bureaucratic elites of Homeland states in the name of the liberation movement (Niehaus 1997; Ralushai Commission 1996; Ritchken 1988).

Shortly after winning office in 1994, the newly elected ANC government of the Northern Province (now Limpopo), the area most affected by witchcraft-related violence, instituted a Commission of Inquiry into Witchcraft Violence and Ritual Murders, known as the Ralushai Commission after its chair, Professor Nkhumeleni Ralushai. The commission's 1996 report documents the extent of antiwitchcraft violence and recommended an overhaul of the Suppression of Witchcraft Act in order to recognize the reality of witchcraft. The national Commission on Gender Equality held numerous meetings and conferences to raise awareness of violence against suspected witches, who were predominantly older women. As the premier of the Northern Province said at a conference on witchcraft violence in September 1998: "Individuals are taking the law into their own hands in the name of justice. Our people have resorted to violent and criminal actions in dealing with those they believe to be witches" (SAPA 1998). Witches were being burnt alive by mobs of young people, usually by means of the notorious "necklace" of a car tire doused with petrol perfected as a means of terrorizing informers during the struggle against apartheid.

Although people in the affected communities were apparently satisfied that injustices were being rectified by the killing of these witches, they agreed that it was wrong for rampaging mobs of schoolchildren to kill people (Delius 1996, 191ff.; Niehaus 2001, 156).[8] This was not the proper

---

7. See, e.g., Apter 1993; Auslander 1993.

8. This was also a common theme of interviews I conducted in the region in 1990 and 1991. Older people I spoke to were torn between gratitude for the work the youth were do-

procedure. As the main black daily newspaper of South Africa, the *Sowetan*, editorialized on February 10, 1994, after one such incident when three elderly women were burnt to death by a mob of schoolchildren: "It is not part of the African tradition to allow youths to inflict punishment on those who are believed to be enemies of the tribe or village." "African tradition" in these matters, by all accounts, involved judicial procedures conducted under the auspices of political authority in which accusations were tested against evidence in order that justice might be seen to be done. Yet, while everyone can agree that rampaging mobs of schoolchildren is not the best way to solve a community's problems, finding a way of securing justice for people who feel themselves assaulted by witchcraft is not easy. In the witch-killing movements that swept the region now known as Limpopo (formerly the Lebowa Homeland and then the Northern Province) in the 1980s and early 1990s, young people took the lead in ridding the community of occult enemies in the same way they led the struggle to overthrow apartheid and the Homeland leaders they denounced as puppets of the apartheid regime (Ritchken 1988).

The ethnographic record of this part of the world contains many descriptions of judicial processes relating to witchcraft. These historical descriptions embody a definite sense of what justice consists of in procedures relating to witchcraft, a sense that would be endorsed by participants in contemporary conflicts such as those surrounding the death of MaNdlovu. The first requirement of justice in these affairs demands an independent and impartial adjudicator to preside over the proceedings. In the precolonial context, the chief or king was the person playing this role, though missionary critics often pointed out that since the chief stood to gain by confiscating the property of witches and had a strong motive to convict anyone whose wealth in cattle challenged his chiefly preeminence, his impartiality could not always be guaranteed (Kingon 1919). Assuming that the office of impartial adjudicator could be filled, justice demanded that both the accuser and the accused have the right to account for themselves before him.

The second condition of justice in cases of witchcraft is the requirement of evidence. Accusations of occult injury, like all accusations of wrongdoing must be supported by evidence—as the Street Committee in Snake Park insisted when MaNdlovu appeared before them. Being predicated upon secrecy, witchcraft is not the easiest thing to prove. The most convincing proof is when the accused is caught in the act of deploying dangerous *muthi*. If

---

ing in ridding the community of evil, discomfort at the upending of social authority, and fear for their own safety should they be targeted as witches.

someone was found with *muthi* in another person's yard at night, especially if the accused person was naked at the time, the accuser would have strong evidence. From time to time people do in fact find suspicious substances in their yards or smeared on their walls, suggesting efforts at witchcraft, but it is not easy to catch the culprits in the act. Techniques of deploying *muthi,* moreover, do not always leave a trace or require physical contact. Houses could be searched for incriminating evidence of *muthi,* but hundreds of thousands of traditional healers and their clients will also have *muthi* in their houses for purposes of healing. When I mentioned this to Mr. Zondi one afternoon when he was in the middle of a diatribe about the necessity of police action against witches, he suggested that suspected witches' homes could be searched and any *muthi* discovered tested for poisonous properties by forcing the suspect to drink it. Innocent people, he insisted, would be unscathed. Witches would either refuse to drink or die (Ashforth 2000a, 129).

Ultimately, the possibilities of nefarious action with *muthi* are such that in most instances of suffering only a diviner capable of perceiving the invisible agencies at work can determine whether or not witchcraft is in effect. Thus, divination must be an integral part of the judicial process in cases of witchcraft. Few people in these parts doubt the theoretical possibility of obtaining "objective" evidence regarding the use of *muthi* by means of divination—this, after all, is the central procedure of traditional healing. Most, however, treat the activities of particular diviners with skepticism. Hence, in cases where witchcraft accusations must be tested, the impartiality of the diviner must be secured.[9] The traditional method of doing this is to take the complaint to a distant diviner with no connections to either the parties in dispute or the community in which they live. Another way of "proving" the validity of a diviner's finding is to seek corroboration from others. The logic is simple: if two or more independent diviners confirm a story, surely it must be the truth.

Whether or not formal proceedings take place, accusations of witchcraft are usually tested by assessments of the motives and characters of those involved. Most of the time, indeed, these are all there is to go on, and usually such assessments are drawn from the raw materials of gossip and rumor. In formal proceedings, witnesses attest to the characters, motives, and activities of suspected witches and their accusers. Testimony by witnesses, however, is inherently limited since the acts of witchcraft are

9. For a discussion of the ways in which divination can serve to pervert justice in modern African witchcraft trials, see Fisiy and Geschiere 1990.

mostly perpetrated in secret. If the witch was not caught in the act, the testimony of witnesses may say more about their own relations with the accused rather than the truth about the supposed witch's actions. Ultimately, neither divination nor testimony by witnesses can satisfy the demands of justice and truth. For the truth to be revealed, the witch must confess. Nothing satisfies the demand for justice in cases of witchcraft as much as confession. As the authors of the fifteenth-century handbook on witchcraft prosecutions, the *Malleus Maleficarum,* noted, "common justice demands that a witch should not be condemned to death unless she is convicted by her own confession" (Krämer and Sprenger 1486, 161). Most people who take witch finding seriously in Africa would agree.[10]

Since the costs of witchcraft suspicions are high for the accused, his or her family, and the community as a whole, justice also demands that serious costs are levied upon those who make false accusations. False accusations must be punished. Before proceedings began in the chiefly courts of old, accusers were commonly required to provide the chief with a specified number of cattle, which would be forfeited if the accusations were found not proven.

Finally, when witchcraft accusations are found proven, the witch, or witches, must be punished. The form of this punishment need not be death, though the fact that most witches are presumed to be intent on killing their victims means that the death penalty is usually thought appropriate. Furthermore, since the witch has access to enormous secret power, death is the only sure way to prevent future evil. Indeed, since many people worry that witches may even strike from beyond the grave, they see a need to kill them in such a way as to prevent this—hence the favored practice of burning.

If procedures for dealing with witchcraft embodied these safeguards to test the truth of accusations, most people who worry about living in a world with witches would be satisfied in the quest for justice. Colonial rule and apartheid made securing justice in cases of witchcraft difficult, if not impossible. In postapartheid South Africa, where the Constitution guarantees basic human rights and the regime is committed to the rule of law, these criteria of justice cannot be fulfilled. No matter how culturally sensitive a court system might want to be—and South African courts have long taken the belief in witchcraft into account as a mitigating factor in sentencing

---

10. See, for examples, Willis 1970. Fisiy and Geschiere (1990, 147) report that in Cameroonian witch trials, the role of the diviner has come to supplant the requirement of confession and has resulted in a pervasive sense of an "unholy alliance" between witch doctors and powerful elites.

(Nel et al. 1992)—there is simply no getting around the fact that the category of the person to which the term "human" in modern doctrines of human rights refers is not a being capable of inflicting harm in the manner widely presumed by people who speak of witchcraft.

The willingness of South African courts to accept belief in witchcraft as an extenuating factor in sentencing has not been altogether ungrudging. In the early decades of the twentieth century, judges were inclined to make an example of people who executed witches in an effort to stamp out what they saw as barbarism (Chanock 2001, 326–327). Later courts have sometimes been lenient in sentencing people who genuinely believed they were killing witches, though many white judges still subscribe to old notions of progress and the necessity of weaning Africans from their harmful superstitions. For example, in sentencing a group of six young men who were part of a mob of youths who burnt two old men to death as witches in February 1990 in a village of the former Venda Homeland, Justice van der Walt, while admitting the belief in witchcraft as an extenuation, made the following statement:

> What I have said is not an absolute rule of the law, it is simply a way of application of the law, influenced by social norms as they exist at a given time. But social norms develop over the time and are expected to develop and especially to become more civilised as time goes on. So that I want to say for their information and for information of everybody else who may be so inclined as they are, and who may have the same beliefs as they have that the time most probably is approaching rapidly where a civilised system of justice cannot allow their cognition of such out-dated beliefs as a norm for application of the law. (Ralushai Commission 1996, 238; see also Minaar 1998, 3)

For people who live in a world with witches, the willingness of a person to practice witchcraft automatically cancels their rights to membership in the human community; indeed, it negates their claim to be considered human. If witches are something other than human, they can hardly claim human rights to protect themselves from the righteous anger and justice of the community. As a traditional healer in Soweto once ruefully put it to me regarding witches: "now they have these human rights, so you can't just kill them" (Ashforth 1998b, 523). He had no doubt that witches did not deserve these rights and should be killed.

Where cases of witchcraft have entered the formal judicial system in Africa, the results have generally not been salutary for the health of that system or the cause of justice (Ciekawy 1997; Geschiere 1994).[11] Courts are used mostly by the wealthy and powerful to protect themselves both from the fear that others are attacking them through witchcraft because of jealousy about their wealth and from accusations that they have amassed wealth by means of sorcery themselves. As we saw in the case of MaNdlovu, however, a person accused of witchcraft in contemporary South Africa has few options with which to defend herself. If the rumors take hold of the popular imagination, the best she, or he, can hope for is a sort of social death. The worst is the fate that befell Mrs. Mhlongo, Chafunya's mother, when the mob of schoolchildren hacked her to death and burnt her home. In either case, calling the police is not much help.

Law Reform and Witchcraft

In South Africa in recent years a number of proposals have been made to revise the laws pertaining to witchcraft to make them consonant with Africans' insistence on the reality of "evil forces." The most comprehensive of these was a proposal to revise the Suppression of Witchcraft Act (no. 3 of 1957 as amended by Act no. 50 of 1970) by the Commission of Inquiry into Witchcraft Violence and Ritual Murders, the Ralushai Commission. Having reached the conclusion that "no one can now argue that witchcraft is a myth which can only exist in the minds of the ignorant," the Ralushai Commission revised the act in an effort to devise legislation capable of protecting people accused of witchcraft and inhibiting unrestrained witch-finding campaigns while at the same time recognizing the reality of "supernatural" crimes (Ralushai Commission 1996, 56). Article 1(a) of their proposed "Witchcraft Control Act" recommends punishing with a prison term of up to three years (or R 3,000 fine) any person who "*without any reasonable or justifiable cause* imputes to any other person the causing, by supernatural means, of any death, disease in or injury or damage to any person or thing, or who names or indicates any other person as a wizard or witch" (Ralushai Commission 1996, 55, emphasis added). Clauses (b) and (c) of the same article make it a similar offense to use "supernatural power, witchcraft, sorcery, enchantment or conjuration"

11. For a discussion of "informal" policing of witches and the dilemmas facing the legal system of recognizing the realities of witchcraft, see Harnischfeger 2000; Mavhungu 2000; Motshekga 1984. For an attempt to reconcile the claims of "tradition" and "modernity" in relation to courts and witchcraft, see Chavunduka 1980.

to name a witch or employ a "witch-doctor, witch-finder or any other person" for the same purpose.

While naming a witch is to be made a serious offense under the Ralushai Commission's proposed Witchcraft Control Act, practicing, or pretending to practice, witchcraft is made even more serious. Any person who "does any act which creates a reasonable suspicion that he is engaged in the practice of witchcraft" (1[d]) or "professes a knowledge of witchcraft, or the use of charms, and advises any person how to bewitch, injure or damage any person or thing, or supplies any person with any means of witchcraft" (1[e]), or who uses such means to "bewitch, injure or damage any person or thing" (1[e]), shall be guilty of an offense punishable by a maximum of four years imprisonment or R 4,000 fine. Less serious offenses under the proposed legislation would be collecting money to employ a witch finder and forcing any "witch-doctor or witch-finder" to divulge the name of a witch. These offenses would be punished by the maximum of two years or R 2,000.

Nothing came of the Ralushai Commission's recommendations on law reform. The Ralushai report was commissioned by the minister of Safety and Security of the Northern Province, whereas the legislation it was proposing to revise was the responsibility of the national Parliament. The national government has preferred to treat witchcraft as primarily a problem of social violence, one particularly prevalent in the Northern Province. Its law reform efforts, such as they are, have been devoted to the issue of regulating traditional healers, a matter also highlighted by the Ralushai Commission and which I shall discuss in the following chapter. The commission's insistence that the threat of practicing witchcraft, the "reasonable suspicion" that someone is actually practicing it, and the pretense of practicing it should be made equally punishable reveals the fundamental structure of insecurity in everyday life regarding the use of occult power. This standard of "reasonable suspicion" is their way of avoiding the thorny problems of evidence. For as the report points out in its discussion of this proposed legislation, "the most vexing problem surrounding witchcraft is that the activities of a witch cannot be witnessed by naked eyes" (unless, as they also point out, the witch is "caught naked inside someone's yard") (Ralushai Commission 1996, 57). This vexing problem of evidence notwithstanding, the report recognized the need to punish witches as paramount.

Advocate Seth Nthai, the minister of Safety and Security of what was then known as the Northern Province, to whom the Ralushai report was submitted, agreed with the commission that "it goes without saying that practitioners of witchcraft should be brought to trial and means for this should be contained in the envisaged legislation . . . [to] make our justice system more responsive to the plight of victims of witchcraft related crimes" (Nthai 2001, 162). Nthai, however, considered that the proper place for witchcraft trials to be conducted was within the purview of "traditional courts" rather than the formal "justice system." Arguing in a paper presented to the 1999 Law Reform Commission and Commission on Gender Equality conference "Witchcraft Violence and the Law," Nthai made a case for revamping traditional courts, along with what he called the "traditional police service," in order to handle witchcraft disputes. Nthai claimed that these courts were inherently concerned with mediation, and therefore traditional authorities, along with "legitimate *sangomas*," could work through these courts to secure justice through mediation in witchcraft cases. Nthai neglected to mention the fact that traditional authorities—insofar as they are genuinely traditional and hold real authority—have no need of enabling legislation to perform their roles.

Mediation, however, is a poor substitute for justice. Who would propose mediation for other forms of murder? As the Zimbabwean scholar and traditional healer Gordon Chavunduka has pointed out, mediation works well enough when the underlying social problems leading to accusations of witchcraft can be resolved through discussion and peace reestablished, but it is not effective in cases when "people become sick and die as a result of witchcraft" (Chavunduka 2001, 164). In cases of actual witchcraft, Chavunduka argues that it is necessary to engage diviners in witch finding, preferably supported by confession of the designated witch, and to punish the person found responsible (Chavunduka 2001, 167–168). Proposals for law reform that prohibit the employment of witch finders, therefore, would not secure justice, nor would reforms that prohibit the severe punishment of witches, for that would leave the murderers free. Rather, he argues, both "traditional" and "modern" courts should be encouraged to hear witchcraft cases in order to prevent victims from taking the law into their own hands. Courts should also be encouraged to employ the services of African specialists in determining the truth of accusations (Chavunduka 2001, 169). The South African legal scholar John Hund has also argued vigorously for a consideration of "legitimate *sangomas*" in the South African legal system, since "state enforcement of a world view which aims to suppress African spiritual beliefs has not worked and is not the answer" to the problem of the escalation of witchcraft violence and the pervasive sense of injustice that arises from the exposure to witchcraft in African life (Hund 2001, 53). His proposal, however, does not resolve the fundamental epistemological challenge of verifying the *sangomas'* accounts in the discursive context of a court.[12]

In 1998, the Commission on Gender Equality, one of a number of independent statutory bodies created by the new constitution, hosted a national conference on witchcraft violence in the Northern Province town of Thohoyandou, former capital of the Venda Homeland, drawing "participation from national and international stakeholders toward ending the scourge of violence associated with witchcraft accusations" (Commission on Gender Equality 1998).[13] On September 10, 1998, the conference adopted what they called the *Thohoyandou Declaration on Ending Witchcraft Violence.* The *Thohoyandou Declaration* marks the first attempt in South African history to place the question of witchcraft and witchcraft violence—which it rightly insists is a "national problem"—on the national political agenda in a way that does not automatically presuppose the absurdity of the belief in witchcraft; it was the first effort to make the national government responsive to the needs of ordinary people in their communities. It met with a resounding silence.

The many difficulties facing the national government in dealing with witchcraft that arise from the ontological chasm between those who view witchcraft as a form of belief and those for whom occult assault is a form of action can be seen in the terms of the *Declaration.* Where it is focused upon violence, the *Declaration* contains nothing objectionable to anyone. The participants in the national conference on witchcraft violence expressed themselves "SHOCKED AND HORRIFIED by the misery suffered by survivors of witchcraft violence" and were "DEEPLY CONCERNED by the escalation in witchcraft violence and the flagrant violation of human rights which it represents." To prevent these abuses the *Declaration* proposes changes in policing, improving education, counseling for victims, and the development of community mediation procedures. None of these proposals are at all controversial. In claiming that "poverty and illiteracy, particularly among women, are a major contributory factor to the superstition and false accusations, which lead to witchcraft violence," the *Declaration* remains true to the modernist principles of education and development. Even the ambiguous qualifier "false" in "false accusations" can be read as an endorsement

12. For further examples of this reasoning, see also Mavhungu 2000.

13. See Appendix 2 for a full text of the *Thohoyandou Declaration.* All quotations here are from this text, published on the Web at http://www.polity.org.za/govdocs/pr/1999/pro324b.html by the Commission on Gender Equality without page or paragraph numbers (Commission on Gender Equality 1998).

of the fact that *all* such accusations are by definition false. Similarly, the *Declaration*'s call for the "economic empowerment of women" as a way of addressing underlying causes of witchcraft violence is nothing that anyone could publicly object to in the new South Africa.

Though they seem to have accepted that the "survivors" of witchcraft violence who presented "graphic testimony" of their misery to the meeting were in fact innocent of the charge of witchcraft, the drafters of the *Declaration* were not persuaded that all such charges must necessarily be false. In calling for reform of the present Suppression of Witchcraft Act, the *Declaration* urges what it calls a "paradigm shift from the current act which operates on a premise that denies the belief in witchcraft." Law reform, in the new paradigm, would bring witchcraft cases into the criminal justice system "so that those who are engaged in harmful practices can be separated out from those who are falsely accused; and so that those who make false accusations can be brought to book." The *Declaration* offers no hints as to how this separation might be effected in practice, other than calling for "clear definitions for words and concepts such as 'witch,' 'wizard' and 'witchcraft.'" The *Declaration* does, however, suggest the establishment of "conciliation and mediation" structures to "resolve underlying tensions" that lead to witchcraft violence. And it also calls for legislation to "control the practice of traditional healing . . . to ensure that the practice of traditional medicine is separated from sinister practices."

The existing legislation, as the *Declaration* notes, does indeed operate "from a premise that denies the belief in witchcraft." Indeed, it does more than merely deny the *belief;* it outlaws the most important practices relating to that belief, to wit: divination and witch finding, accusation, and adjudication. Under the legislation, the hundreds of thousands of healers whom people turn to in search of help for afflictions that are often deemed caused by witchcraft are in breach of the law. To accuse anyone of practicing witchcraft is itself a crime. This latter aspect of the law has resulted in hundreds of accused witches seeking protection from the police in the way MaNdlovu did, placing the police in the invidious position of being seen as aiding enemies of the community.

The *Declaration*'s faith in the power of legislation to establish clarity in defining the essentially contested concepts of witchcraft reveals the extent of the widely held conviction that these are matters of objective reality, not issues of moral judgment or philosophical inquiry. Similarly, as we shall see in more detail in the next chapter, the faith that legislators can regulate the enterprise of traditional healing, founded as it is upon the authority of invisible beings, reveals the extent of the conviction that healers wield objectively verifiable powers and that the spiritual entities from whom they draw their powers are ordinary features of the social landscape—hence, the faith that a legislatively prescribed "Code of Conduct" for traditional healers would ensure that "the practice of traditional medicine is separated from sinister practices." In a related effort, the Commission on Gender Equality sponsored explorations of models of community mediation and reconciliation between parties in witchcraft accusations (Hill and Black 2002). The experience, by all accounts, was valuable. They also launched what they called "Witchcraft Roadshows," which visited villages and towns and held meetings to discuss issues surrounding witchcraft conflict. In July 2000, the commission claimed that these road shows reduced witch killings in the formerly violence-plagued Northern Province/Limpopo (Commission on Gender Equality 2000).

In keeping with the spirit of the times, the *Thohoyandou Declaration* also endorses programs similar to those of the Truth and Reconciliation Commission (TRC) to "resolve underlying tensions" that stimulate accusations and to seek reconciliation between accusers and accused, between perpetrators of witchcraft violence and their victims. Reconciliation and justice, however, as the TRC has found, are two different matters. When applied to the question of actual witchcraft (as distinct from accusations thereof)—or the perpetration of "harmful practices" in the *Declaration*'s language—the TRC model of seeking justice, healing, harmony, and reconciliation through knowing truth (what the TRC refers to in its report as "restorative justice") rather than seeking retribution through punishment (what the TRC report calls "retributive justice") raises fundamental difficulties regarding the determination of this truth. The TRC report expresses the distinction thus:

> We have been concerned, too, that many consider only one aspect of justice. Certainly, amnesty cannot be viewed as justice if we think of justice only as retributive and punitive in nature. We believe, however, that there is another kind of justice—a restorative justice which is concerned not so much with punishment as with correcting imbalances, restoring broken relationships—with healing, harmony and reconciliation. Such justice focuses on the experience of victims; hence the importance of reparation. (TRC 1998, vol. 1, chap. 1, para. 36)

As we have seen in earlier discussions of interpretations of the nature of *muthi*, determining the truth in matters of witchcraft—where the actions of invisible forces cannot be witnessed by ordinary human perception—involves epistemological principles and divinatory practices that engage humans in relations with invisible forces and powers and that are impossible to reconcile with the evidentiary procedures of modern judicial practice upon which the South African legal system is based.

Invisible Evil Powers and the State

Habits of interpreting power that put a premium on divining the true agencies behind the appearance of misfortune are not limited to explicit issues of witchcraft. Relations with the range of invisible forces taken as shaping life in places like Soweto demand a constant vigilance regarding the hidden realities behind the manifest appearances. Effective security cannot be found unless the real force behind the apparent consequences of action is discerned. These habits of interpretation extend also to the interpretation of political power, reinforced by experience of state power during the era of apartheid.

In the days of apartheid, denouncing apartheid as "the System" was a commonplace of political life. Expressing hatred for the System was a staple of the political diet. Obed Kunene, a leading black journalist, articulated well the character of the System when he wrote in response to white critics of the destruction of "facilities" in Black Townships during the 1976 Soweto Uprising:

> Blacks do not destroy facilities. They destroy symbols of the entire system devised by whites for them . . . pass laws with their repugnant manifestations, Bantu Education, job reservation, unequal pay for equal work, no security of tenure, no land ownership rights, poor living conditions, migrant labour, inequitable distribution of the country's wealth, and a denial of the democratic right to decision-making. It is a system that has virtually ruined the fabric of black society, especially in the urban areas. It is abhorred, resented, despised, and hated almost to pathological limits. (Kane-Berman 1978, 48)

Manifested most vividly in the figure of the white policeman, the System was embodied in virtually every aspect of the physical and social environment of Soweto, whose very existence as a segregated residential area was itself a product of White political dominance. The houses in which people lived, for example, had been built by the state; known as "matchboxes," and tiny compared to the homes of Whites in suburbia, they expressed the malevolence of power. The schools the children attended, like the hospital and clinics, were likewise products of the System, as were the roads, pension offices, and so on. Virtually everything except the churches (and even they were supposed to be) was licensed by the state.

Justice and equity were not words black people associated with the System, particularly in the later years of apartheid when organized political resistance became more widespread, for the System was considered in its essence to be nothing more than a mode of imposing unfair disadvantages upon Blacks premised upon racial advantage to Whites. As the Freedom Charter pronounced, "our people have been robbed of their birthright to land, liberty and peace by a form of government founded on injustice and inequality" (Karis and Gerhart 1977, 205). The experience, common to virtually every black adult at some time or other, of being compelled to approach public authorities—especially those involved in the infamous and labyrinthine pass system—as rightless supplicants to arbitrary and capricious, or corrupt, officials inured people to a degree of cynicism about the purposes of public power.

Regardless of the regular protestations of honorable intentions by the white politicians and civic leaders of the apartheid era, and despite the fact that among the myriads of functionaries who composed the System there may have been many genuinely well-intentioned people, black as well as white, working in its offices and agencies, the self-evident and overwhelming fact of the inferior status and conditions imposed upon black people served to bathe the whole in an evil light. No one doubted that the System was evil, it was spoken of as a generalized source of suffering and misfortune. When expressing their hatred for the System, political leaders of the liberation movements and ordinary people alike typically insisted, especially when talking politics with a sympathetic white person, on distinguishing between "the Whites" and "the System." Everyone knew that the System was made by the Whites and was designed to oppress Blacks, but it was not the same thing as the Whites, for not all white people supported apartheid, and, more important, you could hate the System without falling into the racist trap of simply hating white people. Maintaining this distinction was not always easy, especially in the heat of uprisings, when the symbols of the System were embodied in real human beings—as the furor that erupted in 1993 over ANC Youth League president Peter Mokaba's use of the slogan "Kill the Boer, the Farmer!" at political rallies showed.[14] Then,

14. For a semiofficial statement of the ANC's understanding of "the System," prepared for the fiftieth national conference of the party in 1997, see P. Jordan 1997.

witch hunt is wrong, in this view of the world, because witches cannot exist. To name someone as a witch, therefore, and to claim thereby to have found the source of an affliction besetting an individual or community is both absurd and unjust. In South Africa, however, as in the rest of the continent, the business of identifying and neutralizing evil powers named under the rubric "witchcraft" can be a matter of the utmost importance and urgency. As we have seen, the majority of those who bore the brunt of apartheid consider witches and witchcraft to be extremely serious matters—matters of life and death. Discovering the secret source of evil afflicting a community and punishing perpetrators of witchcraft are essential elements of justice—elements that have been denied most communities by the impositions of colonialism and apartheid. Talk of a "witch hunt" as a metaphor for injustice in this context, then, is more than a little curious.

At the same time as denying that it was involved in a witch hunt, the TRC insisted that its project was more than a merely legal and political exercise. Describing the project of the TRC, the chair, Archbishop Tutu, insisted: "The Truth and Reconciliation Commission has a clear political focus and strong legal implications. It is, at the same time, at its heart a deeply theological and ethical initiative. For people of faith, the experience of honesty and mercy, confession and forgiveness, justice and peace, repentance and reconciliation is what *truth and reconciliation are all about*" (Tutu 1996, 7, emphasis in original). By suggesting that the TRC was a "theological and ethical initiative," I assume that Tutu means its purview encompassed an inquiry not only into questions of crimes and "human rights abuses" legally defined but also into the fundamental nature of the evil that was inherent in apartheid as a whole. Generally, in discussions of the TRC and debates over "reconciliation," these "theological" issues concerning the evil that was the crime against humanity of apartheid and its legacy in South Africa have been considered within a broadly Christian framework of confession and forgiveness: those who committed evil acts were called upon to confess and were offered forgiveness in the form of legal amnesty from prosecution.

In its public hearings and report, the TRC also represented itself as part of a "healing process." On February 13, 1996, for instance, before beginning their official work, the commissioners attended an interdenominational religious service in St. George's Cathedral, Cape Town, at which they were implored to "dedicate yourselves to carry out the task that has been entrusted to you with the highest integrity, with impartiality and compassion for all, for the purpose of healing our nation." To this each commissioner affirmed "I will" (Botman and Peterson 1996, 169). This theme of "healing the nation" was repeated ceaselessly throughout the commission's life—and since—by participants and observers of the most diverse sorts. Most people who have taken this talk of healing seriously have interpreted the task in terms of psychotherapeutic discourses about trauma and Christian doctrines of confession.[15] As we have seen, however, for a great many people in South Africa, the work of healing in everyday life is inseparable from questions of justice, since healing often involves struggles against witches and witchcraft, struggles to identify the secret human source of the invisible evil forces causing harm and to repel them while strengthening and protecting the patient against future aggression. How might the work of healing the nation look if viewed in the light of this paradigm of healing?

The TRC's mission had two fundamental aspects. The first was to document particular human rights abuses during the period 1960–1994 by hearing the testimony of victims and witnesses (with a view to recommending reparations) and hearing confessions from perpetrators (with a view to recommending amnesty). The second was to provide an authoritative account of the history of the mandate period to attribute general responsibility for human rights abuses and to account for the general source of the evil that was the "crime against humanity" (as declared by United Nations resolution 556 of December 13, 1984) of apartheid. This they endeavored to do by piecing together the puzzle from accounts of particular abuses gathered from victims and perpetrators while soliciting general statements and testimony from political leaders, government officials past and present, civic leaders, and representatives of key institutions in civil society. The inquiries guiding each of these approaches were augmented and directed by research coordinated by the TRC.

In its efforts to develop "findings" on the history of the conflict, the TRC called for submissions from all major actors and called political leaders to testify. The most important of these were members of the ANC and the National Party. The ANC submitted to the TRC a long statement that, among other things, provided a general overview of the nature of apartheid and the motive force behind the human rights abuses perpetrated by the state in its name. For the ANC, apartheid was a deliberate and malicious evil, a crime against humanity designed to oppress and exploit black people and motivated primarily by the racist ideology of white supremacy: "The simultaneous and interdependent legitimisation of the two inherently anti-human concepts of racial superiority and the colonial state as the concen-

15. The most notable example is the award-winning account by the Afrikaner poet Antjie Krog (1998).

trated expression of the unlimited right to the use of force, of necessity and according to the inherent logic of the system of apartheid, produced the gross violations of human rights by the apartheid state" (African National Congress 1996, chap. 2). From the ANC's perspective, the National Party and its supporters were determined to maintain this system by ever more repressive means and would have done so in perpetuity were they not forced to concede to democratic negotiations in 1990. And yet, the ANC insisted, even after conceding these negotiations, the National Party government still perpetrated a secret war against the people, unleashing a "third force" mandated to create havoc in order to "demobilise [the] mass base so as to weaken the ANC" (African National Congress 1997c).

No such talk of conspiracies or deliberately motivated evil can be found in the former government's submission presented by F. W. de Klerk. In a submission on behalf of the National Party, he argued that the period since 1948 ought to be divided into two periods: the period of apartheid and the period of dismantling apartheid. Regarding the early period, the National Party submission argued that mistakes were made: although the leaders were "good and honorable men . . . as far as the policy of apartheid was concerned, they were deeply mistaken in the course upon which they embarked" (National Party 1996, 4). The National Party submission argued that the mistakenness of the policy of apartheid was realized in the late 1970s. At that time, it claimed, President P. W. Botha began efforts to rectify the mistakes, efforts that were continued by his successor, F. W. de Klerk, and that ultimately led to the elections of 1994 and the end of white rule. While rectifying the mistaken policy of apartheid, however, more mistakes were made. Both Botha and de Klerk, the National Party submission insists, were confronted with a worsening security situation in South Africa at a time when they (and, we should not forget, their supporters in Thatcher's Britain and Reagan's United States, among other places) still feared international communist expansion. While trying to counter this security threat, de Klerk argued, a context was created in which "abuses" by security personnel were not sufficiently discouraged. For these "abuses" he apologized. Few were moved. In the National Party view of apartheid, then, there was no deliberate malice or secret evil conspiracy—just well-intentioned mistakes, understandable lapses of oversight, and isolated cases of abuse.

Adjudicating between these conflicting views of the historic struggle between the forces of apartheid and the forces of liberation, the TRC produced its own synthesis incorporating and rejecting elements of each while framing the whole in its preferred manner. They endorsed the ANC's perspective on apartheid as a crime against humanity and reaffirmed the legitimacy of its armed struggle as a "just war." Nonetheless, they found that ANC supporters and leaders had been guilty of human rights abuses. The problem of interpreting the "conflicts of the past"—the TRC's brief—was complicated by the fact that the vast majority of political killings and other human rights abuses occurred in the period after negotiations began in 1990 in what was called at the time "black-on-black" violence. This was not really a "conflict of the past" like the older struggles between the forces of an oppressive regime and those of the liberation movements. At the time of the TRC hearings, the conflicts between ANC and Inkatha supporters, dating from the mid-1980s in KwaZulu and Natal, were still very much part of the present.

The ANC, along with most black South Africans, insisted that ultimate responsibility for the deaths in political violence during the early 1990s lay with the National Party government. Inkatha members, for most ANC supporters, were mere stooges of the apartheid regime. More sinister, in the view of the ANC, was the secret "Third Force" used by the government to "destabilize" the liberation movement by sowing havoc among its supporters. Through the years of TRC hearings, the ANC strove to convince the TRC of the existence and significance of this Third Force. In October 1997, for example, after the TRC subpoenaed members of the State Security Council, the ANC issued a press release asserting: "The state security council controlled a totalitarian national network which reached into every part of the country. . . . We believe that the members served with subpoenas should provide answers with regard to how security and or third force networks functioned, how extensive they were, what has happened to the networks and what capacity these networks have to destabilise our new democracy" (African National Congress 1997d). The ANC at the time, after three years in government, had no doubt that the networks still existed and were still active. Proof, however, was elusive. Signs of the power of evil networks were everywhere apparent—after all, they "reached into every part of the country." Ultimate responsibility for crime and political violence were attributed, time and again, to a Third Force recruited and controlled by the leaders of the previous regime.[16] But while the TRC and criminal investigations were turning up evidence of individuals involved in hit squads

16. In a press release of April 9, 1997, entitled "Third Force Allegations against the National Party," for example, the ANC reaffirmed its "long held conviction that the former National Party government aided and abetted in the creation of a third force. The ANC has always maintained that the creation of a third force and subsequent activities, which undermined even apartheid laws, was never the work of mavericks within government but was sanctioned at the highest levels of the apartheid state" (1997c).

and secret assistance to the Inkatha Freedom Party, nothing comparable to a comprehensive "totalitarian national network" was found.

As with all theories of conspiracy regarding secret evil forces, whether those of politics or of witchcraft, the perpetrators could be identified by interpreting the evident signs of their action as manifested in misfortune. Confidence in the true attribution of culpability for this suffering, however, requires confession by the perpetrators since the accumulation of empirical evidence always leaves a margin of doubt. Witchcraft and conspiracy both flourish in the shadows of such doubt. De Klerk and the National Party were called upon time and again by the commissioners and the ANC to confess and identify the culprits: "Without the assistance of the NP in identifying these third force networks," the ANC wrote in a media release criticizing the National Party for withdrawing from the TRC process in May 1997, "no other inference can be drawn than that the NP is not interested in the process of reconciliation and healing" (African National Congress 1997e).

De Klerk and the National Party, however, would not confess. Their submission to the TRC claimed that only "some elements" of the security forces were involved in the "fomentation of 'black-on-black' violence." The former president accepted responsibility only to the extent that an otherwise legitimate preoccupation with security in the tumultuous years of the 1980s had created a situation in which these rogue elements could flourish. Rather than confession, de Klerk continued to insist that the idea of a Third Force was a product of the "ANC propaganda machine":

> The ANC and others are now attempting to dismiss all the violence that occurred in the conflict between various black groupings, including its struggle against the IFP, as the result of "Third Force" activities. This is patently absurd. . . .
>
> The Government never adopted a policy to promote "black-on-black" violence. To my knowledge, such a policy was never discussed in the Cabinet or the State Security Council or at any other meeting of any other body that I attended. It has since come to light that some elements within the security forces may have been involved in the fomentation of "black-on-black" violence. It would, however, be ludicrous to suggest that such actions were the prime cause—or even a major cause—of such violence. Support for various organisations, such as Inkatha etc, that were being threatened by the strategies and actions of those responsible for the armed insurrection, should not be confused with support for "black-on-black" violence. (National Party 1997)

Despite repeated entreaties by the chair of the TRC to confess, the National Party leadership had nothing more to say. The doubts remained.

In October 1998, the TRC issued the report of its Human Rights Violations Committee. On the subject of the Third Force, they reported that

> while the involvement of security force individuals and structures in "third force" violence was to some degree corroborated, lines of command and accountability, were not established. It is not clear whether senior security force personnel so involved represented their own, state or right-wing agendas. In a rapidly changing political situation with shifting alliances, it is probable that there were several agendas involved. (TRC 1998, vol. 2, chap. 7, para. 549)

The report added that because "levels of political intolerance were extremely high . . . little instigation was required to generate self-perpetuating cycles of violence" (1998, vol. 2, chap. 7, para. 550). After concluding that "the Commission did not make significant progress in uncovering the forces behind the violence in the 1990s" and calling for further investigation into "intelligence practices" and "front companies," the committee issued a formal finding that

> While there is little evidence of a centrally directed, coherent or formally constituted "third force," a network of security and ex–security force operatives, acting frequently in conjunction with right-wing elements and/or sectors of the IFP, were involved in actions that could be construed as fomenting violence and which resulted in gross violations of human rights, including random and targeted killings. (1998, vol. 2, chap. 7, para. 551, printed in all capitals in the original)

They found that such networks grew out of security force operations in the 1980s in which "partnerships" were established between the security forces and progovernment organizations. They further found

> that such networks functioned at times with the active collusion and/or knowledge of senior security force personnel, and that the former Government, either deliberately or by omission, failed to take sufficient steps to put an end to such practices. (1998, vol. 2, chap. 7, para. 551, printed in all capitals in the original)

Finally:

> The success of "third force" attempts to generate violence was at least in part
> a consequence of extremely high levels of political intolerance, for which all
> parties to the conflict are held to be morally and politically accountable.
> (1998, vol. 2, chap. 7, para. 551, printed in all capitals in the original)

Considering that some 14,000 people died in incidents of political violence between mid-1990 and the elections of April 1994 (TRC 1998, vol. 2,
chap. 7, para. 7), with countless others wounded and displaced from homes
(more than in the rest of the commission's mandate period beginning in
1960) and considering that a significant majority of people in South Africa
can be presumed to endorse the ANC's official position that there was a
Third Force behind the violence, these findings are, to say the least, sloppy.

The TRC reported that it had found "little evidence" of central direction, coherence, or formal constitution of such forces, but it could not say
that such a force did not exist. And while they can point to involvement and
collusion in the violence on the part of senior security officers, which the
government failed to stop, they cannot say whether this failure was deliberate or not. These are not minor points. They do not, however, add up to
the Third Force of popular imagination and ANC propaganda. The findings of the TRC, while equivocating on the subject of the Third Force, implicitly denied the possibility of a singular overarching structure of meaning inherent in this suffering. By attributing responsibility for a good part
of the violence among black people to the ANC's failures as an organization, as well as to the influence of a general context created by the previous
regime, the TRC undermined the narrative the ANC and its supporters
clung to in making sense of their suffering as a deliberately motivated evil,
and thus outraged the ANC leadership in the new government.

If apartheid is understood, as the ANC and its supporters understood
it, as the fundamental explanation for the collective suffering of a whole nation—a *crime* deliberately motivated by the evils of white supremacy and
colonialism, with a secret core of malice capable of unleashing death and
destruction in the form of a Third Force—then a witch hunt, properly understood, is precisely what is needed to both secure justice and neutralize
the evil. Unless it can be demonstrated that the secret source of evil has
been neutralized, no one can be sure that, despite the election of a representative government, the evils of apartheid violence will not continue. As
the ANC KwaZulu-Natal leadership stated in March 1997: "Without the

destruction of the apartheid covert network root and branch, we cannot hope that we can destroy the capacity of the evil forces to unleash violence" (African National Congress 2000). A witch hunt, at least in the sense of a concerted endeavor to reveal the secret source of affliction and to induce those responsible to confess their malicious motives, is precisely what is required to lay such suppositions to rest. Even if the suppositions about secret forces are not true, the logic of the witch hunt demands confession as the foundation of reconciliation. Everyone knows who the people responsible for the suffering in the community are: the National Party government and the apartheid regime. While the TRC induced some of the small fry to confess, the big fish stayed silent. A witch hunt did not happen. The secret remains.

A witch hunt that could have induced the former leaders of apartheid South Africa to confess would have been of the utmost benefit in "healing the nation." For unlike the Christian model of confession, in which God sees the truth of repentance in the sinner's heart despite the appearance of false sorrow (Pascal 1947, 397), the witchcraft paradigm requires confession in order to effect healing, reconcile conflicts within the community, and eliminate the possibility of future harm. The purpose of confession is not simply to secure the legitimacy of punishment, although that is important, or just to smooth the way for the evildoers' reintegration into the community. It is also a practical matter of rectifying the actual harm already caused and preventing further harm from emerging from that source. So the fact that the leadership of the National Party failed to confess their full activities (including their secret activities) and their malicious motives is more than just a galling reminder of their stubborn shamelessness. It leaves the secret intact. The evil source of suffering remains alive and ready to strike again.

12

DEMOCRATIC STATECRAFT
IN A WORLD OF WITCHES

On Democratic Governance: Service Delivery and Witchcraft

In August 1997, after a couple of months immersed in my friend Madumo's struggle against witchcraft and many hours spent with his healer, Mr. Zondi, I interviewed the mayor of Soweto (or, as it was then known, the Southern Metropolitan Local Council), Nandi Mayathula-Khoza. We met in her offices at the Soweto Civic Centre, the old headquarters of the apartheid "puppet" administration of the Soweto City Council. Our discussion at first focused on issues of how the new administration, the first in Soweto's history that had been democratically elected, was coping with the challenges of establishing a responsive and effective government in a place where residents had long been habituated to resisting government and where the struggle against apartheid had been combined with rent strikes and boycotts against service charges (a potent combination of moral righteousness and pecuniary self-interest) that had produced what was now being called a "culture of nonpayment." The mayor spoke proudly of the new council's achievements in providing services for their constituents. She insisted that if the level of services was improved, people would be glad to contribute to the cost of their own social development. I was somewhat skeptical about that, though nonetheless impressed by her evident commitment to the task at hand. But I wanted to talk of witchcraft.

Since my return to Soweto in June of that year, I had been surprised by how conscious my friends were of their exposure to occult assault—and not only poor Madumo, who was in a state of complete social isolation after being accused of killing his mother with witchcraft. In the course of many evenings discussing politics in the new South Africa with people who were worried about witches, I had become accustomed to raising the question of witchcraft and democracy. For most of my friends, after spending the better part of their lives engaged in "the struggle," politics was a register of discourse that was as natural to them as breathing. It involved a well-worn repertoire of issues and ideologies: the "national question," "nonracialism," "black consciousness," "federalism," "socialism," the "national democratic revolution," the "woman question," and so on and so forth. At that time, too, the concept of "service delivery" was beginning to emerge as a theme of everyday political analysis in the shebeens of Soweto, though the notion that "loyal opposition" to an ANC government might be a good thing was as yet unthinkable, as was the idea that a black person could legitimately support any other political organization than the ANC. When issues of witchcraft were on the table, however, as they sometimes were, the talk was of something pertaining to a different realm of action and experience from politics, something personal, speculative, and open ended—a "thing of we Blacks," as the commonplace phrase went. However, if in the course of discussion I raised my thesis about witchcraft and democracy, if I asked my interlocutors whether the fact that democracy is supposed to be "government of, for, and by the people" meant that a democratic government should be doing something about the problem of witches in the community, the connection would usually seem blindingly obvious. Discussion would then focus on what could be done and how.

So, in my interview with the mayor of Soweto, I tried the same argument. Here is the transcript of our discussion:

AA Let me ask you a slightly different question. You might find it somewhat unusual. One of the things that I've noticed—and I've lived here off and on for seven years, and over those years I've come to appreciate that the problem of witchcraft is very central in everyday life. It comes up in different ways at different points of crisis. People are afflicted and there is turmoil about it. When I came back this year I found that people of many different kinds of backgrounds have said to me that witchcraft is much worse than ever, that it's going out of control almost. That since the elections of 1994, the levels of witchcraft are rising continuously. And they point to the increase in jealousy, that now everyone is out for themselves. And certainly the increase in opportunities has not been distributed evenly across the community. Some people are thriving and other people are still suffering and in the same position they were before. So the conditions for jealousy have certainly changed in that period. And people interpret this in terms of witchcraft being caused by jealousy, being motivated by jealousy, and the misfortunes that people suffer—and many of my friends have been suffering quite significant problems which they attribute directly to the witchcraft of relatives and neighbors. Now one of the things that I know about witchcraft is that when one is personally afflicted, one makes reparations to the ancestors, visits an *inyanga,* and gets things put right in a sort of "private" way. The *inyanga's* ancestors, the family's ancestors, work together to bring about a healing of the individual or family to ward off this evil spirit. On the other hand, however, the problem of witches generally in the community, I'm told, is a problem for the community. That is, it's not a job for the ancestors to deal with witches, it's a problem for the community. And I've heard, indeed I was having a discussion with an *inyanga* at Merafe Hostel last week about this, and he was suggesting that each community—Phiri, Mapetla, Senaoane, and so on—should call upon the police to assist them in tracking down and dealing with witches. Now, in this sense, if that is a community problem that people talk about and see as facing the community, do you find as councillors, or at the level of the council, that there has ever been any suggestion that part of your job should be to address this evil that is afflicting the community?

NM No, I haven't really heard of any discussion, or I haven't been involved in any discussion about that. Um. I don't know. I don't know, really. [*She laughs nervously.*] I'm not well conversant with this subject. But I know one thing for sure—that witchcraft is there. Okay. But I haven't been personally inflicted with this problem as such. But if it is generally a problem experienced by members of the community and if the community wants to bring it up to council level, I'm sure council would be more than willing to address that problem and listen to people as to what kind of solution do they want to this problem. And if we can make any contribution towards that, in particular working with the police, because communities are now working with the police, council is working with the police and if they want the problem to be taken up by council, I'm saying we would be more than prepared to deal with that. But the kinds of problems basically that people have been experiencing and putting forward are developmental kinds of projects. Yes, there is witchcraft as a problem, but I'm saying so far, since I've been involved in council, since 1994, I haven't really been involved in a discussion dealing with that problem.

AA You haven't heard of anyone else that's been asked to deal with aspects of this problem?

NM Not within this council, not within the Greater Johannesburg Council or the Southern Metropolitan Local Council.

AA Because one thing that strikes me, and I might be wrong—I hope I'm wrong
—is that there are two things that are taking place. The first is the increase
in the condition for jealousy, and the belief that this is sponsoring or creating more witchcraft. But the other thing is that people see a loss of faith in
inyangas and *sangomas*. People have been paying their money and not getting results. So in a sense there is an increase in evil and a perceived decrease
in the ability to rectify evil. Misfortune is still widespread, suffering is widespread, and *inyangas* and *sangomas* are presumed to be able to go both ways,
if you like: to be able to heal and to be able to kill. And I've got a feeling that
sometime in the future this could become a crisis when people say No, these
people in the community are pretending to help us—

NM Which people are they?

AA The *inyangas* and *sangomas* particularly. That these are the people who are
doing the witchcraft, and they could turn on them. There could be, I feel,
that many of the conditions are there for a witch-finding movement to
emerge in communities.

NM Yeah, it's such an interesting subject, and I think I would like to explore
more about what you are talking about. And it's true that there are those
inyangas and *sangomas* who are genuine and who are healing people. And
it might also be true that there are those that, you know, would be involved—
those that are not genuine, who are not real *inyangas* and *sangomas,* but instead are involved in the witchcraft itself. But I don't have evidence of that
as such. It's something that is being discussed by individual people that I've
actually communicated with at some stage. And it's true also that people are
beginning to lose faith in *sangomas,* in some of the *sangomas* and *inyangas.*
Because their problems sometimes are not solved. Instead, they get worse.
And they move from one *inyanga* to another, paying lots and lots of money,
and their problems remain the same.

AA And their problems are often not of the kind that can be solved by *inyangas*—

NM Sometimes.

AA Like to make the boss at work like me.

NM [*Laughing.*] Yeah. But as I've said before, I really haven't been personally inflicted, and I haven't really personally experienced that. But I know one thing
for sure. Even members of my family have experienced similar problems.
And they've shared those problems with me and at that level then I know it's
taking place and I know it's the biggest problem. But unfortunately it hasn't
come through to the council. But I'm saying that if it's a community problem, and the community's interested, or wants the council to be involved, I
think why not?

AA What sort of response do you think you would get from the white councillors?

NM There are white councillors, some from the National Party, Democratic Party, but we don't have DP here [in the Southern substructure], and there are some white councillors as well within the ANC movement, the democratic organization. And I believe that witchcraft happens everywhere. It happens also in the white community, it happens in the black community. And there are *sangomas* who are white as well as *sangomas* who are black. So it happens almost everywhere.

AA So if it came up at council you'd be able to run a discussion in the council chamber that would be worthwhile.

NM Yeah, I think it would be worthwhile. But now the problem is that we are confined by the ordinance, which actually defines the sorts of functions that we should carry out. And I'm beginning to think, and wonder, if the ordinances would actually allow us to embark on such discussion. But I'm saying if it's a community problem then the council should really entertain a discussion of such. Because we have terms of reference as well for the council, terms of reference for various committees within the council. We also have caucuses. Probably it may be well taken, first, at caucus level. Then if the caucus for various parties can actually decide that "Let's take this up to the council," then I'm sure we can be able to do it, even if the ordinance doesn't spell out that we can actually entertain such problems.

AA One of the things I've been doing is spending time with the local police. I go to a shebeen there in the flats near the barracks and the police come after work. And discussing this issue with them, they find themselves caught in the position where officially witchcraft doesn't exist according to the law. There's the Suppression of Witchcraft Act, but that doesn't address witchcraft, it addresses witchcraft accusations. So it's illegal to accuse somebody of being a witch, but the actual practice of witchcraft is something else. And the police get caught in situations where they have to intervene, and often it comes down to private and unofficial action by them which is beyond the law. It's unofficial and informal policing.

NM [*Chuckles.*] Yeah. And sometimes you'll find in some communities, people deal with that problem themselves and they get to kill, you know, a witch, a person who's considered to be a witch in a particular community. And again, that is considered as taking law into your own hands and it's just not allowed.

AA I know in Senaoane there was a woman killed last year. Do you remember that?

NM I remember there was some case.

AA It was the mother of this gangster, Chafunya.

NM Yes, yes, the Chafunya gang. It's true. But then that was not a witch-related problem; it was crime-related.

AA But *she* was killed because they believed she'd been giving him *muthi* and that was—

NM Okay, to be involved in the criminal activities that he was involved in. No, you are correct. I remember very well. And that also she was allowing those children to carry on the evil work that they were doing. I remember. And obviously those—because it was mainly the youth who stoned that mother to death—I think they were taken to the police station. I think there was a lot that happened. I didn't eventually know everything that happened. But the fact that they killed that mother, that lady, they'd taken the law into their hands. Yeah, it's a big problem. You know, one realizes that it's a big problem when you discuss it with somebody else. Yeah.

AA This is what I was talking about with the police. In such a situation where you have a crowd, especially when it's usually schoolchildren at the forefront of these things, who are targeting a witch—if you step in as police and protect this mother, because she has a right to live under the Constitution and your duty is to uphold the Constitution, in fact from the point of view of the community, you are protecting a witch. And the witch is a source of evil to the community—

NM To the community.

AA And this is a problem that the police, the councillors, and the government are supposed to represent the community and to solve problems facing the community. It's potentially very difficult.

NM It is very difficult. You know, now that we've spoken about it, I think I'll just discuss with other councillors informally and hear what their opinion is about this problem. And probably we could then take it to various caucuses and discuss it and see if we can't really give quality time to it in terms of discussing it and working with the community in coming up with means and ways of resolving this problem.

AA I think it would be an important thing to do. Especially if, as I said, these two processes of the increase in witchcraft and the decrease in faith in *sangomas*, which could easily turn into a targeting—

NM Of *sangomas* themselves and others.

AA And there are so many. Particularly middle-aged women who have been through *ukuthwasa* and who have herbs in their house. They might not necessarily be practicing themselves as *sangomas*. In fact, I think the people who have a practice, and who are publicly known to be practicing, are safer in a sense. But if you just have a mother who five or ten years ago *ukuthwasa*'d and still has the herbs and stuff in the box in the backyard [NM *chuckles*], people can easily turn on her.

NM Yeah. That's true. No, we will look at that. Definitely. It's interesting.[1]

I do not know whether the mayor ever brought the subject of witchcraft up in discussions with her colleagues on the council. When I returned to follow up this discussion with Mayor Mayathula-Khoza the following year, she was accompanied to our interview by her "political adviser," Mr. Pat Nhlapo. He dominated the conversation and prevented discussion of anything other than the many achievements of "service delivery" by the ANC in government.

People in Soweto continue to talk of "politics" in a register that remains largely distinct from the problems of everyday life that are spoken of as "witchcraft." Their leaders, such as Mayor Mayathula-Khoza (who, at this time, in 2004, is speaker of the City of Johannesburg Council), do not make connections between these domains either. This may be their only option. But the risk of ignoring issues of spiritual insecurity in an African context is that people who see their lives as subject to the ravages of "evil forces" may suspect, or continue to doubt, that the practice of democratic government, with its doctrines of "rule of law" and "human rights," doctrines that are very recent in the history of political subjection in this part of Africa, represent alien impositions with little connection to their own needs, particularly their desire for security and justice. They may, indeed, come to suspect that powerful people are using occult forces for purposes of their own enrichment and empowerment at the public's expense.

In the previous chapter we examined some of the legal conundrums that face the new regime and that arise from the problem of witchcraft. We saw how proposals to reform the Suppression of Witchcraft Act so as to recognize the reality of witchcraft and bring accusations of witchcraft into the formal judicial system ran into serious problems of evidence. Short of voluntary confession by a witch, proof of witchcraft is available only to a diviner using occult means. We also saw how in the course of more than a century of the government's denial of the reality of witchcraft, the work of seeking justice for those who found themselves victims of witches had become privatized and delegated to the realm of traditional healing. Traditional healing, however, since it is based upon divination and frequently

1. Interview with Nandi Mayathula-Khoza, mayor of Southern Metropolitan Local Council of Greater Johannesburg, August 4, 1997, by Adam Ashforth. An edited version of this interview was published in Ashforth 1998b, 524–527.

involves the identification of witches, is illegal. Since 1994, the government of the ANC, representing the majority population of South Africa, people for whom traditional healing is part of their lives, has endeavored to regularize the legal position of healing and incorporate traditional healers into the national health systems of the country. We should examine these efforts, then, to see whether, since such healers are one of the first lines of defense against witchcraft, these efforts by the new regime will have any impact upon the sense of injustice aroused by witchcraft. We should also examine whether efforts to reform the educational system to make it more consonant with the values of the once excluded majority are having any impact upon questions of witchcraft.

Regulating Healers in the Postapartheid State

Traditional healing in virtually all its forms has been illegal for more than a century in South Africa. Under the provisions of the Suppression of Witchcraft Act of 1957 (first introduced in 1895, last amended in 1970), all forms of divination are outlawed. Divination is the heart of healing in Africa; therefore, all healing is outlawed. I have been unable to find accounts of the prosecution of healers for contravening this legislation. No doubt healers have been targeted from time to time in the various districts of South Africa, probably when their activities intruded into political matters or complicated the everyday activities of white administrators. By the 1990s, however, healers operated without the slightest concern for contravening the Suppression of Witchcraft Act. The Health Professions Act of 1974 (Act no. 56 of 1974) requires that all health practitioners be registered with an appropriate professional governing body, of which there is none for traditional healers. More recently, the South African Medicines and Medical Devices Regulatory Authority Act of 1998 requires all medicines, including traditional medicines, to be registered with the Medicines Control Council. Despite these laws, traditional healers have only rarely been prosecuted simply for plying their trade. Nonetheless, traditional healers deeply resent their inferior status. They resent the fact that they are not accorded the same respect and government support as medical doctors, despite their conviction and that of their clients that they are providing essential services. Their clients resent the fact that they cannot obtain health insurance coverage for traditional treatments nor present employers with medical certificates from traditional healers. And the new African political elite, ever mindful of the historic denigration of African culture within previous

racist regimes, is insistent that traditional knowledge and culture be accorded proper respect within this African state.

Although the new democratically elected government is strongly committed to rectifying the situation of traditional healers, they have achieved
little in their first decade of office. The difficulty of acting on these matters,
despite a broad agreement on principles, reveals some of the complexities
of dealing with "evil forces" in a modern state.

Shortly after taking office in 1994, the ANC published *A National Health
Plan for South Africa.* In conceiving the plan, the ANC drew on technical support from the World Health Organization and UNICEF. Since the
1970s, both of these organizations have advocated that national governments officially recognize "traditional healers" as partners in health care
and integrate "traditional medicine" into Western biomedical systems. In
the ANC's plan, the new government promised to "seek to establish appropriate mechanisms that will lead to the integration of traditional and other
complementary healers into the National Health Service" (African National Congress 1994, chap. 1).

It is unclear from the plan exactly what is meant by "integration." Many
writers on the subject of relations between medical systems have suggested
that three broad possibilities exist for policy on the matter: full integration (in which case the question of the status of traditional healers within
the health system arises: equal or subordinate to medical doctors?); cooperation, where a degree of common purpose is developed between different kinds of practitioners while each sector retains independence; and par-
allelism, where each remains distinct and independent of the other. The
ANC plan at different points seems to suggest both integration and co-
operation.[2] The ANC's National Health Plan also promised that the government would "investigate the safety and potential benefit of traditional
drugs," while "fostering liaison and cooperation with traditional healers."
The overall aim was to make "traditional healing . . . an integral and recognised part of health care in South Africa. Consumers will be allowed
to choose whom to consult for their health care, and legislation will be
changed to facilitate controlled use of traditional practitioners" (African
National Congress 1994, chap. 3).

Much of the language of this National Health Plan bears the hallmark
of a liberation movement gaining office in a state for the first time and de-

2. For a discussion of these options in the South African context, see Freeman and
Motsei 1992.

termined to set the world to rights at once. ANC offices around the country are littered with thousands of such noble plans gathering dust as the party gets on with the business of governing. The idea of legislating "controlled use of traditional practitioners," for example, is pure fantasy. None of the policy documents on traditional healing provide answers to the question of why, after a century of being outlawed, healers would willingly submit to being "controlled" by Department of Health bureaucrats. The conceptual framework of this National Health Plan, however, is worth examining in detail, as it reveals the orthodoxies of political thinking about issues of traditional healing in postapartheid South Africa. It also reveals why regulation of the industry that manages problems of witchcraft will be difficult to achieve.

Underpinning the plan's policies regarding "traditional practitioners" were the following "tenets":

- People have the right of access to traditional practitioners as part of their cultural heritage and belief system.
- There are numerous advantages in cooperation and liaison between allopathic and traditional health practitioners and interaction will thus be fostered.
- Traditional practitioners often have greater accessibility and acceptability than the modern health sector and this will be used to promote good health for all.
- Traditional practitioners will be controlled by a recognised and accepted body so that harmful practises can be eliminated and the profession promoted.
- Mutual education between the two health systems will take place so that all practitioners can be enriched in their health practises. (African National Congress 1994, chap. 3)

The elementary presumptions of this plan, then, are that there exist two distinct "health systems"—one "modern" and "allopathic" the other "traditional" and part of an African "cultural heritage and belief system"—which can be integrated into a single national health care system under the auspices of the state. To facilitate the policy of integrating the systems, the ANC proposed that negotiations take place between government representatives and traditional practitioners, that legislation be enacted to change the "position and status" of healers, that interaction between practitioners from different health systems be encouraged, that training programs be initiated, and that a "regulatory body for traditional medicine" be established (African National Congress 1994, chap. 3).

The goals and methods of the National Health Plan at first glance seem entirely laudable. Clearly, since many, if not most, black South Africans engage the services of traditional healers from time to time, a democratic government cannot deny them this right. Indeed, coming to power after decades of struggle against a regime that seemed intent upon denigrating the culture of black people—albeit while claiming to respect that of "the Bantu"—the ANC government was keen to insist that the proper status of African tradition be respected. A government committed to the multicultural principles enshrined in the South African Constitution must be prepared to respect the practices of healing widespread among the population. All of this may be laudable, but it ignores some fundamental questions, such as whether or not there are indeed two *systems* of health care, in what sense or senses traditional practitioners are in fact *traditional,* in what sense or senses they are *health care* practitioners (as distinct from, say, religious or spiritual leaders), and to what extent the forms of knowledge and authority underpinning traditional healing are compatible with those institutionalized within modern bureaucratic states. This last point is especially important because a large part of the work of healing involves— in the words of the healers' representatives reporting to the Portfolio Committee on Arts, Culture, Science, and Technology—battling against evil forces of witchcraft.

Healing and Authority

Prospects for state regulation of the healing industry hinge upon the ability of public officials to find ways of connecting principles of authority operative within the state to those operating in the world of healing in all the varieties that are practiced. Policy makers seeking to devise ways for the state to recognize the legitimacy of traditional healing are confounded by the fact that while there are many revered practitioners of what they refer to as "traditional medicine," there are no indigenous written or scholarly traditions in this field. Most of the literature on traditional healing in South Africa has been written by white missionaries, social scientists, and medical practitioners, most of whom write within the disciplines of academic scholarship.[3] While much of this literature is informative and sympathetic,

3. The literature on traditional healing in South Africa has been mainly concerned with efforts to describe particular healing "systems" in distinct ethnic/national groups (e.g., Ashton 1943; H. Ngubane 1977) or to construct a general account that can serve either as a reference point for those engaged with Western biomedicine (e.g., Conco 1972; Hammond-Tooke 1989b; Hewson 1998) or as a means by which respect can be accorded to African

it hardly serves the purpose of building officially recognized training programs or registers for traditional healers. Compared to the body of literature developed by anthropologists, lawyers, officials, and traditional leaders in the field of customary law (Bekker 1989), which has long been recognized (and rewritten) by the state, the material on medical practice would be a flimsy foundation on which to build an edifice of public health administration.[4] Nonetheless, the goal of integrating "medical systems" remains official government policy.

Progress on the tasks of recognizing and regulating healers has been slow. It seems there are some basic impediments to the institutionalization of African healing traditions within a modern national state. In 1995, the ministers of health in the national and provincial governments agreed to conduct hearings into traditional healing with a view to affording healers official recognition (E. Pretorius 1999). In 1996, the Interim Co-ordinating Committee for Traditional Medical Practitioners' Associations made a presentation to the National Council of Provinces "appealing for formal recognition of their system of medicine." The healers told Parliament that their "dignity had been eroded by the colonial and apartheid powers" and reminded them that the official policies of both the ANC and the Department of Health called for official recognition. The Department of Health, however, reported that they were unable to make policy in this regard, as they lacked information and were confounded by the "apparent division within this profession" (Select Committee on Social Services 1998, 4). In re-

---

culture and the injuries of the past redressed (e.g., Gumede 1990; Mutwa 1969). In recent years, primarily in response to the tuberculosis and HIV/AIDS epidemics, a growing body of work has examined questions of how to integrate traditional healers into the biomedical system (e.g., Hopa, Simbayin, and Du Toit 1998; Wilkinson, Gcabashe, and Lurie 1999), although there are few studies of the attitudes and perceptions of physicians and other stakeholders in the biomedical system to traditional healing (Peltzer 2001). Apart from an important body of work on the faith-healing communities of the AICs (Kiernan 1990b; Oosthuizen 1992; Oosthuizen et al. 1989), little has been written on urban innovations in healing (Farrand 1980), the varieties of healing that do not conform with traditional notions and categories such as *sangoma* and *inyanga,* or the ways those healing categories and the practices associated with them have developed in nontraditional ways (Cocks and Dold 2000).

4. Despite the extent and importance of this writing on customary law, many African legal scholars consider the legal foundations of customary law as it became institutionalized in the South African state to be contrary to the true interests and culture of Africans. See, e.g., Majeke 2002. For an account of the recognition of customary law, see Hahlo and Kahn 1960; also Chanock 2001.

sponse to these appeals, hearings were held in 1997 and 1998 under the auspices of the Select Committee on Social Services of the National Council of Provinces and the Portfolio Committee on Health of the National Assembly.

In August 1998, the Select Committee on Social Services presented its report to Parliament. They recommended the creation of a statutory council for traditional healers similar to the bodies regulating other forms of medical practice. The "broad functions" of this body were to be as follows:

1. Registration of all qualifying traditional healers.
2. Promotion of training, research, professionalism and the creation of a traditional medicine data base.
3. Development of an ethical code of conduct and the maintenance of discipline within the profession.
4. Establishment of norms and standards with regard to the practice of traditional healing, including regulating the issuing of medical certificates and tariff levels.
5. Facilitating co-operation among traditional healers, allopathic medical professionals and the government.
6. Regulating anything incidental to traditional medical practice. (Select Committee on Social Services 1998, 5)

In short, the committee did little more than reiterate the policy articulated in the ANC's National Health Plan four years earlier. They gave no indication as to how relevant qualifications might be decided for inclusion in the register or how standards might be maintained other than to pass the task onto another proposed consultative body.

The report recommended recognition of the following four categories of healers:

(a) Inyanga (herbalist or traditional doctor). This is usually a person who uses herbal and other medicinal preparations for treating disease.
(b) Sangoma (diviners). They are trained to communicate with and utilise the powers of ancestors in diagnosing a disease or mishap.
(c) Traditional birth attendants (Ababelekisi). They are usually elderly women who have been midwives for years and are highly respected for their obstetric expertise.
(d) Traditional surgeons (iingcibi). They are usually trained men with experience in conducting traditional circumcision. (Select Committee on Social Services 1998, 6)

The committee offers no guidance as to how the training in communicating and utilizing powers of ancestors might be evaluated by the proposed statutory council. Birth attendants and circumcision surgeons are relatively simple to integrate into the medical system because their work is limited and nothing in the traditions they uphold is incompatible with basic medical principles. Official recognition of their activities, therefore, merely requires promoting proper education for practitioners in the basics of hygiene (such as requiring *iincibi* to use a fresh sterile blade on each initiate) and the ability to quickly recognize complications requiring medical attention. In recent years a number of well-publicized fatalities at circumcision schools have resulted in demands for closer official scrutiny, and several traditional surgeons have been arrested for running unregistered schools where initiates have died. A somewhat more complicated matter involving negotiation between legal cultures embodying different principles concerning the nature of childhood and consent arises from the fact that the circumcision rituals marking the passage of boys to men require a degree of hardship that has always been accompanied by a risk of death: the men now running the circumcision schools risk charges of "child abuse." Teenage boys from schools where teachers are no longer allowed to use corporal punishment sometimes find it difficult to adjust to the strenuous discipline of the circumcision school. These issues, however, can be sorted out quite satisfactorily on a case-by-case basis.[5]

Inyangas and *sangomas,* however, constitute a far more difficult problem for the state because much of their practice is founded on radically different principles from those embodied in biomedical science. Moreover, the committee's distinction between *inyangas* as herbalists and *sangomas* as diviners is deeply problematic. Implicit in the description of healing categories presented in the committee's report is a model of functional differentiation of professions and modes of training that is thoroughly Western and modernist in conception and that ignores the possibility of unseen evil forces acting in both the etiology and the treatment of disease. Such a model presumes that matters such as qualifications, standards, fees, and codes of conduct are products of hierarchical social authority and can be made, therefore, subject to regulation by the state. When a draft Traditional Health Practitioners Bill was finally published in the *Government Gazette* on April 14, 2003, after nearly ten years of formulation and consultation, the proposed legislation was an almost identical transcript of the

5. For a description of a young man's experience at such a school in the 1990s, see Ramphele 2002.

Health Professions Act (Act no. 56 of 1974). The draft bill avoids mention of *inyangas* and *sangomas* or any other category of healer and the various categories of evil forces they see themselves contending with, defining "traditional health practice" instead as

> the performance of a function, activity, process or service that includes the utilization of a traditional medicine or a traditional practice and which has as its object:
> (a) the maintenance or restoration of physical or mental health or function; or
> (b) the diagnosis, treatment or prevention of a physical or mental illness; or
> (c) the rehabilitation of a person so that he or she may resume normal functioning within the family or community;
> (d) the physical or mental preparation of an individual for puberty, adulthood, pregnancy, childbirth, and death.

The main purpose of the bill is to establish procedures for the minister of health to constitute a Council of Traditional Health Care Practitioners and to outline procedures by which this council is supposed to register and regulate healers.

Despite the fact that they number in the hundreds of thousands and perform services very similar to those of traditional healers, the report of the Select Committee on Social Services rejected suggestions that "spiritual healers (abathandazi)" be included in the register, because the committee was "of the view that . . . they are not traditional in nature and their training and accreditation is unclear and ill-defined" (1998, 6). Considering that the training of healers includes communicating with the spirits of the dead and that the procedures used by many healers are constantly being updated and changed, the committee was perhaps being somewhat rash in the judgment that their training was more clearly defined than that of spiritual healers in general. In any event, as officials of the Department of Health discovered when they began discussions of questions of training and certification with healers' organizations, no consensus was possible on the question of what qualifies a person to heal.[6]

6. This issue proved a major bone of contention in discussions between the Department of Health and traditional-healing "stakeholders." At one meeting, on February 20, 2001, in Pretoria, representatives of the department announced that healers would have to take a written exam prior to registration, a suggestion that outraged the less literate healers. The proposal was dropped (Katherine Lee, South African Traditional Healers' Alliance, per-

The powers underpinning virtually every kind of nonmedical healing in South Africa derive from personal relationships with ancestors and other spiritual beings. While there may appear to be regularities and patterns in practice, these patterns are of an entirely different order from those that emerge in systems governed by authoritative institutions such as those of biomedical science and the medical professions. While the policy makers might want to institute more professionalization within the traditional-healing "sector," if they were serious about engaging with the authority structures of such healing practices in the manner understood by the practitioners themselves, they would have to propose a mode of negotiation, not just with "stakeholders" in the sector, but with the ancestors and spirits on whose behalf most of the stakeholders practice. This would not be a simple undertaking, but the policy makers, in their insistence that traditional health care can be regulated by institutions constituted along lines identical to those regulating the medical professions, seem to be assuming that authority deriving from connection with ancestors and other invisible beings can be treated as if coterminous with the secular authority of communities, professions, and the state.

Traditional healers do not operate completely outside structures of ordinary social authority. *Ngoma* rituals, for example, are regulated to some extent within networks of diviners centered on senior healers who teach and initiate others into the calling (Green, Zokwe, and Dupree 1995; H. Ngubane 1981). Although a senior healer could possibly initiate a hundred or more *sangomas* over the course of a long career, these networks are limited in extent. Harriet Ngubane estimated in 1981 that an average Zulu diviner might be in contact with some four hundred fellow diviners from all over the subcontinent over a three- to five-year period (1981, 364). During the process of *ukuthwasa* the senior serves merely as a guide in assisting the afflicted initiate in developing his own relationship with tutelary

---

sonal communication). Since the knowledge embodied in traditional healing has never been transmitted by means of writing, such an examination would be a curious anomaly. An insight into difficulties with the issue of qualifications can be gleaned from the fact that the official Web site of Thamba Administrators, a company set up to administer medical insurance plans for employers that cover the services of traditional healers (who are paid with vouchers), lists under "Requirements" that healers "must have the necessary qualifications as recognised by an approved traditional healers association," and under "Training" states, in boldface: "We need more information about what training you require to become a Traditional Healer" (Thamba Administrators 2001). The company was incorporated in January 1997 and the question remained unanswered four years later when I viewed their Web site.

spirits, who in turn empower his healing practice. Although the influence of seniors and colleagues no doubt remains strong during a *sangoma*'s career, and although there are various recognized grades and statuses among *sangomas*, in theory she or he is dependent for healing power only upon personal spirits. This makes these networks extremely fissiparous. Indeed, I have known healers to boast of having broken away from the senior to whom they were apprenticed and remaining independent of all other human authorities as a way of emphasizing their primary subjection to spiritual power and thus their extraordinary capacity to heal.

The authority structures that emerge within networks of *sangomas*, however, are not hierarchies of the sort that are utilized in modern Western states for certifying and regulating healing practice. Although senior healers exercise a great deal of authority over initiates, there is no power on earth that can prevent people from becoming healers if they feel their ancestors so desire, or prevent them from practicing in ways they believe their ancestors demand. Nor can any person say without fear of contradiction that a particular healer's call is not genuine. It is not impossible to imagine, however, these networks of healers being organized into representative organizations capable of accrediting members such that the entire institution might be regulated more formally. This is the hope underlying current government policy. The proliferation of associations, councils, and advocacy groups representing healers over the past decade in anticipation of a new legal framework, however, suggests that a fertile field for political action exists in this domain. Some estimates put the number of such associations at more than 150 (E. Pretorius 1999).[7] The heart of the matter that representatives of the state feel called upon to resolve, however, the problem of distinguishing genuine healers from charlatans and regulating the use of "harmful medicines," remains intractable.

The figure of the sagacious *sangoma*, guardian of spiritual tradition participating in age-old rituals of the ancestors, dominates the image of traditional healing in public discourse in contemporary South Africa. The major part of the work of healing illness and misfortune in contemporary South Africa, however, is actually carried on outside this domain. Most healing and health maintenance work is done at home, without professional supervision, by people medicating themselves and their families and

7. These groups have tended to be organized on ethnic lines. The two largest organizations, the Interim-Coordinating Council of Traditional Healers (predominantly Xhosa) and the Traditional Healers Organisation of South Africa (predominantly Zulu), have been at loggerheads in the battle for government recognition (Katherine Lee, South African Traditional Healers' Alliance, July 19, 2001, personal communication).

friends with substances obtained from grocery stores, clinics, hospitals, *inyangas'* "surgeries," pharmacies, "African chemist" shops, and streetside *muthi* vendors. In addition to self-medication and ministration, people draw upon an array of nonmedical practitioners and religious entrepreneurs of the most diverse kinds, who offer cures for every ailment and "medicine" to solve every imaginable problem of life. Many of these problems—like the need of students to obtain *muthi* guaranteeing success in examinations; or the need of gamblers for success in the Lotto—would have been unrecognizable to their ancestors. The title *inyanga* is commonly given to all healers who are in neither medical nor religious institutions. This is a crowded marketplace.

Inyangas typically claim two distinct grounds for their healing abilities. On the one hand, they insist on the length and rigor of their training with a master healer. On the other, they claim that their skills with *muthi* derive from their ancestors—either through inheritance of an innate capacity or through direct instruction by means of dreams or both. Judging from the fragmentary information available in the literature on medical mishaps and clinical syndromes associated with traditional healing, the substances and practices of *inyangas* are no longer based solely upon a traditional herbal apothecary. As one of the leading toxicologists of South Africa has recently argued: "there is a need to explode the myth that all of these [traditional remedies] are safe" (Stewart, Steenkamp, and Zuckerman 1998, 513). The facts that healers operate with a radically different concept of etiology and a vastly more expansive interpretation of the agency of substances than is common in pharmacology make it difficult to connect scientific interpretations of medicinal substances with popular healing practices, particularly those geared toward protection from witchcraft. When policy makers invoke the "traditional healer" or "traditional medical practitioner" in their deliberations, they tend to conjure into being the *sangoma* figure representing the wisdom of the ages. Meanwhile, in the townships, squatter camps, and dilapidated slums of the inner cities, so-called *inyangas* are dispensing their *muthi* without restraint.

The term *inyanga* signifies nothing as consistent or orderly as the *ngoma* cult. It is this domain of healing work that policy makers worry about when they talk about integrating "health systems," restraining "harmful practices," and regulating the training, practice, and remuneration of African "health professions." In the discourses of health policy, at least among those who are sympathetic to the enterprise of traditional healing (which is the vast majority of black South Africans and not a few white people), *in-*

yangas are seen as "herbalists" dispensing natural healing products based upon ancient wisdom. And this wisdom is widely considered to constitute a system of knowledge which, in the interests of multicultural justice, must be considered equally valuable as any other, particularly that of "Western" science. For policy makers concerned with traditional healing, particularly those who are sympathetic to the image of the healer as sage, the principal issue is the task of identifying and prosecuting "charlatans."

Distinguishing between the charlatan and the sage, however, is complicated. In popular discourse in places like Soweto, *inyangas* are seen as African scientists whose secret knowledge allows them to perform "miracles." These miracles can be either miracles of harm and death in the manner spoken of as witchcraft or miracles of healing. The only charlatans in this business are those whose miracles fail to happen after they have taken their clients' money. Even the relatively straightforward issue of tariffs and fees, which government policy suggests should be regulated, are related to the dignity and authority of invisible beings. For most healers, the fee is stipulated as a token of respect to their ancestors and is not spoken of as an economic arrangement at all. Of course, if the ancestors are powerful and much in demand, the fee will be high.[8] Discussions of the importance of recognizing traditional healing often refer to its cost advantage in relation to Western medicine as a reason for encouraging official recognition and generally developing the practice.

Questions of cost relating to traditional healing, however, are not at all straightforward. While it may well be the case that the costs of establishing a modern medical practice are greater than those involved in a traditional practice, it is by no means certain that the costs to patients will always be less. Consultations with traditional healers are almost always an ongoing process, more like prolonged psychotherapy in their general structure than a visit to the general practitioner. Cure is never final. There is always some other detail needing attention, resulting in further expense. Moreover, as the practice of healing usually involves mending relations with family, both living and dead, while overcoming forces of evil dispatched by others, the costs of healing include things such as feasts for ancestors and their hungry descendants and reinforcing protections against witches. Such procedures

8. To the best of my knowledge, the economics of fee setting among South African traditional healers has not been explored. In Central Africa, however, Kenneth Leonard has found that the custom of paying healers more if their treatments are successful produces an incentive for healers to strive to provide quality care (Leonard 2001a, 2001b).

can easily run into the thousands of rand. In fact, without spending thousands, it is impossible to be assured that everything that could be done to deal with a particular case of misfortune has been done. At the end of the day, if misfortunes persist, a whole new regime of treatment, even a new healer, and more expense might be required.

The Select Committee on Social Services inquiry into traditional healing noted that the "practice of traditional medicine is officially outlawed" under provisions of the Health Professions Act of 1974. It also noted that until the end of apartheid, "traditional healers were not only degraded and dehumanised but were branded as witches." Yet, despite this outlawing, "large numbers of Africans continued their belief in and trust of traditional medicines" (Select Committee on Social Services 1998, 3). What the committee did not investigate, however, was how healers, having survived decades of official repression, might be induced to cooperate with authorities of the state in a system of regulation and registration that could in theory disqualify them from practicing a calling that had come from their ancestors. Nor does the report or the draft bill of 2003 offer any guidance as to how, if the qualifications for healing include such things as communicating with ancestors, the process of appointment to the statutory council can be guaranteed as "transparent and democratic" (Select Committee on Social Services 1998, 6). In its drive to find a way of according respect to a certain official model of "tradition," the committee neglected the fact that in South Africa there is a large and energetic population of nonmedical therapists practicing varieties of healing they are pleased to call, among other things, "herbal," "spiritual," and "traditional" who are not Africans in the way the present regime understands that term. After the report was tabled in 1998, many of the white healers moved to develop common cause with African traditional healers' associations to lobby jointly for official recognition.[9]

Given that for the past decade the Department of Health has been preoccupied with the AIDS epidemic at the same time as much of the infrastructure of the allopathic medical system has been collapsing, the failure to make progress in regulating traditional healing is not surprising. The

9. A document issued in 2000 by the Professional Traditional Healers Register of South Africa (motto: "Healers United for the Healing of South Africa and the World"), for example, notes that many forms of alternative medicine used in the West (e.g., "Massage, Aromatherapy, Acupuncture, Reflexology, Bach Flower Remedies etc.") originated in Africa and are used by African traditional healers.

AIDS epidemic, however, has also heightened the perception of the need to integrate traditional healers into the public health endeavor. In practice, when policy makers devise plans for the health system, they have mostly ignored traditional healing entirely or else have situated nonmedical healers in a clearly subordinate role.[10] Generally, such plans call for programs to train healers to recognize symptoms of AIDS and illnesses such as tuberculosis, as well as other sexually transmitted diseases, in order to facilitate referrals to biomedical practitioners; they treat traditional healing as a subsidiary activity to Western medicine.[11] However, as illnesses associated with AIDS become more widespread, demand for the services of healers and their remedies is likely to increase substantially. Policing claims for having discovered cures for AIDS will prove a taxing task for authorities.

In the first decade of democratic rule, the most significant legislation pertaining to traditional healers has been the South African Medicines and Medical Devices Regulatory Authority Act (Act no. 132 of 1998), which includes "traditional medicines" under the category "complementary medicines." This act provides for the regulation and registration of all medicines intended for human and animal use. Under its terms, *muthi* must be approved by the Medicines Control Council, who are appointed by the minister of health, and sold with full disclosure of ingredients. The provision has simply been ignored. Healers dispense their remedies without giving a thought to the fact that they are now required to submit their healing potions to the scrutiny of the Medicines Control Council.[12] As the AIDS crisis grows, public interest in traditional *muthi* as remedies is increasing, as are opportunities to profit from their manufacture and sale. There is no sign of an effective regulatory system emerging.

Given that the final authority for healers' activities and the source of their healing gifts lie in the domain of invisible beings, and considering that many of the ailments they treat are considered to have an origin in domains

10. The five-year Strategic Framework plan devised by the national and provincial health departments, for example, makes no mention of traditional or spiritual healers at all. See Department of Health 1999.

11. The Department of Health's AIDS Strategy plan, for example, lists as goals: "Collaborate with traditional healers to improve health care seeking behaviour for STDs" (Goal 2); "Conduct research on the effectiveness of traditional medicines" (Goal 11) (Department of Health 2000).

12. For an example of some of the reactions to this legislation from purveyors of "complementary" medicines, consider this initialism: PHARMAPACT (Peoples Health Alliance Rejecting Medical Authoritarianism, Prejudice, and Conspiratorial Tyranny).

of occult forces, it is difficult to see how bureaucratic regulation can ever be fully effective. Regulatory bodies, however, especially if they control significant financial resources and disciplinary powers, will certainly spawn a whole new field of political activity as groups struggle for control of these resources. The new legislation will also empower the minister of health to grant certain healers an official imprimatur. But while the rhetoric of policy makers invokes models of authority emphasizing the creation of systematic bureaucratic regulation for traditional healing, the most likely prospect for this sector is a continuation of the present unregulated market for healing services coupled with a smaller sector of healers who win control of state resources.

Schools, Science, Sorcery, and Citizenship

Almost everyone between the ages of seven and twenty in South Africa is attending school. About a quarter of the total population of Soweto, for example, is in school (A. Morris 1999b, table 2.2). Many of the younger children are in preschools and crèches, and millions of older young people are attending institutions of higher education. About two-thirds of the current adult population spent ten years or more in school. Older women are likely to have had less schooling than men. By the 1990s, however, this gender disparity had disappeared and girls were attending school in equal numbers to boys. Indeed, girls were more likely to take their matriculation examinations in the 1990s. They were, however, less likely to pass.[13] But those who failed "matric" had plenty of company. Fewer than half of those who took their final matriculation examinations during the 1990s passed (Ministry of Education 1999).

The vast system of public schools maintained and operated by the South African state are not being used as instruments to shape attitudes to and practices of witchcraft in contemporary South Africa. Education policy makers generally have nothing to say about witchcraft, at least as their

13. Of the total number of students taking national matriculation exams in 1996 (as in most years), 56 percent were female, of whom 50.2 percent passed; 44 percent were male, of whom 58.5 percent passed (Anstey 1997). The higher retention rate of girls in Soweto schools is influenced by the fact that whereas boys who drop out before their final year have the option of joining cohorts of age-mates and roving the streets in search of adventure, girls who do not go to school are almost always housebound and face the unrelieved drudgery of housework. Girls still attending school also bear heavy burdens of domestic labor, but at least they have some daily escape.

views are reflected in official documents. Nonetheless, education does affect the ways in which matters of spiritual insecurity are perceived in everyday life. This subject is too immense to deal with in anything but the most summary fashion here. Two aspects of education, however, seem to me crucial in relation to the issues of spiritual insecurity we have been considering in this book. First, the teaching of natural science can influence the ways students form plausible interpretations of the forces shaping the material world. Second, schools can have an effect upon issues of identity through the teaching of citizenship values derived from the history, culture, and identity of social groups.

Most of the children and young people I have known in Soweto love going to school. What they do there, however, has limited value in preparing them for productive and rewarding futures. Besides the widespread disruption of schooling that took place during the years of struggle, when the slogan "No Education before Liberation" was current, and the legacy of unruliness that prompts the authorities of the new regime to issue perennial calls to "restore a culture of learning" in the schools, the quality of Soweto's schools, as with most of the other schools for black children in South Africa, is generally poor. Most people who pass through these schools leave with little more than a basic grasp of the essentials of "book learning," including reading and writing English. Few Soweto schoolchildren at the turn of the century leave school with skills adequate to pursuing further education and training in fields that would allow them to take advantage of future opportunities in the labor market, particularly not in technology sectors, where, according to the Human Sciences Research Council (1999), most employment growth is likely to occur. If a good grasp of the basics of mathematics and physical science is the measure of such preparation, African candidates are pitifully few.

Few black parents today or in the past have had adequate resources to enable their children to succeed educationally. Most are also unable to provide a home environment conducive to success in academic study. In populations that have been denied the benefits of quality education, it is not surprising to find that few people, parents and students alike, are aware of what is needed in order for students to excel. Moreover, among young Sowetans of my acquaintance, pursuing excellence in schoolwork can be a dangerous path, particularly for boys, as the time necessary for devotion to books requires a retreat from social life and the daily work of maintaining networks of supportive comrades. That can easily engender resentment among peers and the accusation of pride, which is a widely accepted pretext for ostracism and which in turn can serve to expose them to violence.[14] In sum, most Sowetans either have been or are still at school, but few are well educated. They are all aware of the power of science, but few are familiar with its principles. This is the foundation for imagining that field of secret endeavor I have described as African science.

Africans in this part of the world have long valued education as a means of mastering the ways of "Whites," the key to social and economic advancement. Educationists, too, have advocated African education as a means of social and cultural transformation. As David Shingler has argued, unlike Afrikaners, for whom "Christian National" education was a primary means of inculcating a sense of national identity, Africans "never saw education as an instrument for preserving an African identity, religion, or language. On the contrary, it was seen as providing a language of global preeminence, as a means of participating in the structure which had been imposed upon them and of obtaining familiarity with a literature and ideas, skills and techniques which were the source of wealth and power" (Shingler 1973, 54).

Almost from the time the first schools were established by missionaries, African demand for schooling has outstripped supply. Mass public education for Africans dates from the midfifties with the introduction of the notorious "Bantu Education," part of the National Party's program of "separate development." Bantu Education had the effect of replacing a small number of reasonably good schools run by religious missions with a large-scale and inferior public system (Hartshorne 1992; Kallaway 1984). And although the Afrikaner nationalists who devised Bantu Education paid lip service to the importance of maintaining African traditions, in practice neither schools nor families were in a position to educate black children systematically in the heritage of their history, traditions, folklore, or anything else of the sort that is currently described under the rubric of indigenous knowledge systems. Indeed, nearly a decade after the first democratic elections brought an "Africanist" government to office, black leaders are bemoaning the ignorance of young people regarding the anti-apartheid struggle that brought them freedom.

The education system, then, leaves most young adults exposed to, but hardly in command of, the rudiments of "White" culture. And while other formal institutions governing youth activities such as churches, sports clubs, political organizations, prisons, clinics, and hospitals exert formative influ-

14. An excellent description of these dynamics can be found in Njabulo Ndebele's short story "The Music of the Violin" (1983).

ences on young lives, they rarely enable young people to master authoritative discourses of interpretation—whether of Western, African, or global provenance—pertaining to the forces shaping their lives.[15] Few young black South Africans are in a position to comprehend the discourses of global economics; fewer still have mastered mathematics or the natural sciences.

Young Sowetans are even less well versed in the traditions of Africa. There are no formal or large-scale institutions serving education in "traditional" or "indigenous" cultural matters, although a small number of families send children (particularly boys) to rural relatives to attend initiation schools. Historically, the education of young people in this part of the world and their socialization into statuses of respectable men and women proceed within three interlocking sets of social relations: the family, including the generalized relations of respect for adult authority expressed in the usage "Mother" and "Father" for all elders, who had corresponding rights and duties to discipline, correct, and instruct all youngsters in their domains; peer groups, age grades, and gender-segregated cohorts of young people, who mimicked the ways of their immediate elders and were sometimes instructed by them explicitly; and the organized authority of politically designated elders and experts who schooled youngsters in the laws and lore applicable to their station in life. Only a tiny minority of young people these days receive anything like a comprehensive education in any of these domains.

From the first efforts by European missionaries to educate Africans through to present efforts to overcome the legacy of Bantu Education in black schools, the central question in debates over what is now called curriculum development has hinged on how the content of what is taught in schools relates to African culture and how the project of schooling relates to the broad project of reconstructing African social life. Central to this question, although not always raised explicitly, has been the question of how the curriculum deals with witchcraft and associated matters pertaining to what I have called spiritual insecurity.

In 1917, for example, the inspector of schools for Natal, Charles Loram, published his revised doctoral dissertation, written while a student of John Dewey's at Columbia Teacher's College. In it, he developed the first argument for establishing a comprehensive education system for South African "Natives." In answer to the question "Why educate the Native?" (the title

---

15. For an extended portrait of the circumstances of young people in the township of New Crossroads in Cape Town, a place similar in many respects to Soweto, see Ramphele 2002.

of his chapter 3), Loram argued that not only was it impossible to avoid
"educating the Native by our contact with him," but "the calls of humanity
and Christianity," advantages to "Europeans," and the prospect of enabling
"Natives" to solve their own problems all demanded the development of
proper education for Africans (Loram 1969, 30). A central part of this project of "Native education," he argued, was the eradication of the belief in
witchcraft:

> One of the greatest blessings which education could bring to the Native
> would be to free him from the dominance and deadening influence of the
> spirit world. The "raw" South African Native has a profound belief in the
> potency of spirits. All the calamities which befall him or his tribe are due to
> malignant spirits. Any Native whose life is out of the ordinary runs the risk
> of being suspected of witchcraft. This is one of the reasons why Natives are
> unwilling to practise at home the arts they have learnt in the service of the
> white man. To remove this blighting influence is one of the tasks of educa-
> tion. (Loram 1969, 31)

Loram quoted approvingly an article by Dr. Neil Macvicar, the medical officer to the Lovedale Mission, who wrote in 1909: "the only way of getting rid
of that dreadful theory ["the ancestral belief in witchcraft"], which can be
really called the curse of the Natives, is to replace in their minds the primi-
tive and dangerous animism by the spiritual, highly moral, philosophical
theism of Christianity" (quoted in Loram 1969, 30).

In 1932, in a foundational document of the "scientific" segregationism
that came into prominence at the time (Ashforth 1990, chap. 3), the Native
Economic Commission (NEC) argued that the very survival of the "Natives" as a people required modernizing the "tribal system" by means of
education to eradicate central cultural precepts. The key "anti-progressive"
features of the tribal system, the NEC argued, were ancestor worship, which
produced too great an emotional attachment to land and cattle; the related
"cattle cult," another "anti-economic inheritance," in which cattle have religious significance and which leads to overstocking and overgrazing; and
witchcraft, which leads to a reluctance to accumulate wealth for fear of being accused of sorcery (Native Economic Commission, paras. 31, 34, 26).
The best way to modernize the tribal system, in the NEC's view, was not
to cast it aside as so much lumber but to "introduce among the Natives a
leaven of social education which will gradually, step by step, free the masses
from their anti-progressive social heritage" (1932, paras. 62, 79). Labor discipline was still seen as the driving force of progress, but in the 1930s and

1940s it became the orthodoxy in discussions of the "Native question" that the state would have to take a more direct role in shaping African society through the instrument of schooling.

These notions of education were integrally connected with propositions concerning the inherent rationality of Natives and their capacity to participate in government as citizens. In the early decades of the twentieth century, after the founding of the Union of South Africa in the aftermath of the Anglo-Boer War, doctrines of political citizenship in the state were premised upon the idea that Natives and "Europeans" differed fundamentally by virtue of levels of "civilisation." Europeans were said to exist at a higher level of civilization; Natives at a lower. Implicit in this ordering of difference was the presumption that progress from one level to another would take place over time and was essentially linear, resulting either from a natural evolution or assisted by deliberate policies of "upliftment" designed by the higher civilization to assist the lower. Citizenship was posited as a reward and accompaniment of "civilisation." Such an account of citizenship served to justify the exclusion of the mass of Africans from political participation outside the designated Native Reserves, where the "tribal system" was to be maintained, while offering the prospect that an African elite might one day find their place in the halls of power. Belief in witchcraft was generally put forward as both an example of and an explanation for the lower level of African civilization.

Consider the attitude of General J. B. M. Hertzog, who was prime minister of South Africa during the 1920s and 1930s and was one of the principal architects of the legal provisions that finally excluded all Africans from the vote, even those formerly deemed "civilised Natives," who had been entitled to a property-based franchise in Cape Province (Lacey 1981). Though he struggled mightily to eradicate the last vestiges of African political participation, the "Cape Native Franchise," Hertzog was not, or so his colleague in government and biographer Oswald Pirow insists, opposed in principle to self-government for Africans.[16] Rather, like most "Europeans" of his time, he saw the test of that right as being the test of civilization. Civilization, however, was not something that he or his biographer considered Africans were going to accede to at anytime soon. The reason for this, in Hertzog's view, was the prevalence of a "general belief in witchcraft and

---

16. In his biography of the prime minister, Pirow writes that Hertzog "insisted that no native state should come into being anywhere in Africa until its inhabitants were fully capable of self-government. In this connection the determinative factor would be not the acquisition of the white man's booklearning but of his ethical conceptions" (Pirow 1937, 193).

associated phenomena" (Pirow 1937, 196). Hertzog considered this belief
to be deep-rooted, even among educated Africans, leading him to the conclusion that "with so-called civilised natives, almost without exception their
civilisation was only skin deep" (Pirow 1937, 196). Pirow proceeds to re-
count an anecdote Hertzog told him about one of his farm workers explaining why he had to move his homestead to avoid trouble from spirits
in an old burial place. Pirow quotes Hertzog: "That shows how far civilisation has gone with a native who normally would be described as a civilised
man and a Christian. It emphasises how careful we must be before we place
duties and responsibilities on them which they are incapable of carrying"
(Pirow 1937, 197).

When the Afrikaner nationalists began advocating their policy of apartheid in the late 1940s, with its doctrine of "separate development" for distinct African nations, each located in its own "Homeland," to justify black
exclusion from citizenship in the central states, African belief in witchcraft
ceased to be referred to in official discourse as evidence of their inability to
govern themselves. The basic attitude toward "superstition," however, remained strong. From the nationalist perspective, Africans (then referred to
as "Bantu") were entitled to develop the intrinsic qualities of their distinctive, and God-given, "cultures" in their own Homelands until such time as
the culture reached self-awareness as a "nation," at which point they would
qualify for self-government. For the people developing these schemes for
legitimating political domination, the fact that Africans believed in witchcraft was of no particular interest (other than representing another aspect
of a more fundamental cultural difference). Ideologists of apartheid, such
as W. W. M. Eiselen, were adamant that modernization of "Bantu culture"
was necessary in order for socioeconomic development to take place, and
the presumption of all modernizers—British colonial, Afrikaner, and African alike—has been that science and technology would drive out superstition (Eiselen 1948; Commission on Native Education 1951). In the view of
Afrikaner nationalists, however, the form of that modernization would be
a matter for African intellectuals to determine in the process of uplifting
their own people. Consequently, after the 1940s there is little talk of witchcraft in relation to basic questions of African citizenship.

When the National Party came to power in 1948, with their policy of
apartheid, they brought a radically different conception of education to
bear on the program of reengineering African life. Afrikaner nationalism
had been forged in the crucible of conflict with the financially and culturally dominant British. For the nationalists, education was primarily a matter of preserving and advancing the distinctiveness of their own culture, ex-

pressed in their own national language, Afrikaans. Whereas the general thrust of missionary education of Africans had been geared toward instruction in English and the rudiments of European schooling, the Afrikaner nationalists proposed a model of education designed to protect and develop the distinctiveness of "Bantu" culture. In 1951, the Commission on Native Education issued its report, a document which was to become the foundation of the Bantu Education system that governed black South African education until the mid-1990s. Chaired by the social anthropologist and son of missionaries W. W. M. Eiselen, who was to become secretary of native affairs under Hendrik F. Verwoerd and one of the few men who deserve the title "architect of apartheid," the commission proposed that the fundamental aim of "Bantu education . . . is the development of a modern progressive culture, with social institutions which will be in harmony with one another and with the evolving conditions of life to be met in South Africa, and with the schools which must serve as effective agents in this process of development" (Commission on Native Education 1951, 765).

While the nationalists proclaimed the aims of education as promoting the "development of a modern progressive culture," the greater part of their program was aimed at reproducing distinct ethnic identities. The Eiselen report contains none of the old language about "eradicating superstition." In place of that formula the nationalists substituted generalities about "development" and the "tremendous cultural leap such as the South African Bantu are called upon to make" (Commission on Native Education 1951, 764). The school system that was created in the name of Bantu Education—which critics, citing Prime Minister Verwoerd, denounced as designed to perpetuate the subordination of Africans as "hewers of wood and drawers of water"—certainly helped foster new forms of African culture, flowering most dramatically in the school-based youth uprisings of the 1970s and 1980s, but they were nothing like what Eiselen had in mind.

In the postapartheid era, as the government of the ANC struggles to transform the institutions of mass education bequeathed by Eiselen and Verwoerd in order to serve the vision of a multicultural democratic citizenship, no one talks of the need to eradicate beliefs in witchcraft and superstition as objects of education policy. Education policy, nevertheless, directly bears upon the issues of spiritual insecurity, primarily in relation to science and religious education.

In February 2000, for example, the minister of education, Kader Asmal, convened a committee of advisers—styling it the "Working Group on Values in Education"—to inquire into and recommend the "appropriate values South Africa ought to embrace in its primary and secondary educational

institutions . . . for the shaping more broadly of the quality of national character to which we as a people in a democracy wish to aspire" (Working
Group on Values in Education 2000, 1). The values the Working Group decided to promote (without giving reasons for their choices) were equity, tolerance, multilingualism, openness, accountability, and honor. A year later,
after a period of "national debate" (a debate that prompted only 3 out of
29,000 schools to submit responses to the document on values in education), another ministerial working group produced *Manifesto on Values,
Education and Democracy* (Gevisser and Morris 2001), which managed to
find ten core values in the Constitution that should be included in the curriculum.[17] The project was envisioned as part of the effort of "moral regeneration." Nowhere in the postapartheid manifestos on values or in any
other statement of educational philosophy or curriculum development that
I have been able to find do the words "witchcraft," "sorcery" or any other
variant of local terms for occult powers appear.

Occasionally, education policy documents will make a reference to
"indigenous knowledge systems" and "African traditional religion," along
with the importance of considering them in the curriculum. The "Natural
Sciences Learning Area" in the "outcomes based" Curriculum 2005, for
example, proposes a "learning outcome" of "Understanding science and
technology in the context of history and indigenous knowledge" in a way
that situates indigenous practices on a continuum of linear development of
scientific knowledge from tradition to modernity (Isaac 2002, 114). When
references are made to indigenous practices in discussions of the relation
between science and religion, a gesture will usually be made toward "African religion" or "indigenous religious traditions," though very few participants in the educational reform debates seem to have any real interest or
expertise in this field, and I have yet to see any practical recommendations
about how these inclusions might be made.[18] None of these documents, nor
any other plan for curriculum reform that I have been able to find, men-

17. These values were democracy, social justice, equality, nonracism and nonsexism,
ubuntu (human dignity), an open society, accountability (responsibility), the rule of law, respect, and reconciliation (Gevisser and Morris 2001, 1).

18. A partial exception to this is the work of the Ugandan educationalist Catherine
Odora Hoppers, who served as an adviser on indigenous knowledge systems to Parliament's
Portfolio Committee on Arts, Culture, Science, and Technology and who has suggested that
a consideration of the "core African philosophy of Ubuntu" would lead to a "re-animation
and humanisation of science" in such a way as to "help science recover its sense of dwelling,
its sense of caring, crying, laughter and joy" (Odora Hoppers 2002a, 85–86). See also Odora
Hoppers 2002c.

tions how teachers might deal with issues pertaining to spiritual insecurity in the classroom. The Ralushai Commission on witchcraft violence made some recommendations regarding education, but only to "liberate people mentally to refrain from participating in the killing and causing harm resulting from their belief in witchcraft," not to alter the underlying principles of "belief" (Ralushai Commission 1996, 60).

The manifestos on values have mostly been ignored in practice. One of the main reasons these values programs have had little impact is that they focus entirely upon the values that should be dispensed to "learners" without addressing the problem of reconstructing the value schemes of the legions of teachers who were themselves products of the apartheid educational system (Jansen 2003). Nonetheless, they reveal important contours of official thinking. The Working Group on Values emphasized as one of its three "considerations of educational philosophy" the centrality of science:

> our educational philosophy should provide learners with the tools to solve the many problems that come with being human throughout the life cycle. We believe that these tools are the same as the tools of science, broadly understood, which are to bring all knowledge, however tentative and imperfect, of a problem, to bear on finding its rational solution. It is to treat problems as challenges to be solved through knowledge and understanding, rather than as unbearable burdens to be endured without solution. The will and courage to approach life in this manner does not simply reside in science, but in the spirituality of humanity that defines our attitude to life. (Working Group on Values in Education 2000, chap. 1)

The other two "key elements" they suggested were "to develop the intellectual abilities and critical faculties among all of the children and young adults in our schools" and "inclusiveness" (2000, 1). Later in the report the point is repeated: "A command over elementary science adds value. A grasp of environment patterns, the basic physics of the cosmology [*sic*], human biology and the engineering logic of the built environment enhance the ability of the individual to function and to exercise a mastery over his or her fate" (2000, chap. 5). A real "command over elementary science" as well as adding value would render worthless much of the *muthi* that is currently in use and require a rethinking of many of the presumptions underpinning relations with substances and spirits such as those described in previous chapters. About this, however, the Working Group is silent.

By far the greatest clamor over the teaching of science in postapartheid schools has been aroused by the question of evolution, with the most noise being made by conservative and predominantly white Christian groups, influenced and supported by their counterparts in the United States. These groups are angered by the fact that the curriculum, which for generations had been shaped by "Christian National" Calvinist precepts, is being updated in line with scientific principles and humanist precepts.[19] At the turn of the twenty-first century, while conservative Christian white parents are agitating against the teaching of evolution, the cultural and religious impact of science education upon the way African children interpret the powers operating in their world is being completely ignored in the debates on curriculum development.

19. For accounts of these debates, see Chidester 2002; Chisholm 2003; Jansen 2003; Lever 2002.

Epilogue

Dimensions of Insecurity

Why are we poor? Why are we suffering? Why are our young people dying? Who is to blame? Why are they doing this? Who can save us?

Everyday life in Soweto and other places in southern Africa throws up such questions about the meaning of misfortune without respite. In this book I have sought to show how suppositions about "witchcraft" provide plausible answers for people, answers people can live with and work with as they turn to various forms of spiritual power in search of solace and safety. The general purpose of my inquiries has been to begin reflecting on the implications of the quest for spiritual security in a world of witches for the project of democracy in an African state.

Ultimately, the dimension of insecurity that I am calling "spiritual" is shaped by epistemological concerns—doubts and uncertainties aroused by both the inherent indeterminacy of "invisible forces" and the existence of competing, and often contradictory, schemes and authorities for interpreting their nature and actions in a context of widespread ignorance about how best to act. In contemporary Soweto, people live with a vivid apprehension that their sufferings and misfortunes can be products of natural, spiritual, or personal forces and events. Distinguishing which forces are responsible for misfortunes, however, can be extremely difficult. People are only rarely able to reach an assessment of the causes of their misfortunes without someone close to them disagreeing strongly over the nature of their suffering and the best course for treatment. Thus, I have spent a great deal of time in the preceding chapters examining the sorts of questions that arise in the course of everyday life regarding these forces, the outlines of the various plausible interpretations available, and the varieties of authority promising assistance in managing problems of life I term "spiritual insecurity." I have suggested that the notion of "African science" has come to occupy a central place in establishing the plausibility of statements concerning the potentials of *muthi* in its dialectical guises of both poison and medicine. I also speculated that the current investment in research into indigenous knowledge systems pertaining to traditional healing as "science" might—by virtue of the dialectical nature of *muthi*—also lend greater credence to popular speculation about witchcraft as African science.

One of the reasons I have insisted on referring to the complex of problems involving the actions of invisible forces in everyday life as *spiritual* insecurity is because for most people the fundamental ground of security and prosperity in life is sought in relations with invisible beings. The spirit world of contemporary Soweto, however, as in other places in Africa, not to mention the rest of the planet, is an extraordinarily complex domain, with correspondingly complex varieties of faith and forms of religious organization that offer different forms of access to spiritual power and thus security. For more than a century the principal issue of spiritual life among Africans in this part of the world has concerned relations between Jesus and the ancestors. The power of ancestors has been transformed both by the advent of new understandings of the spirit world presented by Christian missions and by the transformation of African political, community, and family life. Ordinary people, especially in urban areas such as Soweto, generally have access to a smaller domain of ancestral powers than their forebears apparently did. Their access to these beings has also been transformed by the steady erosion of paternal authority and capacity in families. Mothers, and maternal ancestors, seem to be playing a far greater role in the affairs of family security than in the past. Ancestors are also under increasing assault from the varieties of Pentecostalism that are spreading rapidly throughout Africa.

Perhaps the most complex domain of action by invisible forces is the terrain of the self, or the "inner" realms of being commonly spoken of in Christian-inflected terms as the "soul." All of the social and spiritual transformations described above in relation to the spirit world and invisible forces have created a fertile field for anxiety when people contemplate the vulnerability of inner realms of being to external forces. A paradigmatic example of this is Madumo's dreaming that his mother wanted him to clean her grave—only to learn from his *inyanga* that the dream had been implanted by witchcraft to lead him into contact with deadly *muthi*. The possibility that malicious individuals can hijack a person's mind, will, and deepest desires by nefarious means and turn them against that person opens up a field of vulnerability that is inadequately accounted for in the language of psychology. These possibilities also give rise to questions about personal responsibility that are difficult to resolve within the discourses of modern jurisprudence. They also complicate the business of living in a world with witches.

One of the most difficult problems arising in the study of witchcraft in contemporary Soweto is created by the fact that people talk about witchcraft least when it matters most. For this reason, the principal method used in the sociological study of witchcraft in Africa throughout the twentieth century—the analysis of patterns of accusation—is of only limited value in understanding the significance of fears of witchcraft in the context of everyday life. Witchcraft discourse in contemporary Soweto flourishes mostly in the medium of gossip, and it is through gossip that the essential secrecy at the heart of the fear of witchcraft is plumbed. The epistemological double bind that arises in the course of living in a world with witches—created by the fact that both the motive and the means of witchcraft are secret—means that life must be lived in terms of a presumption of malice. This makes jealousy a deadly force, and one much to be feared, as well as limiting the possibilities of social trust.

These fears of the powers of others to cause harm by secretly deploying invisible forces create fundamental problems of justice in everyday life that neither community organizations nor the postapartheid state are well placed to resolve. Traditional healing promises a limited form of justice akin to revenge: in treating a victim of witchcraft, healers promise that the evil forces will be returned to their source to kill the witch who dispatched them. The problem of social justice, however, remains. Efforts to seek justice in communities afflicted by fears of witchcraft tend to be informal, ad hoc, and sporadic. Meanwhile, a pervasive sense of suffering as injustice permeates social life. In a world of witches, all conflicts have an occult dimension. Occult force, like physical violence, is akin to what the political activists used to call a "terrain of struggle." Many weapons are available to persons seeking to cause harm or protect themselves from it. When justice is unobtainable, violence breeds violence in a cycle of revenge; witchcraft also breeds witchcraft.

Spiritual Insecurity and Political Power in Postapartheid South Africa

Harm and death caused to citizens have long been considered the legitimate interests of states. In the history of modern democratic states, the idea that political authorities should be devoted to advancing the security and welfare of citizens has long been lauded as the organizing principle of public power, the bedrock of political legitimacy. Protecting citizens from threats of violence, whether from outsiders or fellow citizens, serves as *the* foundational principle of public power. State involvement in matters of economic security such as the alleviation of poverty, the encouragement of economic development, or the regulation of market excesses has also come to be taken for granted in modern politics as fundamental to the welfare of both states and citizens. Further, as understanding of the relationship between sanitation, infection, and public health has advanced with the development of scientific medicine, public policy relating to problems of medical insecurity has come to occupy an important place in the everyday politics of modern states. Questions of spiritual insecurity, however, though they remain potent in the lives of many modern citizens, have been largely excluded from the public domain and relegated to a sphere designated as "religion" that has to do with matters of "faith" and "belief," which are understood as essentially private and personal, not as matters of public safety.

Belief in witchcraft presents severe challenges for the project of democratic government within a modern state. A democratic regime cannot acknowledge the legitimacy of "informal" efforts to seek justice in the face of witchcraft, but if authorities prevent communities from securing their own forms of justice while refusing to address the underlying problem of occult violence, they open themselves to the charge that they are either ignoring dangers facing the community or in league with the evil forces themselves. In postapartheid South Africa, efforts to reform laws on witchcraft and healing to recognize the reality of witchcraft, while retaining punishment for unsubstantiated accusations against suspected witches, have been unsuccessful. These proposals generally fail to address the problem that the formal legal system enshrines principles of evidence that cannot take cognizance of the expertise of diviners. The problem of officially recognizing diviners and traditional healers has also engaged the efforts of policy makers. Forms of authority underpinning traditional healing and faith healing are not obviously amenable to regulation by bureaucratic principles. The actions of people proclaiming themselves subject only to higher authorities have always proved difficult for secular political power.

The 1996 Constitution of South Africa grants every person the right to freely practice the religion of her or his choice. Apostolic/Zionist and Pentecostalist churches are the fastest growing and most significant religious movement in South Africa. People are drawn to these churches by the promise of healing and the "holistic" solutions they offer to the problems of life involving witchcraft, pollution, and the activities of other invisible evil forces in their communities. The Zionist and Apostolic churches offer modes of managing the dangers of evil forces in collective rituals and communal action that are, by virtue of belonging to the sphere of religion, outside the public domain. Thus, although these churches are continually dealing with matters their members treat as issues of public safety and security, from the point of view of the state they are dealing with private matters of religious belief. To some degree, the constitutional establishment of a separation between church and state protects government from the need to intervene in matters of spiritual insecurity. Leaving these matters as the sole province of religious authorities, however, does not obviate the problem of the pervasive sense of injustice aroused by spiritual insecurity. Indeed, the proliferation of healing churches of the Spirit type indicates a failure of secular authority.

Since issues of spiritual insecurity pervade virtually every aspect of social life, acts of government also impinge upon them, sometimes in unexpected ways. The ending of apartheid, for example, produced for many people in Soweto a sense that witchcraft was increasing and that occult violence was running rampant. The increasing socioeconomic inequalities over the past decades in the black South African population, a product of government policy as much as anything, have also contributed to a sense of insecurity. Education policy, health policy, AIDS policy, economic development policies, and more shape the distribution of social jealousy, the distribution of misfortunes, and the resources available for people to interpret the forces shaping their lives and mediate the conflicts that arise in the course of living them. I do not pretend to be able to predict exactly how these will play out in the future. I hope I have shown, however, that issues pertaining to spiritual insecurity will remain a feature of social life in this part of Africa for the foreseeable future and will shape the practice of politics and government in this new African state.

From Security to Identity

Although I have spent hundreds of pages exploring the negative dimensions of life, the everyday negations of the comity that makes community possible, I must remind my reader that these sad facts are not all there is to life in Soweto, or South Africa, or Africa as a whole. As I pointed out at the beginning, the account presented in this book is partial. It draws from my own personal experience and expresses nothing so much as my own struggle to understand these issues as they have touched my own life. One day, perhaps, I shall try to portray the strength of the bonds of love and the power of joy that infuse everyday life in Soweto. The intensity of these positive dimensions of life makes these negative worlds seem so shocking. Perhaps that is what lends credence to suppositions about the dangerous occult forces that unleash the power of hate.

When I began trying to write about witchcraft in Soweto more than a decade ago, I had no idea it would be so difficult. I assumed one simply had to describe what people said about it, how they acted in relation to it, and what the consequences of their thoughts and actions were. But I did not fully appreciate the depths of my friends' sense of their own ignorance of these matters, a sense that is widely shared by black South Africans, judging from the range of recent calls for authoritative definitions of the nature of "witches" and "witchcraft" to be discovered by official inquiries and enshrined in law. Unfortunately, no such clarity is possible. "Witchcraft" is an essentially contested concept—doubly so for naming an activity born in secrecy.

Africans living in a world of witches at the turn of the twenty-first century also live in the same world as the rest of us—whoever we might be. They enjoy, as much as they are able, the miracles of modern science, the bounties of capitalism, and the benefits of democracy—not to mention the love of Jesus, the fear of God, and the power of the Holy Spirit as well as of innumerable other invisible beings. That I was surprised by this world of witchcraft when I first encountered Soweto reveals nothing so much as the depths of an ignorance fostered in the lecture halls and libraries of some fine universities. I hesitate to indict my stupidity. For I was, and remain, not alone. If such stupidity were a hanging crime, the gallows would be overburdened with social scientists, each dangling his or her own slew of presumptions about modernity, rationality, and secularity.

The fact that the modern state in Western Europe emerged from the crucible of religious conflict lent credence to particular configurations of state and church that allowed a degree of autonomy for the managers of spiritual security while establishing a symbiotic relationship between the political orders of the sacred realm and those in the sphere of mundane affairs. Euro-American histories of relations between what is comfortably called church and state, human institutions shaping the domains of gods and men into distinct territories (stamping out the witches in the process), accompanied by millennium-long narratives of the struggle to organize human affairs into a manageable mass under a unified God lording it over a single state for each singular nation comprised of solitary individuals getting on with their business, have produced enormously powerful ways of understanding human affairs. Those of us inhabiting such "bleakly monotheistic worlds," to reprise Peter Brown, are left helpless (one might almost say "eyeless in Gaza") when confronted with the passions of those who worry about witches, dream of the virgins rewarding their martyrdom, or await the rapture of the Saved in their reunion with Jesus. At the dawn of the twenty-first century, the openings salvos of a new Holy War announce to all that this failure to understand can have tragic consequences. Yet, though the thunder of cosmic rage resounds worldwide, ears like mine battle even to hear noise.

Throughout this book I have struggled (haltingly, inadequately, I readily admit; at times, sorry to say, overweeningly) to attempt to leap the ontological chasm between the bleak world devoid of deity that I inhabit as a simpleminded modern man and the teeming universe of contending agencies that is the home of most of my friends. I know I did not succeed. For I have tried to leap this chasm without submitting to belief, without surrendering to the wisdom of those who would teach the truth about life on the other side. I have tried to imagine what it might be like to live in real relations with the invisible beings they talk of and live with. As a white South African physician friend once said to me: "the difference between you and me is that you talk about witchcraft as if it could be real. I know that it *is* real. And it's helluva dangerous." He knows this as a Christian. I have tried to take seriously what I have heard said and seen done in relation to entities I cannot begin to imagine. I went this far because I eventually came to realize that, had I but a little more skill in logic than, alas, I possess, I could show that all the precepts upon which I have been content to live my life in a world without witches are demonstrably as baseless as those supporting my friends as they make their way through witch-ridden worlds.

And yet we all seem to get along, sort of.

I remain convinced, however, that it is better to live in a world without witches. I remain convinced that my inability to accept the reality of invisible evil forces leaves me free in important material ways: free from the fear that my neighbors can harm me, free from the fear of cosmic agencies of evil, free from the need to supplicate unto equally invisible entities in order to secure the welfare and prosperity of myself and those I love.

Such freedom is a luxury. Its enjoyment, like that of most luxuries, is predicated upon security. Spiritual insecurity becomes so confounding for the secular humanist such as myself when persons who, it seems to me, should have little to fear, whose lives, if not altogether luxurious, are unperturbed by poverty, violence, political oppression, or disease, bow themselves wholeheartedly in obeisance to what seem to me phantasmal deities or profess fear of attack from vengeful spirits or invisible evil forces. The secular humanist impulse is to reduce all these strangenesses to matters of belief, a business that goes on in the mind—itself an entity that emerges from the biochemical quirks of our brains. Our inclination is to frame these issues as matters of cultural and religious identity.

To focus exclusively on identity and religious belief, however, is to miss the distinction between identity and security: a difference between discourses and practices that establish, or celebrate, *who* I am and those that preserve the fact *that* I am. When people are confronted with threats to their existence or fears for the lives and well-being of those they love, observances and rituals that seem to an outsider like expressions of belief and identity are as often as not pressing matters of survival and security. When people are satisfied that they are not about to be killed, they seem more inclined to neglect their spiritual obligations, though when life is lived in real relationships with entities such as those I prefer to call "invisible," these entities tend to impose demands of their own that those who live in relations with them find hard to refuse. What I like to think of as freedom, then, may in fact be the recklessness my friends in Soweto say it is. If I was not something of an outsider, despite our connections, they might also complain that my recklessness threatens their peace and security in relations with invisible beings. They might consider my tolerance of their beliefs a dangerous insult to the powers upon which they know we all depend. I would still like to see the rituals they perform in pursuit of security, however, change into expressions of mere identity in a world free of fear. I don't see this happening.

Appendix 1: The Literature on Soweto—a Brief Excursus

Considering the symbolic significance of the South Western Townships (Soweto) and the bulk of writing about South Africa that was produced in the final decades of apartheid, the literature on the history, politics, and culture of Soweto is sparse. Most of the writing about Soweto focuses on its place in the story of the struggle against apartheid, with little attention to the character of life as it was actually lived there. While the significance of the antiapartheid struggle cannot be denied, equally as significant for this part of the world has been the emergence throughout the twentieth century of distinctive forms of African urban life in Soweto, as in other towns and cities. Representations of this life are scarce in the available literature.

Soweto was a product of bureaucratic power. A former mayor of Johannesburg, Patrick Lewis, under whose stewardship the greater part of Soweto was built (while he was chairman of the Non-European Affairs Committee of the Johannesburg City Council), published an essay in 1966 describing the building of the township as the creation of a "city within a city." In 1990 Lewis's principal lieutenant in the making of Soweto, W. J. P. Carr, the manager of Johannesburg's Non-European Affairs Department (NEAD), published a memoir of the building of the townships. Although self-justifying in the manner of political memoirs everywhere (he particularly bemoans the decline of township administration after the National Party in the central government wrested control of Soweto from the more liberal United Party administration in the Johannesburg City Council in the late 1960s), Carr's book is a good account of the public housing project that became Soweto (Carr 1990). Another bureaucrat's memoirs can be found in the embittered account of one David Grinker, written in 1986 after he was fired from his position of town secretary by the Diepmeadow City Council (one of the three constituent local government units at the time) as a result of disputes with the black mayor (Grinker 1986). Grinker's career as an administrator of the township began in the era of white supremacy and spanned the beginnings of black local self-government. His tale is revealing as an account of the tensions generated between rising black elites and white people in established positions of power, a story that has surely been repeated a thousand times in recent years. For surveys of public policies in relation to Soweto through the early eighties, see Mandy 1984, 173; P. Morris 1980. For an account of Soweto's place in the Johannesburg metropolis at the turn of the millennium, see Beavon 1997.

After the schoolchildren protesting the use of Afrikaans in schools sparked the 1976 Soweto Uprising, Soweto became an internationally recognized symbol of racial injustice and a focus of media attention, generating miles of videotape and acres of newsprint. In the late 1970s and early 1980s a number of more substantial accounts appeared that detailed the origins of the conflict and showed how it boded ill for the future of apartheid; notable among these accounts are those by the journalist John Kane-Berman (1978) and the exiled Trotskyist historian Baruch Hirson (1979). An official commission of inquiry also published a report on the "unrest" (Republic of South Africa 1977). More recently, efforts have been made to capture memories of the uprising through oral history interviews and personal memoirs (Ndlovu 1997; Brink et al. 2001). The Russian Africanist Valentin Gorodnov published an account of Soweto in 1983, which was translated into English in 1988 for the benefit of "freedom lovers and revolutionaries" everywhere. All of this was grist for the "how long will South Africa survive?" mill (R. Johnson 1977), but no one predicted what was going to happen. An evangelical preacher named Clark L. Gittens responded to the 1976 Soweto Uprising by publishing an account of the influence of Satan in Sowetan life and politics but failed to spark a wide debate or concerted response to the problem (Gittens 1978). From the late 1970s through the 1980s, virtually everything written about Soweto was framed in terms of either policies for avoiding further "unrest" or explaining and celebrating "resistance."

Soweto was never particularly popular as a field site for research students and social scientists at local universities, in part because of the restrictions on access imposed by officials and in part because of political turmoil after 1976, so there is little ethnographic or sociological literature about the place. Most of the unpublished theses are limited studies produced for degrees in social work and psychology at the Afrikaans universities. Most of these works contain prefaces bemoaning the impositions of officialdom which restricted the writers to fleeting visits to the township in order to interview generally suspicious and uninformative "informants." They are generally superficial as a result. In the late 1970s, the anthropologist Philip Mayer, one of the preeminent scholars of urban African life at the time, wrote a book-length study of Sowetan social life based upon interviews conducted in 1965 and 1975–76 that contains a wealth of information about local attitudes to class, race, and ethnicity. It was never published (Mayer 1979). By the time he finished it, interest in such subtleties was submerged beneath the commitment to resistance and revolt. Mayer's unpublished Soweto book belongs in the small class of literature on urban African life, to which he was a major contributor in the three-part series entitled *Xhosa in Town: Studies of the Bantu-Speaking Population of East London, Cape Province,* which he edited for Oxford University Press in the early 1960s. Although there are several studies of other black townships (Phillips 1938; Hellmann 1948; Longmore 1959; Mayer 1961; B. Pauw 1963; Wilson and Mafeje 1963; Brandel-Syrier 1978), Mayer's unpublished work is the only general sociological study of Soweto. This genre of sociological and anthropological writing, based as it was upon fieldwork by white people among people who were presumed culturally different from Whites, was killed by the upsurge of political resistance to a political order that insisted upon difference. It was replaced by a form of social history, centered in the History Workshop at the University of the Witwatersrand, which was composed predominantly of white scholars whose interest in the ordinary lives of ordinary black people was strongly influenced by the political imperative of revealing the omnipresence of resistance through time and, though its most sophisticated practitioners denied it, giving "voice to the voiceless" (Delius and Bozzoli 1991). (For a general survey of writing about Africans in South African cities, see Maylam 1995.) The History Workshop is responsible for the best general work on Soweto, a documentary video and book, both entitled *Soweto, a History,* which appeared in the mid- to late 1990s.

In 1980, the Urban Foundation (an organization that was founded by liberal business leaders in the wake of the 1976 Soweto Uprising and that financed, among other things, the development of middle-class "suburbs" in Soweto) published a detailed survey of conditions in Soweto highlighting the need for improvement (P. Morris 1980). For nearly two decades this was the most accurate and comprehensive source of information about the township. In 1997, when the newly elected local government found itself with no idea of such basic information as how many people lived in the region, the Department of Sociology at the University of the Witwatersrand was commissioned by the new mayor of Soweto to produce a demographic and social survey (A. Morris 1999b; University of the Witwatersrand Department of Sociology 1997). Although somewhat limited by its research brief, the Wits Survey provides by far the most detailed contemporary picture of Sowetan life and is used extensively in this book. The picture that emerges from the Wits Survey is one of a working-class city where life is tough but not impossible.

Some glimpses of the character of life in the township can be gleaned from creative literature and memoirs, such as Mzamane 1982, 1986; Sikakane 1977. Most of the creative literature by Sowetan writers was written at a time when committed artists saw their task as one of advancing the struggle by means of "culture," with the result that, as Njabulo Ndebele has pointed out, "the writing's probing into the South African experience has been largely superficial" (1994, 28). Ndebele's own stories, published in a collection entitled *Fools, and Other Stories* (1983), though not, for the most part, set in Soweto, do give a sense of the breadth of life, particularly because he writes about the tensions that emerge around class divisions within township society.

A generally more vibrant picture of township life emerges from the writings of an earlier generation of black writers associated with *Drum* magazine, although they were focused more upon the life of Sophiatown, the polyglot, privately owned black slum in Johannesburg's western suburbs, than official "townships" like Soweto. The finest of these writers was Can Themba (Themba 1985). For me, the images of the "swarming, cacophonous, strutting, brawling, vibrating life" (Themba 1985, 104) conjured up for earlier eras by writers like Themba, or Nat Nakasa, Bloke Modisane, and Modikwe Dikobe, still ring true for Soweto today. I am not aware of any novels or stories published in the 1990s that convey as strong a sense of the texture of life as it is lived in Soweto. In the 1990s, the publishers who brought the struggle literature into the world went broke, and the previously vibrant genres of township struggle theater and poetry (whose crowning achievement was the international hit musical *Sarafina*) died out. At the end of that decade, Mzwakhe Mbuli, the "People's Poet," whose strident verses accompanied by the danceable beats of his band had been emblematic of the era of the struggle, was in prison serving a sentence for bank robbery. As for the people, they were glued to their televisions watching American soap operas such as the *Bold and the Beautiful* (or, as my sardonic friend Nono calls it, "The Bold and the Bloody Fools") and locally produced African-language soap operas featuring situations representing the glittering lives of the new black elites in all the contortions of sex and intrigue made popular the world over by their American progenitors.

Photographic portraits of township life in Soweto can be found in the works of Peter Magubane (Magubane, Bristow, and Motjuwadi 1990) and Santu Mofokeng (Carlin 1990). See also Lanning, Roake, and Horning 2003. Mofokeng's recent work is his project entitled *Chasing Shadows*, which is the first major photographic exploration of the spiritual life of black South Africa and has been an inspiration for this book.

Appendix 2: The Thohoyandou Declaration on Ending Witchcraft Violence, Issued by the Commission on Gender Equality

10 September 1998

WE, THE PARTICIPANTS IN THE NATIONAL CONFERENCE ON WITCHCRAFT VIO-LENCE convened by the Commission on Gender Equality in Thohoyandou, Venda, from 6 to 10 September 1998.

SHOCKED AND HORRIFIED by the misery suffered by survivors of witchcraft violence, so graphically conveyed in the first hand testimonies made by fellow participants who survived such scourges on the first day of this conference

DEEPLY CONCERNED by:

- the escalation in witchcraft violence and the flagrant violation of human rights which it represents;
- its disproportionate effects on women, the aged, and the weakest members of our society;
- the particular effects of witchcraft violence on the disabled, whose disabilities are frequently ascribed to witchcraft;
- the escalation in witchcraft violence related to HIV/AIDS;
- the silence which surrounds witchcraft violence because it often occurs in remote rural areas and is deemed less urgent than urban-based crime such as bank robberies and car high jacks;
- the apparent inability of the criminal justice system to address this problem;
- and its negative effects on development which add to the enormous burdens on women, who constitute the majority of the poor and the dispossessed.

FIRMLY BELIEVING that at the heart of democracy is the right of all men and women to live without fear of threat to their lives;

RECOGNISING that this is a national problem which is by no means confined to the Northern Province;

CONDEMN such violence in the strongest possible terms;

COMMEND the bold efforts which have been made by the provincial government, NGOs, religious groups and other stakeholders in the Northern Province to confront the problem by taking up the recommendations of the Commission of Inquiry into Witchcraft Violence and Ritual Murders in the Northern Province (the Ralushai report); launching public education campaigns and intervening to prevent displacements;

FURTHER COMMEND a group of perpetrators and survivors of witchcraft violence who met in the wings of the conference, under the mediation of the Commission on Gender Equality and religious groups, for showing us that reconciliation is possible;

COMMIT ourselves, individually, and as organisations, to adopt a visible leadership stance in ending the scourge of witchcraft violence through signing the attached statement of commitment; and

RECOMMEND THE ADOPTION OF A NATIONAL PLAN OF ACTION FOR ERADICATING WITCHCRAFT VIOLENCE INCLUDING THE FOLLOWING KEY COMPONENTS:

DECLARING THE ERADICATION OF WITCHRAFT VIOLENCE A NATIONAL PRIORITY at the highest political level is crucial to ensuring that the issue is given the prominence it deserves. We request that the Minister of Safety and Security, who will close the conference on behalf of the Deputy President, convey this recommendation to the President for his immediate consideration.

ECONOMIC EMPOWERMENT OF WOMEN: poverty and illiteracy, particularly among women, are a major contributory factor to the superstition and false accusations, which lead to witchcraft violence. The eradication of poverty and illiteracy and achievement of gender equality are central to all strategies for ending this scourge.

STRENGTHENING THE RESPONSE BY THE SOUTH AFRICAN POLICE SERVICE: The current response by the police to witchcraft violence is inadequate. Inves-

tigations into witchcraft violence are often poorly conducted, because of
the reluctance of the police to deal with the issue as well as the fear by witnesses to come forward with evidence. We recommended to the Minister of
Safety and Security and to provincial MEC's for Safety and Security that
the following specific measures be adopted as soon as possible:

- NATIONAL CRIME PREVENTION STRATEGY: Inclusion of the eradication of
  witchcraft violence as a priority at national as well as at provincial level
  in the NCPS so that it is given prominence and a specific budget allocation.
- TRAINING: Special training for police in the handling of witchcraft violence
  as part of the human rights, investigative, crime prevention and intelligence
  training which they receive.
- SPECIAL INVESTIGATIVE UNITS: the establishment of specially trained, dedicated units for investigating witchcraft violence.
- THE HANDLING OF SURVIVORS AT POLICE STATIONS: Survivors of witchcraft violence who seek refuge and help at police stations are often forced
  to wait long hours and are treated with indifference. Procedures and physical arrangements at police stations, especially in areas which are afflicted
  by this problem, should be reviewed to ensure that survivors are treated
  with dignity and are encouraged to lodge their cases.
- HELP LINE: Consideration should be given to establishing a help line for
  survivors which they can access at the nearest police station they are able
  to reach.
- STRENGTHENING POLICE-COMMUNITY CO-OPERATION in ending witchcraft
  violence can be achieved through establishing Community Police Fora
  (where these do not exist); strengthening existing CPF's; the offer of rewards to those who come forward with evidence; and conducting rallies
  at which police interact with the community on this issue.
- PREVENTIVE APPROACHES: Better relations with the community should enable the police to take pre-emptive measures to stop witchcraft violence
  before it occurs.
- ADEQUATE RESOURCES: Because witchcraft violence often occurs in remote areas with no telecommunications, effective policing of the problem
  requires considerable human and financial resources. It is crucial that
  adequate resources be allocated at national and provincial level for this
  purpose.

LEGISLATIVE REFORM: The Witchcraft Suppression Act 3 of 1957 falls short
of a pragmatic approach to the issue of witchcraft, and may in fact be fu-
elling witchcraft violence. Legislative reform is required as a matter of ur-

gency. We call on the government to repeal the Witchcraft Suppression Act
and introduce:

(1) Legislation dealing with the issue of witchcraft, so that those who are engaged in harmful practices can be separated out from those who are falsely
accused; and so that those who make false accusations can be brought to
book. Such legislation would, inter alia,
    • Represent a paradigm shift from the current act which operates from a
    premise that denies the belief in witchcraft; leading to the Issue being
    dealt with outside the criminal justice system.
    • Provide clear definitions for words and concepts such as "witch," "wiz-
    ard" and "witchcraft."
    • Introduce structures to deal with certain witchcraft-related complaints
    by means of conciliation and mediation, thereby attempting to resolve
    underlying tensions.

(2) Legislation to control the practice of traditional healing: which should be
accompanied by a Code of Conduct to ensure that the practice of traditional medicine is separated from sinister practices.

The conference requested the Commission on Gender Equality to convene
a meeting with the Ministry of Justice and other interest groups to initiate
the above legislative reform in October.

VICTIM SUPPORT: At present, there is very little information on what victim
support structures exist, and how accessible these are to survivors of witchcraft violence. We urge that:

• The Department of Welfare and/or NGOs involved in this area undertake
an audit of what facilities exist, and how accessible these are to survivors of
witchcraft violence;
• Survivors of witchcraft violence be included in the Department of Welfare's
Victim Empowerment Programme;
• Mobile Counselling Centers be established to assist those affected by
witchcraft violence.

REINTEGRATION AND RECONCILIATION: Thousands of victims of witchcraft violence have been displaced from their homes and have suffered losses and
damages to their property. Such victims have often lived with the terrible
burden of their memories, without having had the opportunity to be coun-

selled. On the other hand, many perpetrators are living with their guilt. They are looking for ways in which to come forward and seek forgiveness. We call on the government, religious leaders, traditional leaders, independent bodies and NGOs to find ways of reuniting communities which have been divided by witchcraft violence, drawing on the experiences and methods of the Truth and Reconciliation Commission. The following specific measures—many of which emerged from the meeting between survivors and perpetrators in the wings of the conference—are proposed:

- Conducting research on how such reintegration can best be approached.
- Launching pilot project from which lessons can be drawn.
- Providing counselling to survivors and perpetrators.
- Facilitating the return of displaced persons to their homes.
- Assisting survivors and perpetrators to become economically active; and in particular explore the possibility of joint projects between the two.
- Lobby for a special fund for survivors to be awarded reparations.
- Monitor the situation to ensure that violence does not re-occur.

PUBLIC EDUCATION: We recommend the adoption of a comprehensive public education and awareness campaign, which builds on the work already started by the government and NGOs in the Northern Province, and includes the following components:

- Getting perpetrators of the violence (including those who have served prison terms) who have shown contrition to give talks at schools and at other youth fora, discouraging other youth from engaging in such violence.
- Use of drama to highlight the trauma that surrounds witchcraft violence.
- Including education on witchcraft violence in Curricula 2005.
- Launching a pilot project in one of the worst affected areas including videos, debates, pamphlets, the media, essays, competitions etc from which lessons could be learned and extended to the broader public education campaign.

MONITORING AND EVALUATION: We propose that the Commission on Gender Equality convene a task team of all relevant stakeholders to take forward the recommendations made at this conference and to monitor their implementation. This task team should report back on its work at a similar conference in two years time, when it is our fervent hope that there will have been a substantial reduction in witchcraft violence.

Selected Bibliography

Abdool Karim, S. S. 1993. Traditional Healers and AIDS Prevention. *South African Medical Journal* 83(6): 423–425.

Abrahams, Roger D. 1970. A Performance-Centered Approach to Gossip. *Man*, n.s., 5(2): 290–301.

Abt Associates. 2000. *The Impending Catastrophe: A Resource Book on the Emerging HIV/AIDS Epidemic in South Africa.* Johannesburg: Henry J. Kaiser Foundation.

Adler, Glen, and Jonny Steinberg. 2000. *From Comrades to Citizens: The South African Civics Movement and the Transition to Democracy.* Basingstoke, UK: Macmillan.

African National Congress. 1994. *A National Health Plan for South Africa.* (Prepared by the ANC with the technical support of WHO and UNICEF.) Johannesburg: African National Congress.

———. 1996. Statement to the Truth and Reconciliation Commission. Johannesburg: Department of Publicity and Information, African National Congress. www.anc .org.za/ancdocs/misc/trctoc.html.

———. 1997a. Eighty-five Years Old and Still in the Harness (Statement on Anniversary of ANC's Founding). Johannesburg: Department of Publicity and Information, African National Congress. January 8, 1997. http://www.anc.org.za/ancdocs/pr/ 1997/pro108.html

———. 1997b. Organisational Democracy and Discipline in the Movement. African National Congress, Johannesburg. http://www.anc.org.za/ancdocs/discussion/ discipline.html.

———. 1997c. Third Force Allegations against the National Party. April 9, 1997. Johannesburg: Department of Information and Publicity, African National Congress. http://www.anc.org.za/ancdocs/pr/1997/pro409a.html.

———. 1997d. TRC Hearings for Security Members. Johannesburg: African National Congress, Department of Publicity and Information. http://www.anc.org.za/ ancdocs/pr/1997/pr1014a.html.

———. 1997e. The Withdrawal of the National Party from the TRC Process. May 16, 1997. Johannesburg: Department of Publicity and Information, African National Congress. http://www.anc.org.za/ancdocs/pr/1997/pro516c.html.

————. 1998. Submission of the African National Congress to the Truth and Reconciliation Commission in Reply to the Section 30 (2) of Act 34 of 1996 on the TRC "Findings on the African National Congress."

————. 2000. Commission for Religious Affairs. *The ANC and Religion.* Johannesburg: African National Congress.

Anderson, A. M. 1931. *Ukanya: Life Story of an African Girl.* Anderson Indiana: Warner Press.

Anderson, Allan. 1991. *Moya: The Holy Spirit in an African Context.* Pretoria: University of South Africa Press.

————. 1992a. *Bazalwane: African Pentecostals in South Africa.* Pretoria: University of South Africa Press.

————. 1992b. Frederick Modise and the International Pentecost Church: An African Messiah? *Missionalia, the Journal of the Southern African Missiological Society* 20(3): 186–200.

————. 1993a. African Pentecostalism and the Ancestors: Confrontation or Compromise? *Missionalia, the Journal of the Southern African Missiological Society* 21(1): 26–39.

————. 1993b. Prophetic Healing and the Growth of the Zion Christian Church in South Africa. Paper presented at the "New Religious Movements and Independent Churches" conference, July 1993.

————. 1997. African Pentecostal Churches and Concepts of Power. Paper presented at the Africa Forum, Council of Churches for Britain and Ireland, April 1997.

————. 1999. The Lekganyanes and Prophecy in the Zion Christian Church. *Journal of Religion in Africa* 29(3): 285–312.

————. 2000a. Pentecostals and Politics in South Africa: Public Space and Invisible Forces. In *Imaginaires politiques et Pentecôtismes: Afrique/Amérique Latine,* ed. André Corten and André Mary. Paris: Karthala.

————. 2000b. *Zion and Pentecost: The Spirituality and Experience of Pentecostal and Zionist/Apostolic Churches in South Africa.* Pretoria: University of South Africa Press.

————. 2001a. *African Reformation: African Initiated Christianity in the 20th Century.* Trenton: Africa World Press.

————. 2001b. Pentecostals and Apartheid in South Africa during Ninety Years, 1908–1998. *Cyberjournal for Pentecostal-Charismatic Research* 7. http://artsweb.bham.ac .uk/aanderson/Main/papers.htm.

Anderson, Allan, and Gerald J. Pillay. 1997. The Segregated Spirit: The Pentecostals. In Elphick and Davenport 1997.

Anderson, Neil, Sharmila Mhatre, Nzwakie Mqotsi, and Marina Penderis. 2000. *Beyond Victims and Villains: Culture of Sexual Violence in South Johannesburg.* Johannesburg: CIETafrica.

Andersson, Jens. 2002. Sorcery in the Era of "Henry IV": Kinship, Mobility and Mortality in Buhera District, Zimbabwe. *Journal of the Royal Anthropological Institute,* n.s., 8: 425–449.

Anstey, Gillian. 1997. Schoolboys in a Class of Their Own. *Sunday Times* (Johannesburg) Internet ed., May 1, 1997. http://www.suntimes.co.za/edu/educate/girlvboy.htm.

Apter, Andrew. 1993. Atinga Revisited: Yoruba Witchcraft and the Cocoa Economy, 1950–1951. In Comaroff and Comaroff 1993.

Aristotle. 1953. *The Ethics of Aristotle.* Ed. and trans. J. A. K. Thomson Harmondsworth: Penguin Books.

Ashby, G. 1987. Demonic Powers from a High Church Perspective. In *Like a Roaring Lion . . . : Essays on the Bible, the Church and Demonic Powers,* ed. Pieter De Villiers. Pretoria: C. B. Powell Bible Centre.

Ashforth, Adam. 1990. *The Politics of Official Discourse in Twentieth-Century South Africa.* Oxford: Clarendon Press.

———. 1991a. War Party: Buthelezi and Apartheid. *Transition* 52: 56–90.

———. 1991b. The Xhosa Cattle-Killing and the Politics of Memory. *Sociological Forum* 6(3): 579–592.

———. 1992. *Images, Power, and the Politics of Representation: Notes from the South of Africa.* Indian Ocean Centre for Peace Studies Occasional Papers. Perth.

———. 1993. A Letter from Soweto. *Dissent,* Fall, 419–423.

———. 1996a. Down the Old Potch Road to Lekoka Street: State Power and Social Space in Soweto. *Review of Architectural Theory* 1(2): 60–78.

———. 1996b. Of Secrecy and the Commonplace: Witchcraft and Power in Soweto. *Social Research* 64(3): 1183–1234.

———. 1997. Lineaments of the Political Geography of State Formation in Twentieth-Century South Africa. *Journal of Historical Sociology* 10(2): 101–126.

———. 1998a. Reflections on Spiritual Insecurity in a Modern African City (Soweto). *African Studies Review* 41(3): 36–67.

———. 1998b. Witchcraft, Violence, and Democracy in the New South Africa. *Cahiers d'Études Africaine* 38(2–4): 505–532.

———. 1999. Weighing Manhood in Soweto. *Codesria Bulletin* 3/4: 51–58.

———. 2000a. *Madumo, a Man Bewitched.* Chicago: University of Chicago Press.

———. 2000b. Soweto Witch Project. *Transition* 81/82: 22–51.

———. 1995. State Power, Violence, Everyday Life: Soweto. Working Paper no. 210, Center for Studies of Social Change, New School for Social Research, New York.

———. 2001a. AIDS, Witchcraft, and the Problem of Public Power in Post-apartheid South Africa. School of Social Science Occasional Paper no. 10, Institute for Advanced Study, Princeton.

———. 2001b. On Living in a World with Witches: Everyday Epistemology and Spiritual Insecurity in a Modern African City (Soweto). In Moore and Sanders 2001b.

Ashton, E. H. 1943. *Medicine, Magic, and Sorcery among the Southern Sotho.* Rondebosch: University of Cape Town.

Assad, Talal. 1986. The Concept of Cultural Translation in British Social Anthropology. In *Writing Culture: The Poetics and Politics of Ethnography,* ed. James Clifford and George E. Marcus. Berkeley and Los Angeles: University of California Press.

Auslander, Mark. 1993. "Open the Wombs!" The Symbolic Politics of Modern Ngoni Witchfinding. In Comaroff and Comaroff 1993.

Austen, Ralph. 1993. The Moral Economy of Witchcraft: An Essay in Comparative History. In Comaroff and Comaroff 1993.

Bacon, Francis. 1955. Of Envy. In *Selected Writings of Francis Bacon,* ed. Hugh G. Dick. The Modern Library. New York: Random House.

Baier, Annette C. 1986. Trust and Antitrust. *Ethics* 96(2): 231–260.

———. 1992. Trusting People. *Philosophical Perspectives* 6: 137–153.

Baleta, A. 1998. South Africa to Bring Traditional Healers into Mainstream Medicine. *Lancet* 352(9127): 554.

Bannerman-Richter, Gabriel. 1982. *The Practice of Witchcraft in Ghana.* Winona, MN: Apollo Books.

———. 1984. *Don't Cry, My Baby, Don't Cry! Autobiography of an African Witch.* Winona, MN: Apollo Books.

Bate, Stuart C. 1995. *Inculturation and Healing: Coping-Healing in South African Christianity.* Pietermaritzburg, RSA: Cluster Publications.

Beattie, John. 1970. On Understanding Ritual. In *Rationality,* ed. Wilson Bryan. New York: Harper and Row.

Beattie, John, and John Middleton. 1969. *Spirit Mediumship and Society in Africa.* New York: Africana Publishing Corp.

Beavon, Keith. 1997. Johannesburg: A City and Metropolitan Area in Transformation. In *The Urban Challenge in Africa: Growth and Management of Its Large Cities,* ed. Rakodi Carole. Tokyo, New York, and Paris: United Nations University Press.

Becken, H. Jürgen. 1989. African Independent Churches as Healing Communities. In Oosthuizen et al. 1989.

Becker, Heike. 2001. "I Am the Man": Historical and Contemporary Perspectives on Masculinities in Northern Namibia. Paper presented at the "AIDS in Context" conference, University of the Witwatersrand, April 4–7, 2001.

Behrend, Heike, and Ute Luig. 1999. *Spirit Possession, Modernity, and Power in Africa.* Oxford: James Currey; Kampala: Fountain Publishers; Cape Town: David Philip; Madison: University of Wisconsin Press.

Beidelman, Thomas O. 1974. Social Theory and the Study of Christian Missionaries in Africa. *Africa* 44: 235–249.

Bekker, J. C. 1989. *Seymour's Customary Law in Southern Africa.* 5th ed. Cape Town: Juta and Co.

Bekker, Simon, and Richard Gordon Humphries. 1985. *From Control to Confusion: The Changing Role of Administration Boards in South Africa, 1971–1983.* Pietermaritzburg, RSA: Shuter and Shooter.

Berger, Peter L. 1967. *The Sacred Canopy: Elements of a Sociological Theory of Religion.* Garden City, NY: Doubleday.

Berglund, Axel-Ivar. 1976. *Zulu Thought-Patterns and Symbolism.* Bloomington and Indianapolis: Indiana University Press.

Bever, Edward. 2000. Witchcraft Fears and Psychosocial Factors in Disease. *Journal of Interdisciplinary History* 30(4): 573–590.

Bezwoda, W. R., H. Colvin, and J. Lehoka. 1997. Transcultural and Language Problems in Communicating with Cancer Patients in Southern Africa. *Annual of the New York Academy of Science* 809: 119–132.

Bhabha, Homi. 1994. *The Location of Culture.* London and New York: Routledge.

Bhat, R. B., and T. V. Jacobs. 1995. Traditional Herbal Medicine in Transkei. *Journal of Ethnopharmacology* 48(1): 7–12.

Biko, Steve. 1978. *Black Consciousness in South Africa*. Ed. Arnold Millard. New York: Vintage Books.

Bishop, Craig. 1997. *Muti* Passes the Science Test. *Electronic Mail and Guardian* (Johannesburg) Internet ed., October 2, 1997. http://www.web.co.za/mg/news/97oct2/200c-muti.html.

Blackett-Sliep, Y. 1989. Traditional Healers and the Primary Health Care Nurse. *Nursing RSA Verpleging* 4(11): 43–44.

Blankley, William, and Robin Arnold. 2001. Public Understanding of Science in South Africa: Aiming for Better Intervention Strategies. *South African Journal of Science* 97(3/4): 65–70.

Bleek, Wolf. 1976. Witchcraft, Gossip and Death: A Social Drama. *Man*, n.s., 11(4): 526–541.

Blohm, H. 1935. The African Explanation of Witchcraft. Part 6, Xhosa. *Africa* 8: 522–525.

Bodemer, W. 1987. Satanism, Witchcraft and the Occult: A Psychiatrist's View. In *Like a Roaring Lion . . . : Essays on the Bible, the Church and Demonic Powers*, ed. Pieter De Villiers. Pretoria: C. B. Powell Bible Centre.

Bodenstein, J. W. 1977. Toxicity of Traditional Herbal Remedies. *South African Medical Journal* 52(20): 790.

Bond, George Clement, and Diane Ciekawy. 2001. *Witchcraft Dialogues: Anthropological and Philosophical Exchanges*. Athens: Ohio University Press.

Bond, Patrick, George Dor, and Greg Ruiters. 1999. Transformation in Infrastructure Policy from Apartheid to Democracy. Background Research Series, Municipal Services Project, Queens University, Kingston. http://qsilver.queensu.ca/~mspadmin/pages/Project_Publications/Papers/Transfor.pdf.

Bongmba, Elias Kifon. 2001. *African Witchcraft and Otherness: A Philosophical and Theological Critique of Intersubjective Relations*. Albany: State University of New York Press.

Bonner, P. 1993. The Russians on the Reef, 1947–57: Urbanisation, Gang Warfare and Ethnic Mobilisation. In *Apartheid's Genesis, 1934–62*, ed. P. Bonner, P. Delius, and D. Posel. Johannesburg: Ravan Press.

Bonner, Philip, and Lauren Segal. 1998. *Soweto: A History*. Johannesburg: Maskew Miller Longman.

Booyens, J. H. 1982. Observations on the Opinions of Black Matriculants on the Medical Capabilities of Different Types of Medical Practitioners. *South African Medical Journal* 61(21): 795–797.

———. 1989. Aspekte van populêre opvattinge oor diareesiektes onder Tswanasprekende stedelinge [Aspects of the popular attitude about diarrhea among Tswana-speaking urbanites]. *Curationis* 12(3/4): 11–16.

Booysen, Susan. 1994. Democracy, Liberation and the Vote in South Africa's First Democratic Election: The Matla Trust Voter Education Survey. Paper presented at the "Democracy: Popular Precedents, Popular Practice and Popular Culture" history workshop, University of the Witwatersrand, July 13–15, 1994.

Borer, Tristan Ann. 1998. *Challenging the State: Churches as Political Actors in South Africa, 1980–1994.* Notre Dame: University of Notre Dame Press.

Bornman, E., R. van Eeden, and M. Wentzel. 1998. *Violence in South Africa: A Variety of Perspectives.* Pretoria: Human Sciences Research Council.

Bosch, D. J. 1987. The Problem of Evil in Africa: A Survey of African Views on Witchcraft and of the Response of the Christian Church. In *Like a Roaring Lion . . . : Essays on the Bible, the Church and Demonic Powers,* ed. Pieter De Villiers. Pretoria: C. B. Powell Bible Centre.

Botha, B. M., and C. M. McCrindle. 2000. An Appropriate Method for Extracting the Insect Repellent Citronellol from an Indigenous Plant (*Pelargonium Graveolens L'Her*) for Potential Use by Resource-Limited Animal Owners. *Journal of the South African Veterinary Association* 71(2): 103–105.

Botman, H. Russel, and Robin M. Peterson. 1996. *To Remember and to Heal: Theological and Psychological Reflections on Truth and Reconciliation.* Cape Town: Human and Rousseau.

Bradshaw, Debbie, Rob Dorrington, David Bourne, Ria Laubscher, Nadine Nannan, and Ian Timaeus. 2001. AIDS Mortality in South Africa. Paper presented at the "AIDS in Context" conference, University of the Witwatersrand, April 4–7, 2001.

Brandel-Syrier, Mia. 1962. *Black Woman in Search of God.* London: Lutterworth.

———. 1978. *"Coming Through": The Search for a New Cultural Identity.* Johannesburg: McGraw-Hill.

Brewer, John D. 1994. *Black and Blue: Policing in South Africa.* Oxford: Clarendon Press.

Brink, Esabé, Ghandi Malungane, Steve Lebelo, Dumisani Ntshangane, and Sue Krige. 2001. *Soweto 16 June 1976, It All Started with a Dog. . . .* Cape Town: Kwela.

Brookes, Edgar H. 1927. *The History of Native Policy in South Africa from 1830 to the Present Day.* Pretoria: J. L. van Schaik.

Brooks, Alan, and Jeremy Brickhill. 1980. *The Whirlwind before the Storm: The Origins and Development of the Uprising in Soweto and the Rest of South Africa from June to December 1976.* London: International Defence and Aid Fund for Southern Africa.

Brooks, Peter. 2000. *Troubling Confession: Speaking Guilt in Law and Literature.* Chicago: University of Chicago Press.

Broster, Joan A., and Herbert C. Bourn. 1981. *Amagqirha: Religion, Magic, and Medicine in Transkei.* Cape Town: Via Afrika.

Brown, J. Tom. 1926. *Among the Bantu Nomads: A Record of Forty Years Spent among the Bechuana, a Numerous & Famous Branch of the Central South African Bantu, with the First Full Description of Their Ancient Customs, Manners & Beliefs.* With an introduction by A. R. Radcliffe-Brown. London: Seeley Service.

Brown, Joshua, Patrick Manning, Karen Shapiro, Jon Wiener, Belinda Bozzoli, and Peter Delius. 1991. *History from South Africa: Alternative Visions and Practices.* Philadelphia: Temple University Press.

Brown, Peter. 1995. *Authority and the Sacred: Aspects of the Christianisation of the Roman World.* Cambridge: Cambridge University Press.

Brownlee, Charles Pacalt. 1916. *Reminiscences of Karir Life and History and Other Papers.* 2nd ed. Lovedale: Lovedale Press.

Bryant, A. T. 1929. *Olden Times in Zululand and Natal, Containing Earlier Political History of the Eastern-Nguni Clans.* London: Longmans, Green, and Co.

———. 1949. *The Zulu People, as They Were before the White Man Came.* Pietermaritzburg: Shuter and Shooter.

———. 1970. *Zulu Medicine and Medicine-Men.* Cape Town: Struik.

Bührmann, M. V. 1977. Xhosa Diviners as Psychotherapists. *Psychotherapeia* 31: 17–20.

———. 1978. Tentative Views on Dream Therapy by Xhosa Diviners. *Journal of Analytical Psychology* 23(2): 105–121.

———. 1983. Some Psychological Factors in Particular Crimes of Violence in the Black Man. *South African Journal of Criminal Law and Criminology* 7(2): 252–258.

———. 1986. *Living in Two Worlds: Communications between a White Healer and Her Black Counterparts.* Wilmette: Chiron.

———. 1987a. The Feminine in Witchcraft: Part I. *Journal of Analytic Psycholology* 32(2): 139–156.

———. 1987b. The Feminine in Witchcraft: Part II. *Journal of Analytic Psycholology* 32(3): 257–277.

———. 1989. Religion and Healing: The African Experience. In Oosthuizen et al. 1989.

———. 2002. Witchcraft, Witchcraft Beliefs, and the Black People of South Africa. *South African Medical Journal* 68(9): 668–671.

Bunn, David. 1996. The Brown Serpent of the Rocks: Bushman Arrow Toxins in the Dutch and British Imaginations, 1735–1850. In *Transgressing Boundaries: New Directions in the Study of Culture in Africa,* ed. B. Cooper and A. Steyn. Cape Town: University of Cape Town Press.

Burke, Kenneth. 1969. *A Grammar of Motives.* Berkeley and Los Angeles: University of California Press.

Burke, Timothy. 1996. *Lifebuoy Men, Lux Women: Commodification, Consumption, and Cleanliness in Modern Zimbabwe.* Durham, NC: Duke University Press.

Buur, Lars. 1999. Monumental History: Visibility and Invisibility in the Work of the South African Truth and Reconciliation Commission. Paper presented at "The TRC: Commissioning the Past" conference, University of the Witwatersrand, June 11–14, 1999.

Bye, S. N., and M. F. Dutton. 1991. The Inappropriate Use of Traditional Medicines in South Africa. *Journal of Ethnopharmacology* 34(2/3): 253–259.

Bynum, Caroline. 1999. Why All the Fuss about the Body? A Medievalist's Perspective. In *Beyond the Cultural Turn: New Directions in the Study of Society and Culture,* ed. Victoria Bonnell and Lynn Hunt. Berkeley and Los Angeles: University of California Press.

Calderwood, D. M., and Paul H. Connell. 1952. Minimum Standards of Accommodation for the Housing of Non-Europeans in South Africa. *Bulletin of the National Building Research Institute* 8: 1–23.

Caldwell, John C., Pat Caldwell, and Pat Quiggin. 1989. The Social Context of AIDS in Sub-Saharan Africa. *Population and Development Review* 15(2): 185–234.

Caldwell, John C., I. O. Orubuloye, and Pat Caldwell. 1992. Underreaction to AIDS in
Sub-Saharan Africa. *Social Science and Medicine* 34(11): 1169–1182.

Callaway, Henry. 1970. *The Religious System of the Amazulu.* Cape Town: Struik. (Orig.
pub. 1870, Lovedale Press.)

Caltreaux, Karen. 1996. *Standard and Non-standard African Language Varieties in the
Urban Areas of South Africa: Main Report of the STANON Research Programme.*
Pretoria: Human Sciences Research Council.

Campbell, James T. 1995. *Songs of Zion: The African Methodist Episcopal Church in
the United States and South Africa.* New York: Oxford University Press.

Campbell, Susan Schuster. 1998. *Called to Heal: African Shamanic Healers.* Twin
Lakes, WI: Lotus Press.

Cargill, Jenny. 2000. Black Economic Empowerment 1999. Business Map South Africa.
http://www.bmap.co.za/bee/sample_bee_annual.html.

Carlin, John. 1990. Getting by in Soweto: Santo Mofokeng. *Independent Magazine,*
February.

Carlson, Dean W. 1998. Towards the Spiritual Mapping of Dobsonville, Soweto. http://
www.ribbett.com/ghm/pdf_docs/Dobsonville%20Sowto.pdf.

Carr, W. J. P. 1990. *Soweto: Its Creation, Life and Decline.* Johannesburg: South African
Institute of Race Relations.

Casalis, Eugene. 1861. *The Basutos; Or, Twenty Years in South Africa.* London: James
Nisbet.

Case, Anne, and Angus Deaton. 1998. Large Cash Transfers to the Elderly in South
Africa. *Economic Journal* 108(450): 1330–1361.

Centre for Health Policy. 1991. *Traditional Healers in Health Care in South Africa: A
Proposal.* Johannesburg: University of the Witwatersrand, Department of Community Health.

Chanock, Martin. 2001. *The Making of South African Legal Culture, 1902–1936: Fear,
Favour, and Prejudice.* Cambridge: Cambridge University Press.

Chavunduka, G. L. 1980. Witchcraft and the Law in Zimbabwe. *Zambezia* 8(2): 129–147.

———. 2001. The Reality of Witchcraft. *African Legal Studies* 2: 163–169.

Cheetham, R. W., and J. A. Griffiths. 1980. Changing Patterns in Psychiatry in Africa:
With Special Reference to Southern Africa. *South African Medical Journal* 58(4):
166–168.

———. 1982. Sickness and Medicine—an African Paradigm. *South African Medical
Journal* 62(25): 954–956.

Cheetham, W. S., and R. J. Cheetham. 1976. Concepts of Mental Illness amongst the
Rural Xhosa People in South Africa. *Australian and New Zealand Journal of Psychiatry* 10(1): 39–45.

Chidester, David. 1991. *Religions of South Africa.* London and New York: Routledge.

———. 2002. Christianity and Evolution. In *The Architect and the Scaffold: Evolution
and Education in South Africa,* ed. Wilmot James and Lynne Wilson. Cape Town:
Human Sciences Research Council and New Africa Books.

Chidester, David, Chirevo Kwenda, Robert Petty, Judy Tobler, and Darrel Wratten.
1997a. *African Traditional Religion in South Africa: An Annotated Bibliography.*
Westport and London: Greenwood Press.

Chidester, David, Judy Tobler, and Darrel Wratten. 1997b. *Christianity in South Africa: An Annotated Bibliography.* Westport and London: Greenwood Press.

Chilivumbo, Alifeyo B. 1977. The Social Basis of Illness: A Search of Therapeutic Meaning. In *Society in Southern Africa,* ed. B. Helm. Cape Town: Association for Sociology in South Africa.

Chipfakacha, V. G. 1994. The Role of Culture in Primary Health Care: Two Case Studies. *South African Medical Journal* 84(12): 860–862.

———. 1997. STD/HIV/AIDS Knowledge, Beliefs and Practices of Traditional Healers in Botswana. *AIDS Care* 9(4): 417–425.

Chisholm, Linda. 2003. Religion, Science and Evolution in South Africa: The Politics and Construction of the Revised National Curriculum Statement for Schools (Grades R–9). In *The Architect and the Scaffold: Evolution and Education in South Africa,* ed. Wilmot James and Lynne Wilson. Cape Town: Human Sciences Research Council and New Africa Books.

Chris Hani Baragwanath Hospital. 2002. Chris Hani Baragwanath Hospital Statistics for 2000/2001. Chris Hani Baragwanath Hospital, Johannesburg. http://www.chris hanibaragwanathhospital.co.za/statistics.shtml.

Ciekawy, Diane. 1997. Policing Religious Practice in Contemporary Coastal Kenya. *Political and Legal Anthropology Review* 20(1): 62–72.

Cillié Commission. 1978. *South Africa in Travail: The Disturbances of 1976/77.* (Evidence presented by the South Africa Institute of Race Relations to the Cillié Commission of Inquiry into the Riots at Soweto and Other Places during June 1976.) Johannesburg: South African Institute of Race Relations.

Cocks, Michelle, and Anthony Dold. 2000. The Role of "African Chemists" in the Health Care System of the Eastern Cape Province of South Africa. *Social Science and Medicine* 51(10): 1505–1515.

Cocks, Michelle, and V. Moller. 2002. Use of Indigenous and Indigenised Medicines to Enhance Personal Well-Being: A South African Case Study. *Social Science and Medicine* 54(3): 387–397.

Codrington, R. B. 1987. Demonic Powers from an Evangelical Perspective. In *Like a Roaring Lion . . . : Essays on the Bible, the Church and Demonic Powers,* ed. Pieter De Villiers. Pretoria: C. B. Powell Bible Centre.

Colbourn, Theo, Diane Dumanoski, and John Peterson Myers. 1996. *Our Stolen Future: Are We Threatening Our Fertility, Intelligence, and Survival? A Scientific Detective Story.* New York: Penguin Books.

Coleman, James S. 1990. *Foundations of Social Theory.* Cambridge, MA: Belknap Press.

Colenso, J. W. 1884. *Zulu-English Dictionary.* 2nd ed. Pietermaritzburg and Durban, RSA: P. Davis.

Colenso, John William. 1982. *Bringing Forth Light: Five Tracts on Bishop Colenso's Zululand Mission.* Ed. Ruth Edgecombe. Durban and Pietermaritzburg, RSA: University of Natal Press and Killie Campbell Africana Library.

Colson, Elizabeth. 2000. The Father as Witch. *Africa* 70(3): 333–358.

Comaroff, Jean. 1981a. Healing and Cultural Transformation: The Tswana of Southern Africa. *Social Science and Medicine* 15B: 367–378.

———. 1981b. Healing and the Cultural Order: The Case of the Barolong Boo Ratshidi of Southern Africa. *American Ethnologist* 7(4): 637–657.

———. 1985. *Body of Power, Spirit of Resistance: The Culture and History of a South African People.* Chicago: University of Chicago Press.

Comaroff, Jean, and John Comaroff. 1991. *Of Revelation and Revolution.* Vol. 1, *Christianity, Colonialism, and Consciousness in South Africa.* Chicago: University of Chicago Press.

———. 1993. *Modernity and Its Malcontents: Ritual and Power in Postcolonial Africa.* Chicago: University of Chicago Press.

———. 1997. *Of Revelation and Revolution.* Vol. 2, *The Dialectics of Modernity on a South African Frontier.* Chicago: University of Chicago Press.

———. 1999a. Alien-Nation: Zombies, Immigrants and Millennial Capitalism. *Codesria Bulletin* 3/4: 17–28.

———. 1999b. Occult Economies and the Violence of Abstraction: Notes from the South African Postcolony. *American Ethnologist* 26(2): 279–303.

———. 2000. Millenial Capitalism: First Thoughts on a Second Coming. *Public Culture* 12(2): 291–343.

Commission of Inquiry into Witchcraft Violence and Ritual Murders. 1996. *Report of the Commission of Inquiry into Witchcraft Violence and Ritual Murders in the Northern Province of the Republic of South Africa (Ralushai Commission).* Ministry of Safety and Security, Northern Province, RSA.

Commission on Gender Equality. 1998. *The Thohoyandou Declaration on Ending Witchcraft Violence.* Johannesburg: Commission on Gender Equality. http://anc.org.za/anc/newsbrief/1999/news0325.

———. 2000. Decrease in Witchcraft Killings and Violence. Commission on Gender Equality, Johannesburg. http://www.cge.org.za/press/2000/22-7-2000.4.htm.

Commission on Native Education. 1951. *Report of the Commission on Native Education, 1949–1951.* U.G. no. 53/1951. Pretoria.

Conco, W. Z. 1972. The African Bantu Traditional Practice of Medicine: Some Preliminary Observations. *Social Science and Medicine* 6: 283–322.

Connerton, Paul. 1989. *How Societies Remember.* Cambridge: Cambridge University Press.

Cook, P. A. W. 1931. *Social Organisation and Ceremonial Institutions of the Bomvana.* Cape Town: Juta.

Corten, André, and Ruth Marshal-Fratani. 2000. *Between Babel and Pentecost: Transnational Pentecostalism in Africa and Latin America.* London: C. Hurst.

Council of African Instituted Churches. 1999. Testimony before the Truth and Reconciliation Commission, East London, November 18, 1999. Truth and Reconciliation Commission, Human Rights Abuses. http://www.uct.ac.za/depts/ricsa/commiss/trc/caictest.htm.

Couper, J. L. 1990. The Healing Bird. *South African Medical Journal* 78(8): 485–489.

Crankshaw, O., and S. M. Parnell. 2000. *Race, Inequality and Urbanisation in the Johannesburg Region, 1946–1996.* Paper presented at the National Academy of Science workshop, "World Cities in Poor Countries," Washington, DC.

Crawford, T. 1995. Traditional Healers and Psychiatric Health Care. *South African Medical Journal* 85(4): 291–292.

Crossman, Peter, and René Devisch. 2002. Endogenous Knowledge in Anthropological Perspective. In Odora Hoppers 2002c.

Cruise O'Brien, Donal B. 2000. Satan Steps Out from the Shadows: Religion and Politics in Africa. *Africa* 70(3): 520–525.

Crush, Jonathan, Alan Jeeves, and David Yudelman. 1991. *South Africa's Labor Empire: A History of Black Migrancy to the Gold Mines*. Boulder: Westview.

Cullinan, Kerry. 2001. The Media and HIV/AIDS: A Blessing and a Curse. Paper presented at the "AIDS in Context" conference, University of the Witwatersrand, April 4–7, 2001.

Cunningham, Anthony. 1991. The Herbal Medicine Trade: Resource Depletion and Environmental Management for a "Hidden Economy." In *South Africa's Informal Economy*, ed. Eleanor Preston-Whyte and Rogerson Christian Preston-Whyte. Cape Town: Oxford University Press.

Dachs, Anthony J. 1972. Missionary Imperialism: The Case of Bechuanaland. *Journal of African History* 13: 647–658.

Dahl, Robert A. 1989. *Democracy and Its Critics*. New Haven and London: Yale University Press.

Daneel, Marthinus L. 1970. *Zionism and Faith-Healing in Rhodesia: Aspects of African Independent Churches*. The Hague: Mouton.

———. 1971. *Old and New in Southern Shona Independent Churches*. Vol. 1, *Background and Rise of the Major Movements*. The Hague: Mouton.

———. 1974. *Old and New in Southern Shona Independent Churches*. Vol. 2, *Causative Factors and Recruitment Techniques*. The Hague and Paris: Mouton.

———. 1990. Exorcism as a Means of Combating Wizardry: Liberation or Enslavement? *Missionalia, the Journal of the Southern African Missiological Society* 18(1): 220–247.

———. 2001. *African Earthkeepers: Wholistic Interfaith Mission*. New York: Orbis.

Dauskardt, Rolf. 1991. "Urban Herbalism": The Restructuring of Informal Survival in Johannesburg. In *South Africa's Informal Economy*, ed. Eleanor Preston-Whyte and Rogerson Christian Preston-Whyte. Cape Town: Oxford University Press.

Davenport, T. R. H. 1976. The Triumph of Colonel Stallard: The Transformation of the Natives (Urban Areas) Act between 1923 and 1937. *South African Historical Journal* 16(2): 77–89.

Davis, Erik. 1998. *Techgnosis: Myth, Magic, and Mysticism in the Age of Information*. New York: Three Rivers Press.

Davis, Gordon, et al. 1959. *Urban Native Law*. Port Elizabeth, RSA: Grotius.

De Gruchy, John, ed. 1999. *Facing the Truth: South African Faith Communities and the Truth and Reconciliation Commission*. Cape Town: David Philip.

De Heusch, Luc. 1985. *Sacrifice in Africa: A Structuralist Approach*. Trans. Linda O'Brien and Alice Morton. Bloomington: Indiana University Press.

de Jongh van Arkel, J. T. 1987. Pastoral Counselling and Demonology. In *Like a Roar-

ing Lion . . . : Essays on the Bible, the Church and Demonic Powers, ed. Pieter De Villiers. Pretoria: C. B. Powell Bible Centre.

de Jongh, Michael. 1990. Veracity and Validity in Black Urban Research in South Africa: Problems of Practicability and Perception. In *Truth Be in the Field: Social Science Research in Southern Africa,* ed. Pierre Hugo. Pretoria: University of South Africa Press.

Delius, P. 1984. Sebatagomou: Migrant Organisation, the ANC, and the Sekhukuneland Revolt. *Journal of Southern African Studies* 15(4).

Delius, Peter. 1996. *A Lion amongst Cattle: Reconstruction and Resistance in the Northern Transvaal.* Portsmouth, NH: Heinemann; Johannesburg: Ravan Press.

———. 2001. Witches and Missionaries in the 19th Century Transvaal. *Journal of Southern African Studies* 27(3): 429–443.

Delius, Peter, and Belinda Bozzoli. 1991. Radical History and South African Society. In Brown et al. 1991.

Department of Education. 2001. *National Strategy for Mathematics, Science and Technology Education.* Pretoria: Department of Education.

Department of Health. 1997. White Paper for the Transformation of the Health System in South Africa. Pretoria.
http://www.polity.org.za/govdocs/white_papers/health.html.

———. 1999. Health Sector Strategic Framework, 1999–2004. Pretoria. http://196.36 .153.56/doh/docs/policy/framewrk/.

———. 2000. HIV/AIDS/STD Strategic Plan for South Africa, 2000–2005. Pretoria. http://196.36.153.56/doh/docs/index.html.

———. 2001. Directorate of Health Systems Research and Epidemiology. *Summary Report: National HIV Sero-prevalence Survey of Women Attending Ante-natal Clinics in South Africa.* Pretoria.

De Villiers, Pieter. 1987. *Liberation Theology and the Bible.* Pretoria: University of South Africa Press.

Dewar, David, and Vanessa Watson. 1991. Urban Planning and the Informal Sector. In *South Africa's Informal Economy,* ed. Eleanor Preston-Whyte and Rogerson Christian Preston-Whyte. Cape Town: Oxford University Press.

Dick, B., and P. J. Murray. 1978. Traditional Healers and the Medical Profession. *South African Medical Journal* 53(9): 311–312.

Dickinson, G. 1999. Traditional Healers Face Off with Science. *Canadian Medical Association Journal* 160(5): 629.

Digby, Anne, and Helen Sweet. 2002. Nurses as Culture Brokers in Twentieth-Century South Africa. In *Plural Medicine, Tradition and Modernity, 1800–2000,* ed. Waltraud Ernst. London and New York: Routledge.

Dilger, Hansjoerg. 2001. "Living PositHIVely in Tanzania": The Global Dynamics of AIDS and the Meaning of Religion for International and Local AIDS Work. Paper presented at the "AIDS in Context" conference, University of the Witwatersrand, April 4–7, 2001.

Dilika, F., P. D. Bremner, and J. J. Meyer. 2000. Antibacterial Activity of Linoleic and Oleic Acids Isolated from *Helichrysum Pedunculatum:* A Plant Used during Circumcision Rites. *Fitoterapia* 71(4): 450–452.

Doke, C. M. 1961. Scripture Translation into Bantu Languages. In *Contributions to the History of Bantu Languages,* ed. D. T. Cole and C. M. Doke. Johannesburg: Witwatersrand University Press.

Doke, C. M., D. M. Malcolm, J. M. Sikakana, and B. W. Vilakazi. 1990. *English-Zulu, Zulu-English Dictionary.* Combined ed. Johannesburg: Witwatersrand University Press.

Donders, G. G., H. G. De Wet, and E. De Jonghe. 2000. Images in Infectious Diseases in Obstetrics and Gynecology: Lethal Sepsis due to Traditional Healing. *Infectious Disease in Obstetrics and Gynecology* 8(2): 76.

Donkers, Ando, and Murray Renata. 1997. Prospects and Problems Facing Traditional Leaders in South Africa. In *The Rights of Indigenous People: A Quest for Coexistence,* ed. De Villiers Bertus. Pretoria: Human Sciences Research Council.

Dorrington, Rob, David Bourne, Debbie Bradshaw, Ria Laubscher, and Ian Timaeus. 2001. *The Impact of HIV/AIDS on Adult Mortality in South Africa.* Technical Report, Burden of Disease Research Unit. Tygerberg: Medical Research Council.

Douglas, Mary. 1966. *Purity and Danger: An Analysis of Concepts of Pollution and Taboo.* New York: Praeger.

———. 1970a. Introduction: Thirty Years after *Witchcraft, Oracles and Magic.* In Douglas 1970.

———, ed. 1970b. *Witchcraft Confessions and Accusations.* London: Tavistock.

———. 1991. Witchcraft and Leprosy: Two Strategies of Exclusion. *Man,* n.s., 26(4): 723–736.

Doull, John. 2001. Toxicology Comes of Age. *Annual Review of Pharmacology and Toxicology* 41: 1–21.

Dowdall, T. 1982. Behavior Therapy in South Africa: A Review. *Journal of Behavior Therapy and Experimental Psychiatry* 13(4): 279–286.

Dowson, Thomas A., and David Lewis-Williams. 1994. *Contested Images: Diversity in Southern African Rock Art Research.* Johannesburg: Witwatersrand University Press.

Drewes, Siegfried, and Marion Horn. 2002. The African Potato *Hypoxis Hemerocallidea* (*Hypoxidacea*): Myth or Miracle *Muthi.* http://www.akita.co.za/mnp/africanpotato.htm.

Drexler, Madeline. 2002. *Secret Agents: The Menace of Emerging Infections.* Washington, D.C.: Joseph Henry Press (National Academy of Science).

Dube, D. 1989. A Search for Abundant Life: Health, Healing and Wholeness in Zionist Churches. In Oosthuizen et al. 1989.

Dugard, John. 1999. Dealing with Crimes of a Past Regime: Is Amnesty Still an Option? Paper presented at "The TRC: Commissioning the Past" conference, University of the Witwatersrand, June 11–14, 1999.

Duncan, A. C., A. K. Jager, and J. van Staden. 1999. Screening of Zulu Medicinal Plants for Angiotensin Converting Enzyme (ACE) Inhibitors. *Journal of Ethnopharmacology* 68(1–3): 63–70.

Dunn, J. P., J. E. Krige, R. Wood, P. C. Bornman, and J. Terblanche. 1991. Colonic Complications after Toxic Tribal Enemas. *British Journal of Surgery* 78(5): 545–548.

du Plessis, J. S. 1987. Demonic Bondage. In *Like a Roaring Lion . . . : Essays on the*

Bible, the Church and Demonic Powers, ed. Pieter De Villiers. Pretoria: C. B. Powell Bible Centre.

du Plooy, W. J., M. R. Jobson, E. Osuch, L. Mathibe, and P. Tsipa. 2001. Mortality from Traditional Medicine Poisoning: A New Perspective from Analysing Admissions and Deaths at Ga-Rankuwa Hospital. *South African Journal of Science* 97(3/4): 70–77.

du Toit, Brian M. 1980. Religion, Ritual, and Healing among Urban Black South Africans. *Urban Anthropology* 9(1): 21–49.

———. 1998. Modern Folk Medicine in South Africa. *South African Journal of Ethnology* 21(4): 145–152.

Dyzenhaus, David. 1999. With the Benefit of Hindsight. Paper presented at "The TRC: Commissioning the Past" conference, University of the Witwatersrand, June 11–14, 1999.

Eales, Kathy. 1991. Gender Politics and the Administration of African Women in Johannesburg, 1903–1939. Department of History, University of the Witwatersrand.

Edelstein, Melville Leonard. 1972. *What Do Young Africans Think? An Attitude Survey of Urban African Matric. Pupils in Soweto with Special Reference to Stereotyping and Social Distance: A Sociological Study.* Johannesburg: South African Institute of Race Relations.

Edgar, Robert. 1988. *Because They Chose the Plan of God: The Story of the Bulhoek Massacre.* Johannesburg: Ravan Press.

Edgar, Robert, and Hilary Sapire. 2000. *African Apocalypse: The Story of Nontetha Nkwekwe, a Twentieth-Century South African Prophet.* Athens: Ohio University Center for International Studies; Johannesburg: Witwatersrand University Press.

Edgerton, Robert B. 1971. A Traditional African Psychiatrist. *Southwestern Journal of Anthropology* 27: 259–278.

Edmunds, Marion. 1996. Masakhane Gets a Second Chance. *Weekly Mail and Guardian* (Johannesburg) Internet ed., June 9, 1996. http://www.sn.apc.org/wmail/issues/960906/NEWS29.html.

Edwards, F. S. 1983. Healing and Transculturation in Xhosa Zionist Practice. *Culture Medicine and Psychiatry* 7(2): 177–198.

Edwards, S. D. 1986. Traditional and Modern Medicine in South Africa: A Research Study. *Social Science and Medicine* 22(11): 1273–1276.

———. 1989. Traditional and Modern Medicine in Southern Africa: Some Reflective and Research Considerations. In Oosthuizen et al. 1989.

Edwards, S. D., P. W. Grobbelaar, N. V. Makunga, P. T. Sibaya, L. M. Nene, S. T. Kunene, and A. S. Magwaza. 1983. Traditional Zulu Theories of Illness in Psychiatric Patients. *Journal of Social Psychology* 121(2nd half): 213–221.

Eiselen, W. W. M. 1932a. The Art of Divination as Practiced by the Bamasemola (Part 1). *Bantu Studies* 6: 1–29.

———. 1932b. The Art of Divination as Practiced by the Bamasemola (Part 2). *Bantu Studies* 6: 251–263.

———. 1948. The Meaning of Apartheid. *Race Relations* 15(3): 69–86.

Eisenstadt, S. N. 1956. Ritualized Personal Relations: Blood Brotherhood, Best Friends, Compadre, etc.: Some Hypotheses and Suggestions. *Man* 56: 90–95.

Ellen, Roy, and Holly Harris. 1996. Concepts of Indigenous Environmental Knowledge in Scientific and Development Studies Literature: A Critical Assessment. Paper presented at the East-West Environmental Linkages Network Workshop 3, Canterbury, May 8–10, 1996.

———. 2000. Introduction to *Indigenous Environmental Knowledge and Its Transformation: Critical Anthropological Perspectives*, ed. Roy Ellen and Holly Harris. Amsterdam: Harwood.

Elliot, J. 1984. Black Medical Students and African Cosmological Beliefs. *Africa Insight* 14(2): 109–112.

Eloff, J. N. 2001. Antibacterial Activity of Marula (*Sclerocarya Birrea* (A. Rich.) *Hochst.* Subsp. *Caffra* (Sond.) *Kokwaro*) (Anacardiaceae) Bark and Leaves. *Journal of Ethnopharmacology* 76(3): 305–308.

Elphick, Richard. 1995. Writing Religion into History: The Case of South African Christianity. In *Missions and Christianity in South African History*, ed. Henry Bredekamp and Robert Ross. Johannesburg: Witwatersrand University Press.

———. 1997. Introduction: Christianity in South African History. In Elphick and Davenport 1997.

Elphick, Richard, and Rodney Davenport, eds. 1997. *Christianity in South Africa: A Political, Social, and Cultural History*. Perspectives on Southern Africa, no. 55. Berkeley and Los Angeles: University of California Press; Cape Town: David Philip.

Emdon, Erica. 1993. Privatisation of State Housing, with Special Focus on the Greater Soweto Area. *Urban Forum* 4(2): 1–13.

Engelke, Mathew. 2002. The Problem of Belief: Evans-Pritchard and Victor Turner on "the Inner Life." *Anthropology Today* 18(6): 3–8.

Englund, Harri. 1996. Witchcraft, Modernity, and the Person. *Critique of Anthropology* 41: 225–239.

Etherington, Norman. 1978. *Preachers, Peasants and Politics in Southeast Africa, 1835–1880: African Christian Communities in Natal, Pondoland and Zululand*. London: Royal Historical Society.

———. 1979. The Historical Sociology of Independent Churches in South East Africa. *Journal of Religion in Africa* 10(2): 108–126.

———. 1983. Missionaries and the Intellectual History of Africa: A Historical Survey. *Itinerario* 7: 116–143.

———. 1987. Missionary Doctors and African Healers in Mid-Victorian South Africa. *South African Historical Journal* 19(77): 91.

Evans, Ivan. 1999. To Forgive and to Forget: Racial Memory in South Africa and the US. Paper presented at "The TRC: Commissioning the Past" conference, University of the Witwatersrand, June 11–14, 1999.

Evans-Pritchard, E. E. 1937. *Witchcraft Oracles and Magic among the Azande*. Oxford: Clarendon Press.

———. 1956. *Nuer Religion*. Oxford: Clarendon Press.

Everatt, David. 2000. From Urban Warrior to Market Segment? Youth in South Africa, 1990–2000. *Development Update* 3(2). http://www.interfund.org.za/UpdateVol3 No2.htm.

Farrand, Dorothy. 1980. An Analysis of Traditional Healing in Suburban Johannesburg. MA thesis, Department of Psychology, University of the Witwatersrand.

———. 1984. Is a Combined Western and Traditional Health Service for Black Patients Desirable? *South African Medical Journal* 66(20): 779–780.

———. 1988. *Idliso:* A Phenomenological and Psychiatric Comparison. PhD diss., Department of Psychology, University of the Witwatersrand.

Fashole-Luke, E. W. 1976. The Quest for African Christian Theologies. In *Third World Theologies,* ed. G. H. Anderson and T. F. Stransky. Mission Trends, no. 3. New York: Paulist Press.

Fatnowna, Scott, and Harry Pickett. 2002a. Establishing Protocols for an Indigenous-Directed Process. In Odora Hoppers 2002c.

———. 2002b. Indigenous Contemporary Knowledge Development through Research. In Odora Hoppers 2002c.

———. 2002c. The Place of Indigenous Knowledge Systems in the Post-postmodern Integrative Paradigm Shift. In Odora Hoppers 2002c.

Faure, Véronique. 2001. Notes on the Occult in the New South Africa. *African Legal Studies* 2: 170–176.

Favret-Saada, Jeanne. 1980. *Deadly Words: Witchcraft in the Bocage.* Trans. Catherine Cullen. Cambridge: Cambridge University Press.

Feierman, Steven. 1985. Struggles for Control: The Social Roots of Health and Healing in Modern Africa. *African Studies Review* 28(2/3): 73–147.

———. 1994. Healing, Civil Society, and Colonial Conquest. Paper presented at the "Democracy: Popular Precedents, Popular Practice and Popular Culture" History Workshop conference, University of the Witwatersrand, July 13–15, 1994.

———. 1999. Colonizers, Scholars, and the Creation of Invisible Histories. In *Beyond the Cultural Turn: New Directions in the Study of Society and Culture,* ed. Victoria Bonnell and Lynn Hunt. Berkeley and Los Angeles: University of California Press.

Feierman, Steven, and John M. Janzen. 1992. *The Social Basis of Health and Healing in Africa.* Berkeley and Los Angeles: University of California Press.

Fennell, C. W., and J. van Staden. 2001. *Crinum* Species in Traditional and Modern Medicine. *Journal of Ethnopharmacology* 78(1): 15–26.

Fernandes, D. B. 1970. Medicine and the Zulu. *Practitioner* 205(225): 73–79.

Fernandez, James W. 1967. Divinations, Confessions, Testimonies: Zulu Confrontations with the Social Superstructure. Occasional Paper no. 9. Institute for Social Research, University of Natal, Durban.

———. 1982. *Bwiti: An Ethnography of the Religious Imagination in Africa.* Princeton: Princeton University Press.

Ferrante, A. M., J. A. Fernandez, and N. S. N. Loh. 1999. Crime and Justice Statistics for Western Australia: 1998. Crime Research Centre Statistical Report. University of Western Australia, Perth. http://www.law.ecel.uwa.edu.au/crc/stats/stats_report_1998.pdf.

Field, Sean. 1999. Memory, the TRC and the Significance of Oral History in Post-apartheid South Africa. Unpublished paper.

Fields, Karen. 1982. Political Contingencies of Witchcraft in Colonial Central Africa:

Culture and the State in Marxist Theory. *Canadian Journal of African Studies* 16: 567–581.

Finnegan, William. 1988. *Dateline Soweto: Travels with Black South African Reporters.* New York: Harper and Row.

Firth, Raymond. 1969. Foreword to *Spirit Mediumship and Society in Africa,* ed. John Beattie and John Middleton, ix–xxx. New York: Africana Publishing Corp.

Fisher, C., and L. A. Hurst. 1967. Attitudes to Mental Health in a Sample of Bantu-Speaking Patients at Baragwanath Hospital, Johannesburg. *Topical Problems in Psychiatry and Neurology* 5: 179–204.

Fisiy, Cyprian. 1998. Containing Occult Practices: Witchcraft Trials in Cameroon. *African Studies Review* 41(3): 143–163.

Fisiy, Cyprian, and Peter Geschiere. 1990. Judges and Witches, or How Is the State to Deal with Witchcraft? Examples from Southeastern Cameroon. *Cahiers d'Études Africaines* 118: 135–156.

Fisiy, Cyprian, and Michael Rowlands. 1990. Sorcery and Law in Modern Cameroon. *Culture and History* 6: 63–84.

Flisher, Alan, Wasima Fisher, and Hasina Subedar. 2000. Mental Health. In *South African Health Review, 1999,* ed. Nicholas Crisp and Antoinette Ntuli. Durban: Health Systems Trust.

Foner, Eric. 1994. Race, Democracy, and Citizenship in Nineteenth-Century America. Paper presented at the "Democracy: Popular Precedents, Popular Practice and Popular Culture" History Workshop conference, University of the Witwatersrand, July 13–15, 1994.

Forster, Peter Glover. 1998. Religion, Magic, Witchcraft, and AIDS in Malawi. *Anthropos* 93: 537–545.

Fortes, M. 1965. Some Reflections on Ancestor Worship in Africa. In *African Systems of Thought,* ed. M. Fortes and G. Dieterlen. Oxford: Oxford University Press.

Foster, George M. 1967. Peasant Society and the Image of Limited Good. *American Anthropologist* 67: 293–315.

———. 1972. The Anatomy of Envy: A Study in Symbolic Behavior. *Current Anthropology* 13(2): 165–202.

Foukaridis, G. N., G. L. Muntingh, and E. Osuch. 1994. Application of Diode Array Detection for the Identification of Poisoning by Traditional Medicines. *Journal of Ethnopharmacology* 41(3): 135–146.

Foukaridis, G. N., E. Osuch, L. Mathibe, and P. Tsipa. 1995. The Ethnopharmacology and Toxicology of *Urginea sanguinea* in the Pretoria Area. *Journal of Ethnopharmacology* 49(2): 77–79.

Fourie, Bernard. 2001. The Burden of Tuberculosis in South Africa. Medical Research Council, National Tuberculosis Research Programme, Tygerberg. http://www.sahealthinfo.org/Publications/body_tb/body_body_tb.htm.

Frankel, Philip. 1979a. Municipal Transformation in Soweto: Race, Politics, and Maladministration in Black Johannesburg. *African Studies Review* 22(2): 49–63.

———. 1979b. The Politics of Passes: Control and Change in South Africa. *Journal of African Studies* 17(2): 199–217.

Freeman, M., and M. Motsei. 1992. Planning Health Care in South Africa—Is There a Role for Traditional Healers? *Social Science and Medicine* 34(11): 1183–1190.

Friedson, Steven M. 1996. *Dancing Prophets: Musical Experience in Tumbuka Healing.* Chicago: University of Chicago Press.

Froise, Marjorie. 1996. *South African Christian Handbook, 1996–97.* Pretoria: World Mission Centre.

Fukuyama, Francis. 1995. *Trust: The Social Virtues and the Creation of Prosperity.* New York: Free Press.

Gadamer, Hans Georg. 1994. *Truth and Method.* Trans. Joel Weinsheimer and Donald G. Marshall. 2nd, rev. ed. New York: Continuum.

Gaitskell, Deborah. 1997. Power in Prayer and Service: Women's Christian Organizations. In Elphick and Davenport 1997.

Gallison, Peter. 1997. *Image and Logic: A Material Culture of Microphysics.* Chicago: University of Chicago Press.

Garner, Robert. 2000. Religion as a Source of Social Change in the New South Africa. *Journal of Religion in Africa* 30(3): 310–343.

Gaybba, B. 1987. The Development in Biblical Times of Belief in Demons and Devils and the Theological Issue Raised by Such a Development. In *Like a Roaring Lion . . . : Essays on the Bible, the Church and Demonic Powers,* ed. Pieter De Villiers. Pretoria: C. B. Powell Bible Centre.

Gcabashe, Lindelihle. 2000. The Involvement of Traditional Healers in TB and HIV Efforts in South Africa. AF-AIDS. http://www.hivnet.ch:8000/africa/af-aids/viewR?666.

Gear, Sasha. 2001. Sex, Sexual Violence and Coercion in Men's Prisons. Paper presented at the "AIDS in Context" conference, University of the Witwatersrand, April 4–7, 2001.

Geertz, Clifford. 1962. The Rotating Credit Association: A "Middle Rung" in Development. *Economic Development and Cultural Change* 10(3): 241–263.

———. 1973. Religion as a Cultural System. In *The Interpretation of Culture,* ed. Clifford Geertz. New York: Basic Books.

———. 1983. Common Sense as a Cultural System. In *Local Knowledge: Further Essays in Interpretive Anthropology,* ed. Clifford Geertz. New York: Basic Books.

———. 2000. *Available Light: Anthropological Reflections on Philosophical Topics.* Princeton: Princeton University Press.

Gelfand, Michael. 1967. Medical Aspects of Witchcraft Practice amongst the Shona. *Central African Journal of Medicine* 13(11): 266–268.

Gelfand, Michael, S. Mavi, and R. B. Drummond. 1978. The Role of the Witchdoctor in African Health Care. *Leech* 48(2): 16–18.

Gellner, Ernest. 1970. Concepts and Society. In *Rationality,* ed. Wilson Bryan. Key Concepts in the Social Sciences. New York: Harper and Row.

———. 1974. *Legitimation of Belief.* Cambridge: Cambridge University Press.

Geschiere, Peter. 1997. *The Modernity of Witchcraft.* Charlottesville: University Press of Virginia.

Geschiere, Peter, and Cyprian Fisiy. 1994. Domesticating Personal Violence: Witchcraft, Courts and Confessions in Cameroon. *Africa* 64(3): 323–341.

Gevisser, Mark, and Michael Morris. 2001. *Manifesto on Values, Education and Democracy.* Ed. Wilmot James. Cape Town: Cape Argus Teach Fund for the Department of Education.

Gibson, James L., and Amanda Gouws. 1999. Truth and Reconciliation in South Africa: Attributions of Blame and the Struggle over Apartheid. *American Political Science Review* 93(3): 501–517.

Gifford, Paul. 1998. *African Christianity: Its Public Role.* Bloomington and Indianapolis: Indiana University Press.

Ginsburg, Rebecca. 1996. "Now I Stay in a House": Renovating the Matchbox in Apartheid-Era Soweto. *African Studies* 55(2): 127–140.

Ginzburg, Carlo. 1983. *The Night Battles: Witchcraft and Agrarian Cults in the Sixteenth and Seventeenth Centuries.* Baltimore: Johns Hopkins University Press.

Girvin, S. D. 1987. Race and Race Classification. In *Race and the Law in South Africa,* ed. A. Rycroft. Cape Town: Juta.

Gittens, Clark L. 1978. *Soweto . . . but God!* Pretoria: Dorothea Mission.

Glaser, Clive. 1994. *Youth Culture and Politics in Soweto, 1958–76.* Cambridge: Cambridge University Press.

———. 2000. *Bo-Tsotsi: The Youth Gangs of Soweto, 1935–1976.* Cape Town: David Philip.

Gluckman, Max. 1955. *Custom and Conflict in Africa.* Oxford: Blackwell.

———. 1963. Gossip and Scandal. *Current Anthropology* 4(3): 307–316.

———. 1968. Psychological, Sociological, and Anthropological Explanations of Witchcraft and Gossip: A Clarification. *Man,* n.s., 3(1): 20–34.

Goffman, Erving. 1959. *The Presentation of Self in Everyday Life.* Garden City, NY: Doubleday.

———. 1963. *Stigma Notes on the Management of Spoiled Identity.* Englewood Cliffs, NJ: Prentice-Hall.

Goldblatt, Beth, and Sheila Meintjes. 1999. Women: One Chapter in the History of South Africa? A Critique of the Truth and Reconciliation Commission Report. Paper presented at "The TRC: Commissioning the Past" conference, University of the Witwatersrand, June 11–14, 1999.

Goodhew, David. 2000. Growth and Decline in South Africa's Churches. *Journal of Religion in Africa* 30(2): 344–369.

Goodman, Tanya, and Max Price. 1999. Continuing the TRC Project: The Use of Internal Reconciliation Commissions to Facilitate Organisational Transformation—The Case of Wits Health Sciences Faculty. Paper presented at "The TRC: Commissioning the Past" conference, University of the Witwatersrand, June 11–14, 1999.

Goody, Esther. 1970. Legitimate and Illegitimate Aggression in a West African State. In Douglas 1970b.

Gorodnov, Valentin P. 1988. *Soweto: Life and Struggles of a South African Township.* Trans. David Skvirsky. Moscow: Progress Publishers.

Govender, Prega. 2001. Sigcau Brews Secret AIDS *Muti. Sunday Times* (Johannesburg) Internet ed., July 22, 2001. http://www.suntimes.co.za/2001/07/22/news/news09.htm.

Govere, J., D. N. Durrheim, Toit N. Du, R. H. Hunt, and M. Coetzee. 2000. Local

Plants as Repellents against *Anopheles arabiensis,* in Mpumalanga Province, South Africa. *Central African Journal of Medicine* 46(8): 213–216.

Green, Edward C. 1997. Purity, Pollution and the Invisible Snake in Southern Africa. *Medical Anthropology* 17: 83–100.

———. 1999. *Indigenous Theories of Contagious Disease.* Walnut Creek: Altamira Press.

———. 2000. Male Circumcision and HIV Infection. *Lancet* 355: 927.

Green, E. C., B. Zokwe, and J. D. Dupree. 1995. The Experience of an AIDS Prevention Program Focused on South African Traditional Healers. *Social Science and Medicine* 40(4): 503–515.

Grierson, D. S. and A. J. Afolayan. 1999a. Antibacterial Activity of Some Indigenous Plants Used for the Treatment of Wounds in the Eastern Cape, South Africa. *Journal of Ethnopharmacology* 66(1): 103–106.

———. 1999b. An Ethnobotanical Study of Plants Used for the Treatment of Wounds in the Eastern Cape, South Africa. *Journal of Ethnopharmacology* 67(3): 327–332.

Griffiths, J. A., and R. W. Cheetham. 1982. Priests before Healers—An Appraisal of the ISangoma or ISanusi in Nguni Society. *South African Medical Journal* 62(25): 959–960.

Grinker, David. 1986. *Inside Soweto.* Johannesburg: Eastern Enterprises.

Grundlingh, Louis. 2001. A Critical Historical Analysis of Government Responses to HIV/AIDS in South Africa as Reported in the Media, 1983–1994. Paper presented at the "AIDS in Context" conference, University of the Witwatersrand, April 4–7, 2001.

Gumede, M. V. 1978. Traditional Zulu Practitioners and Obstetric Medicine. *South African Medical Journal* 53(21): 823–825.

———. 1990. *Traditional Healers: A Medical Practitioner's Perspective.* Johannesburg: Skotaville.

Gungubele, Mondli. 1997. ANC Daily News Briefing, June 6, 1997. http://www.anc.org.za/anc/newsbrief/1997/news0606.

Gyeke, Kwame. 1997. *Tradition and Modernity: Philosophical Reflections on the African Experience.* New York: Oxford University Press.

Hahlo, H. R., and Ellison Kahn. 1960. Recognition of Native Law and Creation of Native Courts. In *The Union of South Africa: The Development of Its Laws and Constitution,* by H. R. Hahlo and Ellison Kahn. London: Steven and Sons.

Halbwachs, Maurice. 1962. *Sources of Religious Sentiment.* New York: Free Press.

———. 1992. *On Collective Memory.* Trans. Donald N. Levine. Chicago: University of Chicago Press.

Hall, Elsje J. 1985. Gesondheidsvoorligting—Twee Kulture. *Curationis* 8(1): 27–31.

Hall, James. 1995. *Sangoma: My Odyssey into the Spirit World of Africa.* New York: Touchstone Books.

Hallen, B., and J. O. Sodipo. 1986. *Knowledge, Belief, and Witchcraft: Analytic Experiments in African Philosophy.* London: Ethnographica.

Haltman, Karen. 1999. Cultural History and the Challenge of Narrativity. In *Beyond the Cultural Turn: New Directions in the Study of Society and Culture,* ed. Victoria Bonnell and Lynn Hunt. Berkeley and Los Angeles: University of California Press.

Hamber, Brandon. 1999. Past Imperfect; Strategies for Dealing with Past Political Violence in Northern Ireland, South Africa and Countries in Transition. Paper presented at "The TRC: Commissioning the Past" conference, University of the Witwatersrand, June 11–14, 1999.

Hamilton, Carolyn. 1994. "Zoolacratism" and "Cannibalism": A Discussion of Historical Disposition toward the "Shakan" Model of Social Order and Political Rights. Paper presented at the "Democracy: Popular Precedents, Popular Practice and Popular Culture" History Workshop conference, University of the Witwatersrand, July 13–15, 1994.

Hammond-Tooke, [W.] David. 1970. Urbanization and the Meaning of Misfortune. *Africa* 40(1): 25–38.

———, ed. 1974a. *The Bantu-Speaking Peoples of Southern Africa.* London: Routledge and Kegan Paul.

———. 1974b. The Cape Nguni Witch Familiar as a Mediatory Construct. *Man,* n.s., 9(1): 128–136.

———. 1975. *Command or Consensus: The Development of Transkeian Local Government.* Cape Town: David Philip.

———. 1978. Do the South-Eastern Bantu Worship Their Ancestors? In *Social System and Tradition in Southern Africa,* ed. J. Argyle and E. M. Preston-Whyte. Cape Town: Oxford University Press.

———. 1985. Who Worships Whom: Agnates and Ancestors among Nguni. *African Studies* 44(1): 47–64.

———. 1989a. The Aetiology of Spirit in Southern Africa. In Oosthuizen et al. 1989.

———. 1989b. *Rituals and Medicines: Indigenous Healing in South Africa.* Johannesburg: A. D. Donker.

———. 2002. The Uniqueness of Nguni Mediumistic Divination in Southern Africa. *Africa* 72(2): 277–292.

Handelman, Don. 1973. Gossip in Encounters: The Transmission of Information in a Bounded Social Setting. *Man,* n.s., 8(2): 210–227.

Hardin, Russell. 2002. *Trust and Trustworthiness.* New York: Russell Sage Foundation.

Harnischfeger, Johannes. 2000. Witchcraft and the State in South Africa. *Anthropos* 95: 99–112.

Harries, Patrick. 2001. *Work, Culture, and Identity: Migrant Laborers in Mozambique and South Africa, c. 1860–1910.* London: Heinemann.

Harris, Grace Gredys. 1986. *Casting out Anger.* Prospect Park, IL: Waveland Press.

Hartshorne, Ken. 1992. *Crisis and Challenge: Black Education, 1910–1990.* Cape Town: Oxford University Press.

Harvey, Ibrahim. 2000. Parks, AIDS and the Media. *Daily Mail and Guardian* (Johannesburg) Internet ed., November 17, 2000. http://www.mg.co.za/mg/za/features/harvey/001117-harvey.html.

Haule, Cosmos. 1969. *Bantu "Witchcraft" and Christian Morality: The Encounter of Bantu Uchawi with Christian Morality, an Anthropological and Theological Study.* Nouvelle Revue de Science Missionaire, Supplementa 16. Schoneck-Beckenreid.

Hayes, Stephen. 1992. African Independent Churches: Judgement through Terminology. *Missionalia, the Journal of the Southern African Missiological Society* 20(2): 139–146.

————. 1995. Christian Responses to Witchcraft and Sorcery. *Missionalia, the Journal of the Southern African Missiological Society* 23(3): 339–354.

Haysom, Nicholas. 1981. Towards an Understanding of Prison Gangs. Cape Town: University of Cape Town, Institute of Criminology.

Heald, Suzette. 1991. Divinatory Failure: The Religious and Social Role of Gisu Diviners. *Africa* 61(3): 299–317.

Heggenhougen, H. K., and L. Shore. 1986. Cultural Components of Behavioural Epidemiology: Implications for Primary Health Care. *Social Science and Medicine* 22(11): 1235–1245.

Hellmann, Ellen. 1937. The Native in the Towns. In Schapera 1937.

————. 1940. *The Problems of Urban Bantu Youth.* Johannesburg: South African Institute of Race Relations.

————. 1948. *Rooiyard: A Sociological Survey of an Urban Native Slum Yard.* Cape Town: Oxford University Press.

————. 1971. *Soweto: Johannesburg's African City.* Johannesburg: South African Institute of Race Relations.

Hendricks, Fred. 1999. Amnesty and Justice in Post Apartheid South Africa: How Not to Construct a Democratic Normative Framework. Paper presented at "The TRC: Commissioning the Past" conference, University of the Witwatersrand, June 11–14, 1999.

Henningsen, Gustav. 1980. *The Witches' Advocate: Basque Witchcraft and the Spanish Inquisition (1609–1614).* Reno: University of Nevada Press.

Henry, Yazir. 1999. A Space Where Healing Begins. Paper presented at "The TRC: Commissioning the Past" conference, University of the Witwatersrand, June 11–14, 1999.

Hess, Stuart. 1998. Traditional Healers in South Africa. *Update* 37. Online journal of Health Systems Trust. http://www.hst.org.za/update/37/policy.htm.

Hewlett, Barry S. 2001. The Cultural Contexts of Ebola in Northern Uganda: A Preliminary Report. Washington State University, Vancouver. http://www.vancouver.wsu.edu/fac/hewlett/ebola.html.

Hewson, Mariana G. 1998. Traditional Healers in Southern Africa. *Annals of Internal Medicine* 128: 1029–1034. http://www.acponline.org/journals/annals/15jun98/soafrica.htm.

Higginson, John. 1999. "Making Short Work of Tradition": Popular Rural Protest and the State of Emergency in Bophutatswana, Marico and Rustenburg, as Perceived by TRC Witnesses, 1977–1993. Paper presented at "The TRC: Commissioning the Past" conference, University of the Witwatersrand, June 11–14, 1999.

Higgs, P., and M. P. Van Niekerk. 2002. The Programme for Indigenous Knowledge Systems (IKS) and Higher Educational Discourse in South Africa: A Critical Reflection. *South African Journal of Higher Education* 16(3): 38–49.

Hill, Michele B., and Greg Black. 2002. The Killing and Burning of Witches in South Africa: A Model of Community Rebuilding and Reconciliation. In *Culturally-*

Based Interventions: Alternative Approaches to Working with Diverse Populations, ed. J. Ancis. New York: Brunner Routledge.

Hindson, Doug. 1987. *Pass Controls and the Urban African Proletariat in South Africa.* Johannesburg: Ravan Press.

Hirson, Baruch. 1979. *Year of Fire, Year of Ash: The Soweto Revolt, Roots of a Revolution?* London: Zed.

Hodgson, Janet. 1990. "Don't Fence Me In": Some Problems in the Classification of African Religious Movements. In *Exploring New Religious Movements,* ed. Andrew F. Walls and W. R. Schenk. Elkhart: Mission Focus.

Hoehne, K. A. 1990. Initiative: A Neglected Psychosocial Dimension. *Social Psychiatry and Psychiatric Epidemiology* 25(2): 101–107.

Hoernlé, A. Winifred. 1931. Introduction to *The Bavenda,* ed. Hugh A. Stayt. Oxford: Oxford University Press for the International Institute of African Languages and Cultures.

———. 1937. Magic and Medicine. In Schapera 1937.

Holdstock, T. Len. 1979. Indigenous Healing in South Africa: A Neglected Potential. *South African Journal of Psychology* 9: 118–124.

———. 1981. Indigenous Healing in South Africa and the Person-Centered Approach of Carl Rogers. *Curare* 4: 31–46.

———. 2000. *Re-examining Psychology: Critical Perspectives and African Insights.* London and Philadelphia: Routledge.

Holland, Heidi. 2001. *African Magic: Traditional Ideas That Heal a Continent.* Johannesburg: Penguin.

Hollis, Martin. 1970a. The Limits of Irrationality. In *Rationality,* ed. Wilson Bryan. New York: Harper and Row.

———. 1970b. Reason and Ritual. In *Rationality,* ed. Wilson Bryan. New York: Harper and Row.

Hollis, Martin, and Steven Lukes. 1982. *Rationality and Relativism.* Cambridge: MIT Press.

Honwana, Alcinda. 1997. Spirit Possession and the Politics of Religious Healing in Mozambique. Paper presented at the "Proselytization and Religious Pluralism in Africa" conference, Dakar, Senegal.

Hookway, Christopher. 2001. Epistemic Akrasia and Epistemic Virtue. Unpublished paper.

Hoosen, Sarah, and Anthony Collins. 2001. Women, Culture and AIDS: How Discourses of Gender and Sexuality Affect Safe Sex Behaviour. Paper presented at the "AIDS in Context" conference, University of the Witwatersrand, April 4–7, 2001.

Hopa, M., L. C. Simbayin, and C. D. Du Toit. 1998. Perceptions on Integration of Traditional and Western Healing in the New South Africa. *South African Journal of Psychology* 28(1): 8–15.

Horrell, Muriel. 1960. *The Liquor Laws as They Affect Africans and Coloured and Asian People.* No. 8-1960. Johannesburg: South African Institute of Race Relations.

Horton, Robin. 1970. African Traditional Thought and Western Science. In *Rationality,* ed. Wilson Bryan. New York: Harper and Row.

————. 1993. *Patterns of Thought in Africa and the West: Essays on Magic, Religion, and Science.* Cambridge: Cambridge University Press.

Horwitz, Simonne. 2001. Migrancy and HIV/AIDS: A Historical Perspective. Paper presented at the "AIDS in Context" conference, University of the Witwatersrand, April 4–7, 2001.

Hountondji, Paulin. 1983. *African Philosophy: Myth and Reality.* Bloomington: Indiana University Press.

————. 2002. Knowledge Appropriation in a Post-colonial Context. In Odora Hoppers 2002c.

Hubert, Henri, and Marcel Mauss. 1981. *Sacrifice: Its Nature and Function.* Trans. W. D. Halls. Chicago: University of Chicago Press.

Huddle, Ken, and Asher Dubb. 1994. *Baragwanath Hospital: 50 Years, a Medical Miscellany.* Johannesburg: Department of Medicine, Baragwanath Hospital.

Hudson, Peter. 1999. Liberalism, Democracy and Transformation in South Africa. Paper presented at "The TRC: Commissioning the Past" conference, University of the Witwatersrand, June 11–14, 1999.

Human Rights Watch. 2001. Scared at School: Sexual Violence against Girls in South African Schools. http://www.hrw.org/reports/2001/safrica/.

Human Rights Watch/Africa and Human Rights Watch Women's Rights Project. 1995. *Violence against Women in South Africa: The State Response to Domestic Violence and Rape.* New York: Human Rights Watch.

Human Sciences Research Council. 1999. *Employment Forecasts till 2003.* Pretoria: Human Sciences Research Council.

Humphries, Richard Gordon, and Shubane Kehla. 1989. A Tale of Two Squirrels: The 1988 Local Government Elections and Their Implications. In *South Africa at the End of the Eighties: Policy Perspectives,* ed. University of the Witwatersrand Centre for Policy Studies. Johannesburg: University of the Witwatersrand Centre for Policy Studies.

Hund, John. 2000. Witchcraft and Accusations of Witchcraft in South Africa: Ontological Denial and the Suppression of African Justice. *Comparative and International Law Journal of Southern Africa* 33(3): 366–389.

————. 2001. African Witchcraft and Western Law: Ontological Denial and the Suppression of African Justice. *African Legal Studies* 2: 22–59.

Hund, John, and M. Kotu-Rammopo. 1983. Justice in a South African Township: The Sociology of the Makgotla. *Comparative and International Law Journal of Southern Africa* 16: 179–208.

Hunt, Nancy Rose. 1999. *A Colonial Lexicon of Birth Ritual, Medicalization, and Mobility in the Congo.* Durham, NC: Duke University Press.

Hunter, Monica. 1961. *Reaction to Conquest: Effects of Contact with Europeans on the Pondo of South Africa.* 2nd ed. London: Oxford University Press, for the International African Institute.

Hutchings, A., and S. E. Terblanche. 1989. Observations on the Use of Some Known and Suspected Toxic Liliiflorae in Zulu and Xhosa Medicine. *South African Medical Journal* 75(2): 62–69.

Hutchings, A., and J. van Staden. 1994. Plants Used for Stress-Related Ailments in Traditional Zulu, Xhosa and Sotho Medicine. Part 1, Plants Used for Headaches. *Journal of Ethnopharmacology* 43(2): 89–124.

Hyslop, Jonathan. 1994. The Prophet Van Rensburg's Vision of Nelson Mandela: White Popular Religious Culture and Response to Democratisation. Paper presented at the "Democracy: Popular Precedents, Popular Practice and Popular Culture" History Workshop conference, University of the Witwatersrand, July 13–15, 1994.

———. 1999. Shopping during a Revolution: Entrepreneurs, Retailers and "White" Identity in South Africa's Democratic Transition. Paper presented at "The TRC: Commissioning the Past" conference, University of the Witwatersrand, June 11–14, 1999.

Ijsselmuiden, C. B. 1983. Beliefs and Practices concerning Measles in Gazankulu. *South African Medical Journal* 63(10): 360–363.

Irish, Jenny. 2002. *Policing for Profit: The Future of South Africa's Private Security Industry.* Pretoria: Institute for Security Studies.

Isaac, Dev. 2002. The Structure of the Natural Sciences Learning Area Statement and Opportunities within It for Teaching and Learning of Evolution. In *The Architect and the Scaffold: Evolution and Education in South Africa,* ed. Wilmot James and Lynne Wilson. Cape Town: Human Sciences Research Council and New Africa Books.

Jager, A. K., A. Hutchings, and J. van Staden. 1996. Screening of Zulu Medicinal Plants for Prostaglandin-Synthesis Inhibitors. *Journal of Ethnopharmacology* 52(2): 95–100.

James, William. 1897. *The Will to Believe and Other Essays in Popular Philosophy.* New York and London: Longmans, Green, and Co.

James, Wilmot, and Linda Van de Vijver. 2001. *After the TRC: Reflections on Truth and Reconciliation in South Africa.* Cape Town: David Philip; Athens: Ohio University Press.

Jansen, Jonathan D. 2003. The Politics of Salvation: Pushing the Limits of the Rainbow Curriculum. Unpublished paper.

Janzen, John M. 1978. *The Quest for Therapy in Lower Zaire.* Berkeley and Los Angeles: University of California Press.

———. 1992. *Ngoma: Discourses of Healing in Central and Southern Africa.* Berkeley and Los Angeles: University of California Press.

Jarvie, I. C., and Joseph Agassi. 1970. The Problem of Rationality and Magic. In *Rationality,* ed. Wilson Bryan. New York: Harper and Row.

Jedrej, M. C., and Rosalind Shaw. 1992. *Dreaming, Religion, and Society in Africa.* Leiden: E. J. Brill.

Jeeves, Alan. 1975. The Control of Migratory Labour in the South African Gold Mines in the Era of Kruger and Milner. *Journal of Southern African Studies* 2(1): 3–29.

Jeffery, Anthea. 1999. *The Truth about the Truth Commission.* Johannesburg: South African Institute for Race Relations.

Jingoes, Stimela Jason. 1975. *A Chief Is a Chief by the People: The Autobiography of Stimela Jason Jingoes, Recorded and Compiled by John and Cassandra Perry.* London: Oxford University Press.

John Paul II. 1998. Encyclical Letter Fides et Ratio of the Supreme Pontiff John Paul II to the Bishops of the Catholic Church on the Relationship between Faith and Reason. September 14, 1998. The Holy See, the Vatican. http://www.vatican.va/holy_father/john_paul_ii/encyclicals/documents/hf_jp-ii_enc_15101998_fides-et-ratio_en.html.

Johnson, R. W. 1977. *How Long Will South Africa Survive?* London: Macmillan Press.

Johnston, M. 1977. Folk Beliefs and Ethnocultural Behavior in Pediatrics: Medicine or Magic. *Nursing Clinics of North America* 12(1): 77–84.

Jones, J. S. 1998. Bringing Traditional Healers into TB Control. *South African Medical Journal* 88(8): 929.

Jonker, Cor. 1992. Sleeping with the Devil: Christian Re-interpretation of Spirit Possession in Zambia. *Etnofoor* 5(1/2): 213–233.

Jordan, A. L. 1980. *The Wrath of the Ancestors.* Trans. from the original Xhosa by the author with the help of Priscilla P. Gordon. Alice: Lovedale Press.

Jordan, Bobby. 2000. AIDS Deaths Rocketing in Johannesburg. *Sunday Times* (Johannesburg) Internet ed., May 28, 2000. http://www.suntimes.co.za/2000/05/28/news/gauteng/njhb03.htm.

———. 2002. The Superbugs That Won't Lie Down and Die. *Sunday Times* (Johannesburg) Internet ed., June 16, 2002. http://www.suntimes.co.za/2002/06/16/news/news23.asp.

Jordan, Pallo. 1997. The National Question in Post-1994 South Africa (A Discussion Paper in Preparation for the ANC's 50th National Conference, Mafikeng, 1997). http://www.anc.org.za/ancdocs/discussion/natquestion.html.

Joubert, Jan-Jan. 2001. Spat over Vlakplaas "Cleansing." *Beeld* (Johannesburg), December 14, 2001.

Jung, Courtney. 2000. *Then I Was Black: South African Political Identities in Transition.* New Haven: Yale University Press.

Junod, Henri A. 1910. Les conceptions physiologiques des Bantoes Sud-Africains et leurs tabous. *Revue d'Ethnographie et Sociologie* 1: 126–169.

———. 1962a. *The Life of a South African Tribe.* Vol. 1, *Social Life.* New Hyde Park, NY: University Books.

———. 1962b. *The Life of a South African Tribe.* Vol. 2, *Mental Life.* New Hyde Park, NY: University Books.

Kaido, T. L., D. J. Veale, I. Havlik, and D. B. Rama. 1997. Preliminary Screening of Plants Used in South Africa as Traditional Herbal Remedies during Pregnancy and Labour. *Journal of Ethnopharmacology* 55(3): 185–191.

Kaigh, Frederick. 1947. *Witchcraft and Magic of Africa.* London: Richard Lesley and Co.

Kairos Theologians. 1985. *The Kairos Document: A Challenge to the Church.* Johannesburg: Skotaville.

Kale, R. 1995. Traditional Healers in South Africa: A Parallel Health Care System. *British Medical Journal* 310(6988): 1182–1185.

Kallaway, Peter. 1984. An Introduction to the Study of Education for Blacks in South Africa. In *Apartheid and Education,* ed. Peter Kallaway. Johannesburg: Ravan Press.

Kambizi, L., and A. J. Afolayan. 2001. An Ethnobotanical Study of Plants Used for the Treatment of Sexually Transmitted Diseases (*Njovhera*) in Guruve District, Zimbabwe. *Journal of Ethnopharmacology* 77(1): 5–9.

Kane-Berman, John. 1978. *Soweto Black Revolt, White Reaction.* Johannesburg: Ravan Press.

Kanuma, Shyaka. Good Admin's the Best *Muti. Weekly Mail and Guardian* (Johannesburg), March 22, 2002.

Kapferer, Bruce. 1997. *The Feast of the Sorcerer: Practices of Consciousness and Power.* Chicago: University of Chicago Press.

Kaplan, Temma. 1999. Truth without Reconciliation in Chile: Testimonies of the Tortured and the Case against Augusto Pinochet. Paper presented at "The TRC: Commissioning the Past" conference, University of the Witwatersrand, June 11–14, 1999.

Karis, Thomas G., and Gail M. Gerhart. 1977. *From Protest to Challenge.* Vol. 3. Stanford: Stanford Institution Press, Stanford University.

Karp, Ivan, and D. A. Masolo. 2000. *African Philosophy as Cultural Inquiry.* Bloomington: Indiana University Press.

Katsoulis, L. C., D. J. Veale, and I. Havlik. 2000. The Pharmacological Action of *Rhoicissus tridentata* on Isolated Rat Uterus and Ileum. *Phytotherapy Research* 14(6): 460–462.

Kelly, J. C. 1995. Co-operation between Traditional Healers and Medical Personnel. *South African Medical Journal* 85(7): 686.

Kelmanson, J. E., A. K. Jager, and J. van Staden. 2000. Zulu Medicinal Plants with Antibacterial Activity. *Journal of Ethnopharmacology* 69(3): 241–246.

Keswa, E. R. G. 1975. Outlawed Communities: A Study of Contra-acculturation among Black Criminals in South Africa. Unpublished paper.

Keteyi, Xolile. 1998. *Inculturation as a Strategy for Liberation: A Challenge for South Africa.* Pietermaritzburg, RSA: Cluster Publications.

Kidd, Dudley. 1969. *Savage Childhood.* New York: Negro Universities Press.

Kiernan, James P. 1974. Where Zionists Draw the Line: A Study of Religious Exclusiveness in an African Township. *African Studies* 33(2): 79–90.

———. 1976. Prophet and Preacher: An Essential Partnership in the Work of Zion. *Man,* n.s., 11: 356–366.

———. 1976. The Work of Zion: An Analysis of an African Zionist Ritual. *Africa* 46: 340–356.

———. 1977. Poor and Puritan: An Attempt to View Zionism as a Collective Response to Urban Poverty. *African Studies* 36(1): 31–41.

———. 1978a. Is the Witchdoctor Medically Competent? *South African Medical Journal* 53(26): 1072–1073.

———. 1978b. Saltwater and Ashes: Instruments of Curing among Some Zulu Zionists. *Journal of Religion in Africa* 9(1): 27–32.

———. 1979. The Weapons of Zion. *Journal of Religion in Africa* 10(1): 11–21.

———. 1982. The "Problem of Evil" in the Context of Ancestral Intervention in the Affairs of the Living in Africa. *Man,* n.s., 17: 287–301.

———. 1984. A Cesspool of Sorcery: How Zionists Visualize and Respond to the City. *Urban Anthropology* 13(3): 219–236.

———. 1987. The Role of the Adversary in Zulu Zionist Churches. *Religion in Southern Africa* 8(1): 3–13.

———. 1990a. African and Christian: From Opposition to Mutual Accommodation. In *Amidst Apartheid: Selected Perspectives on the Church in South Africa,* ed. M. Prozesky. New York: St. Martins.

———. 1990b. *The Production and Management of Therapeutic Power in Zionist Churches within a Zulu City.* Lewiston: Edwin Mellen.

———. 1991. Wear 'n' Tear and Repair: The Colour Coding of Mystical Mending in Zulu Zionist Churches. *Africa* 61(1): 26–39.

———. 1994. The Healing Community and the Future of the Urban Working Class. *Journal for the Study of Religion* 7(1): 49–64.

———. 1995a. The African Independent Churches. In *Living Faiths in South Africa,* ed. M. Prozesky and J. De Gruchy. Cape Town: David Philip.

———. 1995b. The Truth Revealed or the Truth Assembled: Reconsidering the Role of the African Diviner in Religion and Society. *Journal for the Study of Religion* 8(2): 3–21.

Kiguwa, S. N. W. 1999. National Reconciliation and Nation Building: Reflections on the TRC in Post Apartheid South Africa. Paper presented at "The TRC: Commissioning the Past" conference, University of the Witwatersrand, June 11–14, 1999.

Kindra, Jaspreen. 2001. "I Need to Keep People Fighting": Former KZN "Warlord" Thomas Shabalala's Tryst with Tragedy Is Helping Break the Stigma Attached to Aids. *Mail and Guardian* (Johannesburg), March 30, 2001.

———. 2002. Aids Drugs Killed Parks, Says ANC. *Weekly Mail and Guardian* (Johannesburg) Internet ed., March 22, 2002. http://www.sn.apc.org/wmail/issues/020322/OTHER102.html.

Kingon, J. R. L. 1919. The Transition from Tribalism to Individualism. *South African Journal of Science* 16: 113–157.

Kistner, Wolfram. 1999. Reconciliation in Dispute. Paper presented at "The TRC: Commissioning the Past" conference, University of the Witwatersrand, June 11–14, 1999.

Klaaren, Jonathan. 1999. A Second Organisational Amnesty? Paper presented at "The TRC: Commissioning the Past" conference, University of the Witwatersrand, June 11–14, 1999.

Klaaste, Aggrey. 1986. A Stake in the System. *New Internationalist* 159. http://www.oneworld.org/ni/issue159/stake.htm.

Kleinman, Arthur. 1980. *Patients and Healers in the Context of Culture: An Exploration of the Borderland between Anthropology, Medicine, and Psychiatry.* Berkeley and Los Angeles: University of California Press.

Kluckhohn, Clyde. 1944. *Navaho Witchcraft.* Boston: Beacon Press.

Kohler, M. 1941. *The Izangoma Diviners.* Pretoria: Union of South Africa, Department of Native Affairs.

Kohnert, Dirk. 1996. Magic and Witchcraft: Implications for Democratization and Poverty-Alleviating Aid in Africa. *World Development* 24(8): 1347–1355.

———. 2001. Witchcraft and the Democratization of South Africa. *African Legal Studies* 2: 177–182.

Kok, Pieter. 2002. Internal Migration and Urbanisation in South Africa: Issues of Research, Policy and Development. Human Sciences Research Council. http://www.hsrc.ac.za/corporate/FocusOn/pckok.html.

König, A. 1987. Theological Response to Ashby, Codrington, Gaybba and Möller. In *Like a Roaring Lion . . . : Essays on the Bible, the Church and Demonic Powers,* ed. Pieter De Villiers. Pretoria: C. B. Powell Bible Centre.

Kopytoff, I. 1971. Ancestors as Elders. *Africa* 41: 129–142.

Kors, Alan C., and Edward Peters, eds. 1972. *Witchcraft in Europe, 1100–1700: A Documentary History.* Philadelphia: University of Pennsylvania Press.

Koziell, A. B., and I. F. Laurenson. 1988. Witchdoctors in Africa. *British Medical Journal (Clinical Research Edition)* 296(6616): 179–181.

Krämer, Heinrich, and Jacob Sprenger. 1486. The *Malleus Maleficarum.* In Kors and Peters 1972.

Krige, Eileen Jensen. 1936. *The Social System of the Zulus.* London: Longman and Green.

Krige, J. D. 1944. The Magical Thought-Pattern of the Bantu in Relation to Health Services. *African Studies* 3(1): 1–13.

Kritzinger, J. J. 1993. The Numbers Game: Independent Churches. *Africa Insight* 23(4): 249.

Krog, Antjie. 1998. *Country of My Skull.* New York: Times Books.

Kros, C. J. 1999. "Putting the History Books Straight": Reflections on Rewriting Biko. Paper presented at "The TRC: Commissioning the Past" conference, University of the Witwatersrand, June 11–14, 1999.

Kruger, Albert. 1983. *Lansdown's South African Liquor Law.* 5th ed. Cape Town: Juta.

Kubukeli, P. 1997. A "Traditional" Traditional Healer: Philip Kubukeli. Interview by Jonathan Spencer Jones. *South African Medical Journal* 87(7): 917.

Kuckertz, Heinz. 1983. Symbol and Authority in Mpondo Ancestor Religion, Part 1. *African Studies* 42: 113–132.

———. 1984. Symbol and Authority in Mpondo Ancestor Religion, Part 2. *African Studies* 43: 1–17.

———. 1990. *Creating Order: The Image of the Homestead in Mpondo Social Life.* Johannesburg: Witwatersrand University Press.

Kulkarni, Anu. 1999. Truth Commissions: Institutional Strategies for Trust Construction and Conflict Management. Paper presented at "The TRC: Commissioning the Past" conference, University of the Witwatersrand, June 11–14, 1999.

Kuper, Adam. 1982. *Brides for Cattle: Bridewealth and Marriage in Southern Africa.* London: Routledge and Kegan Paul.

Kuper, Hilda. 1947. *An African Aristocracy: Rank among the Swazi.* London: Oxford University Press, for the International African Institute.

Kymlicka, Will. 1995. *Multicultural Citizenship: A Liberal Theory of Minority Rights.* Oxford: Clarendon Press.

Lacey, Marian. 1981. *Working for Boroko.* Johannesburg: Ravan Press.

Lagerwerf, Leny. 1987. *Witchcraft, Sorcery, and Spirit Possession: Pastoral Responses in Africa.* Gweru: Mambo Press.

La Hausse, Paul. 1984. The Struggle for the City: Alcohol, The Ematsheni and Popular Culture in Durban, 1902–1936. MA thesis, University of Cape Town.

Lambrecht, Ingo. 2002. Cultural Artifacts and the Oracular Trance States of the Sangoma in South Africa. In *Art and Oracle: African Art and Rituals of Divination,*

ed. Alisa LaGamma. New York: Metropolitan Museum of Art. http://www.met
   museum.org/explore/oracle/essay.html.

Lamont, D. L., and J. A. Duflou. 1988. Copper Sulfate: Not a Harmless Chemical.
   American Journal of Forensic Medical Pathology 9(3): 226–227.

Landman, Willem A., Johann Mouton, and Khanyisa H. Nevhutalu. 2001. Chris Hani
   Baragwanath Hospital Ethics Audit, vol. 2. Ethics Institute of South Africa Research Reports. Pretoria. http://www.ethicsa.org/CHBHFinalReport021101-
   10H40.pdf.

Language Plan Task Group. 1996. Towards a National Language Plan for South Africa: Summary of the Final Report of the Language Plan Task Group. Ministry of
   Arts, Culture, Science, and Technology, Pretoria. http:www.polity.org.za/govdocs/
   reports/langtag.html.

Lanning, Mark, Neil Roake, and Glynis Horning. 2003. *Life—Soweto Style.* Cape
   Town: Struik.

Lanternari, Vittorio. 1963. *The Religions of the Oppressed: A Study of Modern Messianic Cults.* Trans. Lisa Sergio. New York: Alfred A. Knopf.

Lanz, Henry. 1936. Metaphysics of Gossip. *International Journal of Ethics* 46(4): 492–
   499.

Last, Murray. 1992. On the Importance of Knowing about Not Knowing: Observations
   from Hausaland. In Feierman and Janzen.

Latour, Bruno. 1993. *We Have Never Been Modern.* Cambridge: Harvard University
   Press.

Laubscher, B. J. F. 1937. *Sex, Custom, and Psychopathology: A Study of South African
   Pagan Natives.* London: Routledge and Kegan Paul.

Lecky, William Edward Hartpole. 1891. *History of the Rise and Influence of the Spirit of
   Rationalism in Europe.* Rev. ed. 2 vols. New York: D. Appleton.

Leclerc-Madlala, Suzanne. 1994. Zulu Health, Cultural Meanings, and the Reinterpre-
   tation of Western Pharmaceuticals. Paper presented at the Association of Anthropology in South Africa conference, University of Durban-Westville, Durban.

———. 1997. Infect One, Infect All: Zulu Youth Response to the AIDS Epidemic in
   South Africa. *Medical Anthropology* 17(4): 363–380.

Lederle, H. I. 1987. Better the Devil You Know? Seeking a Biblical Basis for the Soci-
   etal Dimension of Evil and/or the Demonic Life in the Pauline Concept of the
   "Powers." In *Like a Roaring Lion ... : Essays on the Bible, the Church and Demonic
   Powers,* ed. Pieter De Villiers. Pretoria: C. B. Powell Bible Centre.

Lee, S. G. 1969. Spirit Possession among the Zulu. In Beattie and Middleton 1969.

Leonard, Kenneth L. 2001a. African Traditional Healers: The Economics of Healing.
   IKNotes 32. http://www.worldbank.org/afr/ik/iknt32.pdf.

———. 2001b. African Traditional Healers: Incentives and Skill in Health Care Delivery. Discussion Papers Series 9798-13, Department of Economics, Columbia
   University.

Le Roux, A. G. 1973. Psychopathology in Bantu Culture. *South African Medical Journal* 47(43): 2077–2083.

Lever, Jeffrey. 2002. Science, Evolution and Schooling in South Africa. In *The Architect and the Scaffold: Evolution and Education in South Africa,* ed. Wilmot James

and Lynne Wilson. Cape Town: Human Sciences Research Council and New Africa Books.

Lewis, Patrick. 1966. *"City within a City": The Creation of Soweto.* Johannesburg: Johannesburg City Council.

Liebenberg, Ian. 1999. Comparative International Perspectives: The TRC in South Africa—Some Tentative Observations. Paper presented at "The TRC: Commissioning the Past" conference, University of the Witwatersrand, June 11–14, 1999.

Liehardt, Godfrey. 1961. *Divinity and Experience: The Religion of the Dinka.* Oxford: Oxford University Press.

Lin, J., A. R. Opoku, M. Geheeb-Keller, A. D. Hutchings, S. E. Terblanche, A. K. Jager, and J. van Staden. 1999. Preliminary Screening of Some Traditional Zulu Medicinal Plants for Anti-inflammatory and Anti-microbial Activities. *Journal of Ethnopharmacology* 68(1–3): 267–274.

Lin, J., T. Puckree, and T. P. Mvelase. 2002. Anti-diarrhoeal Evaluation of Some Medicinal Plants Used by Zulu Traditional Healers. *Journal of Ethnopharmacology* 79(1): 53–56.

Lindsey, K., A. K. Jager, D. M. Raidoo, and J. van Staden. 1999. Screening of Plants Used by Southern African Traditional Healers in the Treatment of Dysmenorrhoea for Prostaglandin-Synthesis Inhibitors and Uterine Relaxing Activity. *Journal of Ethnopharmacology* 64(1): 9–14.

Livingstone, David. 1857. *Missionary Travels and Researches in Africa; Including a Sketch of Sixteen Years' Residence in the Interior of Africa and a Journey From the Cape of Good Hope to Loanda on the West Coast; Thence Across the Continent, Down the River Zambesi, to the Eastern Ocean.* London: Murray.

Longmore, Laura. 1958. Medicine, Magic, and Witchcraft among Urban Africans on the Witwatersrand. *Central African Journal of Medicine* 4(6): 242–249.

———. 1959. *The Dispossessed: A Study of the Sex-Life of Bantu Women in and around Johannesburg.* London: Jonathon Cape.

———. 1997. My Doctor and My Gods. *Journal of Alternative and Complementary Medicine* 3(4): 391–395.

Loram, C. T. 1931. Foreword to Cook 1931, ix–x.

———. 1969. *The Education of the South African Natives.* New York: Negro Universities Press. (Orig. pub. 1917.)

Lotter, J. M. 1988. Prison Gangs in South Africa: A Description. *South African Journal of Sociology* 19(2): 67–75.

Louw, Antoinette, and Charles D. H. Parry. 1999. *The MRC/ISS 3-Metros Arrestee Study.* Tygerberg: Medical Research Council of South Africa.

Louw, Dap A., and Engela Pretorius. 1995. The Traditional Healer in a Multicultural Society: The South African Experience. In *Spirit versus Scalpel: Traditional Healing and Modern Psychotherapy,* ed. Leonore Loeb Adler and B. Runi Mukherji. Westport: Bergin and Garvey.

Louw, Dirk J. 1997. *Ubuntu:* An African Assessment of the Religious Other. *Paideia, Philosophy in Africa.* http://www.bu.edu/wcp/Papers/Afri/AfriLouw.htm.

Lubisi, Dumisani. 2000. Mob Goes Wild after Mozzies Are "Bewitched." *Sunday Times* (Johannesburg), January 16, 2000, p. 16.

Luhmann, Niklas. 1979. *Trust and Power: Two Works by Niklas Luhmann.* New York: John Wiley.

Lukes, Steven. 1970. Some Problems about Rationality. In *Rationality,* ed. Wilson Bryan. New York: Harper and Row.

Lukhaimane, Elias K. 1980. The Zion Christian Church of Ignatius (Engenas) Lekganyang, 1924–1948: An African Experiment with Christianity. MA thesis, Department of History, University of the North.

Lukhele, Andrew Kehla. 1990. *Stokvels in South Africa: Informal Savings Schemes by Blacks for the Black Community.* Johannesburg: Amagi.

Lusu, T., N. Buhlungu, and H. Grant. 2001. The Attitudes of Parents to Traditional Medicine and the Surgeon. *South African Medical Journal* 91(4): 270–271.

Luyckx, V. A., R. Ballantine, M. Claeys, F. Cuyckens, H. Van den Heuvel, R. K. Cimanga, A. J. Vlietinck, M. E. De Broe, and I. J. Katz. 2002. Herbal Remedy-Associated Acute Renal Failure Secondary to Cape Aloes. *American Journal of Kidney Disease* 39(3): E13.

Mabille, A., and H. Dieterlen. 1961. *Southern Sotho–English Dictionary.* Reclassified, revised, and enlarged by R. A. Paroz. Morija: Morija Sesuto Book Depot.

Mabin, Alan. 1992. Dispossession, Exploitation, and Struggle: An Historical Overview of South African Urbanisation. In *The Apartheid City and Beyond: Urbanization and Social Change in South Africa,* ed. David M. Smith. London: Routledge.

Mabina, M. H., J. Moodley, and S. B. Pitsoe. 1997. The Use of Traditional Herbal Medication during Pregnancy. *Tropical Doctor* 27(2): 84–86.

Macfarlane, Alan. 1970. *Witchcraft in Tudor and Stuart England: A Regional and Comparative Study.* London: Routledge and Kegan Paul.

Maclean, C. B. 1906. *A Compendium of Kafir Laws and Customs, Including Genealogical Tables of Kafir Chiefs and Various Tribal Census Returns.* Grahamstown: J. Slater.

Madi, Phinda Mzwakhe. 1997. *Black Economic Empowerment in the New South Africa: The Rights and the Wrongs.* Randburg: Knowledge Resources.

Maduna, Penuell. 1993. Popular Perceptions of Policing among Blacks in South Africa. In *Policing the Conflict in South Africa,* ed. M. L. Mathews, Philip B. Heymann, and A. S. Mathews. Gainesville: University of Florida Press.

Mafeje, Archie. 1975. Religion, Class, and Ideology in South Africa. In *Religion and Social Change in Southern Africa,* ed. M. G. Whisson and M. E. West. Cape Town: David Philip.

Magubane, Peter. 1998. *Vanishing Cultures of South Africa: Changing Customs in a Changing World.* Cape Town: Struik.

Magubane, Peter, David Bristow, and Stan Motjuwadi. 1990. *Soweto: Portrait of a City.* London: New Holland.

Mahomedy, M. C., Y. H. Mahomedy, P. A. Canham, J. W. Downing, and D. E. Jeal. 1975. Methaemoglobinaemia Following Treatment Dispensed by Witch Doctors: Two Cases of Potassium Permanganate Poisoning. *Anaesthesia* 30(2): 190–193.

Maimela, Simon. 1987. *Proclaim Freedom to My People: Essays on Religion and Politics.* Johannesburg: Skotaville Publishers.

Mair, Lucy. 1969. *Witchcraft.* New York: McGraw-Hill.

Majeke, A. M. S. 2002. Towards a Culture-Based Foundation for Indigenous Knowledge Systems in the Field of Custom and Law. In Odora Hoppers 2002c.

Makgoba, M. W. 2000. HIV/AIDS: The Peril of Pseudoscience. *Science* 288(5469): 1171.

Makhubu, Paul. 1988. *Who Are the Independent Churches?* Johannesburg: Skotaville Publishers.

Malala, Justice. 1999. Blacks in Business: Robin Hoods or Just Greedy? *Sunday Times* (Johannesburg), Internet ed., March 21, 1999. http://www.suntimes.co.za/1999/03/21/insight/in03.htm.

Malala, Josephine. 2001. The Perceptions of the Body Illness and Disease amongst Sex Workers in Hillbrow. Paper presented at the "AIDS in Context" conference, University of the Witwatersrand, April 4–7, 2001.

Malan, Rian. 1990. *My Traitor's Heart: A South African Exile Returns to Face His Country, His Tribe, and His Conscience.* New York: Atlantic Monthly Press.

Maluleke, Tinyiko Sam. 1996. African Culture, African Intellectuals, and the White Academy in South Africa. *Religion and Theology* 3(1): 19–42. http://www.unisa.ac.za/dept/press/rt/31/sam.html.

———. 1998. Epilogue to Keteyi 1998.

Mamdani, Mahmood. 1996. *Citizen and Subject: Contemporary Africa and the Legacy of Late Colonialism.* Princeton: Princeton University Press.

Mandela, Nelson. 1992. Speech to the Free Ethiopian Church of Southern Africa, Potchefstroom. December 14, 1992. http://www.anc.org.za/ancdocs/history/mandela/sp921214.html.

———. 1997. Address by President Mandela at the Launch of the National Campaign for Learning and Teaching, Soweto. February 20, 1997. Pretoria: Office of the President.

———. 1999. Address by President Nelson Mandela to Parliament. February 5, 1999. http://usaembassy.southafrica.net/Mandela/speeches1999/nm0205.htm.

Mander, Myles. 1998. Marketing of Indigenous Medicinal Plants in South Africa: A Case Study in Kwazulu-Natal. Food and Agriculture Organization, Rome. http://www.fao.org/docrep/W9195E/w9195e00.htm.

Mandy, Nigel. 1984. *A City Divided: Johannesburg and Soweto.* Johannesburg: Macmillan.

Manganyi, N. C. 1974. Health and Disease: Some Topical Problems of Sociocultural Transition. *South African Medical Journal* 48(21): 922–924.

Mankazana, E. M. 1979. A Case for the Traditional Healer in South Africa. *South African Medical Journal* 56(23): 1003–1007.

Marais, G., and R. van der Kooy, eds. 1986. *South Africa's Urban Blacks: Problems and Challenges.* Pretoria: Centre for Management Studies, School of Business Leadership, University of South Africa.

Market Research Africa. 1968. *An African Day: A Second Study of Life in the Townships.* Johannesburg: Market Research Africa.

Marks, Monique. 1993. Identity and Violence amongst Activist Diepkloof Youth, 1984–1993. Department of Sociology, University of the Witwatersrand.

———. 1995a. Alternative Policing Structures? A Look at Youth Defence Structures in Gauteng in 1995. Centre for the Study of Violence and Reconciliation Occasional Paper, Johannesburg.

———. 1995b. We Are Fighting for the Liberation of Our People: Justifications of Violence by Activist Youth in Diepkloof Soweto. *Temps Modernes* 585: 133–158.

Marlin-Curiel, Stephanie. 1999. Truth and Consequences: Art in Response to the Truth and Reconciliation Commission. Paper presented at "The TRC: Commissioning the Past" conference, University of the Witwatersrand, June 11–14, 1999.

Martin, Ruth. 1989. *Witchcraft and the Inquisition in Venice, 1550–1650.* Oxford: Blackwell.

Marwick, M. G. 1962. Problems of African Urbanisation. In *Man in Africa: Lectures Delivered at the Winter School of the National Union of South African Students at the University of Natal, July 1961,* 18–20. Cape Town: National Union of South African Students.

Marwick, Max. 1982. *Witchcraft and Sorcery.* Middlesex, UK: Penguin Books.

Maseko, Bheki. 1988. Mamlambo. In *From South Africa: New Writing, Photographs, and Art,* ed. David Bunn and Jane Taylor. Chicago: University of Chicago Press.

Mashatile, Paul. 1999. MEC Speech on Occasion of the Handover of Title Deeds in Soweto. August 24, 1999. Gauteng Department of Housing, Johannesburg. http://www.housing.gpg.gov.za/pages/mecspeechetitelrelease.htm.

Mashelkar, R. A. 2002. The Role of Intellectual Property in Building Capacity for Innovation for Development. In Odora Hoppers 2002c.

Masika, P. J., W. van Averbeke, and A. Sonandi. 2000. Use of Herbal Remedies by Small-Scale Farmers to Treat Livestock Diseases in Central Eastern Cape Province, South Africa. *Journal of the South African Veterinary Association* 71(2): 87–91.

Maslowski, J., Jansen van Rensburg, and N. Mthoko. 1998. A Polydiagnostic Approach to the Differences in the Symptoms of Schizophrenia in Different Cultural and Ethnic Populations. *Acta Psychiatrica Scandavica* 98(1): 41–46.

Masoga, Mogomme Alpheus. 1995. Toward Sacrificial-Cleansing Ritual in South Africa: An Indigenous African View. Unpublished paper.

Masolo, D. A. 1994. *African Philosophy in Search of Identity.* Bloomington and Indianapolis: Indiana University Press.

Mathiane, Nomavenda. 1990. *Beyond the Headlines: Truths of Soweto Life.* Johannesburg: Southern Book Publishers.

Mavhungu, Khaukanani. 2000. Heroes, Villains and the State in South Africa's Witchcraft Zone. *African Anthropologist* 7(1): 114–129.

Maxwell, David. 1999. Historicizing Christian Independency: The Southern African Pentecostal Movement, c. 1908–60. *Journal of African History* 40: 243–264.

May, Julian, ed. 1998. Poverty and Inequality in South Africa: Report Prepared for the Office of the Executive Deputy President and the Inter-ministerial Committee for Poverty and Inequality. http:www.polity.org.za/govdocs/reports/poverty.html.

Mayekiso, Mzwanele. 1996. *Township Politics: Civic Struggles for a New South Africa.* New York: Monthly Review Press.

Mayer, Philip. 1961. *Townsmen or Tribesmen: Conservatism and the Process of Urban-ization in a South African City.* Cape Town: Oxford University Press.

———. 1970. Witches. In *Witchcraft and Sorcery: Selected Readings,* ed. Max Marwick. Harmondsworth, UK: Penguin.

———. 1979. Soweto People and Their Social Universes. Unpublished. Typescript in Human Sciences Research Council library, Pretoria.

Maylam, Paul. 1995. Explaining the Apartheid City: 20 Years of South African Urban Historiography. *Journal of Southern African Studies* 21(1): 19–38.

Mbeki, Thabo. 1996. Statement of Deputy President Thabo Mbeki on Behalf of the African National Congress on the Occasion of the Adoption by the Constitutional Assembly of the "Republic of South Africa Constitution Bill 1996." May 8, 1996. Republic of South Africa, National Assembly. http://www.anc.org.za/ancdocs/history/mbeki/1996/sp960508.html.

———. 1998. Statement of Deputy President Thabo Mbeki at the Opening of the De-bate in the National Assembly on "Reconciliation and Nation Building." May 28, 1998. Republic of South Africa, National Assembly. http://www.anc.org.za/ancdocs/history/mbeki/1998/sp980529.html.

———. 1999. Prologue. In *African Renaissance: The New Struggle,* ed. Malegapuru William Makgoba. Sandton and Cape Town: Mafube and Tafelberg.

Mbiti, John S. 1980. The Encounter of Christian Faith and African Religion. *Christian Century* 97(27): 817–820.

———. 1989. *African Religions and Philosophy.* 2nd rev. and enl. ed. Oxford: Heine-mann International.

McAllister, Patrick. 1992. Beer Drinking and Labor Migration in the Transkei: The Invention of a Ritual Tradition. In *Liquor and Labor in Southern Africa,* ed. Jona-than Crush and Charles Ambler. Athens: Ohio University Press.

McCallum, Taffy Gould. 1993. *White Woman Witchdoctor: Tales from the African Life of Rae Graham.* Miami: Fielden Books.

McCord, Margaret. 1997. *The Calling of Katie Makhanya: A Memoir of South Africa.* New York: John Wiley.

McVann, A., I. Havlik, P. H. Joubert, and F. S. Monteagudo. 1992. Cardiac Glycoside Poisoning Involved in Deaths from Traditional Medicines. *South African Medical Journal* 81(3): 139–141.

Mda, Zakes. 2000. *The Heart of Redness.* Cape Town: Oxford University Press.

Medlen, L. 1991. Science or Sangoma? *Nursing RSA Verpleging* 6(7): 3.

Meister, Robert. 1999. After Evil: Moral Logics of National Recovery in the TRC *Final Report.* Paper presented at "The TRC: Commissioning the Past" conference, Uni-versity of the Witwatersrand, June 11–14, 1999.

Melland, Frank. 1935. Ethical and Political Aspects of African Witchcraft. *Africa* 8: 495–503.

Meyer, Birgit. 1999. *Translating the Devil: Religion and Modernity among the Ewe in Ghana.* Trenton: Africa World Press.

Meyer, J. J., and F. Dilika. 1996. Antibacterial Activity of *Helichrysum pedunculatum* Used in Circumcision Rites. *Journal of Ethnopharmacology* 53(1): 51–54.

Mfusi, M. J. H. 1990. Soweto Zulu Slang: A Sociolinguistic Study of an Urban Vernacular in Soweto. BA honours thesis, University of South Africa.

Michie, C. A., M. Hayhurst, G. J. Knobel, J. M. Stokol, and B. Hensley. 1991. Poisoning with a Traditional Remedy Containing Potassium Dichromate. *Human and Experimental Toxicology* 10(2): 129–131.

Middleton, John. 1967. *Magic, Witchcraft, and Curing.* Garden City, NY: Natural History Press.

Middleton, John, and E. H. Winter. 1963. *Witchcraft and Sorcery in East Africa.* London: Routledge and Kegan Paul.

Milingo, Emmanuel. 1984. *The World in Between: Christian Healing and the Struggle for Spiritual Survival.* Ed. Mona Macmillan. London: Hurst.

Mill, J. S. 1859. *On Liberty, Representative Government, the Subjection of Women.* London: Oxford University Press.

Miller, F. P. 1987. Pentecostal Perspectives on the Activity of Demonic Powers. In *Like a Roaring Lion . . . : Essays on the Bible, the Church and Demonic Powers,* ed. Pieter De Villiers. Pretoria: C. B. Powell Bible Centre.

Mills, C. Wright. 1940. Situated Actions and Vocabularies of Motive. *American Sociological Review* 5(6): 904–913.

Minaar, Anthony. 1998. Witchpurging and *Muti* Murders in South Africa with Specific Reference to the Northern Province. Paper presented at South African Police Service Occult Crime Unit Workshop on Occult- and Witchcraft-Related Crime, Paarl Police College, Paarl.

Minaar, Anthony, Marie Wentzel, and Catherine Payze. 1998. Witch Killing with Specific Reference to the Northern Province of South Africa. In *Violence in South Africa: A Variety of Perspectives,* ed. E. Bornman, R. van Eeden, and M. Wentzel. Pretoria: Human Sciences Research Council.

Ministry of Education. 1999. Status Report for the Minister of Education. Pretoria. http://education.pwv.gov.za/Archives/StatusReport.htm.

Ministry of Transport. 1997. Second Draft White Paper on the Road Accident Fund. Pretoria. http://www.polity.org.za/govdocs/white_papers/mmf.html.

Mkhize, H. B. 1989. The Umthandazi—Prayer-Healer. In Oosthuizen et al. 1989.

Mkhwanazi, I. 1989. The ISangoma as Psycho-therapist. In Oosthuizen et al. 1989.

Mndende, Nokuzola. 1999. From Underground Praxis to Recognized Religion: Challenges Facing African Religions. In *Religion and Politics in South Africa: From Apartheid to Democracy,* ed. Abdulkader Tayob and Wolfram Weisse. Munich: Waxmann.

Moffat, Robert. 1842. *Missionary Labours and Scenes in Southern Africa.* London: John Snow.

Mofolo, Thomas. 1931. *Chaka: An Historical Romance.* Trans. from Sesuto by F. H. Dutton. London: Oxford University Press, for the International Institute of African Languages and Cultures.

[Mokaba, Peter?]. 2002. Castro Hlongwane, Caravans, Cats, Geese, Foot and Mouth and Statistics: HIV/AIDS and the Struggle for the Humanisation of the African. Discussion document circulated within ANC branches, reputedly authored by Peter Mokaba with input from Thabo Mbeki.

Molema, Samuel Modiri. 1920. *The Bantu Past and Present: An Ethnographical and Historical Study of the Native Races of South Africa.* Edinburgh: W. Green and Son.

———. 1950. *Chief Moroka: His Life, His Times, His Country, and His People.* Cape Town: Methodist Publishing House.

———. 1966. *Montshiwa: Barolong Chief and Patriot (1814–1896).* Cape Town: Struik.

Möller, F. P. 1987. Pentecostal Perspectives on the Activity of Demonic Powers. In *Like a Roaring Lion . . . : Essays on the Bible, the Church and Demonic Powers,* ed. Pieter De Villiers. Pretoria: C. B. Powell Bible Centre.

Moolman, Maurice. 1990. *From Town to Township: Regional Service Councils Assessed.* Johannesburg: South African Institute of Race Relations.

Moore, D. A., and N. L. Moore. 1998. Paediatric Enema Syndrome in a Rural African Setting. *Annals of Tropical Paediatrics* 18(2): 139–144.

Moore, Henrietta, and Todd Sanders. 2001a. Magical Interpretations and Material Realities: An Introduction. In Moore and Sanders 2001.

———. 2001b. *Magical Interpretations, Material Realities: Modernity, Witchcraft, and the Occult in Postcolonial Africa.* London: Routledge.

Moral Regeneration Committee. 2000. Freedom and Obligation: A Report on the Moral Regeneration Workshops I and II. http://www.polity.org.za/htm1/govdocs/reports/morals.htm.

Moral Regeneration Movement. 2003. Moral Regeneration Movement to Launch Moral Charter Campaign. Press statement, January 29, 2003. Johannesburg.

Morar, N. S., and S. S. Abdool Karim. 1998. Vaginal Insertion and Douching Practices among Sex Workers at Truck Stops in KwaZulu-Natal. *South African Medical Journal* 88(4): 470.

Morrell, Robert. 1998. Of Boys and Men: Masculinity and Gender in Southern African Studies. *Journal of Southern African Studies* 24(4): 605–630.

Morris, Alan. 1999a. *Bleakness and Light: Inner-City Transition in Hillbrow, Johannesburg.* Johannesburg: Witwatersrand University Press.

———, ed. 1999b. *Change and Continuity: A Survey of Soweto in the Late 1990s.* Johannesburg: Department of Sociology, University of the Witwatersrand.

Morris, K. 2001. Treating HIV in South Africa—a Tale of Two Systems. *Lancet* 357(9263): 1190.

Morris, Pauline. 1980. *Soweto: A Review of Existing Conditions and Some Guidelines for Change.* Johannesburg: Urban Foundation.

———. 1981. *A History of Black Housing in South Africa.* Johannesburg: South Africa Foundation.

Mosala, Itumeleng J., and Buti Tlhagale. 1986. *The Unquestionable Right to Be Free: Black Theology from South Africa.* Johannesburg: Skotaville Publishers.

Motala, M. B. 1989. The Relative Influence of Participation in Zionist Church Services on the Emotional State of Participants. In Oosthuizen et al. 1989.

Motlana, N. 1988. The Tyranny of Superstition. *Nursing RSA* 3(1): 17–18.

Motshekga, Mathole S. 1984. The Ideology behind Witchcraft and the Principle of Fault in Criminal Law. *Codicillus* 35(2): 4-14.

Mqotsi, L. 2002. Science, Magic and Religion as Trajectories of the Psychology of Projection. In Odora Hoppers 2002c.

Mshana, Robert. 2002. Globalisation and Intellectual Property Rights. In Odora Hoppers 2002c.

Mtalane, L. J., L. R. Uys, and E. M. Preston-Whyte. 1993. The Experience of Terminal Illness among Zulu Speaking Patients and Their Families. *International Journal of Nursing Studies* 30(2): 143–155.

Mthembu, C. 1981. Some Aspects of Traditional Beliefs as They Affect Tuberculosis Treatment. *Curationis* 4(3): 28.

Mtshali, Thokozani. I Have Seen My Family Die of Aids but No One Believes It. *Sunday Times* Internet ed. April 28, 2002. http://www.sundaytimes.co.za/2002/04/28/insight/ino4.asp.

Mudimbe, V. Y. 1988. *The Invention of Africa*. Bloomington and Indianapolis: Indiana University Press.

———. 1994. *The Idea of Africa*. Bloomington and Indianapolis: Indiana University Press.

Mufamadi, Thembeka. 1999. A Reflection on the Process of Research and Writing on Human Rights Violations in Venda. Paper presented at "The TRC: Commissioning the Past" conference, University of the Witwatersrand, June 11–14, 1999.

Mugo, Micere Gitae. 1999. African Culture in Education for Sustainable Development. In *African Renaissance: The New Struggle,* ed. William Malegapuru Makgoba. Sandton and Cape Town: Mafube and Tafelberg.

Murray, Colin. 1987. Displaced Urbanization: South Africa's Rural Slums. *African Affairs* 86: 311–329.

Mutwa, Credo Vusa'mazulu. 1969. *My People: The Writings of a Zulu Witchdoctor.* London: Anthony Blond.

———. 2002. The Sangoma's Lore of the Soul. *African Legal Studies* 2: 61–77.

Mzamane, Mbulelo. 1982. *The Children of Soweto.* Johannesburg: Ravan Press.

———. 1986. *Hungry Flames and Other Black South African Short Stories.* London: Longman.

Nathan, Laurie. 1989. Troops in the Townships, 1984–1987. In *War and Society: The Militarisation of South Africa,* ed. Jacklyn Cock and Laurie Nathan. Cape Town and Johannesburg: David Philip.

National Building Research Institute. 1954. *Research Studies on the Costs of Urban Bantu Housing.* Pretoria: South African Council for Scientific and Industrial Research.

National Party. 1996. Submission to the Truth and Reconciliation Commission by Mr. F. W. de Klerk, Leader of the National Party.

———. 1997. Second Submission of the National Party to the Truth and Reconciliation Commission.

National Research Foundation. 2001. Call for Proposals in Indigenous Knowledge Systems, 2002.

Native Economic Commission. 1932. *Report of Native Economic Commission, 1930–1932.* U.G. no. 22/1932. Pretoria.

Naudé, C. M. B., M. M. Grobbelaar, and H. F. Snyman. 1996. *The Second International Crime (Victim) Survey in Johannesburg: Summary of Research Findings.* Department of Criminology, University of South Africa, Pretoria.

Naude, Piet. 1995. *The Zionist Christian Church in South Africa: A Case-Study in Oral Theology*. Lewiston: Edwin Mellen.

Ndebele, Njabulo S. 1983. *Fools, and Other Stories*. Johannesburg: Ravan Press.

———. 1994. *South African Literature and Culture: Rediscovery of the Ordinary*. Manchester: Manchester University Press.

Ndlovu, Sifiso. 1997. *The Soweto Uprisings: Counter-memories of June 1976*. Johannesburg: Ravan Press.

Needham, Rodney. 1972. *Belief, Language, and Experience*. Chicago: University of Chicago Press.

Neke, Gael. 1999. (Re)Forming the Past: South African Art Bound to Apartheid. Paper presented at "The TRC: Commissioning the Past" conference, University of the Witwatersrand, June 11–14, 1999.

Nel, C. J., T. Verschoor, F. J. W. Calitz, and P. H. J. J. van Rensburg. 1992. The Importance of an Anthropological Perspective in Relevant Trials of Apparently Motiveless Murders. *South African Journal of Ethnology* 15(3): 85–92.

Newman, W. J., N. F. Moran, R. D. Theakston, D. A. Warrell, and D. Wilkinson. 1997. Traditional Treatments for Snake Bite in a Rural African Community. *Annals of Tropical Medicine and Parasitology* 91(8): 967–969.

New York City Police Department CompStat Unit. 2002. CompStat Report Covering the Week of 01/07/2002 through 01/13/2002. Vol. 9, no. 2. New York City Police Department. www.nyc.gov/html/nypd/pdf/.

Ngubane, Harriet. 1977. *Body and Mind in Zulu Medicine: An Ethnography of Health and Disease in Nyuswa-Zulu Thought and Practice*. London: Academic Press.

———. 1981. Clinical Practice and Organization of Indigenous Healers in South Africa. *Social Science and Medicine* 15(3): 361–366.

Ngubane, Jordan K. 1974. *Ushaba, the Hurtle to Blood River: A Zulu Umlando*. Washington, DC: Three Continents Press.

Niehaus, Isak A. 1997. Witchcraft, Power and Politics: An Ethnographic Study of the South African Lowveld. Ph.D. diss., Department of Social Anthropology, University of the Witwatersrand.

———. 2000. Witches and Zombies in the South African Lowveld: Symbolic Discourse, Accusation and Subjectivity. Unpublished paper.

———. 2001. *Witchcraft, Power, and Politics: Exploring the Occult in the South African Lowveld*. Cape Town: David Philip.

Normann, Hans, Ina Snyman, and Morris Cohen. 1996. *Indigenous Knowledge and Its Uses in South Africa*. Pretoria: Human Sciences Resource Council.

Nthai, Seth A. 2001. Witchcraft Violence—the Need for New Legislation. *African Legal Studies* 2: 158–162.

Ntshangase, Kruschev Dumisani Jombolo. 1993. The Social History of Isicamtho. MA thesis, Department of African Languages, University of the Witwatersrand.

Ntuli, P. Pitika. 2002. Indigenous Knowledge and the African Renaissance. In Odora Hoppers 2002c.

Nzimakwe, D. 1996. Primary Health Care in South Africa: Private Practice Nurse Practitioners and Traditional Healers Form Partnerships. *Journal of the American Academy of Nurse Practitioners* 8(7): 311–316.

Odora Hoppers, Catherine. 2000. Indigenous Knowledge and the Integration of Knowledge Systems: Towards a Conceptual and Methodological Framework. (A discussion document prepared by Dr. Catherine A. Odora Hoppers, coordinator of the Human Sciences Research Council project "A Comparative Study of the Development, Integration and Protection of Knowledge Systems in the Third World," initiated in consultation with the Parliamentary Portfolio Committee on Arts, Culture, Science, and Technology of the Parliament of South Africa, endorsed by the Science Councils of South Africa.) Pretoria: Human Sciences Research Council. http://www.dst.gov.za/programmes/indigenous_knowledge/iksdoc.pdf.

———. 2002a. The Evolution/Creationism Debate: Insights and Implications from the Indigenous Knowledge Systems Perspective. In *The Architect and the Scaffold: Evolution and Education in South Africa,* ed. Wilmot James and Lynne Wilson. Cape Town: Human Sciences Research Council and New Africa Books.

———. 2002b. Indigenous Knowledge and the Integration of Knowledge Systems. In Odora Hoppers 2002c.

———. 2002c. *Indigenous Knowledge and the Integration of Knowledge Systems: Towards a Philosophy of Articulation.* Claremont, RSA: New Africa Books.

———. 2002d. Psychoanalysis, the Enigma of Human Behaviour and the Contribution of Indigenous Knowledges. In Odora Hoppers 2002c.

Office of the City Manager. 2000. *iGoli2002: Making Greater Johannesburg Work.* Office of the City Manager, Greater Johannesburg Metropolitan Council. http://www.igoli.gov.za/iGoli%202002/Outline/Booklet%202/Booklet2.htm.

O'Mahony, D., and M. Steinberg. 1995. A Population-Based Survey of Obstetric Practices among Rural Women in the Bizana District, Transkei. *South African Medical Journal* 85(11): 1168–1171.

O'Meara, Dan. 1996. *Forty Lost Years: The Apartheid State and the Politics of the National Party, 1948–1994.* Athens: Ohio University Press.

Oosthuizen, Gerhardus C. 1968. *Post-Christianity in Africa: A Theological and Anthropological Study.* Grand Rapids: William B. Eerdmans.

———. 1987. The Interpretation of and Reaction to Demonic Powers in Indigenous Churches. In *Like a Roaring Lion . . . : Essays on the Bible, the Church and Demonic Powers,* ed. Pieter De Villiers. Pretoria: C. B. Powell Bible Centre.

———. 1989. Indigenous Healers within the Context of African Independent Churches. In Oosthuizen et al. 1989.

———. 1992. *The Healer-Prophet in Afro-Christian Churches.* Leiden: E. J. Brill.

Oosthuizen, Gerhardus C., S. D. Edwards, W. H. Wessels, and I. Hexham. 1989. *Afro-Christian Religion and Healing in Southern Africa.* African Studies, vol. 8. Lewiston: Edwin Mellen.

Oosthuizen, Gerhardus C., and Irving Hexham. 1991. *Afro-Christian Religion at the Grassroots in Southern Africa.* Lewiston: Edwin Mellen.

Opoku, A. R., M. Geheeb-Keller, J. Lin, S. E. Terblanche, A. Hutchings, A. Chuturgoon, and D. Pillay. 2000. Preliminary Screening of Some Traditional Zulu Medicinal Plants for Antineoplastic Activities versus the *HepG2* Cell Line. *Phytotherapy Research* 14(7): 534–537.

Osborne, R., A. Grove, P. Oh, T. J. Mabry, J. C. Ng, and A. A. Seawright. 1994. The Magical and Medicinal Usage of *Stangeria eriopus* in South Africa. *Journal of Ethnopharmacology* 43(2): 67–72.

Oskowitz, B. 1991. Bridging the Communication Gap between Traditional Healers and Nurses. *Nursing RSA Verpleging* 6(7): 20–22.

Packard, Randall M. 1981. *Chiefship and Cosmology: An Historical Study of Political Competition.* Bloomington: Indiana University Press.

Paine, Robert. 1967. What Is Gossip About? *Man,* n.s., 2(2): 278–285.

Parkin, David, ed. 1985. *The Anthropology of Evil.* Oxford: Blackwell.

Parnell, Susan. 1993. Johannesburg Slums and Racial Segregation in South African Cities, 1910–1937. PhD diss., Department of Geography, University of the Witwatersrand.

Parry, Charles D. H. 1997. Alcohol Misuse and Public Health: A 10-Point Action Plan. Part 1. Medical Research Council Policy Briefs, Medical Research Council, Tygerberg.

Parry, Charles D. H., and Anna L. Bennetts. 1999. *Alcohol Policy and Public Health in South Africa.* Cape Town: Oxford University Press.

Partain, Jack. 1986. Christians and Their Ancestors: A Dilemma of African Theology. *Christian Century* 103(36): 1066–1069.

Pascal, Blaise. 1947. *Pascal's Pensées.* Trans. H. F. Stewart. New York: Random House.

Patel, V., T. Musara, T. Butau, P. Maramba, and S. Fuyane. 1995. Concepts of Mental Illness and Medical Pluralism in Harare. *Psychological Medicine* 25(3): 485–493.

Patterson, Orlando. 1994. Freedom, Slavery and the Modern Construction of Rights. Paper presented at the "Democracy: Popular Precedents, Popular Practice and Popular Culture" History Workshop conference, University of the Witwatersrand, July 13–15, 1994.

Pauw, Berthold A. 1963. *The Second Generation: A Study of the Family among Urbanized Bantu in East London.* Cape Town: Oxford University Press.

———. 1974. Ancestor Beliefs and Ritual among Urban Africans. *African Studies* 33(2): 99–111.

———. 1975. *Christianity and Xhosa Tradition: Belief and Ritual among Xhosa-Speaking Christians.* Oxford: Oxford University Press.

———. 1980. Recent South African Anthropology. *Annual Review of Anthropology* 9: 315–338.

Pauw, C. M. 1995. African Independent Churches as a "People's Response" to the Christian Message. *Journal for the Study of Religion* 8(1): 3–25.

Peden, Margie, and Alex Butchart. 2000. Trauma and Injury. In *South African Health Review 1999,* ed. Nicholas Crisp and Antoinette Ntuli. Durban: Health Systems Trust.

Peek, Philip M., ed. 1991. *African Divination Systems: Ways of Knowing.* Bloomington and Indianapolis: Indiana University Press.

Peires, J. B. 1989. *The Dead Will Arise: Nongqawuse and the Great Xhosa Cattle-Killing Movement of 1856–7.* Johannesburg: Ravan Press.

———. 1994. Unsocial Bandits: The Stock Thieves of Qumbu and Their Enemies. Paper presented at the "Democracy: Popular Precedents, Popular Practice and Popular Culture" History Workshop conference, University of the Witwatersrand, July 13–15, 1994.

———. 1999. Secrecy and Violence in Rural Tsolo. Paper presented at the annual meeting of the South African Historical Association, University of the Western Cape.

———. 2000. Traditional Leaders in Purgatory: Local Government in Tsolo, Qumbu and Port St. Johns, 1990–2000. *African Studies* 59(1): 97–114.

Pelser, Eric. 2000. Operation Crackdown: The New Policing Strategy. *Nedbank ISS Crime Index* 4(2). http://www.iss.co.za/Pubs/CRIMEINDEX/00VOL4NO2/Operat Crackdown.html.

Peltzer, Karl. 1999. Faith Healing for Mental and Social Disorder in the Northern Province of South Africa. *Journal of Religion in Africa* 29(4): 387–402.

———. 2000a. Community Perceptions on the Witchcraft Suppression Act in South Africa. *South African Journal of Criminal Justice* 13(3): 312–318.

———. 2000b. Perceived Treatment Efficacy of the Last Experienced Illness Episode in a Community Sample in the Northern Province, South Africa. *Curationis* 23(1): 57–60.

———. 2001. Attitudes of Physicians toward Traditional Healing, Faith Healing and Alternative Medicine in Rural South Africa. *Medicine Journal* (Internet Issue). http://www.medpharm.co.za/tmj/2001/aug_01/attitudes.html.

Peltzer, Karl, L. B. Khoza, M. E. Lekhuleni, S. N. Madu, V. I. Cherian, and L. Cherian. 2001. Concepts and Treatment for Diabetes among Traditional and Faith Healers in the Northern Province, South Africa. *Curationis* 24(2): 42–47.

Peters, Edward. 1978. *The Magician, the Witch, and the Law.* Philadelphia: University of Pennsylvania Press.

Petersen, Robin M. 1995. Time, Resistance, and Reconstruction: Rethinking Kairos Theology. PhD diss., University of Chicago Divinity School.

Pettersson, Olof. 1953. *Chiefs and Gods: Religious and Social Elements in the South Eastern Bantu Kingship.* Lund: C. W. K. Gleerup.

Phillips, Ray. 1938. *The Bantu in the City: A Study of Cultural Adjustment on the Witwatersrand.* Alice, Cape Province: Lovedale Press.

Piazza-Georgi, Barbara. 1999. A Profile of the Self-Employed in Soweto in Mid-1999, with Gender Disaggregation. Department of Economics, University of the Witwatersrand, Johannesburg. http://www.wits.ac.za/economics/ersa/Policy%20Papers/PP15.pdf.

———. 2000. Human and Social Capital in Soweto in 1999, Preliminary Report on Field Study, Background, and Descriptive Statistics. Department of Economics, University of the Witwatersrand, Johannesburg. http://www.wits.ac.za/economics/ersa/Policy%20Papers/PP4.pdf.

Pillay, A. L., and A. K. Akoo. 1993. Health Beliefs in South Africa. *Perceptual and Motor Skills* 76(3, pt. 2): 1190.

Pillay, C. C., A. K. Jager, D. A. Mulholland, and J. van Staden. 2001. Cyclooxygenase Inhibiting and Anti-bacterial Activities of South African *Erythrina* Species. *Journal of Ethnopharmacology* 74(3): 231–237.

Pinnock, Don, with Dudu Douglas-Hamilton. 1997. *Gangs, Rituals, and Rites of Passage.* Cape Town: African Sun with University of Cape Town Institute of Criminology.

Pirie, G. H. 1984. Letters, Words, Worlds: The Naming of Soweto. *African Studies Journal* 43: 43–51.

———. 1992. Travelling under Apartheid. In *The Apartheid City and Beyond: Urbanization and Social Change in South Africa,* ed. David M. Smith. London: Routledge.

Pirow, Oswald. 1937. *James Barry Munnik Hertzog.* Cape Town: Howard Timmins.

Pitje, G. M. 1950a. Traditional Systems of Male Education among Pedi and Cognate Tribes, Part 1. *African Studies* 9(2): 53–76.

———. 1950b. Traditional Systems of Male Education among Pedi and Cognate Tribes, Part 2. *African Studies* 9(3): 105–124.

———. 1950c. Traditional Systems of Male Education among Pedi and Cognate Tribes, Part 3. *African Studies* 9(4): 194–201.

Pityana, Barney. 1999. The Renewal of African Moral Values. In *African Renaissance: The New Struggle,* ed. William Malegapuru Makgoba. Sandton and Cape Town: Mafube and Tafelberg.

Platzky, R., and J. Girson. 1993. Indigenous Healers and Stuttering. *South African Journal of Communication Disorders* 40: 43–48.

Poggenpoel, M. 1993. Trends in Community Psychiatry. *Nursing RSA Verpleging* 8(4): 35–37, 42.

Polanyi, Michael. 1995. *Personal Knowledge: Towards a Post-critical Philosophy.* Chicago: University of Chicago Press.

Population Division of the United Nations Secretariat. 2000. World Urbanization Prospects: The 1999 Revision. ESA/P/WP/161. United Nations, New York. http://www .un.org/Depts/unsd/social/hum-set.htm.

Portfolio Committee on Arts, Culture, Science, and Technology. 2000. Report of the Portfolio Committee on Arts, Culture, Science, and Technology on Indigenous Knowledge Systems. National Assembly, Cape Town. http://www.polity.org.za/ govdocs/reports/committees/newreports.htm.

Potgieter, A. H., M. G. S. Pierides, A. E. de la Porte, and A. D. Geel. 1987. Multiprofessional Case Representation: The Case of David H. In *Like a Roaring Lion . . . : Essays on the Bible, the Church and Demonic Powers,* ed. Pieter De Villiers. Pretoria: C. B. Powell Bible Centre.

Pretorius, Cornia. 1999. Yizo Gets Gold Stars and Black Marks. *Sunday Times* (Johannesburg) Internet ed., November 14, 1999. http://www.suntimes.co.za/1999/11/14/ arts/ane07.htm.

———. 2000. Soweto Shakes Off the Ashes of June 16. *Sunday Times* (Johannesburg) Internet ed., January 9, 2000. http://www.suntimes.co.za/2000/01/09/insight/ino1.htm.

Pretorius, Engela. 1991. Traditional and Modern Medicine Working in Tandem. *Curationis* 14(4): 10–13.

———. 1999. Traditional Healers. In *South African Health Review, 1999,* ed. Nicholas Crisp and Antoinette Ntuli. Durban: Health Systems Trust.

Pretorius, Engela, G. W. de Klerk, and H. C. J. van Rensburg. 1991. The Traditional Healer in South Africa Health Care. ASS/BBS-27. Co-operative HSRC Programme, Affordable Social Provision. Human Sciences Resource Council, Pretoria.

Pretorius, H. L. 1995. *Historiography and Historical Sources regarding African Indige-
  nous Churches in South Africa.* Lewiston: Edwin Mellen.
Pretorius, H. W. 1995. Mental Disorders and Disability across Cultures: A View from
  South Africa. *Lancet* 345(8949): 534.
Pretorius, Hennie, and Lizo Jafta. 1997. "A Branch Springs Out": African Initiated
  Churches. In Elphick and Davenport 1997.
Professional Traditional Healers Register of South Africa. 2000. Important News
  for All Healers. Steenberg. http://www.spiritualworld.co.za/FrontPageArticles/
  importantnewsforallhealers.htm.
Proust, Marcel. 1983. *Rememberance of Things Past,* vol. 2. New York: Penguin Books.
Putnam, Robert. 1993. *Making Democracy Work: Civic Traditions in Modern Italy.*
  Princeton: Princeton University Press.
———. 2000. *Bowling Alone: The Collapse and Revival of American Community.* New
  York: Simon and Schuster.
Quine, Willard Van Orman. 1960. *Word and Object.* Cambridge: Technology Press of
  the Massachusetts Institute of Technology.
Rakate, Phenyo. 1999. Transitional Justice in South Africa and the Former Yugoslavia
  —a Critique. Paper presented at "The TRC: Commissioning the Past" conference,
  University of the Witwatersrand, June 11–14, 1999.
Ralushai Commission. *See* Commission of Inquiry into Witchcraft Violence and Ritual
  Murders.
Ramogale, Marcus, and Sello Galane. 1997. Faith in Action: Mokhukhu of the Zion
  Christian Church. In *Articles from the 1997 Festival of American Folklife Program
  Book.* Washington: Smithsonian Institution. http://www.folklife.si.edu/festival/
  fest97/1997progbook.htm.
Ramolefe, A. M. R. 1969. Sesotho Marriage, Guardianship, and the Customary-Law
  Heir. In *Ideas and Procedures in African Customary Law,* ed. Max Gluckman.
  London: Oxford University Press, for the International African Institute.
Ramphele, Mamphela. 1993. *A Bed Called Home.* Cape Town: David Philip.
———. 1996. *Across Boundaries: The Journey of a South African Woman Leader.* New
  York: Feminist Press at the City University of New York.
———. 2000. Teach Me How to Be a Man: An Exploration of the Definition of Masculinity. In *Violence and Subjectivity,* ed. Veena Das, Arthur Kleinman, Mamphela
  Ramphele, and Pamela Reynolds. Berkeley and Los Angeles: University of California Press.
———. 2001. Citizenship Challenges for South Africa's Young Democracy. *Daedalus*
  130(1): 1–17.
———. 2002. *Steering by the Stars: Being Young in South Africa.* Cape Town: Tafelberg.
Reader, D. H. 1961. *The Black Man's Portion: History, Demography, and Living Con-
  ditions in the Native Locations of East London, Cape Province.* Cape Town: Oxford
  University Press, on behalf of the Institute of Social and Economic Research,
  Rhodes University.
Redding, Sean. 1992. Beer Brewing in Umtata: Women, Migrant Labor, and Social
  Control in a Rural Town. In *Liquor and Labor in Southern Africa,* ed. Jonathan
  Crush and Charles Ambler. Athens: Ohio University Press.

Redfield, Robert. 1941. *The Folk Culture of Yucatan.* Chicago: University of Chicago Press.

Rees, Anthony. 1999. Biodiversity and Intellectual Property Rights: Implications for Indigenous People of South Africa. May 4, 1999. Traditional Healers Organization for Africa. http://www.mamiwata.com/rights.html.

Reis, Ria. 2000. The "Wounded Healer" as Ideology: The Work of Ngoma in Swaziland. In Van Dijk, Reis, and Spierenburg 2000.

Republic of South Africa. 1977. Report of the Commission of Inquiry into the Riots at Soweto and Other Places in the Republic of South Africa during June 1976 (Cillié Commission). Pretoria: Republic of South Africa.

———. 1995. Promotion of National Unity and Reconciliation Act. No. 34 of 1995.

———. 1998. The White Paper on Local Government. Department of Provincial and Local Government, Pretoria. http://www.local.gov.za/DCD/dcdindex.html.

———. 2001. National Strategy for Mathematics, Science, and Technology Education in General and Further Education. Department of Education, Pretoria. http://education.pwv.gov.za/DoE_Sites/Maths%20and%20Science/Final-doc.pdf.

Reynolds, Pamela. 1996. *Traditional Healers and Childhood in Zimbabwe.* Athens: Ohio University Press.

Rich, Paul B. 1978. Ministering the White Man's Needs: The Development of Urban Segregation in South Africa, 1913–1923. *African Studies* 37(2): 177–192.

———. 1984. *White Power and the Liberal Conscience: Racial Segregation and South African Liberalism, 1921–1960.* Johannesburg: Ravan Press.

Ritchken, Edwin. 1988. Comrades, Witches and the State: Popular Mobilisation and Organisation in Mapulaneng. Paper presented to Association for Sociology in South Africa annual conference.

———. 1989. The Meaning of Rural Political Violence: The Meaning of the Anti-witchcraft Attacks. Centre for the Study of Violence and Reconciliation, paper 5. University of the Witwatersrand, Johannesburg.

———. 1994. Leaders and Conflict in Bushbuckridge, 1978–1990: Struggles to Define Moral Economies in the Context of Rapidly Transforming Political Economies. PhD diss., Department of Political Science, University of the Witwatersrand.

Roberts, C. Clifton. 1935. Witchcraft and Colonial Legislation. *Africa* 8: 488–494.

Robertson, B. A., and A. Kottler. 1993. Cultural Issues in the Psychiatric Assessment of Xhosa Children and Adolescents. *South African Medical Journal* 83(3): 207–208.

Rodseth, F. R., F. van Heerden, and J. E. Jennings. 1951. Native Housing Research in South Africa. *Bulletin of the National Building Research Institute* 6: 1–8. Pretoria: South African Council for Scientific and Industrial Research, National Building Research Institute.

Rogers, Howard. 1933. *Native Administration in the Union of South Africa.* Pretoria: Union of South Africa, Department of Native Affairs.

Rogerson, C. M., and D. M. Hart. 1986. The Survival of the "Informal Sector": The Shebeens of Black Johannesburg. *GeoJournal* 12(2): 153–166.

Rogerson, Christian. 1992. Drinking Apartheid and the Removal of Beerhalls in Johannesburg, 1939–1962. In *Liquor and Labor in Southern Africa,* ed. Jonathan Crush and Charles Ambler. Athens: Ohio University Press.

Rogerson, Rebecca. 2001. Traditional African Healers: Their Role in the Fight against STDs, HIV and AIDS in South Africa. Paper presented at the "AIDS in Context" conference, University of the Witwatersrand, April 4–7, 2001.

Rorty, Amelie. 1983. Akratic Believers. *American Philosophical Quarterly* 20(2): 175–183.

Rose, E. F. 1972. *Senecio* Species: Toxic Plants Used As Food and Medicine in the Transkei. *South African Medical Journal* 46(30): 1039–1043.

Rose, Sonya. 1999. Cultural Analysis and Moral Discourses: Episodes, Continuities, and Transformations. In *Beyond the Cultural Turn: New Directions in the Study of Society and Culture,* ed. Victoria Bonnell and Lynn Hunt. Berkeley and Los Angeles: University of California Press.

Rouse, Jonathan. 1999. Global Dissemination of Indigenous Knowledge: Contradiction, or the Way Forward? http://www.worldbank.org/afr/ik/global_ik990615.htm.

Roystom, Lauren. 1999. South Africa: The Struggle for Access to the City in the Witwatersrand Region. In *Evictions and the Right to Housing: Experience from Canada, Chile, the Dominican Republic, South Africa, and South Korea,* ed. Antonio Azuela, Emilio Duhau, and Enrique Ortiz. Ottawa: International Development Research Centre.

Russell, Jeffrey Burton. 1988. *The Prince of Darkness: Radical Evil and the Power of Good in History.* Ithaca: Cornell University Press.

Sachs, Wulf. 1947. *Black Hamlet.* New York: Little, Brown, and Co.

Sampson, H. F. 1969. *The White-Faced Huts: Witchcraft in the Transkei.* Johannesburg: Voortrekkerpers.

Sanders, Todd. 2003. Reconsidering Witchcraft: Postcolonial Africa and Analytic (Un)-Certainties. *American Anthropologist* 105(2): 338–352.

Sanneh, Lamin. 1989. *Translating the Message: The Missionary Impact on Culture.* Maryknoll: Orbis.

———. 1993. *Encountering the West: Christianity and the Global Cultural Process; The African Dimension.* Maryknoll: Orbis.

SAPA. *See* South African Press Association.

Sarakinski, Mike. 1987. The Ideology and Politics of African Capitalists. *Africa Perspective* 1(3/4): 43–61.

Saunders, Christopher. 1988. *Making of the South African Past: Major Historians on Race and Class.* Cape Town: David Philip.

Savage, A. 1982. Do-It-Yourself Medicine. *British Medical Journal (Clinical Research Edition)* 285(6341): 560–561.

Schapera, I. 1934. *Western Civilization and the Natives of South Africa: Studies in Culture Contact.* London: Routledge.

———, ed. 1937. *The Bantu-Speaking Tribes of South Africa: An Ethnographical Survey.* Cape Town: Maskew Miller.

———. 1938. *A Handbook of Tswana Law and Custom: Compiled for the Bechuanaland Protectorate Administration.* London: Oxford University Press, for the International Institute of African Languages and Cultures.

———. 1947. *Migrant Labour and Tribal Life: A Study of Conditions in the Bechuanaland Protectorate.* London: Oxford University Press.

———. 1950. *Married Life in an African Tribe.* London: Faber and Faber.

———. 1953. *The Tswana.* London: International African Institute.

———. 1956. *Government and Politics in Tribal Societies.* London: Watts.

———. 1970. *Tribal Innovators: Tswana Chiefs and Social Change, 1795–1940.* London: University of London, Athlone Press.

Schatzberg, Michael G. 2001. *Political Legitimacy in Middle Africa: Father, Family, Food.* Bloomington: Indiana University Press.

Scheler, Max. 1998. *Ressentiment.* Trans. Lewis B. Coser and William W. Holdheim. Wisconsin: Marquette University Press.

Scheper-Hughes, Nancy. 1995. Who's the Killer? Popular Justice in a South African Squatter Camp. *Social Justice* 22(3): 143–164.

Schimlek, Francis. 1950. *Witchcraft Versus Medicine.* Marianhill: Marianhill Mission Press.

Schneider, David M. 1984. *A Critique of the Study of Kinship.* Ann Arbor: University of Michigan Press.

Schneider, Helen. 2002. On the Fault-Line: The Politics of AIDS Policy in Contemporary South Africa. *African Studies* 61(1): 145–167.

Schoffeleers, Mathew. 1991. Ritual Healing and Political Acquiescence: The Case of the Zionist Churches in Southern Africa. *Africa* 61(1): 1–25.

Schreuder, Derek M. 1976. The Cultural Factor in Victorian Imperialism: A Case-Study of the British "Civilising Mission." *Journal of Imperial and Colonial History* 4: 283–317.

Schultze, Wilhelm Georg. 1997. The Origin and Legal Nature of the *Stokvel. South African Mercantile Law Journal* 9(1): 18–29.

Schutte, A. G. 1972. Thapelo Ya Sephiri: A Study of Secret Prayer Groups in Soweto. *African Studies* 31(4): 245–260.

Schweitzer, G. 1978. Body and Mind in Zulu Medicine. *South African Medical Journal* 54(15): 593.

Seekings, Jeremy. 1986. Why Is Soweto Different? African Studies Seminar Paper, University of the Witwatersrand, Johannesburg.

———. 1989. People's Courts and Popular Politics. *South African Review* 5.

Segal, I. 1988. The Trauma of the Urban Experience. *Journal of the Royal College of Physicians, London* 22(1): 45–47.

Segal, I., and L. O. Tim. 1979. The Witchdoctor and the Bowel. *South African Medical Journal* 56(8): 308–310.

Segal, I., L. O. Tim, D. G. Hamilton, H. H. Lawson, A. Solomon, F. Kalk, and S. A. Cooke. 1979. Ritual-Enema-Induced Colitis. *Diseases of the Colon and Rectum* 22(3): 195–199.

Segal, Lauren. 1992. The Human Face of Violence: Hostel Dwellers Speak. *Journal of Southern African Studies* 18(1): 191–231.

Select Committee on Social Services. 1998. Report of the Select Committee on Social Services on Traditional Healers. No. 144-1998, August 4. Parliament of the Republic of South Africa, Cape Town. Hansard. www.polity.org.za/govdocs/parliament/papers/ta/1998/ta1111.html.

Serote, Mongane Wally. 1998. Initiatives for Protection of Rights of Holders of Traditional Knowledge, Indigenous Peoples and Local Communities. WIPO/INDIP/RT/ 98/4C, World Intellectual Property Organization, Geneva. http://www.wipo.org/ eng/meetings/1998/indip/rt98_4c.htm.

Setiloane, Gabriel M. 1973. Modimo: God among the Sotho-Tswana. *Journal of Theology for Southern Africa* 4: 6–17.

———. 1976. *The Image of God among the Sotho-Tswana.* Rotterdam: A. A. Balkema.

———. 1988. African Views on Birth. *Nursing RSA* 3(7): 43–45.

Sewell, William H., Jr. 1999. The Concept(s) of Culture. In *Beyond the Cultural Turn: New Directions in the Study of Society and Culture,* ed. Victoria Bonnell and Lynn Hunt. Berkeley and Los Angeles: University of California Press.

Shaw, Mark. 2002. *Crime and Policing in Post-apartheid South Africa.* Bloomington: Indiana University Press.

Shaw, Mark, and Peter Gastrow. 2001. Stealing the Show? Crime and Its Impact in Post-apartheid South Africa. *Daedalus* 130(1): 235–258.

Shaw, Rosalind. 1990. The Invention of "African Traditional Religion." *Religion* 20(339): 353.

———. 1991. Splitting Truths from Darkness: Epistemological Aspects of Temne Divination. In Peek 1991.

———. 2002. *Memories of the Slave Trade: Ritual and the Historical Imagination in Sierra Leone.* Chicago: University of Chicago Press.

Shingler, David John. 1973. Education and Political Order in South Africa, 1902–1961. PhD diss., Yale University.

Shorter, Aylward. 1985. *Jesus and the Witchdoctor: An Approach to Healing and Wholeness.* Maryknoll: Orbis.

Sidley, P. 1996. Botched Circumcisions Lead to Arrest for Murder. *British Medical Journal* 313(7058): 647.

Siebane, Alpheus, and Makgotho Selby. My Mother-in-Law Turned into a Dog. *Sunday Times* (Johannesburg) Internet ed., May 16, 1999. http:www.suntimes.co.za/1999/ 05/16/news/gauteng/njhb10.htm.

Sikakane, Joyce. 1977. *A Window on Soweto.* London: International Defense and Aid Fund.

Simmel, Georg. 1950. *The Sociology of Georg Simmel.* Ed. Kurt H. Wolf. New York: Free Press.

———. 1964. *Conflict and the Web of Group-Affiliations.* New York: Free Press.

Simon, C. 1991. Innovative Medicine—a Case Study of a Modern Healer. *South African Medical Journal* 79(11): 677–678.

Simon, C., and M. Lamla. 1991. Merging Pharmacopoeia: Understanding the Historical Origins of Incorporative Pharmacopoeial Processes among Xhosa Healers in Southern Africa. *Journal of Ethnopharmacology* 33(3): 237–242.

Simon, Lilian. 1993. *Inyanga: Sarah Mashele's Story.* Johannesburg: Justified Press.

Sisulu, Walter. 1998. Foreword to *Soweto: A History,* ed. Philip Bonner and Lauren Segal. Cape Town: Maskew Miller Longman.

Sklar, Richard. 1994. The Significance of Mixed Government in Southern African Studies: A Preliminary Assessment. Paper presented at the "Democracy: Popular

Precedents, Popular Practice and Popular Culture" History Workshop conference, University of the Witwatersrand, July 13–15, 1994.

Slovo, Joe. 1976. South Africa: No Middle Road. In *Southern Africa: The New Politics of Revolution*, ed. Basil Davidson, Joe Slovo, and Anthony R. Wilkinson. Harmondsworth, UK: Penguin.

Smith, M. T., N. R. Crouch, N. Gericke, and M. Hirst. 1996. Psychoactive Constituents of the Genus *Sceletium* N.E.Br. and Other Mesembryanthemaceae: A Review. *Journal of Ethnopharmacology* 50(3): 119–130.

Smyth, A., M. Martin, and J. Cairns. 1995. South Africa's Health: Traditional Healers May Cause Dangerous Delays. *British Medical Journal* 311(7010): 948.

Snyman, T., M. J. Stewart, and V. Steenkamp. 2001. A Fatal Case of Pepper Poisoning. *Forensic Science International* 124(1): 43–46.

Soga, John Henderson. 1930. *The South-Eastern Bantu (Abe-Nguni, Aba-Mbo, Ama-Lala)*. Johannesburg: Witwatersrand University Press.

Soggot, Mungo. 1997. SANCO Crippled by Debt. *Weekly Mail and Guardian* (Johannesburg) Internet ed., April 25, 1997. http://www.sn.apc.org/wmail/issues/970425/NEWS4.html.

Solleder, G. 1974. Clinical Observations on Toxic Effects of Xhosa Medicine. *South African Medical Journal* 48(57): 2365–2368.

Somers, Margaret. 1999. The Privatization of Citizenship: How to Unthink a Knowledge Culture. In *Beyond the Cultural Turn: New Directions in the Study of Society and Culture*, ed. Victoria Bonnell and Lynn Hunt. Berkeley and Los Angeles: University of California Press.

Sommerville, William. 1979. *William Sommerville's Narrative of His Journeys to the Eastern Cape Frontier and to Lattakoe, 1799–1802*. Ed. Edna Barlow and Frank Barlow. Cape Town: Van Riebeck Society.

South African Law Commission. 1999. Community Dispute Resolution Structures. Report 87. Pretoria.

———. 2000. Customary Law. Report 93 (project 90). Pretoria.

South African Native Affairs Commission. 1905. *Report of the South African Native Affairs Commission, 1903–5*, vol. 1. Cape Town: Government Printers.

South African Police Service. 1998. CIMC Quarterly Report 1/98. Quarterly Crime Reports. http://www.saps.co.za/8_crimeinfo/198/soweto.htm.

———. 2001. Crime per Police Area for the Period January to December 1994–2001. Pretoria. http://www.saps.org.za/8_crimeinfo/bulletin/942000a/gsoweto.htm.

South African Press Association. 1997. Gauteng Health Department Considers Integrating Traditional Healers. *Daily News Briefs* Internet ed., June 5, 1997. http://www.anc.org.za/anc/newsbrief/1997/news0606.

———. 1998. Witch Hunting in SA Is a New Phenomenon, Conference Hears. ANC Newsbriefs, September 7, 1998. http://www.anc.org.za/anc/newsbrief/1998/news0908.

———. 2001a. Confusion Brewing over Sigcau's AIDS *Muti*. *The Independent* Internet ed., July 23, 2001. http://www.iol.co.za/html/frame_news.php?click_id=79&art_id=qw995902262208B232.

————. 2001b. Northern Province "Witch" Burned Alive. *News24.co.za* Internet. August 14, 2001. http://www.news24.co.za/News24/South_Africa/NorthernProvince/ 0,1113,2-7-834_1065872,00.html.

————. 2002. 15,680 Child Rape Cases Reported Last Year. *Daily Mail and Guardian* (Johannesburg) Internet ed., March 22, 2002.

————. 2003a. Madiba's Vow: To Fight AIDS Forever. *Daily News,* July 17, 2003, p. 1.

————. 2003b. Sangoma-Hiring Wife Gets Life. January 15, 2003. http://iafrica.com/ news/sa/201564.htm.

South African Reserve Bank. 2000. Quarterly Economic Review. http://www.resbank .co.za/Economics/qbul032000/Domes.html#Employment.

Spacks, Patricia. 1985. *Gossip.* New York: Knopf.

Sparg, S. G., J. van Staden, and A. K. Jager. 2000. Efficiency of Traditionally Used South African Plants against Schistosomiasis. *Journal of Ethnopharmacology* 73(1/2): 209–214.

Stacey, Simon. 1999. A "New South Africa": The South African Truth and Reconciliation Commission's Vexed Nation-Building Project. Paper presented at "The TRC: Commissioning the Past" conference, University of the Witwatersrand, June 11–14, 1999.

Stander, I., and C. W. Van Wyk. 1991. Toothbrushing with the Root of *Euclea natalensis. Journal de Biologie Buccale* 19(2): 167–172.

Stapleton, Timothy J. 2001. *Faku: Rulership and Colonialism in the Mpondo Kingdom (c. 1760–1867).* Waterloo: Wilfrid Laurier University Press.

Statistics South Africa. 1998. *The People of South Africa: Population Census, 1996.* Report no. 1. Pretoria: Statistics South Africa.

————. 1999. Census in Brief. 3rd ed. http://www.statssa.gov.za/RelatedInverseSites/ census96/HTML/CIB/census_in_brief.htm.

————. 2002. Causes of Death in South Africa, 1997–2001: Advanced Release of Recorded Causes of Death. P0309.2. http://www.mrc.ac.za/researchreports/causesof death.pdf.

Steenkamp, Vanessa. 2002. Toxicology of Traditional Remedies. *Science in Africa (Online Edition).* http://www.scienceinafrica.co.za/2002/february/toxic.htm.

Steenkamp, Vanessa, M. J. Stewart, S. van der Merwe, M. Zuckerman, and N. J. Crowther. 2001. The Effect of *Senecio latifolius,* a Plant Used as a South African Traditional Medicine, on a Human Hepatoma Cell Line. *Journal of Ethnopharmacology* 78(1): 51–58.

Steenkamp, Vanessa, M. J. Stewart, and M. Zuckerman. 2000. Clinical and Analytical Aspects of Pyrrolizidine Poisoning Caused by South African Traditional Medicines. *Therapeutic Drug Monitoring* 22(3): 302–306.

Stephens, Simon. 2000. Kwaito. In *Senses of Culture: South African Cultural Studies,* ed. Sarah Nuttall and Cheryl-Ann Michael. Cape Town: Oxford University Press.

Stephney, Inez. 1999. The Difference between the Nuremberg Trials and the TRC: A Lesson to Be Learnt? Paper presented at "The TRC: Commissioning the Past" conference, University of the Witwatersrand, June 11–14, 1999.

Stewart, M. J. 2002. South Africa: A Toxicologist's Goldmine. *Therapeutic Drug Monitoring* 24(1): 172–177.

Stewart, M. J., J. J. Moar, J. Mwesigwa, and M. Kokot. 2000. Forensic Toxicology in Urban South Africa. *Clinical Toxicology* 38(4): 415–419.

Stewart, M. J., J. J. Moar, P. Steenkamp, and M. Kokot. 1999. Findings in Fatal Cases of Poisoning Attributed to Traditional Remedies in South Africa. *Forensic Science International* 101(3): 177–183.

Stewart, M. J., V. Steenkamp, and M. Zuckerman. 1998. The Toxicology of African Herbal Remedies. *Therapeutic Drug Monitoring* 20(5): 510–516.

Steyn, M., and A. Muller. 2000. Traditional Healers and Cancer Prevention. *Curationis* 23(3): 4–11.

Straker, Gillian. 1994. Integrating African and Western Healing Practices in South Africa. *American Journal of Psychotherapy* 48(3): 455–467.

Sundkler, Bengt. 1948. *Bantu Prophets in South Africa.* London: Lutterworth.

———. 1961. *Bantu Prophets in South Africa.* 2nd ed. London: Oxford University Press, for the International African Institute.

———. 1976. *Zulu Zion and Some Swazi Zionists.* Oxford: Oxford University Press.

Sundkler, Bengt, and Christopher Steed. 2000. *A History of the Church in Africa.* Cambridge: Cambridge University Press.

Swart, C. 1979. *Swarthebuising Deel I: Gesinsbehuising in Soweto.* Johannesburg: Rand Afrikaanse Universiteit.

Swartz, L. 1985. Issues for Cross-Cultural Psychiatric Research in South Africa. *Culture Medicine and Psychiatry* 9(1): 59–74.

Swift, P. J., and J. I. Strang. 1993. Traditional Healers and AIDS Prevention. *South African Medical Journal* 83(9): 690–691.

Szwed, John. 1966. Gossip, Drinking, and Social Control in a Newfoundland Parish. *Ethnology* 5: 434–445.

Tambiah, S. J. 1990. *Magic, Science and the Scope of Rationality.* Cambridge: Cambridge University Press.

Taussig, Michael T. 1986. *Shamanism, Colonialism, a Study in Terror and Healing and the Wild Man.* Chicago: University of Chicago Press.

———. 1993. *Mimesis and Alterity.* New York and London: Routledge.

Taylor, Charles. 1989. *Sources of the Self: The Making of Modern Identity.* Cambridge: Harvard University Press.

Tema, B. O. 2002. Science Education and Africa's Rebirth. In Odora Hoppers 2002c.

Tempels, Placide R. P. 1948. *La philosophie bantoue.* Trans. A. Rubbens. Paris: Présence Africaine.

———. 1959. *Bantu Philosophy.* With a foreword to the English edition by Margaret Read. Paris: Présence Africaine.

Terreblanche, Christelle. 2001. Death Squad Base Targeted for Healing. *Star* (Johannesburg), November 12, 2001.

Terreblanche, Sampie. 2002. *A History of Inequality in South Africa, 1652–2002.* Durban: University of Natal Press.

Thamba Administrators. 2001. The Traditional Healers: Intervention. http://www .siliconzoo.co.za/previews/thamba/healers.html.

Themba, Can. 1985. *The Will to Die.* Cape Town: David Philip.

Theron, J. P. J. 1987. Some Aspects of the Ministry of Deliverance from Evil Forces.

In *Like a Roaring Lion . . . : Essays on the Bible, the Church and Demonic Powers,* ed. Pieter De Villiers. Pretoria: C. B. Powell Bible Centre.

Thomas, E. Linda. 1994. African Indigenous Churches as a Source of Socio-political Transformation in South Africa. *Africa Today* 41(1): 39–56.

Thorpe, Mark. 2001. Shifting Discourse—Teenage Masculinity and the Challenge for Behavioural Change. Paper presented at the "AIDS in Context" conference, University of the Witwatersrand, April 4–7, 2001.

Tierno, Philip M. 2001. *The Secret Life of Germs: Observations and Lessons from a Microbe Hunter.* New York: Simon and Schuster.

Tilly, Charles. 2002. *Stories, Identities, and Political Change.* Lanham: Rowman and Littlefield.

———. 2003. *The Politics of Collective Violence.* Cambridge: Cambridge University Press.

Tisani, Nomathamsanqa. 1994. Royal by Birth, Ruler by Will of the People: Amaxhosa Royalty Revisited. Paper presented at the "Democracy: Popular Precedents, Popular Practice and Popular Culture" History Workshop conference, University of the Witwatersrand, July 13–15, 1994.

TRC. *See* Truth and Reconciliation Commission.

Truth and Reconciliation Commission. 1998. *The Report of the Truth and Reconciliation Commission.* 5 vols. www.truth.org.za/final/.

Turner, Victor W. 1968. *The Drums of Affliction: A Study of Religious Processes among the Ndembu of Zambia.* Oxford: Clarendon Press.

Tutu, Desmond. 1969. The Ancestor Cult and Its Influence on Ethical Issues. *Ministry,* 103–104.

———. 1996. Foreword to *To Remember and to Heal,* ed. H. Russel Botman and Robin M. Peterson. Cape Town: Human and Rousseau.

UNAIDS. 2000. Report on the Global AIDS Epidemic. UNAIDS, Geneva. http://www .unaids.org/epidemic_update/report/Epi_report.htm.

UNDP. 1994. *Human Development Report 1994.* New York and Oxford: Oxford University Press for the United Nations Development Programme.

University of the Witwatersrand Department of Sociology. 1997. Soweto in Transition Project (Preliminary Report). Johannesburg. Mimeograph.

Uys, L. 2001. HIV/AIDS Care in KwaZulu-Natal, South Africa: An Interview with Dr. Leana Uys. Interviewed by Ellen Giarelli and Linda A. Jacobs. *Journal of the Association of Nurses in AIDS Care* 12(6): 52–67.

van Aarde, A. G. 1987. Demonology in New Testament Times. In *Like a Roaring Lion . . . : Essays on the Bible, the Church and Demonic Powers,* ed. Pieter De Villiers. Pretoria: C. B. Powell Bible Centre.

van Beukering, J. A. 1969. Cantharidin Poisoning: Three Case Reports. *Tropical and Geographical Medicine* 21(1): 30–32.

van Binsbergen, Wim. 2000. Witchcraft in Modern Africa as Virtualized Boundary Conditions of the Kinship Order. December 8, 2000. http:www.geocities.com/africanreligion/witchtxt.htm.

van der Geest, Sjaak, Susan Reynolds Whyte, and Anita Hardon. 1996. The Anthropology of Pharmaceuticals: A Biographical Approach. *Annual Review of Anthropology* 25: 153–178.

van der Linde, I. 1996. Tailor Make the TB Message. *South African Medical Journal* 86(8): 900, 902.

———. 1997. Western and African Medicines Meet. *South African Medical Journal* 87(3): 268, 270.

van der Watt, E., and J. C. Pretorius. 2001. Purification and Identification of Active Antibacterial Components in *Carpobrotus edulis* L. *Journal of Ethnopharmacology* 76(1): 87–91.

Van Dijk, Rijk, Ria Reis, and Marja Spierenburg. 2000. *The Quest for Fruition through Ngoma: Political Aspects of Healing in Southern Africa.* Oxford: James Currey.

van Eeden, A. 1993. The Traditional Healer and Our Future Health System. *South African Medical Journal* 83(6): 441–442.

Vansina, Jan M. 1965. *Oral Tradition: A Study in Historical Method.* Trans. H. M. Wright. Chicago: Aldine.

Van Warmelo, N. J. 1977. *Anthropology of Southern Africa in Periodicals to 1950: An Analysis and Index.* Johannesburg: Witwatersrand University Press.

Varga, C. A., and D. J. Veale. 1997. Isihlambezo: Utilization Patterns and Potential Health Effects of Pregnancy-Related Traditional Herbal Medicine. *Social Science and Medicine* 44(7): 911–924.

Vaughan, Megan. 1991. *Curing Their Ills: Colonial Power and African Illness.* Stanford: Stanford University Press.

Veale, D. J., K. I. Furman, and D. W. Oliver. 1992. South African Traditional Herbal Medicines Used during Pregnancy and Childbirth. *Journal of Ethnopharmacology* 36(3): 185–191.

Veale, D. J., I. Havlik, L. C. Katsoulis, T. L. Kaido, N. S. Arangies, D. W. Olive, T. G. Dekker, K. B. Brookes, and O. V. Doudoukina. 1998. The Pharmacological Assessment of Herbal Oxytocics Used in South African Traditional Medicine. *Biomarkers and Environment* 2(2–3). http://www.cechtuma.cz/bioenv/1998/2-3/c216-en.html.

Verhoef, Grietjie. 2002. Money, Credit and Trust: Voluntary Savings Organisations in South Africa in Historical Perspective. Paper presented at the International Economic History Association congress, Buenos Aires, July 22–26, 2002.

Verotta, L., T. Aburjai, C. B. Rogers, P. Dorigo, I. Maragno, D. Fraccarollo, G. Santostasi, R. M. Gaion, M. Floreani, and F. Carpenedo. 1995. Chemical and Pharmacological Characterization of *Erythrophleum lasianthum* Alkaloids. *Planta Medica* 61(3): 271–274.

Verryn, Trevor. 1981. "Coolness" and "Heat" among the Sotho Peoples. *Religion in Southern Africa* 2: 11–38.

Vilakazi, Absolom. 1965. *Zulu Transformations: A Study of the Dynamics of Social Change.* Pietermaritzburg: University of Natal Press.

———. 1985. *Shembe: The Revitalization of African Society.* Johannesburg: Skotaville Publishers.

Walker, A. R. 2000. African Traditional Healers: The Future? *National Medical Journal of India* 13(4): 213–214.

Walker, A. R., et al. 1990. Obesity in Black Women in Soweto, South Africa. *Journal of the Royal Society of Health* 110: 101–103.

Walker, A. R., B. F. Walker, B. Manetsi, N. G. Tsotetsi, and I. Segal. 1989. Appendicitis in Soweto, South Africa: Traditional Healers and Hospitalization. *Journal of the Royal Society of Health* 109(6): 190–192.

Warren, Mark E., ed. 2001. *Democracy and Trust.* Cambridge: Cambridge University Press.

Watson, A. R., H. M. Coovadia, and K. D. Bhoola. 1979. The Clinical Syndrome of Impila (*Callilepis laureola*) Poisoning in Children. *South African Medical Journal* 55(8): 290–292.

Watt, J. M., and N. J. Van Warmelo. 1930. The Medicines and Practice of a Sotho Doctor. *Bantu Studies* 4: 47–68.

Watts, H. L. 1980. Some Reactions to Illness of Urban Black and Indian Families in Durban: A Summary of an Exploratory Study. *South African Medical Journal* 57(15): 589–591.

Wells, Julia. 1993. *We Now Demand: The History of Women's Resistance to Pass Laws in South Africa.* Johannesburg: Witwatersrand University Press.

Werbner, Richard P. 1977. *Regional Cults.* London: Academic Press.

———. 1989. *Ritual Passage, Sacred Journey: The Process and Organization of Religious Movements.* Washington, DC: Smithsonian Institution Press; Manchester, UK: Manchester University Press.

Wessels, W. H. 1989. Healing Practices in African Independent Churches. In Oosthuizen et al. 1989.

Wessman, R. 1908. *The Bawenda of the Spelonken (Transvaal): A Contribution towards the Psychology and Folklore of African Peoples.* Trans. Leo Weinthal. London: African World.

West, Harry G. 1998. "This Neighbor Is Not My Uncle!" Changing Relations of Power and Authority on the Mueda Plateau. *Journal of Southern African Studies* 24(1): 141–160.

———. 2001. Sorcery of Construction and Socialist Modernization: Ways of Understanding Power in Post-colonial Mozambique. *American Ethnologist* 28(1): 119–150.

West, Harry G., and Scott Kloeck-Jenson. 1999. Betwixt and Between: "Traditional Authority" and Democratic Decentralization in Post-war Mozambique. *African Affairs* 98: 455–484.

West, M. E. 1974. Independence and Unity: Problems of Cooperation between African Independent Church Leaders in Soweto. *African Studies* 33: 121–129.

West, Martin. 1975a. *Bishops and Prophets in an African City: African Independent Churches in Soweto, Johannesburg.* Cape Town: David Philip.

———. 1975b. The Shades Come to Town: Ancestors and Urban Independent Churches. In *Religion and Social Change in Southern Africa,* ed. M. G. Whisson and M. E. West. Cape Town: David Philip.

Westaway, M. S. 1990. Health Complaints, Remedies and Medical Assistance in a Peri-urban Area. *South African Medical Journal* 77(1): 34–36.

White, Hylton. 2001. Value, Crisis, and Custom: The Politics of Sacrifice in a Post-apartheid Countryside. PhD diss., Department of Anthropology, University of Chicago.

White, Luise. 2000. *Speaking with Vampires: Rumor and History in Colonial Africa.* Berkeley and Los Angeles: University of California Press.

Whiteford, A., and M. McGrath. 1994. *Distribution of Income in South Africa.* Pretoria: Human Sciences Research Council.

Whiteford, Andrew, and Dirk Van Seventer. 1999. *Winners and Losers: A Report on South Africa's Changing Income Distribution in the 1990s.* Pretoria: Wharton Econometric Forecasting Associates.

White Paper Working Committee. 1998. White Paper on Local Government. Department of Provincial Affairs and Constitutional Development, Pretoria.

Whiteside, Alan, and Clem Sunter. 2000. *AIDS: The Challenge for South Africa.* Cape Town: Human and Rousseau, Tafelberg.

Wilkinson, D., L. Gcabashe, and M. Lurie. 1999. Traditional Healers as Tuberculosis Treatment Supervisors: Precedent and Potential. *International Journal of Tuberculosis and Lung Disorders* 3(9): 838–842.

Williams, B. G., E. Gouws, and S. S. Abdool Karim. 2000. Where Are We Now? Where Are We Going? The Demographic Impact of HIV/AIDS in South Africa. *South African Journal of Science* 96: 297–300.

Williams, Tag. 1998. Expulsion for the Widow Who Mourned the Wrong Way. *Electronic Mail and Guardian* Internet ed., August 6, 1998. http://www.mg.co.za/mg/news/98aug1/6aug-jehovah.html.

Willis, R. G. 1970. Instant Millennium: The Sociology of African Witch-Cleansing Cults. In Douglas 1970b.

Willoughby, William Charles. 1923. *Race Problems in the New Africa: A Study of the Relations of Bantu and Britons in Those Parts of Bantu Africa Which Are under British Control.* Oxford: Clarendon Press.

———. 1928. *The Soul of the Bantu: A Sympathetic Study of the Magico-Religious Practices and Beliefs of the Bantu Tribes of Africa.* New York: Doubleday.

———. 1932. *Nature Worship and Taboo: Further Studies in "The Soul of the Bantu."* Hartford: Hartford Seminary Press.

Wilson, Bryan. 1970. *Rationality.* New York: Harper and Row.

Wilson, Francis, and Mamphela Ramphele. 1989. *Uprooting Poverty, the South African Challenge: Report for the Second Carnegie Inquiry into Poverty and Development in Southern Africa.* New York: W. W. Norton.

Wilson, Monica. 1951. Witch Beliefs and Social Structure. *American Journal of Sociology* 56(4): 307–313.

———. 1971. *Religion and the Transformation of Society: A Study in Social Change in Africa.* Cambridge: Cambridge University Press.

Wilson, Monica, and Archie Mafeje. 1963. *Langa: A Study of Social Groups in an African Township.* Cape Town: Oxford University Press.

Wilson, Peter. 1974. Filcher of Good Names: An Enquiry into Anthropology and Gossip. *Man,* n.s., 9(1): 93–102.

Winch, Peter. 1970. The Idea of a Social Science. In B. Wilson 1970.

Wiredu, Kwasi. 1996. *Cultural Universals and Particulars: An African Perspective.* Bloomington and Indianapolis: Indiana University Press.

Wittgenstein, Ludwig. 1979. *Remarks on Frazer's "Golden Bough."* Trans. A. C. Miles and Rhees Rush. Atlantic Highlands: Humanities Press.

Wolpe, Harold. 1972. Capitalism and Cheap Labour Power in South Africa: From Segregation to Apartheid. *Economy and Society* 1(4): 425–456.

Wood, R., P. B. Mills, G. J. Knobel, W. E. Hurlow, and J. M. Stokol. 1990. Acute Dichromate Poisoning after Use of Traditional Purgatives: A Report of 7 Cases. *South African Medical Journal* 77(12): 640–642.

Word of Life. 1978. *Ikhonkodensi Yebhayibheli Elingcwele* [Zulu Bible Concordance]. Roodeport: Word of Life Publishers.

Working Group on Values in Education. 2000. Values, Education, and Democracy: Report of the Working Group on Values in Education. http://www.gov.za/reports/2000/education.htm.

World Bank, Sub-Saharan Africa. 2001. Indigenous Knowledge (IK) Program. http://www.worldbank.org/afr/ik/kmpacks.htm.

Worsley, Peter. 1957. *The Trumpet Shall Sound: A Study of "Cargo" Cults in Melanesia.* London: MacGibbon and Kee.

Wright, S. V. 1997. An Investigation into the Causes of Absconding among Black African Breast Cancer Patients. *South African Medical Journal* 87(11): 1540–1543.

Young, W. S. 1980. Herbal-Enema Colitis and Stricture. *British Journal of Radiology* 53(627): 248–249.

Zahan, Dominique. 1979. *The Religion, Spirituality, and Thought of Traditional Africa.* Trans. Kate E. Martin and Lawrence M. Martin. Chicago: University of Chicago Press.

Zion Christian Church. 1999. Testimony before the Truth and Reconciliation Commission, East London. Truth and Reconciliation Commission, Human Rights Committee. http://www.web.uct.ac.za/depts/ricsa/commiss/trc/zcctest.htm.

Zulu, Paulus. 1991. Legitimating the Culture of Survival. In *South Africa's Informal Economy,* ed. Eleanor Preston-Whyte and Rogerson Christian Preston-Whyte. Cape Town: Oxford University Press.

Index

abortion, 81–82

Abt Associates, *Impending Catastrophe,* 106

accusations of witchcraft, 66, 77, 85, 97–100, 114, 249–52, 259; and judicial process, 255–61

African Christianity, 182–92. *See also* churches, African Christian

African Christians: and ancestors, 196–202, 207–9; Bazalwane, 172, 207; "Israelites," 187; and *ngoma* cult, 55; and spirit possession, 228–29. *See also* "prophets"

African culture, respect for, 286–87, 289

African humanism, 85. See also *ubuntu*

African Initiated Church (AIC), 170, 185, 188–93, 204–5, 208, 248–49

African National Congress (ANC), 93n.4, 94, 103–4, 220, 269, 274n.16; *National Health Plan for South Africa,* 287–89; and TRC, 272–78

African philosophy, 115

African potato, 151n.10

African Renaissance, 85, 120, 150

"African science," 120, 124, 137, 142–43, 146–48, 302, 312; and "indigenous knowledge systems," 148–53

Afro-Christianity, 171n.1

age, and suspicions of witchcraft, 75–76, 256

agency: and dirt, 167–69; nonhuman, 118–20, 134–37, 139–43

aggression, among male youth, 40–41

AIDS, 81, 154–56. *See also* HIV/AIDS pandemic

AIDS awareness, 9–10, 47–48, 105–10. *See also* HIV/AIDS pandemic

AIDS treatment, 54n.31. *See also* health care; HIV/AIDS pandemic

akrasia, 126, 126n.5

alcohol abuse, 37, 39, 46n.22, 74

allegations of witchcraft, 65–66, 85

ancestor, use of term, 175

ancestors, 174–76; angry and indifferent, 202–6, 210; as demons, 207–8; as family members, 203, 209–19; honoring of, 194–96, 203, 219–20; maternal, 216, 217n.8; neglect of, 205; paternal, 216; powers of, 220–22; protective role of, 202, 222; range of, 219–20; rejection of, 206–9; relations with, 194–202, 215–17, 219; sleeping, 209

ancestral religion, undermining of, 176

Anderson, Allan, 185, 187–89, 204, 208

Anglican church, 84

antiapartheid struggle, 23–24, 102–4, 191–92, 267–70, 279–80

antiwitchcraft legislation, 253–55, 261–67. *See also* Suppression of Witchcraft Act

anxiety, epistemic, 127